ASTRO-LOGICAL
LOVE

OTHER BOOKS BY
Naura Hayden

1980 ISLE OF VIEW (Say It Out Loud)

A book all about love . . . learning how to care for and love your self, learning how to tune into and feel loved by your Giant Self (God), and learning how to love and be loved by another person so that you can have a happy love life, a fulfilling sex life, and a faithful marriage which will last a lifetime.

1976 EVERYTHING YOU'VE ALWAYS WANTED TO KNOW ABOUT ENERGY . . . BUT WERE TOO WEAK TO ASK

A book about The Human Energy Crisis . . . how to get physically, mentally and emotionally energized so that you can overcome self-doubt, anxiety and depression, and attain all the good things in life that you've dreamed and hoped for . . . and deserve.

1972 THE HIP, HIGH-PROTE, LOW-CAL, EASY-DOES-IT COOKBOOK

A cookbook full of high-protein, low calorie recipes . . . over 200 mouthwatering and nutritious dishes that will keep your appetite satisfied and let you lose weight at the same time, while you really enjoy these delish salads, appetizers, "thoups," meatless main dishes, cakes, pies and lots of other delectables that make eating one of life's greatest pleasures.

Naura Hayden

Bibli O'Phile Publishing Company
New York, New York
Distributed by E.P. Dutton, Inc.

Published by Bibli O'Phile Publishing Company
P.O. Box 5189, New York, New York 10022

Printed in the United States of America

Library of Congress Catalog Card Number: 82-80126

ISBN: 0-942104-00-5

Distributed by E. P. Dutton, Inc.

10 9 8 7 6 5 4 3 2 1

First Edition

To Love . . .
Which is God . . .
Which is Love . . .
Which is God . . .
Which is Love . . .

Contents

Foreword

It happened to me several years ago. I was in bed reading a book about Jackie Kennedy, and in it the author went into detail about JFK's promiscuity. Almost every page told of his sexual escapades—either he was sneaking a woman into the White House or he was being sneaked into a woman's apartment or hotel room. Now I knew JFK was a Gemini, born on May 29th, and I was pretty sure it was 1916, but that's all I knew. Suddenly a flash of insight hit me. He must have his Venus in Gemini too!

Several years before this, I knew a Gemini who was incapable of being faithful to a woman—*any* woman. It was so apparent that this poor male was a compulsive philanderer and really couldn't control his fooling around. I got curious about this and did a chart on him, and found out he also had his Venus in Gemini. Now I must explain that anyone who has his or her Venus in Gemini has a particularly difficult time being faithful to anyone. Not that it's impossible (I don't believe *anything* in life is impossible!), it's just that I've *never* found a person with Venus in Gemini who could ever be faithful. There probably is one somewhere (there *must* be one somewhere), but I've never found him (or her).

Going back to JFK. As I got this flash of insight about his having his Venus in Gemini, I jumped out of bed and rushed for my astrological ephemeris, a chart book. I was sure he was born on May 29th and fairly sure it was 1916, so I looked him up, and alas—it showed he had his Venus in Cancer, which connotes a love of home life, and a need for emotional security within the home. Well, I knew that just couldn't *be,* so I figured I must have made a mistake with the year of his birth. I went to another book and looked it up and I *had* made a mistake—he was born in 1917. So again I looked up his Venus, and sure enough—Venus in Gemini. At that moment, I was convinced that you can definitely predict a person's personality traits and character analysis if you do a chart on that person.

Which means that a lot of promiscuous people will have to change their cheatin' ways or they're going to be *without* mates. Nobody's going to put up with flirting and cheating if there's a way of finding our *before* the relationship begins that a prospective lover is a flirt and a cheat.

However, *some* people dig just the opposite—they love the excitement of never knowing where they stand, they're turned on by a flirtatious lover and they get bored with knowing their mate never looks at another woman or man, so these people can stay away from anyone whose chart shows fidelity and constancy in their character.

You can even plan your children astro-logically! The charts in this book all go up to the year 2000, so if you plan on having a child next year or five years from now, you can conceive him or her at the point where the baby's birth day will be in any Sun Sign, Moon Sign, Venus Sign, etc., that you wish. Figure out which sign is the most compatible with yours and your spouse's, and conceive accordingly. Have a son or daughter whose personality and character will blend in harmoniously with the rest of the family!

I've found I'm attracted to people in certain elements, and also I'm usually able to "sense" what element is strongest in a person's chart. For instance, if I meet someone and we discuss astrology and the person asks if I can tell what is his or her Sun Sign, I always start with trying to sense what element I perceive from that person. And I'm right most of the time. And when I'm not right, I find that element I sensed is strong somewhere else in their chart, like their Moon or Ascendant or Venus.

The elements are Earth, Air, Fire and Water.

Earth people are those with Taurus, Virgo and Capricorn in their charts, and they're always very earthy, basic, fundamental people. Their approach to life is down-to-earth. You can sense a heaviness, a weightiness about them, a strong foundation.

Air people are those with Gemini, Libra and Aquarius in their charts, and they are completely opposite from Earth people. They always have a light and airy quality about them, and their approach to life is more sprightly and buoyant than the other elements. You can sense their mental agility and airiness, and there's a breeziness and a not-tied-down feeling about them.

Fire people are exactly that—fiery—and they are those with Aries, Leo and Sagittarius in their charts. They are very much like fire—blazing, passionate, intense, flaming and excitable. They have an ardent feeling about them, and they approach life with passion and intensity.

Water people are those with Cancer, Scorpio and Pisces in their charts, and they are the sensitive, emotional, feeling ones of the Zodiac. They have the most sensibility, perceptiveness, sympathy and depth of feeling. Their approach to life is one of sensitivity and empathy, or "feeling into" others' feelings. You will sense a depth and a vulnerability about them.

Try it. Next time you meet someone new, try sensing his or her element. It's not a mental, intellectual thing of trying to figure out the element, it's a stilling of your mind and just letting your instinct or intuition or "feeling quality" take over. You can do it with people you've known for years but never knew their birth days. In fact, it's easier with people you know, 'cause you've been around them and you can just close your eyes and try to image-in the element that seems to go with them, to fit their nature.

Then, after you get the element, try for which of the three signs of that element they fit into. For instance, if you've chosen Fire as your friend's element, then try to narrow it down to which Sun Sign he or she belongs:

ARIES: a leader, egocentric, bold, impatient, aggressive, headstrong, impulsive.

LEO: romantic, arrogant, generous, vain, dynamic, tyrannical, dramatic, sunny.

SAGITTARIUS: outspoken, cheerful, frank, tactless, impersonal, enthusiastic, emotionally shallow.

Or if Earth is the element, the Sun Sign might be:

TAURUS: practical, deliberate, plodding, prudent, insensitive, self-reliant, obstinate, earthy.

VIRGO: methodical, witty, critical, quick-thinking, cautious, discriminating, nit-picky.

CAPRICORN: determined, ambitious, perservering, calculating, serious, headstrong, basic.

Or if Air is the element, the Sun Sign might be:

GEMINI: charming, undependable, fun-loving, restless, clever, fickle, dual-natured, unreliable.

LIBRA: logical, indecisive, fair, cooperative, narcissistic, diplomatic, artistic.

AQUARIUS: idealistic, eccentric, progressive, original, stubborn, humanitarian, inventive, willful.

Or if Water is the element, the Sun Sign might be.

CANCER: super-sensitive, moody, sentimental, brooding, home-loving, compassionate, talky.

SCORPIO: secretive, strong, selfish, magnetic, suspicious, demanding, forceful.

PISCES: intuitive, self-indulgent, sensitive, passive, imaginative, mystical, sympathetic.

And after you begin to get more serious about your own feelings and recognize that you *can* sense the elements in a person and hone it down to "feeling" what sign that person fits into and be right every time the more you do it and the more sensitive you become, that's when you'll become more convinced than you've ever been that astrology *is* predictable and people *do* fit into categories.

I did a study of composers of popular songs, and took twenty-seven composers of standard songs, from Irving Berlin to Burt Bachrach. I chose composers who had written a minimum of five standard hits, (and most have over ten). There are lots of composers who've written one or two hits, but I'm interested in those who are really prolific. Out of the twenty-seven, fourteen were Air Signs, six were Water, five were Earth and two were Fire. Out of the individual signs, Aquarius (Air) led with six; Libra (Air) had five; Gemini (Air), Taurus (Earth) and Cancer (Water) had three each. Sagittarius (Fire), Capricorn (Earth) and Scorpio (Water) had two each and Pisces (Water) had one. There were three signs that didn't have a single composer in any of them, Aires (Fire), Leo (Fire) and Virgo (Earth). I found that fascinating.

THE AQUARIANS ARE:

Jerome Kern: "Smoke Gets in Your Eyes," "Old Man River," "All the Things You Are."

Burton Lane: "Old Devil Moon," "On a Clear Day," "Everything I Have Is Yours."

Victor Herbert: "Kiss Me Again," "When You're Away," "Gypsy Love Song."

Harold Arlen: "Over the Rainbow," "Stormy Weather," "I've Got the World on a String."
Walter Donaldson: "Love Me or Leave Me," "Little White Lies," "Yes Sir, That's My Baby."
Jimmy Van Heusen: "Call Me Irresponsible," "Imagination," "It Could Happen to You."

THE LIBRANS ARE:
George Gershwin: "Somebody Loves Me," "I've Got Rhythm," "The Man I Love."
Vincent Youmans: "I Want to Be Happy," "Time on My Hands," "Without a Song."
Vernon Duke: "Taking a Chance on Love," "April in Paris," "I Can't Get Started."
Johnny Green: "Body and Soul," "I Wanna Be Loved," "I Cover the Waterfront."
R. Rainger: "Thanks for the Memory," "Please," "Moanin' Low."

THE GEMINIS ARE:
Cole Porter: "Night and Day," "I Get a Kick Out of You," "Easy to Love."
Fritz Loewe: "I Could Have Danced All Night," "Almost Like Being in Love," "If Ever I Should Leave You."
Sammy Fain: "Secret Love," "That Old Feeling," "I'll Be Seeing You."

THE CANCERS ARE:
Richard Rodgers: "My Funny Valentine," "Lover," "If I Loved You."
Frank Loesser: "Baby, It's Cold Outside," "I've Never Been in Love Before," "Slow Boat to China."
Jimmy McHugh: "I Can't Give You Anything But Love," "Don't Blame Me," "I'm in the Mood for Love."

THE TAUREANS ARE:
Irving Berlin: "Always," "How Deep Is the Ocean," "What'll I Do?"
Duke Ellington: "Mood Indigo," "Don't Get Around Much Anymore," "Sophisticated Lady."
Burt Bacharach: "Close to You," "Alfie," "Walk On By."

THE SAGITTARIANS ARE:
Arthur Schwartz: "By Myself," "Dancing in the Dark," "Something to Remember You By."
Noel Coward: "Mad About the Boy," "I'll See You Again," "Someday I'll Find You."

THE CAPRICORNS ARE:
Jule Styne: "Make Someone Happy," "Just in Time," "I'll Walk Alone."
Harry Warner: "The More I See You," "You're My Everything," "I Only Have Eyes for You."

THE SCORPIOS ARE:
Hoagy Carmichael: "Stardust," "Georgia on My Mind," "The Nearness of You."
Richard Whiting: "Beyond the Blue Horizon," "She's Funny That Way," "My Ideal."

THE PISCES IS:
Kurt Weill: "September Song," "Mack the Knife," "Speak Low."

Air is what sound and music travel on, and air is the element in the Sun Signs of over 54 percent of all the composers in my survey. I have a hunch that many of the Earth and Water and Fire composers have their ascendants in Aquarius (Air), but it's almost impossible to find out, 'cause you have to know the exact time of birth, which most of them don't know. I lucked in the other day when I spoke to Irma Bacharach, Burt's mother, and she told me he was born at exactly 1:15 A.M. I already knew his birthday was May 12, 1929, so I looked up his Ascendant, and sure enough, it was in Aquarius. So his Sun Sign, (which is earth), has Air as his Ascendant, which is Aquarius.

Now my survey on composers was certainly not a complete one—there are many more I'm sure I missed. But I chose what I thought was a well-rounded and representative group, and they wrote what I believe is the majority of popular tunes which have become standards in the twentieth century. As I said, there are many who wrote two or three hit songs, but I eliminated them and used only those who have a *minimum* of five standard hits, and most of my list have more than ten which have lasted through the years and are as played today as when they were first written.

There was another survey done several years ago under the supervision of a psychology professor, Dr. Patricia Greenfield, by an astrologer who identified 87 percent of the character traits of a group of grade school kids, using only astrology for information. Alice Lane was the astrologer, and she did astrological charts on ten second and third grade students whom she had never seen nor met, using only the birth dates and time of birth supplied by their teacher, Alice Lauran.

Then Lane, the astrologer, and Lauran, the teacher, each answered twenty-seven questions about the character traits of each child. When the two separate lists of answers were compared, the astrologer had answered 235 out of 270 questions correctly, which is an 87 percent accuracy rate. She had unerringly described the intelligence, creativity, aggressiveness, and went so far as to say which ones had a tendency to gain weight.

Dr. Greenfield, the psychology professor under whose supervision the survey was done, said that as a result of the survey, her opinions about astrology had totally changed. She said that she hadn't thought that the results would be as positive and as accurate as they turned out to be, and that her skepticism was now giving way to belief.

The science of astrology is based on the fact that the sun and the moon and the earth, and all the other stars and planets, are interrelated and part of a giant cosmic plan or design.

The specific conditions and varied positions of the stars and planets influence the earth and everything and everybody on it by emitting cosmic rays and magnetic forces. All the planets' gravitational and electromagnetic fields of influence in our solar system interact with our sun, and we are the recipients of this interaction and these rays and forces.

Just as we can't see radio waves and sound waves, we can't see cosmic rays. But when we turn on the radio or TV, we experience the sound traveling on those radio waves. We can't see the sun's ultraviolet rays, but when we're outdoors in our swim suits, we experience a sun tan. We can't see infra-red rays, but we can see the outlines of our body's bones and organs in a finished X-ray film. Cosmic rays are as real as radio waves and sound waves and ultra-violet rays and infrared rays. We can't see any of them, but we know they exist by their effects.

We may not know *how* radio waves work, we just know that they do, and we confidently switch on our sets knowing the sound will start.

The same with astrology. You may not understand how cosmic rays and magnetic forces work, but after you do a self-chart and see how accurately it pinpoints *you*, or you do a chart on your family and are amazed at how your spouse was so correctly categorized in personality and character traits, you'll believe in astrology as a tool for self-discovery and other-discovery too. You'll become aware of facets of your self that you never knew existed. Some of these will be positive and some will be negative. It's up to you to accentuate the positive and eliminate the negative (and don't mess with Mr. In-Between, as Johnny Mercer said).

The more I know about astrology, the more I can see how accurate it is. And I believe as you read my book and do charts on your self, your love, your family, friends, etc., you'll develop an even stronger belief in astrology than you might already have.

The reason I call my book ASTRO-LOGICAL LOVE is because astrology *is* logical. The more you delve into it and learn about it, the more you'll see the logic in it. Certain signs have certain traits that they give to those born under them. Librans *do* weigh things because they are able to see both sides of an issue. Ariens *are* egocentric and must lead in what they do. Sagittarians *are* outspoken and very frank about everything.

So let's take the mystique out of astrology, really delve into it and really learn about it, and if this book will lead to that, it will make me very happy, and make millions of people more aware of themselves and of everyone around them, and therefore happier too!

Introduction

ASTRO-LOGICAL LOVE is a book for lovers—lovers who want to find out more about themselves as lovers, and more about their inner selves, and who want to find out more about their lovers' inner selves.

You can do a full chart on your self, find out your strengths and weaknesses so you can capitalize on your strengths and try to change or strengthen your weaknesses. Through self-discipline you can transform any deficiency you might have into power. The first step is to become aware of your pluses and minuses, and you will, once you've read this book and used the information to write your own personal astro-logical chart.

You can look up a prospective mate's birth hour, day and year, and do a full chart on him or her and see how basically compatible you are (or aren't). You can look up your mother's and father's birth dates and do charts on them which will explain a lot about why you had so many problems growing up with your mother and none with your father (or vice versa), or why they never got along and finally split, and maybe find out why your mother's later re-marriage did work out so beautifully, after you do a chart on her second husband.

It's the first book ever written on astrology in which you can find out so much about not only your self, but also everyone close to you, and then look up the birth days of over 5,000 celebrities of the world and maybe learn more about some of *them!*

Once you find their birth days, you can do charts on almost every celebrity who has ever lived and find out exactly what different famous people are (were) like, and why they are (were) motivated to do the things they do (did). You can do a chart on Calvin Coolidge or Calvin Klein, on Otto von Bismarck or Otto Preminger.

There is a list of every day of the year—all 366 of them. When you look up your own birth day, you will find out which celebrities were born on that day. Anywhere from five to eighteen of the most renowned, world-famous people were born on your special day, and it's fun to find out which ones. Was Woody Allen? Or Carly Simon? Or Hank Aaron? Or Catherine the Great?

There are 5,000 names, birth days and years of celebrities also listed by occupations and profession, in every conceivable field—from great writers to rock stars, from master painters to TV personalities, from kings to presidents. You can go back to Sigmund Freud, or Winston and Clementine Churchill, and do charts on them. You can look up Albert Einstein or Mick Jagger, Adolf Hitler or Pope John Paul II, FDR and Eleanor, Burt Reynolds and Dinah Shore and Sally Field (and whoever may be next in his life!). You'll find out why some people are content with one spouse for a lifetime, and others divorce and re-marry at a dizzying speed, and still others prefer a life of aloneness and never get married.

You'll find out why some people are faithful to one mate and others fool around a lot. If you have a relationship with a man or woman who seems incapable of faithfulness and is constantly flirting with the opposite (or same) sex, you can now find out why, and decide if you want to put up with it, or find someone whose chart shows fidelity and trustworthiness.

Many people think that all you need to know is your birth day, which of course tells you your Sun Sign (November 2nd makes you a Scorpio, September 10th makes you a Virgo, etc.), but that's only a fraction of the story of you. After you ascertain your Sun Sign, then you find out your Moon, and your Ascendant, your Mercury, Venus, Mars, Jupiter, Saturn, etc. You are a result of at least ten different planetary placements.

Up till this time, I knew a lot about astrology and believed people fell into definite categories characteristic-wise, but my JFK experience really deepened my belief enormously, because it was the first time I ever worked backwards, or applied empirical logic. It was then that I decided to delve further into astrology and write this book. I feel that every person should have the chance to do a self-chart and also a chart on anyone and everyone who affects his or her life. In this way, maybe we can all learn more about our selves and what helps to make us tick, more about our family, our friends and our lovers and what makes them tick, and when we learn all this, maybe we can all tick better together.

1

Signs of the Zodiac

How to Do a Chart
On Your Self and Others

There are twelve signs of the Zodiac, and within these twelve signs you will find your Sun Sign, your Moon, your Ascendant, your Mercury, your Venus, your Mars, your Jupiter, Saturn, Uranus, Neptune and Pluto. When you learn what your signs are, you will learn much more about your self, and be in a good position to start running your life in an active way, instead of having it run you, while you stand around passively wondering why everything seems to happen *to* you, instead of your *making* things happen in an active and positive and constructive way.

Now for the signs . . .

Your Sun Sign is determined by the day of the month you were born (see page 27 to find your Sun). The Sun represents all the positive, life-giving elements, and rules over and represents your basic essence, your individuality, your conscious mind, and your constitutional life-force. The Sun rules how you are deep within your self, the basic and mainmost expression of your self.

Your Moon Sign is found by the year you were born (see page 41 to find your Moon), and it represents your character, (whereas the Sun rules your individuality, and whichever is stronger in your chart is the dominating factor—in other words, if your Moon is stronger than your Sun, then your character will dominate your individuality). The Moon governs your emotions, your intuitions, your feelings, your inner desires, everything that is receptive in your nature, and this includes your emotional responses as well as your desires and instincts. The Moon represents your subconscious, the darker, deeper side of your character, and you will find many times that a person will be attracted to a mate whose Sun Sign is the same as his or her Moon. Your Moon is the key to your character, instincts and inner desires.

Your Ascendant is determined by the sign that was rising on the Eastern horizon at the exact time (to the hour and minute) of your birth (see page 123 to find your Ascendant). Your Rising Sign (Ascendant) determines your personality, your approach to life, how you express your self, how you will start to find your own personal meaning in your life, how your self is manifested to the rest of the world, how everyone around you sees you—your body, the way you walk and talk, the way you move around, and your mental inclinations and quirks. Many times when you meet people, your Ascendant will be more obvious to them than your Sun Sign. Your Ascendant draws you to what you need to learn in order to become in life what you want to become.

Your Mercury is found in either the sign before your Sun Sign, or the sign right after, or right in your Sun Sign. Mercury is close to the Sun and is never more than 28° from the Sun at any time, (and there are only 30° in every sign). So look on page 130 and determine through reading the three descriptions (one before, one during and one after your Sun Sign) which one really is you. Mercury rules the type of mentality you were born with, your practical reasoning, your sense perception, the agent through which the inner you makes contact with the outer world, your mental processes, your way of working, and also Mercury rules all the different forms of communication, and without communication we would never make friends—or lovers! Mercury is your mind, your link with other people, so it's very important that your Mercury be compatible with your mate's.

Your Venus is found by the year you were born (see page 134 to find your Venus). Venus is the planet that influences your love life and your sex life more than any other planet, because it links you to the emotional impressions you receive from outside your self. Whatever sign your Venus is in will define your attitude to these emotional impressions, and how you'll react toward feelings of love and intimacy. Venus has the strongest influence over romance and marriage. When your Venus is in a strong placement, you will almost always have a great capacity for love and a life full of affection. Venus rules everything to do with love—friendship, courtship, romance, marriage, divorce and, of course, intimacy (which so many people are afraid of, and which I go into at great lengths in my last book, *Isle of View*, (*Say It Out Loud*) which is *all* about love).

Your Mars is determined by the year you were born (see page 168 to find your Mars). Mars symbolizes force, action, fervor, heat, aggression, potency—WOW!!! Whatever sign your Mars is in will show how the forces of energy in your life will be expressed, where your energy will most naturally flow, and how you can best use that energy in your life. It rules the strength of your sex drive, your courage, vigor and potency, and is a planet of great power and energy. This can be constructive energy or destructive energy, depending on how you channel it. Used well, Mars can be a tremendous creative force in your romance and in your life.

Your Jupiter is determined by the year you were born (see page 188 to find your Jupiter). Jupiter is your opportunity sign. It rules the superconscious, and has a great effect on your reasoning powers and on your understanding of your mind and spirit and how your feelings are shaped. Jupiter is your antenna, your feeler, for opportunity and chance, and depending on where it's found in your chart, fame, fortune and ambitions (including love ambitions) will turn out the way you want them.

Your Saturn is found by the year you were born (see page 194 to find your Saturn). Saturn is the planet of self-preservation and defense, of form and organization and justice, and gives the ability and talent to analyze a situation and then to use great determination in reaching a goal. Whatever sign your Saturn is in will decide how you will use your powers of self-preservation, and whether you will be defensive in your strivings, or whether you will turn your defenses into ambitions and goals. A good motto for Saturn is, "Your best defense is a good offense," or even better, "Desire without determination and hard work will bring you nothing." Your Venus may be more influential in attracting love, but Saturn's influence will help you to keep that love.

Your Uranus is found by the year you were born (see page 199 to find your Uranus). Uranus is the revolutionary planet which rules the unusual and the innovative, the unexpected and everything futuristic and visionary. It never lets any one condition last too long, and rules your ability to be creatively original, and to respond to change. Mighty changes can happen overnight under Uranus' influence.

Your Neptune is determined by the year you were born (see page 204 to find your Neptune). Neptune governs anyone who is sensitive, imaginative and a dreamer, especially poets, artists, musicians and mystics. Neptune rules your intuition, spirituality and extra-sensory perception, and this is of great help to anyone in business, where snap decisions are often called for.

Your Pluto is found by the year you were born (see page 208 to find your Pluto). Pluto is the planet of mystery and extremes, and makes possible new conditions to replace old ones. Sometimes we'll find things leaving our lives, obstacles which were stopping us from seeing or doing what we want. As we become more aware of our selves and of astrology, we'll find that in looking back on world changes (which of course affect each one of us), Pluto was the force causing these changes . . .

When you make up an astro-logical chart on your self, usually you will be manifesting many of the characteristics associated with your Sun Sign. However, each placement of every planet in your chart has an influence on every other placement. For instance, if a person's Moon or Ascendant (or any of the other planetary signs) is stronger than the Sun Sign, then the person will express a lot of the other, stronger sign. If a person were born the beginning of June and is a Gemini, but has a Taurus Moon, he'll express lots of Taurus' determination and money-making abilities which would overpower Gemini's feet-not-quite-on-the-ground qualities and tendencies of undependability, (but not Gemini's charm—*nothing* could overpower that!!!).

Or if you were born in early March, which is Pisces, a very receptive, idealistic and sensitive sign, but you have a Leo Moon (or Ascendant, etc.), you'll express many of Leo's tendencies of leadership, magnetism and great strength.

But even if the other signs aren't stronger than your Sun Sign, they're still going to influence you greatly in many ways. So just knowing your Sun Sign is not enough. All the other signs in your chart affect each other, and affect you.

You may wonder how a person can have two opposite tendencies—like someone who has Aquarius (an Air Sign) as his Sun Sign, which makes him eccentric and fame-seeking, and then has his Moon in Capricorn (an Earth Sign), which makes him practical, hard-working and determined. He will express the eccentricity and the need for fame, but will also have the practicality and staying-power of Capricorn, which will lessen *some* of the eccentricity of Aquarius.

But what if a person is a *double* placement (meaning two placements in the same sign)? For instance, what if someone is a *double* Gemini and has a Capricorn Moon? That is, someone with her Sun and Ascendant in Gemini with a Capricorn Moon. The Gemini tendencies to be fey and charming and irresponsible would be twice as obvious, and the Capricorn drive and determination and persistence would be less obvious—but it would still be there. Now what if a person is a *triple* Gemini (having three placements in Gemini, like the Sun, the Ascendant and Venus), or maybe even a quadruple Gemini, and has only one placement in Capricorn? The drive and determination would still be there, but it would less strong. Or if a person were a Capricorn, and very intense about success, and very driving toward a goal, and had a Gemini Ascendant, the drive of Capricorn would be predominant, but the charm of Gemini would shine through (whereas with a Virgo Ascendant, there wouldn't be much charm, but there would be lots of perfectionism and practicality, and a terrific eye for detail).

Or let's say you're an Aries, which makes you energetic and bold and aggressive, but very egocentric, and you have a Libra Moon. Well, your Libra tendencies of equality and fair play would lessen your egocentric ways and would make you a friendlier and more selfless person. And then mix in a Taurus Venus, and that would draw you to money and also make you a faithful spouse.

Now I've known triple Aries people and quadruple Librans, and all that does is intensify their positive qualities, but it also intensifies their negative qualities. The egotism of a triple Aries is not to be believed (it needs *constant* attention), but also the dynamism and brilliant ideas are incredible. A quadruple Libran can't make up his mind if his life depended on it (Librans weigh everything—Libra is the Scales, the Balance), but also he's a wonderfully fair person. Unfortunately, the rest of his chart is *all* Air Signs (Gemini and Aquarius), so his feet aren't really on the ground, and he doesn't get too much accomplished.

Let me give a made-up example of a person. Let's say she has her Sun in Leo, which gives her great magnetism, flamboyance and warmth, mixed with arrogance and pride. Her Moon is in Capricorn, and this gives her enormous drive toward success, and also makes her inclined to put business ahead of romance and possibly unite with someone who can help her in her climb, rather than for true love. Add a Virgo Mercury and she looks to details in what she does and becomes analytical in her observations. Her Ascendant is Aquarius, so she's inclined to donate some of her time and money to help needy people, and she's also a little eccentric in many ways. Her Venus is in Cancer, which makes her emotional and caring, and family and home life are important to her. This lessens her inclination to marry for money or power (but doesn't take it away), and gives her a sensitivity to balance her Leo pride. Her Mars is in Libra and gives her a romantic aura about her self, and makes her an eager and enthusiastic lover who delights in pleasuring her mate. Her Jupiter is in Sagittarius, and she loves to travel and loves communications, choosing TV as her career.

Or take a guy who's a Cancer, and very warm and loving and open and emotional, and give him a Virgo Moon, which makes him unemotional and nit-picky. So what happens? Well, he's not quite as warm and loving a Cancer as he would be with a Taurus Moon, and the Virgo Moon makes him critical and detail-conscious along with his warmth and lovingness, which he wouldn't be with a Leo Moon. Leo Moon people have a regal quality about them, and a sunny disposition.

Or let's imagine a Sagittarius who's about as outspoken and frank as a person can be, and not very emotional, and give her a Pisces Moon which will make her more receptive and more a feeling person with emotional depth that Sagittarians don't have (or want!). A Pisces Moon also gives her a dual side to her character (Pisces is two fish, one swimming upstream and the other swimming downstream), and if she's not using and directing her forces on positive action outside her self, they'll be directed within, and she'll be inclined to be self-indulgent and self-pitying and leaning toward alcohol—or some other drug—for strength. Now let's imagine an Aquarian Ascendant to make her a little eccentric, with new and original ideas bubbling in her brain. Add a Scorpio Mercury and she tends to be secretive in what she does, loves crossword & jigsaw puzzles, adores figuring out "whodunits" and solving *any* mysteries, and can be a tad sarcastic in conversations. Now let's give her a Scorpio Venus, which gives her a complex about her desirability with men, so she's unsure of her sexuality and is inclined to fool around a lot and has to prove her self with each new encounter.

So you can see that knowing your Sun Sign is only *part* of the story. Every other planetary placement affects you. And I think you'll find out lots and lots of things about your self that might have been mystifying you for years—maybe for your whole life. It's so exciting to realize, "Aha! So *that's* why I'm so good at making money—or writing poetry—or sticking to something till I finally get it." While writing this book, I discovered I have Virgo in my chart (which I never knew before because the chart I had read had an error in it, and then when I started doing the charts for this book, I found the error and found Virgo). My Virgo in Mercury explains why I'm terribly analytical and such a stickler for detail. I want whatever I'm working on to be *perfect*—I mean each and every little detail. And now I know why.

It's fascinating—fun—and you're going to find so many facets of your personality explained that you'll probably be amazed.

And don't forget that it points out and makes you aware of some negative qualities that maybe you weren't too sure you had. And now that you *are* aware of them, you'd sure like to get rid of them. Well, you can always use a little self-discipline and boot them right out of your life. And then again, you might find some terrific qualities that stand out. And now that you've been made aware of them, you can work on 'em and make them stand out even *more*. Either way, you *are* going to learn about your self.

And maybe, just maybe, when you discover that your mother's Sun in Aries and Moon in Scorpio (both signs ruled by Mars, the god of war!) made her difficult to live with; well, maybe you'll realize that the guilt you've felt all your life, 'cause you fought with her constantly, is ridiculous. You fought with her 'cause she *was* difficult to live with and you sure don't need a psychiatrist to convince you of that, or to work on getting rid of your guilt. *Now* you know there's nothing to be guilty about.

Or maybe you'll find out that Pisces people are dreamers and romantics, and are often poetic, intuitive and super-sensitive. And you're a Pisces. And your father made your life miserable 'cause he wanted you to take over his business, but you couldn't *force* your self to run a chain of fast food places and help sling hamburgers whenever the counterman didn't show up. So ever since you turned to moviemaking, you and your dad haven't been speaking, and he's never forgiven you for snubbing the family biz. He doesn't understand you now, and he's *never* understood you, and to tell the truth, you've never understood your self either. But now that you read about Pisces, you see your self and your nature and your character, and now you understand why it was *impossible* to work with your father. Your nature is not french fries and burgers, it's poetry on film. So there's one less shrink appointment.

Now, obviously, not everyone who finds out his or her inclinations and tendencies via astrology will be rid of all doubts and guilts, but it will help. After all, why do we go to a psychiatrist? He or she doesn't tell us what to do—they get us talking about our selves and unfolding past histories which hopefully we can piece together to help us understand what we're all about. To know our selves is the most important function of life—because if we don't know what makes us the persons we are, then we can't like our selves (we can't like *or* dislike what we don't know). And I'm totally convinced that the bottom line for happiness is in liking our selves. If we *don't* like our selves, we can't like anyone else (and it's not that we wouldn't try, or that we don't want to, it's really *impossible* to like other people if we don't like our selves).

So astrology can enlighten us about our strengths, (which we can strengthen even more once we become super-aware of them), and about our weaknesses, (which we can try to eliminate through self-discipline once we become super-aware of what they are).

The next step with ASTRO-LOGICAL LOVE is to do a chart on your self. As soon as you've done your self-chart, and read the different planetary influences on your character and personality and entire life in every other area, then you should do a chart on the love of your life. Then do your mother and father and sisters and brothers, and all your friends. And *don't* leave out your enemies. How can you know how to handle problems they've already caused and future ones they may try to cause, if you don't understand them and understand what makes them your enemies? You can't deal with something until you know it.

So—learn all about your self, your loves, your family, your friends and your enemies. And you'll be in a good position to start running your life, maybe for the first time, instead of having it run you!

2

Your 12 Sun Signs and Chart

The Sun represents all the positive, life-giving elements, and rules over and represents your basic essence, your individuality, the person you are striving to become either consciously or unconsciously, the attributes you need to become that person, your conscious mind and your constitutional life-force.

The Sun rules how you are deep within your self, the basic and mainmost expression of your self.

Your Sun Sign is determined by the day and month you were born. Your Sun Chart is on the following page.

Your Sun Chart

ARIES	March 21 through April 20
TAURUS	April 21 through May 21.
GEMINI	May 22 through June 21
CANCER	June 22 through July 23
LEO	July 24 through August 23
VIRGO	August 24 through September 23
LIBRA	September 24 through October 23
SCORPIO	October 24 through November 22
SAGITTARIUS	November 23 through December 21
CAPRICORN	December 22 through January 20
AQUARIUS	January 21 through February 19
PISCES	February 20 through March 20

Your 12 Sun Signs

ARIES

Aries is the first sign of the Zodiac as the Sun crosses into spring. You are the first Fire Sign (for excitement) and the first Cardinal Sign (for action), and you are ruled by the planet Mars. You Ariens are the pioneers, the leaders, the innovators, quick and original dynamos, full of energy and enthusiasm. You love to be first in everything you do, and you often show the way to some of the slower, more methodical signs. You aren't as tenacious as you could be, and sometimes rush into a new venture before you've completed a past one because you get bored with it, lose all interest and run off in another, more exciting direction. Aries is the baby of the Zodiac, the first sign, and sometimes you act like an infant—yelling and screaming and throwing tantrums till you get your own way. Aries is the Ram, and the most egocentric of all the signs (just as a baby is egocentric, you are conscious only of your self and think the world revolves around you).

You are always honest and open in your dealings and always go all the way (you're not a halfway person). Once you've decided to go with something, you go. You have a quick temper, but you don't hold a grudge.

Your ego, more than in any other sign, needs to be constantly reassured, and you sometimes have an exaggerated sense of your self. The positive Arien is an initiator, self-assured, a go-getter, full of enthusiasm and imagination. The negative possibilities are intolerance of others' ideas, impatience, and an inability to look ahead before you leap into a project.

Ariens are true extroverts and adventurers, always looking for new ideas, new loves and new worlds to conquer.

Red is usually your favorite color, and some of you go all the way with this—not necessarily in dress, but in whole rooms done in red—furniture, walls, carpets, etc. You're a red person.

Aries rules the head, the top of the body, the first part of the body. Aries likes to be first always. Aries must be a leader. It's very difficult for you to take orders. You want to lead, not follow, and you have all the qualities of leadership, including an enormous amount of optimism.

TAURUS

Taurus is the second sign of the Zodiac, an Earth Sign (very earthy and practical), and a fixed sign (the most fixed and unyielding of all the signs). It is ruled by Venus, the goddess of love. You Taureans are practical, down-to-earth, determined, very patient, conservative and often materialistic. You have a quiet, affectionate way about you, and are basically introverts, depending on your own intuition and animal instinct to show you the way in any endeavor. You depend on your feelings about a person or a thing, rather than on your mind or intellect.

You are a plodder who will almost always be a success once you've decided what it is you really want out of life. You will stick to your goal even after everyone else has given up, till you get what you want.

Taurus is a money sign, and you are very money-conscious—in fact, Taurus rules money. Your Taurus nature understands money more than any other sign, and rarely will a Taurean be a charity case.

You are possessive and need to feel that people and things belong to you. You are very rigid in your ideas, and once your mind is made up, it takes an enormous amount of arguing or discussing to convince you that maybe you were wrong and maybe you'll change your mind.

The positive Taurean has tremendous magnetism and is warm, open, loyal, very compassionate and has a great deal of patience. The negative Taurean is self-indulgent, eats and drinks too much, is stubborn, satisfied with the status quo and has a terrible temper.

Taurus is represented by the Bull, and like a bull you like to be left alone sniffing the flowers (like Ferdinand), but let someone press you or try to force you to do something you don't want to do and you become incredibly obstinate. And if they push you too hard, you will go into a tremendous rage, and change from Ferdinand the sniffer to Ferdinand the snorter, and paw the ground and charge into anything in your way.

Don't push a Taurean, or goad him or her too far, or you'll be sor-ry!

GEMINI

Gemini is the third sign of the Zodiac, an Air Sign (for intellect), and a Mutable Sign (for adaptability), and it's the sign of the Twins—the most fun, unpredictable and charming of all the signs. Gemini is ruled by Mercury, and rules the chest and arms. You are clever, never dull, always stimulating and exciting, quick-witted and alert mentally. Your active mind is easily bored, so you always need variety to keep life from becoming tedious to you.

Because you're a dual sign (the Twins), you are versatile and are usually jumping from one thing to another, but with your dual nature you are indecisive, which leads you to be dissatisfied easily and frustrated a lot of the time, and discontented most of the time.

A negative Gemini is emotionally detached and always a tease, promising more than will be delivered. Also, with your Peter Pan kind of personality, you don't like to accept responsibility. You are a will-o-the-wisp who doesn't want to be tied down—a free spirit who wants to remain free to be able to sometimes be one Twin and sometimes the other one. You can be a split personality with two completely different sides to your self. The truth is not very important to you, and you bend it often. With your wild imagination, you don't really think you're lying—you usually think you're telling the truth.

Most Geminis use words as a weapon, and they love to argue on any subject. Because they are extremely mental, they distrust emotions. Love for them can be a mental thing instead of a feeling thing, which is sometimes a shock to their mates. Gemini treasures friends more than lovers, for with a lover one must make more of an emotional commitment, which Gemini hates.

You Geminis don't like anyone to know exactly where you stand, so often you disguise your real motives. You love to confuse everyone and keep 'em guessing—that keeps you from being pinned down. But you're such charmers (and you really are), that you get away with it. In fact, your charm lets you get away with a lot more than any other sign. People love and forgive you no matter what you do. It's almost impossible to stay mad at a Gemini no matter how awful the slight or wrong doing, 'cause with your fey, childlike quality, you always appear so guileless. And you're always smiling. And impetuous. You usually do whatever strikes you at the moment, with little thought of the results. Well, why not? Nobody ever *stays* made at you, right? You love being around people and parties 'cause you love to talk, and you're always fun and witty.

CANCER

Cancer is the fourth sign of the Zodiac, the second Cardinal Sign (For activity), and the first Water Sign (for emotion), and is ruled by the Moon. You are the most home-loving and domestic of all the signs. Your love, when given, is very strong, and it would take your partner's doing something very extreme to make you break up your marriage or relationship.

You are super-sensitive, and because of this, you make a very good business person, instinctively knowing what will please the public and how you can bring this about.

Because you are ruled by the Moon and are so much affected by it (more than any other sign), you are restless, changeable, emotional and very romantic, and because you are so sensitive, you build a shell around your self (out of necessity) to protect that sensitivity, and withdraw into it when someone criticizes you unjustly (in your opinion) or insults you. Most Cancerians, when you've accomplished something of note, drop the shell, for the accomplishment builds your ego and lessens your anxiety, so you don't need as much protection.

One of the negative aspects of your sign is that you have a tendency to be overly possessive, and this is because you have a basic anxiety within you that makes you insecure and sometimes clinging. You will never give up something you love.

You are easily hurt and wear your heart on your sleeve. Your manner is usually shy and soft-spoken, an introvert.

Cancers don't like casual affairs, love the home, are usually good cooks and make terrific parents.

Cancers have a GREAT sense of humor, better than most of the other signs, and you do like to talk.

You have a strong "taking care" kind of nature, you are extremely loyal to your family and friends and you're a great friend to have. When you love, you love deeply.

LEO

Leo is the fifth sign of the Zodiac, the second Fire Sign (for excitement), and the second fixed sign (for determination), and is ruled by the Sun. You are a strong and forceful personality, a born leader and a true extrovert. You have great personal charm, are very dramatic and love an audience. You have all the attributes of a showman—you are flamboyant and know how to please a crowd. You will never be overlooked *wherever* you are—your very presence commands all eyes be turned on you. Strangely enough, with all these extroverted ways, you generally basically stay pretty conventional.

Your negative traits would be insensitivity, arrogance, conceit, and because of your great strength, you can become a pushy, ruthless person. Unless you find a mate who has as much enthusiasm, energy, zest and passion as you, you will tend to deliberately overshadow and bully that person too much and too far, so that the relationship is ended. You have an unquenchable thirst for personal glory, and you have a weakness for wanting only people who feed your ego and flatter your vanity to be near you. You are very much a peacock who loves to preen and who needs and expects applause all the time. All of you Leos want and strive for centerstage so you can be the "star" with all your supporting actors around you.

Despite all your ego and demands for attention, you are probably the most generous of all the signs, and very romantic. You make a wonderful, warm and caring friend, and will go far out of your way to help solve a friend's problem. You have unbelievable endurance and can outlast many people at many things. You have enormous confidence in your self and what you do, and are demonstrative and affectionate most of the time.

Leo is the Lion, is inherently imperious, and acts like the king or queen of the forest. Leos *feel* superior and regal. You *never* lean on other people—you love them to lean on you. You thrive on responsibility, particularly toward those weaker than you. Being around the helpless makes you feel good 'cause you can step in and help. Sometimes you may complain about everybody needing you and depending on you, but you need their need. It makes you feel strong and good to help.

Leos are lots of fun and, like the Sun, they enjoy spreading warmth to the world. You are basically self-assured, so much so that you do occasionally lack understanding and empathy toward those around you, and see no reason why you shouldn't just do what you want and then tell everyone about it afterwards, without discussion or opinions. It's part of feeling "regal," but will make many difficulties in your life. Because you *are* magnanimous, you get away with a lot, but with more cooperation in your attitude, you'll find your natural optimism, generosity and warmth will bring you what you really want in life.

VIRGO

Virgo is the sixth sign of the Zodiac, the second Earth Sign, and the second Mutable Sign (for adaptability), and is ruled by Mercury, the planet of reason and intellect. You are a practical and realistic person, very conscientious and a hard worker. Because you are endowed with quickness of mind and an abundance of logic, you are able to handle problem conditions that would confound most people or try their patience. You have a real talent for analyzing things right down to the core. You are a dissector who likes to get to the bottom of things to understand them better. You have a good analytical mind and are able to discriminate finely. You do lean toward hanging on to the past and not letting go of those past things you're finished and done with. You are not an emotional sign, and your attitude toward love is realistic, practical and conscientious. In fact, you're conscientious about most everything, and really love to work. You're a detail person, but you tend to be overly critical about a lot of things.

You aren't an experimenter when it comes to love, and you're not a terribly romantic or feeling person. Because you're sometimes overly critical, this can end a blossoming love affair before it hardly gets started. But as critical as you may be with others, you're even more so with your self.

You are extremely quick mentally (because of Mercury's influence), and you know what the other person's saying before he's finished saying it. You're very resilient mentally, physically and emotionally, and because of your practicality, you will rarely let yourself stay depressed— you'll find a way to get back up again fast. You are never impetuous, but clearly and carefully figure things out before you take action.

Earthy Virgos are very dependable and sincere. You're usually not terribly generous with money or with your affections—you give your love slowly and steadily. You're not really demonstrative with lots of hugs and kisses, but when you *do* love, it's deep and lasting. And when you have someone you consider to be a real friend, there's nothing you won't do for that person. Yours is a basic nature and you're down-to-earth about everything you do.

You are very discriminating, have an eye for detail, and are very clean and neat and needing those close to you to be exceptionally clean and neat too. You have a lot of friends because even though you do tend to be fuss-budgets, you are very giving to those who have earned your trust.

LIBRA

Libra is the seventh sign of the Zodiac, the second Air Sign (for intellect), the third Cardinal Sign (for activity), rules the kidneys and is ruled by Venus.

Librans, more than any other sign, think of other people and how to help them. Libra is the sign of human relationships, and you Librans will instinctively look for and need a partner, be it a love partner or a business partner. Because you have such a need for a partner, you can sometimes become overly possessive.

Librans have an obsession to be loved and admired, and respond eagerly to affection, praise and admiration, and need harmony above all else. Scenes of violence or loud arguments offend Libra's sensitivity. Because of your need of harmony, sometimes you will go to extremes to attain it, even lying or procrastinating. To keep the scales balanced (and not to let them tip too far in either direction) is usually the most difficult task before you, and because of this, you will usually find it's difficult to make a decision. You have the talent to weigh everything (and you love justice), so you tend to forever vacillate between two ways of action—weighing one side and seeing all the advantages and disadvantages, then doing the same for the other side.

Librans are very demonstrative and need signs of love. Your need for love is never-ending, and without it you feel unwanted. You hate arguments or any signs of discontent. You need a partner who will not only love you, but let you know you are loved.

Librans are people of action—doers, not only thinkers. But you *must* get your own way. You get unnaturally depressed if you don't. A negative aspect of Libra is that you're very narcissistic and self-involved, and get bored if you're not the center of attention.

Librans are very intelligent and love to concentrate on deep matters. You love books and love to have them around you. You are gentle and need gentle things and gentle people surrounding you. When you keep the scales in balance, you create a harmony within your self that touches everyone around you.

SCORPIO

Scorpio is the eighth sign of the Zodiac, the third Fixed Sign (for determination), and the second Water Sign (for emotion), is ruled by Mars and is represented by the Eagle and the Scorpion.

You are strong-willed, dynamic, passionate and extremely invincible. You are very determined and know just what you want and how you're going to get it. You have the talent for complete concentration and can become totally absorbed in what you're doing. You are very self-controlled and extremely secretive. You tend to be suspicious of everything and everyone.

You are able to make very quick decisions and have strong intuitive powers.

Scorpios are thought to be the sexiest sign in the Zodiac. Your sign rules the genitals, and you are very sex-conscious. You are passionate in everything you do—making love, making war, or making success. You are the most extreme sign of the Zodiac (the Eagle and the Scorpion), and there is never a middle ground for you. Everything is black or white—you either hate or love—there's no gray area. You never go halfway, but your passion is all inside, rigidly controlled on the outside, till someone touches you emotionally and is able to win your confidence and love.

You are intellectually curious and very intense about everything you do.

Your negative tendencies are your suspiciousness and your secrecy, which you carry to an extreme. You also tend to be uncontrollably jealous, have a terrible temper and can be extremely cruel to someone you feel has hurt you. Your latent violence can erupt when least expected, and many Scorpios are into sadism. You can be the most selfish of all the signs, but also the most magnetic—again, you are either the Scorpion or the Eagle. The Scorpion is your lower self, crawling on the ground, crude and vulgar, and the Eagle is your higher self, intuitive and dynamic, soaring high above the earth.

Scorpios are terribly possessive of things and people. You are fierce in your obsessive need to control things, which you do slowly and always very surely. Most of you emotionally involved Scorpios cannot see anything any way but your own way. You're possessive but you don't want to be possessed (unlike Cancers, who are possessive and need to *be* possessed). The *most* important thing for you Scorpios is to make certain you soar like the Eagle and never crawl like the Scorpion. This you can do through self-awareness and self-control, using your enormous determination and willpower to bring it about.

SAGITTARIUS

Sagittarius is the ninth sign of the Zodiac, the third Mutable Sign (for adaptability) and the third Fire Sign (for excitement), rules the thighs and is ruled by Jupiter.

You are an extremely honest person, a straight-shooter (you are represented by the Archer) who will have a hard time lying or being evasive. Sometimes you may hurt those around you by your bluntness, which could (and maybe should) be softened a little with kindness.

You are the philosopher of the Zodiac. You love to find out what goes on inside people, what motives make them do what they do. You are able to accept most things if you find out the reason behind them. You must find out what makes things tick, what are the causes behind the effects.

You love to travel and should as much as you can. It stimulates you and keeps you on your toes.

You try not to let those around you know when the going gets tough, and you keep fairly optimistic most of the time. You will keep things moving so there won't be a dull moment.

You're an adventurer, a truth-seeker, and you're very clever, with a dry and wry sense of humor.

Sagittarians love animals—all kinds of animals, from dogs and cats to turtles and gerbils. And you are all idealists who love to defend causes you believe in. You charge in where angels fear to tread, and you're dauntless. Right is right and you want to right every wrong.

Sagittarians can be tactless in your blunt truth-telling, but you're never consciously or deliberately cruel. People may think what you're saying is cruel, but it's only thoughtless.

You really don't have time for sentiment. Your love life tends to be a surface romance, but you'll never lie about it. You're truthful but not very sentimental. In fact, you *hate* gushy people, and get almost ill when you're forced to be around them. You're more likely to go after a casual relationship than tie yourself down. Sagittarians love to travel and see the world, and this goes for relationships too. But once you *do* find the ideal mate, your love won't be fickle. Yours will be an open, honest and honorable love.

CAPRICORN

Capricorn is the tenth sign of the Zodiac, the fourth Cardinal Sign (for action), the third Earth Sign (for practicality), is ruled by Saturn and rules the knees. Your symbol is the Mountain Goat, and this animal will *always* get to the top of the mountain, where the Bull or the Ram might not make it.

You are very practical and constructive, you have a basic charm without the frou-frou, and you are extremely determined. Capricorns can set your minds on a goal, and even though it may take years, you'll just never give up and you'll always eventually get what you want.

You're conventional and conservative (the most conservative of all the signs), and prefer your love life within marriage. You have a deep need for respect of everyone around you, and you will do everything in your power to earn that respect.

You have a strong sense of responsibility, and when someone has done something for you, you never forget it and will at some point repay in kind.

You are very concerned about what others think of you, which makes you self-conscious and self-centered. Although you do think highly of your self (and you feel justified in this because you work hard attaining honor), you are not a vain person.

Capricorns are hard workers, organizers, and quietly determined people who will always reach your goals because of your determination (like the Mountain Goat). You are enormously ambitious and will always try to advance your self and further your career. Many Capricorns marry for prestige or money, and are not above using others to climb the ladder of success (lots of us do this to some degree, but Capricorns do it unconsciously, and almost always).

Capricorns are late bloomers, and real success usually comes later in life. You love your family and will do anything and everything to keep it together. It's not easy for you to express affection, and you will never be swept off your feet romantically. You're not impetuous, but believe in slow and steady and gradual relationships. Lots of Capricorns will tell you they don't want a birthday present or a compliment, but don't believe it. You Capricorns need very much to be told you're terrific and to be reminded that you are loved. It's just that you keep most of your needs and your love deep within your selves, showing it only to those you trust. Despite your lack of great passion, you are probably quietly the best sexual performer of all the signs.

AQUARIUS

Aquarius is the eleventh sign of the Zodiac, the fourth Fixed Sign (for determination), the third Air Sign (for intellect), is ruled by the planet Uranus and rules the ankles.

You are the most original, unique and completely unpredictable of all the signs. You also are the most interested in your fellow man, a true humanitarian.

You are extremely tenacious and have an incredible persistence in carrying your ideas all the way to a successful conclusion.

Aquarians are very inventive, more than any other sign, and your powers of concentration are amazing. You are able to rid your mind totally of all else but your goal and go after it with a singleness of purpose unknown to any other sign.

The negative qualities of Aquarius are egocentricity, spitefulness, hogging the spotlight (and you can do this better than anyone else, even better than egocentric Aries). You can be stubborn, conceited and overly independent. You do need a sense of freedom about you, because you can't stand the thought of being hemmed in. But you're also very gentle, empathic (you really *can* feel into other people's feelings), sympathetic and kind.

You Aquarians like people a lot, and like to mingle at parties. But you don't have many close friends, even though friendship is very important to you. And once you're married, you'll almost always be faithful. You're dependable and honest in love, and when you commit yourself, you really mean it and do everything in your power to make the relationship last.

Aquarians' memories are not so terrific, but you really don't need one—you've got so much going on inside your head, so many new and original ideas that it's a waste to hang on to the old when you need room for all the new ideas.

Aquarians are a mix of practicality and eccentricity—and *all* Aquarians are eccentric. But that's the best part of your charm. You take offense at other's remarks and are overly sensitive in this area, but your great sensitivity is just another facet of your charm.

You usually keep people guessing—you're *full* of surprises. And you're so progressive, usually years ahead of everyone else in so many areas. You're wonderfully honest, usually cheerful and totally original.

PISCES

Pisces is the twelfth sign of the Zodiac, the fourth Mutable Sign (for adaptability), the third Water Sign (for emotion), is ruled by the planet Neptune and rules the feet.

You are the most receptive of all the signs, but there are two of you—the Two Fishes going in different directions, one swimming upstream and one swimming downstream, and these are the two opposites within you, the positive you and the negative you. The positive is romantic, sensuous, cheerful, kind, sensitive and intuitive, and the negative can be clinging, undependable, overly emotional, whining, bad-tempered and very weak liars. When the Piscean is totally self-centered, all your positives turn into your negatives. But the duality in Pisces is not in two personalities or two desires like Geminis have. The Two Fishes symbolize the option given Pisces—to swim to the top and reach all the longed-for goals, or to swim to the bottom and never reach any goals.

Because your nature makes you receptive, you are easily depressed, and you must be careful about the people you have around you. If they are lazy and complaining, you will have a tendency to take on these characteristics, but if you take care to associate with energetic and cheerful people, you will tend to become more energetic and cheerful too. You can consciously make an effort to get rid of negative people in your life and try to cultivate only positive people.

Most Pisceans procrastinate and make excuses for doing tomorrow what they should take care of today. Again, try to associate only with doers, people of action who will embarrass you if you try to procrastinate around them.

You need love constantly and are much happier married than single.

The Pisces who are swimming with the tide (and have gotten rid of the against-the-current fish) are stronger and self-sufficient and very intuitive and mystical, and make a great partner.

Pisceans are spiritual people and are often shy. You have fantastic intuitive powers and a mystical feeling about you. You really do need a lot of love, and you have a lot of love to give.

You are wonderfully perceptive and your greatest strength is your compassion. You can literally "feel" another's pain and anguish, and you are such a loving person with such incredible emotional depths that you will almost always give of your time and your self to help another in need. You are not a realist, you are more of a dreamer, but life *without* a dream is a bore. And every Pisces should always remember that dreams cost nothing *unless* you want them to come true. With just a *small* amount of work behind each one of your fantasies, it could be brought to life. You have within you the gigantic power of your vivid imagination (much stronger than most other people's), which can propel you to the success you desire.

3

Your 12 Moon Signs and Chart

The Moon governs your emotions, your intuitions, your feelings, your inner desires, everything that is receptive in your nature, and this includes your emotional responses as well as your desires and instincts. The Moon represents your subconscious, the darker, deeper side of your character, and you will find many times that a person will be attracted to a mate whose Sun Sign is the same as his or her Moon (I've found in my experience that this usually doesn't work out).

Your Moon is the key to your character, your instincts and your inner desires.

Your Moon Sign is determined by the year you were born. Your Moon Chart is on the following pages.

If you can't find your exact birth day on the chart, then use the date preceding your birth day.

For example, if the chart has Jan. 1 Taurus and Jan. 3 Gemini, and your birth day is Jan. 2 (not listed on chart), then use Jan. 1 Taurus as your Moon Sign.

Your Moon Chart

1850

JAN	FEB	MAR	APR	MAY	JUN	JUL	AUG	SEP	OCT	NOV	DEC
1 LEO	1 LIB	1 LIB	1 SAG	1 CAP	1 AQU	1 PIS	1 TAU	1 CAN	1 LEO	1 LIB	1 SCO
2 VIR	3 SCO	2 SCO	3 CAP	3 AQU	2 PIS	2 ARI	3 GEM	3 LEO	3 VIR	3 SCO	3 SAG
4 LIB	5 SAG	5 SAG	6 AQU	6 PIS	5 ARI	4 TAU	5 CAN	5 VIR	5 LIB	6 SAG	5 CAP
7 SCO	8 CAP	7 CAP	8 PIS	8 ARI	7 TAU	6 GEM	7 LEO	7 LIB	7 SCO	8 CAP	8 AQU
9 SAG	10 AQU	10 AQU	11 ARI	10 TAU	9 GEM	8 CAN	9 VIR	9 SCO	9 SAG	10 AQU	10 PIS
12 CAP	13 PIS	12 PIS	13 TAU	13 GEM	11 CAN	10 LEO	11 LIB	12 SAG	11 CAP	13 PIS	13 ARI
14 AQU	15 ARI	15 ARI	15 GEM	15 CAN	13 LEO	12 VIR	13 SCO	14 CAP	14 AQU	15 ARI	15 TAU
17 PIS	18 TAU	17 TAU	17 CAN	17 LEO	15 VIR	15 LIB	15 SAG	17 AQU	17 PIS	18 TAU	17 GEM
19 ARI	20 GEM	19 GEM	19 LEO	19 VIR	17 LIB	17 SCO	18 CAP	19 PIS	19 ARI	20 GEM	19 CAN
21 TAU	22 CAN	21 CAN	22 VIR	21 LIB	20 SCO	19 SAG	20 AQU	22 ARI	21 TAU	22 CAN	21 LEO
23 GEM	24 LEO	23 LEO	24 LIB	23 SCO	22 SAG	22 CAP	23 PIS	24 TAU	24 GEM	24 LEO	24 VIR
26 CAN	26 VIR	25 VIR	26 SCO	26 SAG	24 CAP	24 AQU	25 ARI	26 GEM	26 CAN	26 VIR	26 LIB
28 LEO	28 LIB	27 LIB	28 SAG	28 CAP	27 AQU	27 PIS	28 TAU	29 CAN	28 LEO	28 LIB	28 SCO
30 VIR		30 SCO	30 SAG	31 AQU	29 PIS	29 ARI	30 GEM	30 CAN	30 VIR	30 LIB	30 SAG
31 VIR		31 SCO			30 PIS	31 ARI	31 GEM		31 VIR		31 SAG

1851

JAN	FEB	MAR	APR	MAY	JUN	JUL	AUG	SEP	OCT	NOV	DEC
1 SAG	1 AQU	1 AQU	1 ARI	1 TAU	1 CAN	1 LEO	1 LIB	1 SCO	1 CAP	1 AQU	1 PIS
2 CAP	3 PIS	2 PIS	3 TAU	3 GEM	4 LEO	3 VIR	3 SCO	2 SAG	4 AQU	3 PIS	3 ARI
4 AQU	5 ARI	5 ARI	6 GEM	5 CAN	6 VIR	5 LIB	6 SAG	4 CAP	6 PIS	5 ARI	5 TAU
7 PIS	8 TAU	7 TAU	8 CAN	7 LEO	8 LIB	7 SCO	8 CAP	7 AQU	9 ARI	8 TAU	7 GEM
9 ARI	10 GEM	9 GEM	10 LEO	9 VIR	10 SCO	9 SAG	10 AQU	9 PIS	11 TAU	10 GEM	10 CAN
11 TAU	12 CAN	12 CAN	12 VIR	12 LIB	12 SAG	12 CAP	13 PIS	12 ARI	14 GEM	12 CAN	12 LEO
14 GEM	14 LEO	14 LEO	14 LIB	14 SCO	14 CAP	14 AQU	15 ARI	14 TAU	16 CAN	15 LEO	14 VIR
16 CAN	16 VIR	16 VIR	16 SCO	16 SAG	17 AQU	17 PIS	18 TAU	17 GEM	18 LEO	17 VIR	16 LIB
18 LEO	18 LIB	18 LIB	18 SAG	18 CAP	19 PIS	19 ARI	20 GEM	19 CAN	21 VIR	19 LIB	18 SCO
20 VIR	20 SCO	20 SCO	21 CAP	20 AQU	22 ARI	22 TAU	23 CAN	21 LEO	23 LIB	21 SCO	20 SAG
22 LIB	23 SAG	22 SAG	23 AQU	23 PIS	24 TAU	24 GEM	25 LEO	23 VIR	25 SCO	23 SAG	23 CAP
24 SCO	25 CAP	24 CAP	26 PIS	25 ARI	27 GEM	26 CAN	27 VIR	25 LIB	27 SAG	25 CAP	25 AQU
26 SAG	28 AQU	27 AQU	28 ARI	28 TAU	29 CAN	28 LEO	29 LIB	27 SCO	29 CAP	28 AQU	27 PIS
29 CAP		29 PIS	30 ARI	30 GEM	30 CAN	30 VIR	31 SCO	29 SAG	31 AQU	30 PIS	30 ARI
31 AQU		31 PIS		31 GEM		31 VIR		30 SAG			31 ARI

1852

JAN	FEB	MAR	APR	MAY	JUN	JUL	AUG	SEP	OCT	NOV	DEC
1 TAU	1 GEM	1 CAN	1 LEO	1 LIB	1 SAG	1 CAP	1 AQU	1 ARI	1 TAU	1 GEM	1 LEO
4 GEM	2 CAN	3 LEO	2 VIR	3 SCO	4 CAP	3 AQU	2 PIS	3 TAU	3 GEM	2 CAN	4 VIR
6 CAN	5 LEO	5 VIR	4 LIB	5 SAG	6 AQU	5 PIS	4 ARI	6 GEM	5 CAN	4 LEO	6 LIB
8 LEO	7 VIR	7 LIB	6 SCO	7 CAP	8 PIS	8 ARI	7 TAU	8 CAN	8 LEO	6 VIR	8 SCO
10 VIR	9 LIB	9 SCO	8 SAG	9 AQU	11 ARI	10 TAU	9 GEM	10 LEO	10 VIR	8 LIB	10 SAG
12 LIB	11 SCO	11 SAG	10 CAP	12 PIS	13 TAU	13 GEM	12 CAN	13 VIR	12 LIB	10 SCO	12 CAP
15 SCO	13 SAG	13 CAP	12 AQU	14 ARI	16 GEM	15 CAN	14 LEO	15 LIB	14 SCO	12 SAG	14 AQU
17 SAG	15 CAP	16 AQU	14 PIS	17 TAU	18 CAN	18 LEO	16 VIR	17 SCO	16 SAG	14 CAP	16 PIS
19 CAP	18 AQU	18 PIS	17 ARI	19 GEM	20 LEO	20 VIR	18 LIB	19 SAG	18 CAP	17 AQU	19 ARI
21 AQU	20 PIS	21 ARI	20 TAU	22 CAN	22 VIR	22 LIB	20 SCO	21 CAP	20 AQU	19 PIS	21 TAU
24 PIS	22 ARI	23 TAU	22 GEM	24 LEO	25 LIB	24 SCO	22 SAG	23 AQU	23 PIS	21 ARI	24 GEM
26 ARI	25 TAU	26 GEM	24 CAN	26 VIR	27 SCO	26 SAG	24 CAP	25 PIS	25 ARI	24 TAU	26 CAN
29 TAU	28 GEM	28 CAN	27 LEO	28 LIB	29 SAG	28 CAP	27 AQU	28 ARI	28 TAU	26 GEM	29 LEO
31 GEM	29 GEM	31 LEO	29 VIR	30 SCO	30 SAG	30 AQU	29 PIS	30 TAU	30 GEM	29 CAN	31 VIR
			30 VIR	31 SCO		31 AQU	31 PIS		31 GEM	30 CAN	

1853

JAN	FEB	MAR	APR	MAY	JUN	JUL	AUG	SEP	OCT	NOV	DEC
1 VIR	1 SCO	1 SCO	1 CAP	1 AQU	1 ARI	1 TAU	1 GEM	1 LEO	1 VIR	1 SCO	1 SAG
2 LIB	2 SAG	2 SAG	2 AQU	2 PIS	3 TAU	3 GEM	2 CAN	3 VIR	2 LIB	3 SAG	3 CAP
4 SCO	5 CAP	4 CAP	5 PIS	4 ARI	5 GEM	5 CAN	4 LEO	5 LIB	4 SCO	5 CAP	4 AQU
6 SAG	7 AQU	6 AQU	7 ARI	7 TAU	8 CAN	8 LEO	6 VIR	7 SCO	6 SAG	7 AQU	6 PIS
8 CAP	9 PIS	8 PIS	9 TAU	9 GEM	10 LEO	10 VIR	9 LIB	9 SAG	8 CAP	9 PIS	9 ARI
10 AQU	11 ARI	11 ARI	12 GEM	12 CAN	13 VIR	12 LIB	11 SCO	11 CAP	11 AQU	11 ARI	11 TAU
13 PIS	14 TAU	13 TAU	15 CAN	14 LEO	15 LIB	15 SCO	13 SAG	13 AQU	13 PIS	14 TAU	14 GEM
15 ARI	16 GEM	16 GEM	17 LEO	17 VIR	17 SCO	17 SAG	15 CAP	16 PIS	15 ARI	16 GEM	15 CAN
17 TAU	19 CAN	18 CAN	19 VIR	19 LIB	19 SAG	19 CAP	17 AQU	18 ARI	18 TAU	19 CAN	19 LEO
20 GEM	21 LEO	21 LEO	21 LIB	21 SCO	21 CAP	21 AQU	19 PIS	20 TAU	20 GEM	21 LEO	21 VIR
22 CAN	23 VIR	23 VIR	23 SCO	23 SAG	23 AQU	23 PIS	21 ARI	23 GEM	23 CAN	24 VIR	23 LIB
25 LEO	26 LIB	25 LIB	25 SAG	25 CAP	25 PIS	25 ARI	24 TAU	25 CAN	25 LEO	26 LIB	26 SCO
27 VIR	28 SCO	27 SCO	27 CAP	27 AQU	28 ARI	28 TAU	26 GEM	28 LEO	27 VIR	28 SCO	28 SAG
29 LIB		29 SAG	30 AQU	29 PIS	30 TAU	30 GEM	29 CAN	30 VIR	30 LIB	30 SAG	30 CAP
31 SCO		31 CAP		31 ARI		31 GEM	31 LEO		31 LIB		31 CAP

1854

JAN	FEB	MAR	APR	MAY	JUN	JUL	AUG	SEP	OCT	NOV	DEC
1 AQU	1 ARI	1 ARI	1 TAU	1 GEM	1 LEO	1 VIR	1 SCO	1 SAG	1 AQU	1 PIS	1 TAU
3 PIS	4 TAU	3 TAU	2 GEM	2 CAN	3 VIR	3 LIB	3 SAG	2 CAP	3 PIS	2 ARI	4 GEM
5 ARI	6 GEM	5 GEM	4 CAN	4 LEO	5 LIB	5 SCO	6 CAP	4 AQU	5 ARI	4 TAU	6 CAN
7 TAU	9 CAN	8 CAN	7 LEO	7 VIR	8 SCO	7 SAG	8 AQU	6 PIS	8 TAU	6 GEM	9 LEO
10 GEM	11 LEO	11 LEO	9 VIR	9 LIB	10 SAG	9 CAP	10 PIS	8 ARI	10 GEM	9 CAN	11 VIR
12 CAN	14 VIR	13 VIR	12 LIB	11 SCO	12 CAP	11 AQU	12 ARI	10 TAU	12 CAN	11 LEO	14 LIB
15 LEO	16 LIB	15 LIB	14 SCO	13 SAG	14 AQU	13 PIS	14 TAU	13 GEM	15 LEO	14 VIR	16 VIR
17 VIR	18 SCO	17 SCO	16 SAG	15 CAP	16 PIS	15 ARI	16 GEM	15 CAN	17 VIR	16 LIB	18 SAG
20 LIB	20 SAG	20 SAG	18 CAP	17 AQU	18 ARI	17 TAU	19 CAN	18 LEO	20 LIB	18 SCO	20 CAP
22 SCO	22 CAP	22 CAP	20 AQU	19 PIS	20 TAU	20 GEM	21 LEO	20 VIR	22 SCO	21 SAG	22 AQU
24 SAG	25 AQU	24 AQU	22 PIS	22 ARI	23 GEM	22 CAN	24 VIR	22 LIB	24 SAG	23 CAP	24 PIS
26 CAP	27 PIS	26 PIS	24 ARI	24 TAU	25 CAN	25 LEO	26 LIB	25 SCO	26 CAP	25 AQU	26 ARI
28 AQU	28 PIS	28 ARI	27 TAU	26 GEM	28 LEO	27 VIR	28 SCO	27 SAG	28 AQU	27 PIS	28 TAU
30 PIS		30 TAU	29 GEM	29 CAN	30 VIR	30 LIB	31 SAG	29 CAP	31 PIS	29 ARI	31 GEM
31 PIS		31 TAU	30 GEM	31 LEO	31 VIR			30 CAP		30 ARI	

1855

JAN	FEB	MAR	APR	MAY	JUN	JUL	AUG	SEP	OCT	NOV	DEC
1 GEM	1 LEO	1 LEO	1 VIR	1 SCO	1 SAG	1 AQU	1 PIS	1 TAU	1 GEM	1 LEO	1 VIR
2 CAN	4 VIR	3 VIR	2 LIB	4 SAG	2 CAP	3 PIS	2 ARI	3 GEM	2 CAN	4 VIR	3 LIB
5 LEO	6 LIB	5 LIB	4 SCO	6 CAP	4 AQU	6 ARI	4 TAU	5 CAN	5 LEO	6 LIB	6 SCO
7 VIR	9 SCO	8 SCO	6 SAG	8 AQU	6 PIS	8 TAU	6 GEM	7 LEO	7 VIR	8 SCO	8 SAG
10 LIB	11 SAG	10 SAG	9 CAP	10 PIS	8 ARI	10 GEM	9 CAN	10 VIR	10 LIB	11 SAG	10 CAP
12 SCO	13 CAP	12 CAP	11 AQU	12 ARI	11 TAU	12 CAN	11 LEO	12 LIB	12 SCO	13 CAP	13 AQU
14 SAG	15 AQU	14 AQU	13 PIS	14 TAU	13 GEM	15 LEO	14 VIR	15 SCO	15 SAG	15 AQU	15 PIS
17 CAP	17 PIS	16 PIS	15 ARI	17 GEM	15 CAN	17 VIR	16 LIB	17 SAG	17 CAP	17 PIS	17 ARI
19 AQU	19 ARI	18 ARI	17 TAU	19 CAN	18 LEO	20 LIB	19 SCO	20 CAP	19 AQU	19 ARI	19 TAU
20 PIS	21 TAU	20 TAU	19 GEM	21 LEO	20 VIR	22 SCO	21 SAG	22 AQU	21 PIS	22 TAU	21 GEM
23 ARI	23 GEM	23 GEM	21 CAN	24 VIR	23 LIB	25 SAG	23 CAP	24 PIS	23 ARI	24 GEM	23 CAN
25 TAU	26 CAN	25 CAN	24 LEO	26 LIB	25 SCO	27 CAP	25 AQU	26 ARI	25 TAU	26 CAN	26 LEO
27 GEM	28 LEO	28 LEO	26 VIR	29 SCO	27 SAG	29 AQU	27 PIS	28 TAU	27 GEM	28 LEO	28 VIR
30 CAN		30 VIR	29 LIB	31 SAG	29 CAP	31 PIS	29 ARI	30 GEM	30 CAN	30 LEO	31 LIB
31 CAN		31 VIR	30 SCO		30 CAP		31 ARI		31 CAN		

1856

JAN	FEB	MAR	APR	MAY	JUN	JUL	AUG	SEP	OCT	NOV	DEC
1 LIB	1 SAG	1 SAG	1 AQU	1 PIS	1 TAU	1 GEM	1 LEO	1 LIB	1 SCO	1 SAG	1 CAP
2 SCO	3 CAP	2 CAP	2 PIS	2 ARI	2 GEM	2 CAN	3 VIR	4 SCO	4 SAG	2 CAP	2 AQU
5 SAG	5 AQU	4 AQU	4 ARI	4 TAU	4 CAN	4 LEO	5 LIB	6 SAG	6 CAP	5 AQU	4 PIS
7 CAP	7 PIS	6 PIS	6 TAU	6 GEM	7 LEO	6 VIR	8 SCO	9 CAP	8 AQU	7 PIS	6 ARI
9 AQU	9 ARI	8 ARI	8 GEM	8 CAN	9 VIR	9 LIB	10 SAG	11 AQU	11 PIS	9 ARI	8 TAU
11 PIS	11 TAU	10 TAU	10 CAN	10 LEO	11 LIB	11 SCO	12 CAP	13 PIS	13 ARI	11 TAU	10 GEM
13 ARI	14 GEM	12 GEM	13 LEO	13 VIR	14 SCO	14 SAG	15 AQU	15 ARI	15 TAU	13 GEM	13 CAN
15 TAU	16 CAN	14 CAN	15 VIR	15 LIB	16 SAG	16 CAP	17 PIS	17 TAU	17 GEM	15 CAN	15 LEO
17 GEM	18 LEO	17 LEO	18 LIB	18 SCO	19 CAP	18 AQU	19 ARI	19 GEM	19 CAN	17 LEO	17 VIR
20 CAN	21 VIR	19 VIR	20 SCO	20 SAG	21 AQU	20 PIS	21 TAU	21 CAN	21 LEO	20 VIR	19 LIB
22 LEO	23 LIB	22 LIB	23 SAG	22 CAP	23 PIS	22 ARI	23 GEM	24 LEO	23 VIR	22 LIB	22 SCO
25 VIR	26 SCO	24 SCO	25 CAP	25 AQU	25 ARI	24 TAU	25 CAN	26 VIR	26 LIB	25 SCO	25 SAG
27 LIB	28 SAG	27 SAG	27 AQU	27 PIS	27 TAU	27 GEM	27 LEO	29 LIB	28 SCO	27 SAG	27 CAP
30 SCO	29 SAG	29 CAP	30 PIS	29 ARI	29 GEM	29 CAN	30 VIR	30 LIB	31 SAG	30 CAP	29 AQU
31 SCO		31 AQU		31 TAU	30 GEM	31 LEO	31 VIR				31 PIS

1857

JAN	FEB	MAR	APR	MAY	JUN	JUL	AUG	SEP	OCT	NOV	DEC
1 PIS	1 TAU	1 TAU	1 CAN	1 LEO	1 LIB	1 SCO	1 SAG	1 AQU	1 PIS	1 TAU	1 GEM
3 ARI	3 GEM	2 GEM	3 LEO	3 VIR	4 SCO	4 SAG	2 CAP	3 PIS	3 ARI	3 GEM	3 CAN
5 TAU	5 CAN	4 CAN	5 VIR	5 LIB	6 SAG	6 CAP	5 AQU	6 ARI	5 TAU	5 CAN	5 LEO
7 GEM	7 LEO	7 LEO	8 LIB	8 SCO	9 CAP	8 AQU	7 PIS	8 TAU	7 GEM	7 LEO	7 VIR
9 CAN	10 VIR	9 VIR	10 SCO	10 SAG	11 AQU	11 PIS	9 ARI	10 GEM	9 CAN	10 VIR	9 LIB
11 LEO	12 LIB	11 LIB	13 SAG	13 CAP	14 PIS	13 ARI	11 TAU	12 CAN	11 LEO	12 LIB	12 SCO
13 VIR	15 SCO	14 SCO	15 CAP	15 AQU	16 ARI	15 TAU	13 GEM	14 LEO	13 VIR	15 SCO	14 SAG
16 LIB	17 SAG	17 SAG	18 AQU	17 PIS	18 TAU	17 GEM	16 CAN	16 VIR	16 LIB	17 SAG	17 CAP
18 SCO	20 CAP	19 CAP	20 PIS	19 ARI	20 GEM	19 CAN	18 LEO	19 LIB	18 SCO	20 CAP	19 AQU
21 SAG	22 AQU	21 AQU	22 ARI	21 TAU	22 CAN	21 LEO	20 VIR	21 SCO	21 SAG	22 AQU	22 PIS
23 CAP	24 PIS	24 PIS	24 TAU	23 GEM	24 LEO	24 VIR	22 LIB	24 SAG	23 CAP	25 PIS	24 ARI
26 AQU	26 ARI	26 ARI	26 GEM	25 CAN	26 VIR	26 LIB	25 SCO	26 CAP	26 AQU	27 ARI	26 TAU
28 PIS	28 TAU	28 TAU	28 CAN	28 LEO	29 LIB	28 SCO	27 SAG	29 AQU	28 PIS	29 TAU	28 GEM
30 ARI		30 GEM	30 LEO	30 VIR	30 LIB	31 SAG	30 CAP	30 AQU	30 ARI	30 TAU	30 CAN
31 ARI		31 GEM		31 VIR			31 CAP		31 ARI		31 CAN

1858

JAN	FEB	MAR	APR	MAY	JUN	JUL	AUG	SEP	OCT	NOV	DEC
1 LEO	1 VIR	1 LIB	1 SCO	1 SAG	1 AQU	1 PIS	1 ARI	1 GEM	1 CAN	1 VIR	1 LIB
3 VIR	2 LIB	4 SCO	3 SAG	2 CAP	4 PIS	3 ARI	2 TAU	2 CAN	2 LEO	2 LIB	2 SCO
6 LIB	4 SCO	6 SAG	5 CAP	5 AQU	6 ARI	6 TAU	4 GEM	4 LEO	4 VIR	5 SCO	4 SAG
8 SCO	7 SAG	9 CAP	8 AQU	7 PIS	8 TAU	8 GEM	6 CAN	7 VIR	6 LIB	7 SAG	7 CAP
11 SAG	10 CAP	11 AQU	10 PIS	10 ARI	10 GEM	10 CAN	8 LEO	9 LIB	8 SCO	10 CAP	9 AQU
13 CAP	12 AQU	14 PIS	12 ARI	12 TAU	12 CAN	12 LEO	10 VIR	11 SCO	11 SAG	12 AQU	12 PIS
16 AQU	14 PIS	16 ARI	14 TAU	14 GEM	14 LEO	14 VIR	12 LIB	13 SAG	13 CAP	15 PIS	14 ARI
18 PIS	17 ARI	18 TAU	16 GEM	16 CAN	16 VIR	16 LIB	15 SCO	16 CAP	16 AQU	17 ARI	17 TAU
20 ARI	19 TAU	20 GEM	18 CAN	18 LEO	19 LIB	18 SCO	17 SAG	18 AQU	18 PIS	19 TAU	19 GEM
23 TAU	21 GEM	22 CAN	21 LEO	20 VIR	21 SCO	21 SAG	20 CAP	21 PIS	21 ARI	21 GEM	21 CAN
25 GEM	23 CAN	24 LEO	23 VIR	22 LIB	23 SAG	23 CAP	22 AQU	23 ARI	23 TAU	23 CAN	23 LEO
27 CAN	25 LEO	27 VIR	25 LIB	25 SCO	26 CAP	26 AQU	25 PIS	25 TAU	25 GEM	25 LEO	25 VIR
29 LEO	27 VIR	29 LIB	28 SCO	27 SAG	29 AQU	28 PIS	27 ARI	27 GEM	27 CAN	27 VIR	27 LIB
31 VIR	28 VIR	31 SCO	30 SAG	30 CAP	30 AQU	31 ARI	29 TAU	30 CAN	29 LEO	30 LIB	29 SCO
				31 CAP			31 GEM		31 VIR		31 SCO

1859

JAN	FEB	MAR	APR	MAY	JUN	JUL	AUG	SEP	OCT	NOV	DEC
1 SAG	1 CAP	1 AQU	1 PIS	1 ARI	1 GEM	1 CAN	1 VIR	1 SCO	1 SAG	1 CAP	1 AQU
3 CAP	2 AQU	4 PIS	2 ARI	2 TAU	3 CAN	2 LEO	3 LIB	3 SAG	3 CAP	2 AQU	2 PIS
6 AQU	4 PIS	6 ARI	5 TAU	4 GEM	5 LEO	4 VIR	5 SCO	6 CAP	6 AQU	4 PIS	4 ARI
8 PIS	7 ARI	8 TAU	7 GEM	6 CAN	7 VIR	6 LIB	7 SAG	8 AQU	8 PIS	7 ARI	7 TAU
11 ARI	9 TAU	11 GEM	9 CAN	8 LEO	9 LIB	8 SCO	9 CAP	11 PIS	11 ARI	9 TAU	9 GEM
13 TAU	11 GEM	13 CAN	11 LEO	11 VIR	11 SCO	11 SAG	12 AQU	13 ARI	13 TAU	11 GEM	11 CAN
15 GEM	14 CAN	15 LEO	13 VIR	13 LIB	14 SAG	13 CAP	15 PIS	16 TAU	15 GEM	14 CAN	13 LEO
17 CAN	16 LEO	17 VIR	15 LIB	15 SCO	16 CAP	16 AQU	17 ARI	18 GEM	17 CAN	16 LEO	15 VIR
19 LEO	18 VIR	19 LIB	18 SCO	17 SAG	18 AQU	18 PIS	19 TAU	20 CAN	20 LEO	18 VIR	17 LIB
21 VIR	20 LIB	21 SCO	20 SAG	20 CAP	21 PIS	21 ARI	22 GEM	22 LEO	22 VIR	20 LIB	19 SCO
23 LIB	22 SCO	24 SAG	22 CAP	22 AQU	23 ARI	23 TAU	24 CAN	24 VIR	24 LIB	22 SCO	22 SAG
25 SCO	24 SAG	26 CAP	25 AQU	25 PIS	26 TAU	25 GEM	26 LEO	26 LIB	26 SCO	24 SAG	24 CAP
28 SAG	27 CAP	28 AQU	27 PIS	27 ARI	28 GEM	28 CAN	28 VIR	28 SCO	28 SAG	27 CAP	27 AQU
30 CAP	28 CAP	31 PIS	30 ARI	29 TAU	30 CAN	29 LEO	30 LIB	30 SCO	30 CAP	29 AQU	29 PIS
31 CAP				31 TAU		31 VIR	31 LIB		31 AQU	30 AQU	31 PIS

1860

JAN	FEB	MAR	APR	MAY	JUN	JUL	AUG	SEP	OCT	NOV	DEC
1 ARI	1 TAU	1 GEM	1 LEO	1 VIR	1 SCO	1 SAG	1 AQU	1 PIS	1 ARI	1 GEM	1 CAN
3 TAU	2 GEM	2 CAN	3 VIR	2 LIB	3 SAG	2 CAP	3 PIS	2 ARI	2 TAU	3 CAN	3 LEO
5 GEM	4 CAN	4 LEO	5 LIB	4 SCO	5 CAP	5 AQU	6 ARI	5 TAU	4 GEM	5 LEO	5 VIR
7 CAN	6 LEO	6 VIR	7 SCO	6 SAG	7 AQU	7 PIS	8 TAU	7 GEM	7 CAN	8 VIR	7 LIB
9 LEO	8 VIR	8 LIB	9 SAG	9 CAP	10 PIS	10 ARI	11 GEM	10 CAN	9 LEO	10 LIB	9 SCO
11 VIR	10 LIB	10 SCO	11 CAP	11 AQU	12 ARI	12 TAU	13 CAN	12 LEO	11 VIR	12 SCO	11 SAG
14 LIB	12 SCO	13 SAG	14 AQU	13 PIS	15 TAU	15 GEM	15 LEO	14 VIR	13 LIB	14 SAG	13 CAP
16 SCO	14 SAG	15 CAP	16 PIS	16 ARI	17 GEM	17 CAN	17 VIR	16 LIB	15 SCO	16 CAP	15 AQU
18 SAG	17 CAP	17 AQU	19 ARI	18 TAU	19 CAN	19 LEO	19 LIB	18 SCO	17 SAG	18 AQU	18 PIS
20 CAP	19 AQU	20 PIS	21 TAU	21 GEM	21 LEO	21 VIR	21 SCO	20 SAG	19 CAP	21 PIS	20 ARI
23 AQU	22 PIS	22 ARI	23 GEM	23 CAN	24 VIR	23 LIB	23 SAG	22 CAP	22 AQU	23 ARI	23 TAU
25 PIS	24 ARI	25 TAU	26 CAN	25 LEO	26 LIB	25 SCO	26 CAP	24 AQU	24 PIS	26 TAU	25 GEM
28 ARI	27 TAU	27 GEM	28 LEO	27 VIR	28 SCO	27 SAG	28 AQU	27 PIS	27 ARI	28 GEM	28 CAN
30 TAU	29 GEM	30 CAN	30 VIR	29 LIB	30 SAG	30 CAP	31 PIS	29 ARI	29 TAU	30 CAN	30 LEO
31 TAU		31 CAN		31 LIB		31 CAP		30 ARI	31 TAU		31 LEO

1861

JAN	FEB	MAR	APR	MAY	JUN	JUL	AUG	SEP	OCT	NOV	DEC
1 VIR	1 SCO	1 SCO	1 CAP	1 AQU	1 PIS	1 ARI	1 GEM	1 CAN	1 LEO	1 LIB	1 SAG
3 LIB	4 SAG	3 SAG	4 AQU	3 PIS	2 ARI	2 TAU	3 CAN	2 LEO	2 VIR	2 SCO	3 CAP
5 SCO	6 CAP	5 CAP	6 PIS	6 ARI	5 TAU	4 GEM	6 LEO	4 VIR	4 LIB	4 SAG	6 AQU
7 SAG	8 AQU	7 AQU	9 ARI	8 TAU	7 GEM	7 CAN	8 VIR	6 LIB	6 SCO	6 CAP	8 PIS
10 CAP	11 PIS	10 PIS	11 TAU	11 GEM	10 CAN	9 LEO	10 LIB	8 SCO	8 SAG	8 AQU	10 ARI
12 AQU	13 ARI	12 ARI	14 GEM	13 CAN	12 LEO	11 VIR	12 SCO	10 SAG	10 CAP	10 PIS	13 TAU
14 PIS	16 TAU	15 TAU	16 CAN	16 LEO	14 VIR	14 LIB	14 SAG	12 CAP	12 AQU	13 ARI	15 GEM
17 ARI	18 GEM	17 GEM	18 LEO	18 VIR	16 LIB	16 SCO	16 CAP	15 AQU	14 PIS	15 TAU	18 CAN
19 TAU	20 CAN	20 CAN	21 VIR	20 LIB	18 SCO	18 SAG	18 AQU	17 PIS	17 ARI	18 GEM	20 LEO
22 GEM	23 LEO	22 LEO	23 LIB	22 SCO	20 SAG	20 CAP	21 PIS	19 ARI	19 TAU	20 CAN	22 VIR
24 CAN	25 VIR	24 VIR	25 SCO	24 SAG	23 CAP	22 AQU	23 ARI	22 TAU	22 GEM	23 LEO	26 LIB
26 LEO	27 LIB	26 LIB	27 SAG	26 CAP	25 AQU	24 PIS	26 TAU	24 GEM	24 CAN	25 VIR	27 SCO
28 VIR	28 LIB	28 SCO	29 CAP	28 AQU	27 PIS	27 ARI	28 GEM	27 CAN	27 LEO	27 LIB	29 SAG
30 LIB		30 SAG	30 CAP	31 PIS	29 ARI	29 TAU	30 CAN	29 LEO	29 VIR	29 SCO	31 CAP
31 LIB					30 ARI	31 TAU	31 CAN	30 LEO	31 LIB	30 SCO	

1862

JAN	FEB	MAR	APR	MAY	JUN	JUL	AUG	SEP	OCT	NOV	DEC
1 CAP	1 PIS	1 PIS	1 TAU	1 GEM	1 CAN	1 LEO	1 LIB	1 SAG	1 CAP	1 PIS	1 ARI
2 AQU	3 ARI	2 ARI	4 GEM	3 CAN	2 LEO	2 VIR	2 SCO	3 CAP	2 AQU	3 ARI	3 TAU
4 PIS	5 TAU	5 TAU	6 CAN	6 LEO	4 VIR	4 LIB	5 SAG	5 AQU	4 PIS	5 TAU	5 GEM
7 ARI	8 GEM	7 GEM	9 LEO	8 VIR	7 LIB	6 SCO	7 CAP	7 PIS	7 ARI	8 GEM	8 CAN
9 TAU	10 CAN	10 CAN	11 VIR	10 LIB	9 SCO	8 SAG	9 AQU	9 ARI	9 TAU	10 CAN	10 LEO
12 GEM	13 LEO	12 LEO	13 LIB	12 SCO	11 SAG	10 CAP	11 PIS	12 TAU	12 GEM	13 LEO	13 VIR
14 CAN	15 VIR	14 VIR	15 SCO	14 SAG	13 CAP	12 AQU	13 ARI	14 GEM	14 CAN	15 VIR	15 LIB
16 LEO	17 LIB	17 LIB	17 SAG	16 CAP	15 AQU	14 PIS	15 TAU	17 CAN	17 LEO	18 LIB	17 SCO
19 VIR	19 SCO	19 SCO	19 CAP	18 AQU	17 PIS	17 ARI	18 GEM	19 LEO	19 VIR	20 SCO	19 SAG
21 LIB	21 SAG	21 SAG	21 AQU	21 PIS	19 ARI	19 TAU	20 CAN	22 VIR	21 LIB	22 SAG	21 CAP
23 SCO	24 CAP	23 CAP	23 PIS	23 ARI	22 TAU	22 GEM	23 LEO	24 LIB	23 SCO	24 CAP	23 AQU
25 SAG	26 AQU	25 AQU	26 ARI	26 TAU	24 GEM	24 CAN	25 VIR	26 SCO	25 SAG	26 AQU	25 PIS
27 CAP	28 PIS	27 PIS	28 TAU	28 GEM	27 CAN	27 LEO	28 LIB	28 SAG	27 CAP	28 PIS	28 ARI
29 AQU		30 ARI	30 TAU	31 CAN	29 LEO	29 VIR	30 SCO	30 CAP	30 AQU	30 ARI	30 TAU
31 AQU		31 ARI			30 LEO	31 LIB	31 SCO		31 AQU		31 TAU

1863

JAN	FEB	MAR	APR	MAY	JUN	JUL	AUG	SEP	OCT	NOV	DEC
1 GEM	1 CAN	1 CAN	1 VIR	1 LIB	1 SAG	1 CAP	1 PIS	1 ARI	1 GEM	1 CAN	1 LEO
4 CAN	3 LEO	2 LEO	3 LIB	3 SCO	3 CAP	3 AQU	3 ARI	2 TAU	4 CAN	3 LEO	3 VIR
6 LEO	5 VIR	4 VIR	5 SCO	5 SAG	5 AQU	5 PIS	5 TAU	4 GEM	6 LEO	5 VIR	5 LIB
9 VIR	8 LIB	7 LIB	7 SAG	7 CAP	7 PIS	7 ARI	8 GEM	7 CAN	9 VIR	8 LIB	7 SCO
11 LIB	10 SCO	9 SCO	10 CAP	9 AQU	10 ARI	9 TAU	10 CAN	9 LEO	11 LIB	10 SCO	10 SAG
14 SCO	12 SAG	11 SAG	12 AQU	11 PIS	12 TAU	12 GEM	13 LEO	12 VIR	14 SCO	12 SAG	12 CAP
16 SAG	14 CAP	13 CAP	14 PIS	13 ARI	14 GEM	14 CAN	15 VIR	14 LIB	16 SAG	14 CAP	14 AQU
18 CAP	16 AQU	15 AQU	16 ARI	16 TAU	17 CAN	17 LEO	18 LIB	16 SCO	18 CAP	16 AQU	16 PIS
20 AQU	18 PIS	18 PIS	18 TAU	18 GEM	19 LEO	19 VIR	20 SCO	19 SAG	20 AQU	18 PIS	18 ARI
22 PIS	20 ARI	20 ARI	21 GEM	20 CAN	22 VIR	22 LIB	22 SAG	21 CAP	22 PIS	21 ARI	20 TAU
24 ARI	23 TAU	22 TAU	23 CAN	23 LEO	24 LIB	24 SCO	25 CAP	23 AQU	24 ARI	23 TAU	22 GEM
26 TAU	25 GEM	24 GEM	26 LEO	26 VIR	27 SCO	26 SAG	27 AQU	25 PIS	27 TAU	25 GEM	25 CAN
29 GEM	28 CAN	27 CAN	28 VIR	28 LIB	29 SAG	28 CAP	29 PIS	27 ARI	29 GEM	28 CAN	28 LEO
31 CAN		29 LEO	30 VIR	30 SCO	30 SAG	30 AQU	31 ARI	29 TAU	31 CAN	30 LEO	30 VIR
		31 LEO		31 SCO		31 AQU		30 TAU			31 VIR

1864

JAN	FEB	MAR	APR	MAY	JUN	JUL	AUG	SEP	OCT	NOV	DEC
1 LIB	1 SCO	1 SAG	1 AQU	1 PIS	1 TAU	1 GEM	1 CAN	1 VIR	1 LIB	1 SAG	1 CAP
4 SCO	2 SAG	3 CAP	3 PIS	3 ARI	3 GEM	3 CAN	2 LEO	3 LIB	3 SCO	4 CAP	3 AQU
6 SAG	5 CAP	5 AQU	5 ARI	5 TAU	6 CAN	5 LEO	4 VIR	6 SCO	5 SAG	6 AQU	5 PIS
8 CAP	7 AQU	7 PIS	7 TAU	7 GEM	8 LEO	8 VIR	7 LIB	8 SAG	7 CAP	8 PIS	7 ARI
10 AQU	9 PIS	9 ARI	10 GEM	9 CAN	11 VIR	11 LIB	9 SCO	10 CAP	10 AQU	10 ARI	10 TAU
12 PIS	11 ARI	11 TAU	12 CAN	12 LEO	13 LIB	13 SCO	12 SAG	12 AQU	12 PIS	12 TAU	12 GEM
14 ARI	13 TAU	13 GEM	14 LEO	14 VIR	16 SCO	15 SAG	14 CAP	14 PIS	14 ARI	14 GEM	14 CAN
16 TAU	15 GEM	16 CAN	17 VIR	17 LIB	18 SAG	17 CAP	16 AQU	16 ARI	16 TAU	17 CAN	16 LEO
19 GEM	17 CAN	18 LEO	19 LIB	19 SCO	20 CAP	19 AQU	18 PIS	18 TAU	18 GEM	19 LEO	19 VIR
21 CAN	20 LEO	21 VIR	22 SCO	22 SAG	22 AQU	21 PIS	20 ARI	20 GEM	20 CAN	21 VIR	21 LIB
24 LEO	22 VIR	23 LIB	24 SAG	24 CAP	24 PIS	24 ARI	22 TAU	23 CAN	23 LEO	24 LIB	24 SCO
26 VIR	25 LIB	26 SCO	26 CAP	26 AQU	26 ARI	26 TAU	24 GEM	25 LEO	25 VIR	26 SCO	26 SAG
29 LIB	27 SCO	28 SAG	29 AQU	28 PIS	28 TAU	28 GEM	27 CAN	28 VIR	28 LIB	29 SAG	28 CAP
31 SCO	29 SCO	30 CAP	30 AQU	30 ARI	30 TAU	30 CAN	29 LEO	30 LIB	30 SCO	30 SAG	30 AQU
		31 CAP		31 ARI		31 CAP	31 VIR		31 SCO		31 AQU

1865

JAN	FEB	MAR	APR	MAY	JUN	JUL	AUG	SEP	OCT	NOV	DEC
1 AQU	1 ARI	1 TAU	1 GEM	1 CAN	1 VIR	1 LIB	1 SCO	1 CAP	1 AQU	1 ARI	1 TAU
2 PIS	2 TAU	3 GEM	2 CAN	2 LEO	3 LIB	3 SCO	2 SAG	3 AQU	2 PIS	3 TAU	2 GEM
4 ARI	4 GEM	6 CAN	4 LEO	4 VIR	5 SCO	5 SAG	4 CAP	5 PIS	4 ARI	5 GEM	4 CAN
6 TAU	7 CAN	8 LEO	7 VIR	7 LIB	8 SAG	8 CAP	6 AQU	7 ARI	6 TAU	7 CAN	6 LEO
8 GEM	9 LEO	11 VIR	9 LIB	9 SCO	10 CAP	10 AQU	8 PIS	9 TAU	8 GEM	9 LEO	9 VIR
10 CAN	11 VIR	13 LIB	12 SCO	12 SAG	13 AQU	12 PIS	10 ARI	11 GEM	10 CAN	11 VIR	11 LIB
13 LEO	14 LIB	16 SCO	14 SAG	14 CAP	15 PIS	14 ARI	12 TAU	13 CAN	13 LEO	14 LIB	14 SCO
15 VIR	16 SCO	18 SAG	17 CAP	16 AQU	17 ARI	16 TAU	15 GEM	15 LEO	15 VIR	16 SCO	16 SAG
18 LIB	19 SAG	21 CAP	19 AQU	18 PIS	19 TAU	18 GEM	17 CAN	18 VIR	17 LIB	19 SAG	18 CAP
20 SCO	21 CAP	23 AQU	21 PIS	21 ARI	21 GEM	21 CAN	19 LEO	20 LIB	20 SCO	21 CAP	21 AQU
23 SAG	23 AQU	25 PIS	23 ARI	23 TAU	23 CAN	23 LEO	21 VIR	23 SCO	23 SAG	24 AQU	23 PIS
25 CAP	25 PIS	27	25 TAU	25 GEM	25 LEO	25 VIR	24 LIB	25 SAG	25 CAP	26 PIS	25 ARI
27 AQU	27 ARI	29 TAU	27 GEM	27 CAN	28 VIR	28 LIB	26 SCO	28 CAP	27 AQU	28 ARI	27 TAU
29 PIS	28 ARI	31 GEM	29 CAN	29 LEO	30 LIB	30 SCO	29 SAG	30 AQU	30 PIS	30 TAU	29 GEM
31 ARI			30 CAN	31 LEO		31 SCO	31 CAP		31 PIS		31 GEM

1866

JAN	FEB	MAR	APR	MAY	JUN	JUL	AUG	SEP	OCT	NOV	DEC
1 CAN	1 VIR	1 VIR	1 LIB	1 SCO	1 CAP	1 AQU	1 ARI	1 GEM	1 CAN	1 VIR	1 LIB
3 LEO	4 LIB	3 LIB	2 SCO	2 SAG	3 AQU	2 PIS	3 TAU	3 CAN	3 LEO	4 LIB	3 SCO
5 VIR	6 SCO	6 SCO	4 SAG	4 CAP	5 PIS	5 ARI	5 GEM	6 LEO	5 VIR	6 SCO	6 SAG
7 LIB	9 SAG	8 SAG	7 CAP	7 AQU	7 ARI	7 TAU	7 CAN	8 VIR	7 LIB	9 SAG	8 CAP
10 SCO	11 CAP	11 CAP	9 AQU	9 PIS	9 TAU	9 GEM	9 LEO	10 LIB	10 SCO	11 CAP	11 AQU
12 SAG	13 AQU	13 AQU	12 PIS	11 ARI	11 GEM	11 CAN	12 VIR	13 SCO	12 SAG	14 AQU	13 PIS
15 CAP	16 PIS	15 PIS	14 ARI	13 TAU	13 CAN	13 LEO	14 LIB	15 SAG	15 CAP	16 PIS	16 ARI
17 AQU	18 ARI	17 ARI	16 TAU	15 GEM	16 LEO	15 VIR	16 SCO	18 CAP	17 AQU	18 ARI	18 TAU
19 PIS	20 TAU	19 TAU	18 GEM	17 CAN	18 VIR	17 LIB	19 SAG	20 AQU	20 PIS	20 TAU	20 GEM
21 ARI	22 GEM	21 GEM	20 CAN	19 LEO	20 LIB	20 SCO	21 CAP	22 PIS	22 ARI	22 GEM	22 CAN
24 TAU	24 CAN	23 CAN	22 LEO	21 VIR	23 SCO	22 SAG	24 AQU	24 ARI	24 TAU	24 CAN	24 LEO
26 GEM	26 LEO	26 LEO	24 VIR	24 LIB	25 SAG	25 CAP	26 PIS	27 TAU	26 GEM	26 LEO	26 VIR
28 CAN	28 LEO	28 VIR	27 LIB	26 SCO	28 CAP	27 AQU	28 ARI	29 GEM	28 CAN	29 VIR	28 LIB
30 LEO		30 LIB	29 SCO	29 SAG	30 AQU	30 PIS	30 TAU	30 GEM	30 LEO	30 VIR	31 SCO
31 LEO		31 LIB	30 SCO	31 CAP		31 PIS	31 TAU		31 LEO		

1867

JAN	FEB	MAR	APR	MAY	JUN	JUL	AUG	SEP	OCT	NOV	DEC
1 SCO	1 CAP	1 CAP	1 AQU	1 ARI	1 TAU	1 CAN	1 LEO	1 LIB	1 SCO	1 CAP	1 AQU
2 SAG	4 AQU	3 AQU	2 PIS	3 TAU	2 GEM	3 LEO	2 VIR	3 SCO	2 SAG	4 AQU	3 PIS
5 CAP	6 PIS	5 PIS	4 ARI	5 GEM	4 CAN	5 VIR	4 LIB	5 SAG	5 CAP	6 PIS	6 ARI
7 AQU	8 ARI	7 ARI	6 TAU	7 CAN	6 LEO	7 LIB	6 SCO	7 CAP	7 AQU	8 ARI	8 TAU
10 PIS	10 TAU	10 TAU	8 GEM	10 LEO	8 VIR	10 SCO	9 SAG	10 AQU	10 PIS	11 TAU	10 GEM
12 ARI	13 GEM	12 GEM	10 CAN	12 VIR	10 LIB	12 SAG	11 CAP	12 PIS	12 ARI	13 GEM	12 CAN
14 TAU	15 CAN	14 CAN	12 LEO	14 LIB	13 SCO	15 CAP	14 AQU	15 ARI	14 TAU	15 CAN	14 LEO
16 GEM	17 LEO	16 LEO	14 VIR	16 SCO	15 SAG	17 AQU	16 PIS	17 TAU	16 GEM	17 LEO	16 VIR
18 CAN	19 VIR	18 VIR	17 LIB	19 SAG	18 CAP	20 PIS	18 ARI	19 GEM	19 CAN	19 VIR	18 LIB
20 LEO	21 LIB	20 LIB	19 SCO	21 CAP	20 AQU	22 ARI	21 TAU	21 CAN	21 LEO	21 LIB	21 SCO
22 VIR	23 SCO	23 SCO	22 SAG	24 AQU	23 PIS	25 TAU	23 GEM	23 LEO	23 VIR	24 SCO	23 SAG
25 LIB	26 SAG	25 SAG	24 CAP	26 PIS	25 ARI	27 GEM	25 CAN	26 VIR	25 LIB	26 SAG	26 CAP
27 SCO	28 CAP	28 CAP	27 AQU	29 ARI	27 TAU	29 CAN	27 LEO	28 LIB	27 SCO	28 CAP	28 AQU
30 SAG		30 AQU	29 PIS	31 TAU	29 GEM	31 LEO	29 VIR	30 SCO	30 SAG	30 CAP	31 PIS
31 SAG		31 AQU	30 PIS		30 CAN		31 LIB		31 SAG		

1868

JAN	FEB	MAR	APR	MAY	JUN	JUL	AUG	SEP	OCT	NOV	DEC
1 PIS	1 TAU	1 GEM	1 CAN	1 VIR	1 LIB	1 SAG	1 CAP	1 PIS	1 ARI	1 TAU	1 GEM
2 ARI	3 GEM	3 CAN	2 LEO	3 LIB	2 SCO	4 CAP	3 AQU	4 ARI	4 TAU	2 GEM	2 CAN
5 TAU	5 CAN	6 LEO	4 VIR	6 SCO	4 SAG	4 AQU	5 PIS	6 TAU	6 GEM	4 CAN	4 LEO
7 GEM	7 LEO	8 VIR	6 LIB	8 SAG	7 CAP	9 PIS	8 ARI	9 GEM	8 CAN	6 LEO	6 VIR
9 CAN	9 VIR	10 LIB	8 SCO	10 CAP	9 AQU	11 ARI	10 TAU	11 CAN	10 LEO	9 VIR	8 LIB
11 LEO	11 LIB	12 SCO	10 SAG	13 AQU	12 PIS	14 TAU	12 GEM	13 LEO	12 VIR	11 LIB	10 SCO
13 VIR	13 SCO	14 SAG	13 CAP	15 PIS	14 ARI	16 GEM	14 CAN	15 VIR	14 LIB	13 SCO	12 SAG
15 LIB	16 SAG	16 CAP	15 AQU	18 ARI	16 TAU	18 CAN.	17 LEO	17 LIB	16 SCO	15 SAG	15 CAP
17 SCO	18 CAP	19 AQU	18 PIS	20 TAU	19 GEM	20 LEO	19 VIR	19 SCO	19 SAG	17 CAP	17 AQU
19 SAG	21 AQU	22 PIS	20 ARI	22 GEM	21 CAN	22 VIR	21 LIB	21 SAG	21 CAP	20 AQU	20 PIS
22 CAP	23 PIS	24 ARI	23 TAU	24 CAN	23 LEO	24 LIB	23 SCO	24 CAP	23 AQU	22 PIS	22 ARI
24 AQU	26 ARI	26 TAU	25 GEM	26 LEO	25 VIR	26 SCO	25 SAG	26 AQU	26 PIS	25 ARI	25 TAU
27 PIS	28 TAU	29 GEM	27 CAN	28 VIR	27 LIB	29 SAG	27 CAP	29 PIS	28 ARI	27 TAU	27 GEM
29 ARI	29 TAU	31 CAN	29 LEO	31 LIB	29 SCO	31 CAP	30 AQU	30 PIS	31 TAU	29 GEM	29 CAN
31 ARI			30 LEO		30 SCO		31 AQU			30 GEM	31 LEO

1869

JAN	FEB	MAR	APR	MAY	JUN	JUL	AUG	SEP	OCT	NOV	DEC
1 LEO	1 LIB	1 LIB	1 SAG	1 CAP	1 PIS	1 ARI	1 TAU	1 CAN	1 LEO	1 LIB	1 SCO
2 VIR	3 SCO	2 SCO	3 CAP	2 AQU	4 ARI	4 TAU	2 GEM	3 LEO	3 VIR	3 SCO	3 SAG
4 LIB	5 SAG	4 SAG	5 AQU	5 PIS	6 TAU	6 GEM	5 CAN	5 VIR	5 LIB	5 SAG	5 CAP
6 SCO	7 CAP	6 CAP	8 PIS	8 ARI	9 GEM	8 CAN	7 LEO	7 LIB	7 SCO	7 CAP	7 AQU
9 SAG	10 AQU	9 AQU	10 ARI	10 TAU	11 CAN	10 LEO	9 VIR	9 SCO	9 SAG	10 AQU	9 PIS
11 CAP	12 PIS	11 PIS	13 TAU	12 GEM	13 LEO	13 VIR	11 LIB	11 SAG	11 CAP	12 PIS	12 ARI
13 AQU	15 ARI	14 ARI	15 GEM	15 CAN	15 VIR	15 LIB	13 SCO	14 CAP	13 AQU	15 ARI	14 TAU
16 PIS	17 TAU	16 TAU	17 CAN	17 LEO	17 LIB	17 SCO	15 SAG	16 AQU	16 PIS	17 TAU	17 GEM
18 ARI	20 GEM	19 GEM	20 LEO	19 VIR	20 SCO	19 SAG	17 CAP	19 PIS	18 ARI	20 GEM	19 CAN
21 TAU	22 CAN	21 CAN	22 VIR	21 LIB	22 SAG	21 CAP	20 AQU	21 ARI	21 TAU	22 CAN	21 LEO
23 GEM	24 LEO	23 LEO	24 LIB	23 SCO	24 CAP	24 AQU	22 PIS	24 TAU	23 GEM	24 LEO	24 VIR
25 CAN	26 VIR	25 VIR	26 SCO	25 SAG	26 AQU	26 PIS	25 ARI	26 GEM	26 CAN	26 VIR	26 LIB
28 LEO	28 LIB	27 LIB	28 SAG	28 CAP	29 PIS	28 ARI	27 TAU	28 CAN	28 LEO	29 LIB	28 SCO
30 VIR		29 SCO	30 CAP	30 AQU	30 PIS	31 TAU	30 GEM	30 CAN	30 VIR	30 LIB	30 SAG
31 VIR		31 SAG		31 AQU			31 GEM		31 VIR		31 SAG

1870

JAN	FEB	MAR	APR	MAY	JUN	JUL	AUG	SEP	OCT	NOV	DEC
1 CAP	1 AQU	1 PIS	1 ARI	1 TAU	1 CAN	1 LEO	1 LIB	1 SCO	1 CAP	1 AQU	1 PIS
3 AQU	2 PIS	4 ARI	3 TAU	2 GEM	4 LEO	3 VIR	4 SCO	2 SAG	3 AQU	2 PIS	2 ARI
6 PIS	5 ARI	6 TAU	5 GEM	5 CAN	6 VIR	5 LIB	6 SAG	4 CAP	6 PIS	4 ARI	4 TAU
8 ARI	7 TAU	9 GEM	8 CAN	7 LEO	8 LIB	7 SCO	8 CAP	6 AQU	8 ARI	7 TAU	7 GEM
11 TAU	10 GEM	11 CAN	10 LEO	10 VIR	10 SCO	9 SAG	10 AQU	9 PIS	11 TAU	10 GEM	9 CAN
13 GEM	12 CAN	14 LEO	12 VIR	12 LIB	12 SAG	11 CAP	12 PIS	11 ARI	13 GEM	12 CAN	12 LEO
16 CAN	14 LEO	16 VIR	14 LIB	14 SCO	14 CAP	14 AQU	15 ARI	13 TAU	16 CAN	15 LEO	14 VIR
18 LEO	16 VIR	18 LIB	16 SCO	16 SAG	16 AQU	16 PIS	17 TAU	16 GEM	18 LEO	17 VIR	16 LIB
20 VIR	18 LIB	20 SCO	18 SAG	18 CAP	19 PIS	18 ARI	20 GEM	18 CAN	20 VIR	19 LIB	18 SCO
22 LIB	20 SCO	22 SAG	20 CAP	20 AQU	21 ARI	21 TAU	22 CAN	21 LEO	23 LIB	21 SCO	20 SAG
24 SCO	22 SAG	24 CAP	23 AQU	22 PIS	23 TAU	23 GEM	24 LEO	23 VIR	25 SCO	23 SAG	22 CAP
26 SAG	25 CAP	26 AQU	25 PIS	25 ARI	26 GEM	26 CAN	27 VIR	25 LIB	27 SAG	25 CAP	25 AQU
28 CAP	27 AQU	29 PIS	27 ARI	27 TAU	28 CAN	28 LEO	29 LIB	27 SCO	29 CAP	27 AQU	27 PIS
31 AQU	28 AQU	31 ARI	30 TAU	30 GEM	30 CAN	30 VIR	31 SCO	29 SAG	31 AQU	29 PIS	29 ARI
				31 GEM		31 VIR		30 SAG		30 PIS	31 ARI

1871

JAN	FEB	MAR	APR	MAY	JUN	JUL	AUG	SEP	OCT	NOV	DEC
1 TAU	1 GEM	1 CAN	1 LEO	1 VIR	1 SCO	1 SAG	1 AQU	1 ARI	1 TAU	1 GEM	1 CAN
3 GEM	2 CAN	4 LEO	2 VIR	2 LIB	2 SAG	2 CAP	2 PIS	3 TAU	3 GEM	2 CAN	2 LEO
6 CAN	4 LEO	6 VIR	5 LIB	4 SCO	4 CAP	4 AQU	5 ARI	6 GEM	6 CAN	4 LEO	4 VIR
8 LEO	7 VIR	8 LIB	7 SCO	6 SAG	6 AQU	6 PIS	7 TAU	8 CAN	8 LEO	7 VIR	7 LIB
10 VIR	9 LIB	10 SCO	9 SAG	8 CAP	9 PIS	8 ARI	9 GEM	11 LEO	11 VIR	9 LIB	9 SCO
13 LIB	11 SCO	12 SAG	11 CAP	10 AQU	11 ARI	11 TAU	12 CAN	13 VIR	13 LIB	11 SCO	11 SAG
15 SCO	13 SAG	14 CAP	13 AQU	12 PIS	13 TAU	13 GEM	14 LEO	15 LIB	15 SCO	13 SAG	13 CAP
17 SAG	15 CAP	17 AQU	15 PIS	15 ARI	16 GEM	16 CAN	17 VIR	18 SCO	17 SAG	15 CAP	15 AQU
19 CAP	17 AQU	19 PIS	17 ARI	17 TAU	18 CAN	18 LEO	19 LIB	20 SAG	19 CAP	17 AQU	17 PIS
21 AQU	20 PIS	21 ARI	20 TAU	20 GEM	21 LEO	21 VIR	21 SCO	22 CAP	21 AQU	20 PIS	19 ARI
23 PIS	22 ARI	24 TAU	22 GEM	22 CAN	23 VIR	23 LIB	23 SAG	24 AQU	23 PIS	22 ARI	21 TAU
25 ARI	24 TAU	26 GEM	25 CAN	25 LEO	26 LIB	25 SCO	26 CAP	26 PIS	26 ARI	24 TAU	24 GEM
28 TAU	27 GEM	29 CAN	27 LEO	27 VIR	28 SCO	27 SAG	28 AQU	28 ARI	28 TAU	27 GEM	26 CAN
30 GEM	28 GEM	31 LEO	30 VIR	29 LIB	30 SAG	29 CAP	30 PIS	30 ARI	30 GEM	29 CAN	29 LEO
31 GEM				31 SCO		31 AQU	31 PIS		31 GEM	30 CAN	31 LEO

1872

JAN	FEB	MAR	APR	MAY	JUN	JUL	AUG	SEP	OCT	NOV	DEC
1 VIR	1 SCO	1 SCO	1 CAP	1 AQU	1 ARI	1 TAU	1 CAN	1 LEO	1 VIR	1 SCO	1 SAG
3 LIB	4 SAG	2 SAG	2 AQU	2 PIS	2 TAU	2 GEM	3 LEO	2 VIR	2 LIB	3 SAG	2 CAP
5 SCO	6 CAP	4 CAP	5 PIS	4 ARI	5 GEM	5 CAN	6 VIR	5 LIB	4 SCO	5 CAP	4 AQU
7 SAG	8 AQU	6 AQU	7 ARI	6 TAU	7 CAN	7 LEO	8 LIB	7 SCO	6 SAG	7 AQU	6 PIS
9 CAP	10 PIS	8 PIS	9 TAU	9 GEM	10 LEO	10 VIR	11 SCO	9 SAG	9 CAP	9 PIS	9 ARI
11 AQU	12 ARI	10 ARI	11 GEM	11 CAN	12 VIR	12 LIB	13 SAG	11 CAP	11 AQU	11 ARI	11 TAU
13 PIS	14 TAU	13 TAU	14 CAN	14 LEO	15 LIB	14 SCO	15 CAP	14 AQU	13 PIS	13 TAU	13 GEM
15 ARI	17 GEM	15 GEM	16 LEO	16 VIR	17 SCO	17 SAG	17 AQU	16 PIS	15 ARI	16 GEM	15 CAN
18 TAU	19 CAN	17 CAN	19 VIR	18 LIB	19 SAG	19 CAP	19 PIS	18 ARI	17 TAU	18 CAN	18 LEO
20 GEM	22 LEO	20 LEO	21 LIB	21 SCO	21 CAP	21 AQU	21 ARI	20 TAU	19 GEM	21 LEO	20 VIR
23 CAN	24 VIR	22 VIR	23 SCO	23 SAG	23 AQU	23 PIS	23 TAU	2	22 CAN	23 VIR	23 LIB
25 LEO	26 LIB	25 LIB	25 SAG	25 CAP	25 PIS	25 ARI	26 GEM	24 CAN	24 LEO	26 LIB	25 SCO
28 VIR	29 SCO	27 SCO	28 CAP	27 AQU	27 ARI	27 TAU	28 CAN	27 LEO	27 VIR	28 SCO	28 SAG
30 LIB		29 SAG	30 AQU	29 PIS	30 TAU	29 GEM	31 LEO	29 VIR	29 LIB	30 SAG	30 CAP
31 LIB		31 CAP		31 ARI		31 GEM		30 VIR	31 LIB		31 CAP

1873

JAN	FEB	MAR	APR	MAY	JUN	JUL	AUG	SEP	OCT	NOV	DEC
1 AQU	1 ARI	1 ARI	1 GEM	1 CAN	1 LEO	1 VIR	1 SCO	1 SAG	1 AQU	1 PIS	1 TAU
3 PIS	3 TAU	3 TAU	4 CAN	3 LEO	2 VIR	2 LIB	3 SAG	2 CAP	3 PIS	2 ARI	3 GEM
5 ARI	6 GEM	5 GEM	6 LEO	6 VIR	5 LIB	5 SCO	5 CAP	4 AQU	5 ARI	4 TAU	5 CAN
7 TAU	8 CAN	7 CAN	9 VIR	8 LIB	7 SCO	7 SAG	8 AQU	6 PIS	7 TAU	6 GEM	8 LEO
9 GEM	10 LEO	10 LEO	11 LIB	11 VIR	9 SAG	9 CAP	9 PIS	8 ARI	9 GEM	8 CAN	10 VIR
12 CAN	13 VIR	12 VIR	13 SCO	13 SAG	12 CAP	11 AQU	11 ARI	10 TAU	12 CAN	10 LEO	13 LIB
14 LEO	16 LIB	15 LIB	16 SAG	15 CAP	14 AQU	18 PIS	14 TAU	12 GEM	14 LEO	13 VIR	15 SCO
17 VIR	18 SCO	17 SCO	18 CAP	17 AQU	16 PIS	15 ARI	16 GEM	14 CAN	17 VIR	15 LIB	18 SAG
19 LIB	20 SAG	20 SAG	20 AQU	20 PIS	18 ARI	17 TAU	18 CAN	17 LEO	19 LIB	18 SCO	20 CAP
22 SCO	23 CAP	22 CAP	22 PIS	22 ARI	20 TAU	20 GEM	21 LEO	19 VIR	22 SCO	20 SAG	22 AQU
24 SAG	25 AQU	24 AQU	24 ARI	24 TAU	22 GEM	22 CAN	23 VIR	22 LIB	24 SAG	23 CAP	24 PIS
26 CAP	27 PIS	26 PIS	26 TAU	26 GEM	25 CAN	24 LEO	26 LIB	24 SCO	26 CAP	25 AQU	26 ARI
28 AQU	28 PIS	28 ARI	29 GEM	28 CAN	27 LEO	27 VIR	28 SCO	27 SAG	29 AQU	27 PIS	28 TAU
30 PIS		30 TAU	30 GEM	31 LEO	30 VIR	29 LIB	31 SAG	29 CAP	31 PIS	29 ARI	31 PIS
31 PIS		31 TAU				31 LIB		30 CAP		30 ARI	

1874

JAN	FEB	MAR	APR	MAY	JUN	JUL	AUG	SEP	OCT	NOV	DEC
1 GEM	1 LEO	1 LEO	1 LIB	1 SCO	1 SAG	1 AQU	1 PIS	1 TAU	1 GEM	1 LEO	1 VIR
2 CAN	3 VIR	2 VIR	3 SCO	3 SAG	2 CAP	4 PIS	2 ARI	2 GEM	2 CAN	3 VIR	3 LIB
4 LEO	5 LIB	5 LIB	6 SAG	6 CAP	4 AQU	6 ARI	4 TAU	5 CAN	4 LEO	5 LIB	5 SCO
7 VIR	8 SCO	7 SCO	8 CAP	8 AQU	6 PIS	8 TAU	6 GEM	7 LEO	7 VIR	8 SCO	8 SAG
9 LIB	10 SAG	10 SAG	11 AQU	10 PIS	9 ARI	10 GEM	8 CAN	9 VIR	9 LIB	10 SAG	10 CAP
12 SCO	13 CAP	12 CAP	13 PIS	12 ARI	11 TAU	12 CAN	11 LEO	12 LIB	12 SCO	13 CAP	12 AQU
14 SAG	15 AQU	14 AQU	15 ARI	14 TAU	13 GEM	14 LEO	13 VIR	14 SCO	14 SAG	15 AQU	15 PIS
16 CAP	17 PIS	16 PIS	17 TAU	16 GEM	15 CAN	17 VIR	15 LIB	17 SAG	17 CAP	17 PIS	17 ARI
18 AQU	19 ARI	18 ARI	19 GEM	18 CAN	17 LEO	19 LIB	18 SCO	19 CAP	19 AQU	20 ARI	19 TAU
21 PIS	21 TAU	20 TAU	21 CAN	21 LEO	19 VIR	22 SCO	21 SAG	22 AQU	21 PIS	22 TAU	21 GEM
23 ARI	23 GEM	22 GEM	23 LEO	23 VIR	22 LIB	24 SAG	23 CAP	24 PIS	23 ARI	24 GEM	23 CAN
25 TAU	25 CAN	25 CAN	26 VIR	25 LIB	24 SCO	27 CAP	25 AQU	26 ARI	25 TAU	26 CAN	25 LEO
27 GEM	28 LEO	27 LEO	28 LIB	28 SCO	27 SAG	27 AQU	27 PIS	28 TAU	27 GEM	28 LEO	27 VIR
29 CAN		29 VIR	30 LIB	31 SAG	29 CAP	31 PIS	29 ARI	30 GEM	29 CAN	30 VIR	30 LIB
31 LEO		31 VIR			30 CAP		31 TAU		31 LEO		31 LIB

1875

JAN	FEB	MAR	APR	MAY	JUN	JUL	AUG	SEP	OCT	NOV	DEC
1 SCO	1 SAG	1 SAG	1 AQU	1 PIS	1 TAU	1 GEM	1 LEO	1 VIR	1 SCO	1 SAG	1 CAP
4 SAG	3 CAP	2 CAP	3 PIS	3 ARI	3 GEM	2 CAN	3 VIR	2 LIB	4 SAG	3 CAP	3 AQU
6 CAP	5 AQU	4 AQU	5 ARI	5 TAU	5 CAN	5 LEO	5 LIB	4 SCO	7 CAP	5 AQU	5 PIS
9 AQU	7 PIS	7 PIS	7 TAU	7 GEM	7 LEO	7 VIR	8 SCO	7 SAG	9 AQU	8 PIS	7 ARI
11 PIS	9 ARI	9 ARI	9 GEM	9 CAN	9 VIR	9 LIB	10 SAG	9 CAP	11 PIS	10 ARI	9 TAU
13 ARI	12 TAU	11 TAU	11 CAN	11 LEO	12 LIB	11 SCO	13 CAP	12 AQU	13 ARI	12 TAU	11 GEM
15 TAU	14 GEM	13 GEM	13 LEO	13 VIR	14 SCO	14 SAG	15 AQU	14 PIS	16 TAU	14 GEM	13 CAN
17 GEM	16 CAN	15 CAN	16 VIR	15 LIB	17 SAG	17 CAP	18 PIS	16 ARI	18 GEM	16 CAN	15 LEO
20 CAN	18 LEO	17 LEO	18 LIB	18 SCO	19 CAP	19 AQU	20 ARI	18 TAU	20 CAN	18 LEO	18 VIR
22 LEO	20 VIR	20 VIR	21 SCO	20 SAG	22 AQU	21 PIS	22 TAU	20 GEM	22 LEO	20 VIR	20 LIB
24 VIR	23 LIB	22 LIB	23 SAG	23 CAP	24 PIS	24 ARI	24 GEM	22 CAN	24 VIR	23 LIB	22 SCO
26 LIB	25 SCO	24 SCO	26 CAP	25 AQU	26 ARI	26 TAU	26 CAN	25 LEO	26 LIB	25 SCO	25 SAG
29 SCO	28 SAG	27 SAG	28 AQU	28 PIS	28 TAU	28 GEM	28 LEO	27 VIR	29 SCO	28 SAG	27 CAP
31 SAG		29 CAP	30 PIS	30 ARI	30 GEM	30 CAN	30 VIR	29 LIB	31 SAG	30 CAP	30 AQU
		31 CAP		31 ARI		31 CAN	31 VIR	30 LIB			31 AQU

1876

JAN	FEB	MAR	APR	MAY	JUN	JUL	AUG	SEP	OCT	NOV	DEC
1 PIS	1 ARI	1 TAU	1 CAN	1 LEO	1 LIB	1 SCO	1 SAG	1 AQU	1 PIS	1 TAU	1 GEM
4 ARI	2 TAU	2 GEM	3 LEO	2 VIR	3 SCO	3 SAG	2 CAP	3 PIS	3 ARI	3 GEM	3 CAN
6 TAU	4 GEM	5 CAN	5 VIR	5 LIB	6 SAG	5 CAP	4 AQU	5 ARI	5 TAU	5 CAN	5 LEO
8 GEM	6 CAN	7 LEO	7 LIB	7 SCO	8 CAP	8 AQU	7 PIS	8 TAU	7 GEM	8 LEO	7 VIR
10 CAN	8 LEO	9 VIR	10 SCO	9 SAG	11 AQU	10 PIS	9 ARI	10 GEM	9 CAN	10 VIR	9 LIB
12 LEO	10 VIR	11 LIB	12 SAG	12 CAP	13 PIS	13 ARI	11 TAU	12 CAN	11 LEO	12 LIB	11 SCO
14 VIR	13 LIB	13 SCO	15 CAP	14 AQU	16 ARI	15 TAU	14 GEM	14 LEO	13 VIR	14 SCO	14 SAG
16 LIB	15 SCO	16 SAG	17 AQU	17 PIS	18 TAU	17 GEM	16 CAN	16 VIR	16 LIB	17 SAG	16 CAP
19 SCO	17 SAG	18 CAP	20 PIS	19 ARI	20 GEM	19 CAN	18 LEO	18 LIB	18 SCO	19 CAP	19 AQU
21 SAG	20 CAP	21 AQU	22 ARI	21 TAU	22 CAN	21 LEO	20 VIR	20 SCO	20 SAG	21 AQU	21 PIS
24 CAP	22 AQU	23 PIS	24 TAU	23 GEM	24 LEO	23 VIR	22 LIB	23 SAG	23 CAP	24 PIS	24 ARI
26 AQU	25 PIS	25 ARI	26 GEM	25 CAN	26 VIR	25 LIB	24 SCO	25 CAP	25 AQU	26 ARI	26 TAU
28 PIS	27 ARI	28 TAU	28 CAN	27 LEO	28 LIB	28 SCO	26 SAG	28 AQU	28 PIS	29 TAU	28 GEM
31 ARI	29 TAU	30 GEM	30 LEO	30 VIR	30 SCO	30 SAG	29 CAP	30 PIS	30 ARI	30 TAU	30 CAN
		31 GEM		31 VIR		31 SAG	31 AQU		31 ARI		31 CAN

1877

JAN	FEB	MAR	APR	MAY	JUN	JUL	AUG	SEP	OCT	NOV	DEC
1 LEO	1 VIR	1 LIB	1 SCO	1 SAG	1 AQU	1 PIS	1 ARI	1 GEM	1 CAN	1 VIR	1 LIB
3 VIR	2 LIB	3 SCO	2 SAG	2 CAP	3 PIS	3 ARI	2 TAU	2 CAN	2 LEO	2 LIB	2 SCO
5 LIB	4 SCO	6 SAG	4 CAP	4 AQU	6 ARI	5 TAU	4 GEM	5 LEO	4 VIR	4 SCO	4 SAG
8 SCO	6 SAG	8 CAP	7 AQU	7 PIS	8 TAU	8 GEM	6 CAN	7 VIR	6 LIB	7 SAG	6 CAP
10 SAG	9 CAP	11 AQU	9 PIS	9 ARI	10 GEM	10 CAN	8 LEO	9 LIB	8 SCO	9 CAP	9 AQU
12 CAP	11 AQU	13 PIS	12 ARI	12 TAU	12 CAN	12 LEO	10 VIR	11 SCO	10 SAG	11 AQU	11 PIS
15 AQU	14 PIS	16 ARI	14 TAU	14 GEM	14 LEO	14 VIR	12 LIB	13 SAG	12 CAP	14 PIS	14 ARI
18 PIS	16 ARI	18 TAU	16 GEM	16 CAN	16 VIR	16 LIB	14 SCO	15 CAP	15 AQU	16 ARI	16 TAU
20 ARI	19 TAU	20 GEM	19 CAN	18 LEO	18 LIB	18 SCO	16 SAG	18 AQU	17 PIS	19 TAU	18 GEM
22 TAU	21 GEM	22 CAN	21 LEO	20 VIR	21 SCO	20 SAG	19 CAP	20 PIS	20 ARI	21 GEM	21 CAN
25 GEM	23 CAN	25 LEO	23 VIR	22 LIB	23 SAG	23 CAP	21 AQU	23 ARI	22 TAU	23 CAN	23 LEO
27 CAN	25 LEO	27 VIR	25 LIB	24 SCO	25 CAP	25 AQU	24 PIS	25 TAU	25 GEM	25 LEO	25 VIR
29 LEO	27 VIR	29 LIB	27 SCO	27 SAG	28 AQU	28 PIS	26 ARI	27 GEM	27 CAN	28 VIR	27 LIB
31 VIR	28 VIR	31 SCO	29 SAG	29 CAP	30 PIS	30 ARI	29 TAU	30 CAN	29 LEO	30 LIB	29 SCO
			30 SAG	31 CAP		31 ARI	31 GEM		31 VIR		31 SAG

1878

JAN	FEB	MAR	APR	MAY	JUN	JUL	AUG	SEP	OCT	NOV	DEC
1 SAG	1 AQU	1 AQU	1 PIS	1 ARI	1 GEM	1 CAN	1 VIR	1 SCO	1 SAG	1 AQU	1 PIS
3 CAP	4 PIS	3 PIS	2 ARI	2 TAU	3 CAN	2 LEO	3 LIB	3 SAG	3 CAP	4 PIS	3 ARI
5 AQU	6 ARI	6 ARI	4 TAU	4 GEM	5 LEO	4 VIR	5 SCO	5 CAP	5 AQU	6 ARI	6 TAU
7 PIS	9 TAU	8 TAU	7 GEM	6 CAN	7 VIR	6 LIB	7 SAG	8 AQU	7 PIS	9 TAU	8 GEM
10 ARI	11 GEM	10 GEM	9 CAN	9 LEO	9 LIB	8 SCO	9 CAP	10 PIS	10 ARI	11 GEM	11 CAN
12 TAU	13 CAN	13 CAN	11 LEO	11 VIR	11 SCO	11 SAG	11 AQU	13 ARI	12 TAU	14 CAN	13 LEO
15 GEM	16 LEO	15 LEO	13 VIR	13 LIB	13 SAG	13 CAP	14 PIS	15 TAU	15 GEM	16 LEO	15 VIR
17 CAN	18 VIR	17 VIR	15 LIB	15 SCO	15 CAP	15 AQU	16 ARI	18 GEM	17 CAN	18 VIR	17 LIB
19 LEO	20 LIB	19 LIB	17 SCO	17 SAG	18 AQU	18 PIS	19 TAU	20 CAN	20 LEO	20 LIB	20 SCO
21 VIR	22 SCO	21 SCO	19 SAG	19 CAP	20 PIS	20 ARI	21 GEM	22 LEO	22 VIR	22 SCO	22 SAG
23 LIB	24 SAG	23 SAG	22 CAP	21 AQU	23 ARI	23 TAU	24 CAN	24 VIR	24 LIB	24 SAG	24 CAP
25 SCO	26 CAP	25 CAP	24 AQU	24 PIS	25 TAU	25 GEM	26 LEO	26 LIB	26 SCO	26 CAP	26 AQU
27 SAG	28 AQU	28 AQU	27 PIS	26 ARI	28 GEM	27 CAN	28 VIR	28 SCO	28 SAG	29 AQU	28 PIS
30 CAP		30 PIS	29 ARI	29 TAU	30 CAN	29 LEO	30 LIB	30 SAG	30 CAP	30 AQU	31 ARI
31 CAP		31 PIS	30 ARI	31 GEM		31 LEO	31 LIB		31 CAP		

1879

JAN	FEB	MAR	APR	MAY	JUN	JUL	AUG	SEP	OCT	NOV	DEC
1 ARI	1 GEM	1 GEM	1 CAN	1 VIR	1 LIB	1 SAG	1 CAP	1 PIS	1 ARI	1 GEM	1 CAN
2 TAU	4 CAN	3 CAN	2 LEO	3 LIB	2 SCO	3 CAP	2 AQU	3 ARI	2 TAU	4 CAN	3 LEO
5 GEM	6 LEO	5 LEO	4 VIR	5 SCO	4 SAG	5 AQU	4 PIS	5 TAU	5 GEM	6 LEO	6 VIR
7 CAN	8 VIR	7 VIR	6 LIB	7 SAG	6 CAP	7 PIS	6 ARI	8 GEM	7 CAN	8 VIR	8 LIB
9 LEO	10 LIB	9 LIB	8 SCO	9 CAP	8 AQU	10 ARI	9 TAU	10 CAN	10 LEO	11 LIB	10 SCO
12 VIR	12 SCO	11 SCO	10 SAG	11 AQU	10 PIS	12 TAU	11 GEM	12 LEO	12 VIR	13 SCO	12 SAG
14 LIB	14 SAG	13 SAG	12 CAP	14 PIS	12 ARI	15 GEM	14 CAN	15 VIR	14 LIB	15 SAG	14 CAP
16 SCO	16 CAP	16 CAP	14 AQU	16 ARI	15 TAU	17 CAN	16 LEO	17 LIB	16 SCO	17 CAP	16 AQU
18 SAG	19 AQU	18 AQU	16 PIS	19 TAU	18 GEM	20 LEO	18 VIR	19 SCO	18 SAG	19 AQU	18 PIS
20 CAP	21 PIS	20 PIS	19 ARI	21 GEM	20 CAN	22 VIR	20 LIB	21 SAG	20 CAP	21 PIS	21 ARI
22 AQU	23 ARI	23 ARI	21 TAU	24 CAN	22 LEO	24 LIB	22 SCO	23 CAP	22 AQU	23 ARI	23 TAU
25 PIS	26 TAU	25 TAU	24 GEM	26 LEO	25 VIR	26 SCO	25 SAG	25 AQU	25 PIS	26 TAU	26 GEM
27 ARI	28 GEM	28 GEM	27 CAN	28 VIR	27 LIB	28 SAG	27 CAP	27 PIS	27 ARI	28 GEM	28 CAN
30 TAU		30 CAN	29 LEO	31 LIB	29 SCO	30 CAP	29 AQU	30 ARI	30 TAU	30 GEM	31 LEO
31 TAU		31 CAN	30 LEO		30 SCO	31 CAP	31 PIS		31 TAU		

1880

JAN	FEB	MAR	APR	MAY	JUN	JUL	AUG	SEP	OCT	NOV	DEC
1 LEO	1 LIB	1 SCO	1 CAP	1 AQU	1 PIS	1 TAU	1 GEM	1 LEO	1 VIR	1 LIB	1 SAG
2 VIR	3 SCO	3 SAG	3 AQU	3 PIS	2 ARI	4 GEM	3 CAN	4 VIR	3 LIB	2 SCO	3 CAP
4 LIB	5 SAG	5 CAP	6 PIS	5 ARI	4 TAU	6 CAN	5 LEO	6 LIB	6 SCO	4 SAG	5 AQU
6 SCO	7 CAP	7 AQU	8 ARI	8 TAU	6 GEM	9 LEO	7 VIR	8 SCO	8 SAG	6 CAP	8 PIS
8 SAG	9 AQU	9 PIS	10 TAU	10 GEM	9 CAN	11 VIR	10 LIB	10 SAG	10 CAP	8 AQU	10 ARI
11 CAP	11 PIS	12 ARI	13 GEM	13 CAN	12 LEO	14 LIB	12 SCO	13 CAP	12 AQU	10 PIS	12 TAU
13 AQU	13 ARI	14 TAU	15 CAN	15 LEO	14 VIR	16 SCO	14 SAG	15 AQU	14 PIS	13 ARI	15 GEM
15 PIS	16 TAU	17 GEM	18 LEO	18 VIR	16 LIB	18 SAG	16 CAP	17 PIS	16 ARI	15 TAU	17 CAN
17 ARI	18 GEM	19 CAN	20 VIR	20 LIB	18 SCO	20 CAP	18 AQU	19 ARI	19 TAU	17 GEM	20 LEO
19 TAU	21 CAN	22 LEO	23 LIB	22 SCO	20 SAG	22 AQU	20 PIS	21 TAU	21 GEM	20 CAN	22 VIR
22 GEM	23 LEO	24 VIR	25 SCO	24 SAG	22 CAP	24 PIS	23 ARI	24 GEM	23 CAN	22 LEO	25 LIB
24 CAN	26 VIR	26 LIB	27 SAG	26 CAP	24 AQU	26 ARI	25 TAU	26 CAN	26 LEO	25 VIR	27 SCO
27 LEO	28 LIB	28 SCO	29 CAP	28 AQU	27 PIS	28 TAU	27 GEM	29 LEO	28 VIR	27 LIB	29 SAG
29 VIR	29 LIB	30 SAG	30 CAP	30 PIS	29 ARI	31 GEM	30 CAN	30 LEO	31 LIB	29 SCO	31 CAP
31 LIB		31 SAG		31 PIS	30 ARI		31 CAN			30 SCO	

1881

JAN	FEB	MAR	APR	MAY	JUN	JUL	AUG	SEP	OCT	NOV	DEC
1 CAP	1 PIS	1 PIS	1 TAU	1 GEM	1 LEO	1 VIR	1 LIB	1 SAG	1 CAP	1 PIS	1 ARI
2 AQU	2 ARI	2 ARI	3 GEM	3 CAN	4 VIR	4 LIB	2 SCO	3 CAP	2 AQU	3 ARI	2 TAU
4 PIS	5 TAU	4 TAU	5 CAN	5 LEO	6 LIB	6 SCO	5 SAG	5 AQU	5 PIS	5 TAU	5 GEM
6 ARI	7 GEM	6 GEM	8 LEO	8 VIR	9 SCO	8 SAG	7 CAP	7 PIS	7 ARI	7 GEM	7 CAN
8 TAU	10 CAN	9 CAN	10 VIR	10 LIB	11 SAG	10 CAP	9 AQU	9 ARI	9 TAU	10 CAN	9 LEO
11 GEM	12 LEO	11 LEO	13 LIB	12 SCO	13 CAP	12 AQU	11 PIS	11 TAU	11 GEM	12 LEO	12 VIR
13 CAN	15 VIR	14 VIR	15 SCO	14 SAG	15 AQU	14 PIS	13 ARI	14 GEM	13 CAN	15 VIR	14 LIB
16 LEO	17 LIB	16 LIB	17 SAG	16 CAP	17 PIS	16 ARI	15 TAU	16 CAN	16 LEO	17 LIB	17 SCO
18 VIR	19 SCO	19 SCO	19 CAP	19 AQU	19 ARI	19 TAU	17 GEM	18 LEO	18 VIR	19 SCO	19 SAG
21 LIB	22 SAG	21 SAG	21 AQU	21 PIS	21 TAU	21 GEM	20 CAN	21 VIR	21 LIB	22 SAG	21 CAP
23 SCO	24 CAP	23 CAP	23 PIS	23 ARI	24 GEM	23 CAN	22 LEO	23 LIB	23 SCO	24 CAP	23 AQU
25 SAG	26 AQU	25 AQU	26 ARI	25 TAU	26 CAN	26 LEO	25 VIR	26 SCO	25 SAG	26 AQU	25 PIS
27 CAP	28 PIS	27 PIS	28 TAU	27 GEM	29 LEO	28 VIR	27 LIB	28 SAG	28 CAP	28 PIS	27 ARI
29 AQU		29 ARI	30 GEM	30 CAN	30 LEO	31 LIB	30 SCO	30 CAP	30 AQU	30 ARI	30 TAU
31 PIS		31 TAU		31 CAN			31 SCO		31 PIS		31 TAU

1882

JAN	FEB	MAR	APR	MAY	JUN	JUL	AUG	SEP	OCT	NOV	DEC
1 GEM	1 CAN	1 LEO	1 VIR	1 LIB	1 SAG	1 CAP	1 PIS	1 ARI	1 GEM	1 CAN	1 LEO
3 CAN	2 LEO	4 VIR	3 LIB	2 SCO	3 CAP	3 AQU	3 ARI	2 TAU	3 CAN	2 LEO	2 VIR
6 LEO	5 VIR	6 LIB	5 SCO	5 SAG	5 AQU	5 PIS	5 TAU	4 GEM	6 LEO	4 VIR	4 LIB
8 VIR	7 LIB	9 SCO	7 SAG	7 CAP	7 PIS	7 ARI	7 GEM	6 CAN	8 VIR	7 LIB	7 SCO
11 LIB	10 SCO	11 SAG	10 CAP	9 AQU	10 ARI	9 TAU	10 CAN	8 LEO	11 LIB	9 SCO	9 SAG
13 SCO	12 SAG	13 CAP	12 AQU	11 PIS	12 TAU	11 GEM	12 LEO	11 VIR	13 SCO	12 SAG	12 CAP
16 SAG	14 CAP	16 AQU	14 PIS	13 ARI	14 GEM	13 CAN	15 VIR	13 LIB	16 SAG	14 CAP	14 AQU
18 CAP	16 AQU	18 PIS	16 ARI	15 TAU	16 CAN	16 LEO	17 LIB	16 SCO	18 CAP	16 AQU	16 PIS
20 AQU	18 PIS	20 ARI	18 TAU	18 GEM	19 LEO	18 VIR	20 SCO	18 SAG	20 AQU	19 PIS	18 ARI
22 PIS	20 ARI	22 TAU	20 GEM	20 CAN	21 VIR	21 LIB	22 SAG	21 CAP	22 PIS	21 ARI	20 TAU
24 ARI	22 TAU	24 GEM	22 CAN	22 LEO	24 LIB	23 SCO	24 CAP	23 AQU	24 ARI	23 TAU	22 GEM
26 TAU	24 GEM	26 CAN	25 LEO	25 VIR	26 SCO	26 SAG	27 AQU	25 PIS	26 TAU	25 GEM	24 CAN
28 GEM	27 CAN	29 LEO	27 VIR	27 LIB	28 SAG	28 CAP	29 PIS	27 ARI	28 GEM	27 CAN	27 LEO
31 CAN	28 CAN	31 VIR	30 LIB	30 SCO	30 SAG	30 AQU	30 ARI	29 TAU	31 CAN	29 LEO	29 VIR
				31 SCO		31 AQU	31 ARI	30 TAU		30 LEO	31 VIR

1883

JAN	FEB	MAR	APR	MAY	JUN	JUL	AUG	SEP	OCT	NOV	DEC
1 LIB	1 SCO	1 SAG	1 CAP	1 AQU	1 ARI	1 TAU	1 CAN	1 VIR	1 LIB	1 SCO	1 SAG
3 SCO	2 SAG	4 CAP	2 AQU	2 PIS	2 TAU	2 GEM	2 LEO	3 LIB	3 SCO	2 SAG	2 CAP
6 SAG	4 CAP	6 AQU	4 PIS	4 ARI	4 GEM	4 CAN	5 VIR	6 SCO	6 SAG	4 CAP	4 AQU
8 CAP	6 AQU	8 PIS	6 ARI	6 TAU	6 CAN	6 LEO	7 LIB	8 SAG	8 CAP	7 AQU	6 PIS
10 AQU	9 PIS	10 ARI	8 TAU	8 GEM	9 LEO	8 VIR	10 SCO	11 CAP	11 AQU	9 PIS	9 ARI
12 PIS	11 ARI	12 TAU	10 GEM	10 CAN	11 VIR	11 LIB	12 SAG	13 AQU	13 PIS	11 ARI	11 TAU
14 ARI	13 TAU	14 GEM	13 CAN	12 LEO	13 LIB	13 SCO	14 CAP	15 PIS	15 ARI	13 TAU	13 GEM
16 TAU	15 GEM	16 CAN	15 LEO	15 VIR	16 SCO	16 SAG	17 AQU	17 ARI	17 TAU	15 GEM	15 CAN
19 GEM	17 CAN	19 LEO	17 VIR	17 LIB	18 SAG	18 CAP	19 PIS	19 TAU	19 GEM	17 CAN	17 LEO
21 CAN	19 LEO	21 VIR	20 LIB	20 SCO	21 CAP	20 AQU	21 ARI	21 GEM	21 CAN	19 LEO	19 VIR
23 LEO	22 VIR	24 LIB	22 SCO	22 SAG	23 AQU	23 PIS	23 TAU	24 CAN	23 LEO	22 VIR	21 LIB
25 VIR	24 LIB	26 SCO	25 SAG	24 CAP	25 PIS	25 ARI	25 GEM	26 LEO	25 VIR	24 LIB	24 SCO
28 LIB	27 SCO	29 SAG	27 CAP	27 AQU	27 ARI	27 TAU	27 CAN	28 VIR	28 LIB	27 SCO	26 SAG
30 SCO	28 SCO	31 CAP	30 AQU	29 PIS	30 TAU	29 GEM	30 LEO	30 VIR	30 SCO	29 SAG	29 CAP
31 SCO				31 ARI		31 CAN	31 LEO			30 SAG	31 AQU

1884

JAN	FEB	MAR	APR	MAY	JUN	JUL	AUG	SEP	OCT	NOV	DEC
1 AQU	1 ARI	1 TAU	1 GEM	1 LEO	1 VIR	1 LIB	1 SAG	1 CAP	1 AQU	1 ARI	1 TAU
3 PIS	3 TAU	4 GEM	2 CAN	4 VIR	2 LIB	2 SCO	3 CAP	2 AQU	2 PIS	3 TAU	2 GEM
5 ARI	5 GEM	6 CAN	4 LEO	6 LIB	5 SCO	5 SAG	6 AQU	4 PIS	4 ARI	5 GEM	4 CAN
7 TAU	7 CAN	8 LEO	6 VIR	8 SCO	7 SAG	7 CAP	8 PIS	7 ARI	6 TAU	7 CAN	6 LEO
9 GEM	10 LEO	10 VIR	9 LIB	11 SAG	10 CAP	10 AQU	10 ARI	9 TAU	8 GEM	9 LEO	8 VIR
11 CAN	12 VIR	12 LIB	11 SCO	14 CAP	12 AQU	12 PIS	13 TAU	11 GEM	10 CAN	11 VIR	10 LIB
13 LEO	14 LIB	15 SCO	14 SAG	16 AQU	15 PIS	14 ARI	15 GEM	13 CAN	12 LEO	13 LIB	13 SCO
15 VIR	17 SCO	17 SAG	16 CAP	18 PIS	17 ARI	16 TAU	17 CAN	15 LEO	15 VIR	16 SCO	15 SAG
18 LIB	19 SAG	20 CAP	19 AQU	21 ARI	19 TAU	18 GEM	19 LEO	17 VIR	17 LIB	18 SAG	18 CAP
20 SCO	22 CAP	22 AQU	21 PIS	23 TAU	21 GEM	20 CAN	21 VIR	20 LIB	19 SCO	21 CAP	20 AQU
23 SAG	24 AQU	25 PIS	23 ARI	25 GEM	23 CAN	23 LEO	23 LIB	22 SCO	22 SAG	23 AQU	23 PIS
25 CAP	26 PIS	27 ARI	25 TAU	27 CAN	25 LEO	25 VIR	26 SCO	25 SAG	24 CAP	26 PIS	25 ARI
28 AQU	28 ARI	29 TAU	27 GEM	29 LEO	27 VIR	27 LIB	28 SAG	27 CAP	27 AQU	28 ARI	27 TAU
30 PIS	29 ARI	31 GEM	29 CAN	31 VIR	30 LIB	29 SCO	31 CAP	30 AQU	29 PIS	30 TAU	30 GEM
31 PIS			30 CAN			31 SCO			31 ARI		31 GEM

1885

JAN	FEB	MAR	APR	MAY	JUN	JUL	AUG	SEP	OCT	NOV	DEC
1 CAN	1 VIR	1 VIR	1 SCO	1 SAG	1 CAP	1 AQU	1 ARI	1 TAU	1 CAN	1 VIR	1 LIB
2 LEO	3 LIB	3 LIB	4 SAG	3 CAP	2 AQU	2 PIS	3 TAU	2 GEM	3 LEO	4 LIB	3 SCO
5 VIR	5 SCO	5 SCO	6 CAP	6 AQU	5 PIS	4 ARI	5 GEM	4 CAN	5 VIR	6 SCO	5 SAG
7 LIB	8 SAG	7 SAG	9 AQU	8 PIS	7 ARI	7 TAU	7 CAN	6 LEO	7 LIB	8 SAG	8 CAP
9 SCO	10 CAP	10 CAP	11 PIS	11 ARI	9 TAU	9 GEM	9 LEO	8 VIR	9 SCO	10 CAP	10 AQU
12 SAG	13 AQU	12 AQU	13 ARI	13 TAU	11 GEM	11 CAN	11 VIR	10 LIB	12 SAG	13 AQU	13 PIS
14 CAP	15 PIS	15 PIS	16 TAU	15 GEM	13 CAN	13 LEO	13 LIB	12 SCO	14 CAP	16 PIS	15 ARI
17 AQU	18 ARI	17 ARI	18 GEM	17 CAN	15 LEO	15 VIR	16 SCO	14 SAG	17 AQU	18 ARI	18 TAU
19 PIS	20 TAU	19 TAU	20 CAN	19 LEO	18 VIR	17 LIB	18 SAG	17 CAP	19 PIS	20 TAU	20 GEM
21 ARI	22 GEM	21 GEM	22 LEO	21 VIR	20 LIB	19 SCO	20 CAP	19 AQU	22 ARI	22 GEM	22 CAN
24 TAU	24 CAN	23 CAN	24 VIR	23 LIB	22 SCO	22 SAG	23 AQU	22 PIS	24 TAU	24 CAN	24 LEO
26 GEM	26 LEO	26 LEO	26 LIB	26 SCO	24 SAG	24 CAP	26 PIS	24 ARI	26 GEM	26 LEO	26 VIR
28 CAN	28 VIR	28 VIR	29 SCO	28 SAG	27 CAP	27 AQU	28 ARI	27 TAU	28 CAN	29 VIR	28 LIB
30 LEO		30 LIB	30 SCO	31 CAP	29 AQU	29 PIS	30 TAU	29 GEM	30 LEO	30 VIR	30 SCO
31 LEO		31 LIB			30 AQU	31 PIS	31 TAU	30 GEM	31 LEO		31 SCO

1886

JAN	FEB	MAR	APR	MAY	JUN	JUL	AUG	SEP	OCT	NOV	DEC
1 SCO	1 CAP	1 CAP	1 PIS	1 ARI	1 TAU	1 CAN	1 LEO	1 LIB	1 SCO	1 CAP	1 AQU
2 SAG	3 AQU	2 AQU	3 ARI	3 TAU	2 GEM	3 LEO	2 VIR	2 SCO	2 SAG	3 AQU	3 PIS
4 CAP	5 PIS	5 PIS	6 TAU	5 GEM	4 CAN	5 VIR	4 LIB	4 SAG	4 CAP	5 PIS	5 ARI
7 AQU	8 ARI	7 ARI	8 GEM	8 CAN	6 LEO	7 LIB	6 SCO	7 CAP	6 AQU	8 ARI	8 TAU
9 PIS	10 TAU	10 TAU	10 CAN	10 LEO	8 VIR	10 SCO	8 SAG	9 AQU	9 PIS	10 TAU	10 GEM
12 ARI	13 GEM	12 GEM	12 LEO	12 VIR	10 LIB	12 SAG	10 CAP	12 PIS	12 ARI	13 GEM	12 CAN
14 TAU	15 CAN	14 CAN	15 VIR	14 LIB	12 SCO	14 CAP	13 AQU	14 ARI	14 TAU	15 CAN	14 LEO
16 GEM	17 LEO	16 LEO	17 LIB	16 SCO	15 SAG	17 AQU	15 PIS	17 TAU	16 GEM	17 LEO	16 VIR
18 CAN	19 VIR	18 VIR	19 SCO	18 SAG	17 CAP	19 PIS	18 ARI	19 GEM	19 CAN	19 VIR	19 LIB
20 LEO	21 LIB	20 LIB	21 SAG	21 CAP	19 AQU	22 ARI	20 TAU	21 CAN	21 LEO	21 LIB	21 SCO
22 VIR	23 SCO	22 SCO	23 CAP	23 AQU	22 PIS	24 TAU	23 GEM	24 LEO	23 VIR	23 SCO	23 SAG
24 LIB	25 SAG	25 SAG	26 AQU	26 PIS	24 ARI	27 GEM	25 CAN	26 VIR	25 LIB	26 SAG	25 CAP
27 SCO	28 CAP	27 CAP	28 PIS	28 ARI	27 TAU	29 CAN	27 LEO	28 LIB	27 SCO	28 CAP	27 AQU
29 SAG		29 AQU	30 PIS	30 TAU	29 GEM	31 LEO	29 VIR	30 SCO	29 SAG	30 AQU	30 PIS
31 CAP		31 AQU		31 TAU	30 GEM		31 LIB		31 CAP		31 PIS

1887

JAN	FEB	MAR	APR	MAY	JUN	JUL	AUG	SEP	OCT	NOV	DEC
1 PIS	1 TAU	1 TAU	1 CAN	1 LEO	1 LIB	1 SCO	1 CAP	1 AQU	1 ARI	1 TAU	1 GEM
2 ARI	3 GEM	2 GEM	3 LEO	2 VIR	3 SCO	2 SAG	3 AQU	2 PIS	4 TAU	3 GEM	2 CAN
4 TAU	5 CAN	4 CAN	5 VIR	4 LIB	5 SAG	4 CAP	5 PIS	4 ARI	6 GEM	5 CAN	5 LEO
6 GEM	7 LEO	7 LEO	7 LIB	6 SCO	7 CAP	7 AQU	8 ARI	7 TAU	9 CAN	8 LEO	7 VIR
9 CAN	9 VIR	9 VIR	9 SCO	8 SAG	9 AQU	9 PIS	10 TAU	9 GEM	11 LEO	10 VIR	9 LIB
11 LEO	11 LIB	11 LIB	11 SAG	11 CAP	12 PIS	12 ARI	13 GEM	12 CAN	13 VIR	12 LIB	11 SCO
13 VIR	13 SCO	13 SCO	13 CAP	13 AQU	14 ARI	14 TAU	15 CAN	14 LEO	15 LIB	14 SCO	13 SAG
15 LIB	15 SAG	15 SAG	16 AQU	15 PIS	17 TAU	17 GEM	17 LEO	16 VIR	17 SCO	16 SAG	15 CAP
17 SCO	18 CAP	17 CAP	18 PIS	18 ARI	19 GEM	19 CAN	20 VIR	18 LIB	19 SAG	18 CAP	17 AQU
19 SAG	20 AQU	19 AQU	21 ARI	20 TAU	21 CAN	21 LEO	22 LIB	20 SCO	21 CAP	20 AQU	20 PIS
21 CAP	23 PIS	22 PIS	23 TAU	23 GEM	24 LEO	23 VIR	24 SCO	22 SAG	24 AQU	22 PIS	22 ARI
24 AQU	25 ARI	24 ARI	26 GEM	25 CAN	26 VIR	25 LIB	26 SAG	24 CAP	26 PIS	25 ARI	25 TAU
26 PIS	28 TAU	27 TAU	28 CAN	27 LEO	28 LIB	27 SCO	28 CAP	26 AQU	29 ARI	27 TAU	27 GEM
29 ARI		29 GEM	30 LEO	30 VIR	30 SCO	29 SAG	30 AQU	29 PIS	31 TAU	30 GEM	30 CAN
31 TAU		31 GEM		31 VIR		31 SAG	31 AQU	30 PIS			31 CAN

1888

JAN	FEB	MAR	APR	MAY	JUN	JUL	AUG	SEP	OCT	NOV	DEC
1 LEO	1 VIR	1 LIB	1 SAG	1 CAP	1 PIS	1 ARI	1 TAU	1 CAN	1 LEO	1 LIB	1 SCO
3 VIR	2 VIR	2 SCO	2 CAP	2 AQU	3 ARI	3 TAU	2 GEM	3 LEO	3 VIR	3 SCO	3 SAG
5 LIB	4 SCO	4 SAG	5 AQU	4 PIS	6 TAU	5 GEM	4 CAN	5 VIR	5 LIB	5 SAG	5 CAP
7 SCO	6 SAG	6 CAP	7 PIS	7 ARI	8 GEM	8 CAN	7 LEO	7 LIB	7 SCO	7 CAP	7 AQU
10 SAG	8 CAP	8 AQU	10 ARI	9 TAU	11 CAN	10 LEO	9 LIB	9 SCO	9 SAG	9 AQU	9 PIS
12 CAP	10 AQU	11 PIS	12 TAU	12 GEM	13 LEO	13 VIR	11 LIB	11 SAG	11 CAP	12 PIS	11 ARI
14 AQU	13 PIS	13 ARI	15 GEM	14 CAN	15 VIR	15 LIB	13 SCO	14 CAP	13 AQU	14 ARI	14 TAU
16 PIS	15 ARI	16 TAu	17 CAN	17 LEO	18 LIB	17 SCO	15 SAG	16 AQU	15 PIS	16 TAU	16 GEM
19 ARI	17 TAU	18 GEM	20 LEO	19 VIR	20 SCO	19 SAG	17 CAP	18 PIS	18 ARI	19 GEM	19 CAN
21 TAU	20 GEM	21 CAN	22 VIR	21 LIB	22 SAG	21 CAP	20 AQU	20 ARI	20 TAU	21 CAN	21 LEO
24 GEM	22 CAN	23 LEO	24 LIB	23 SCO	24 CAP	23 AQU	22 PIS	23 TAU	23 GEM	24 LEO	24 VIR
26 CAN	25 LEO	25 VIR	26 SCO	25 SAG	26 AQU	25 PIS	24 ARI	25 GEM	25 CAN	26 VIR	26 LIB
28 LEO	27 VIR	27 LIB	28 SAG	27 CAP	28 PIS	28 ARI	27 TAU	28 CAN	28 LEO	29 LIB	28 SCO
31 VIR	29 LIB	29 SCO	30 CAP	29 AQU	30 ARI	30 TAU	29 GEM	30 LEO	30 VIR	30 LIB	30 SAG
		31 SAG		31 AQU		31 TAU	31 GEM		31 VIR		31 SAG

1889

JAN	FEB	MAR	APR	MAY	JUN	JUL	AUG	SEP	OCT	NOV	DEC
1 CAP	1 AQU	1 PIS	1 ARI	1 TAU	1 CAN	1 LEO	1 LIB	1 SCO	1 CAP	1 AQU	1 ARI
3 AQU	2 PIS	3 ARI	2 TAU	2 GEM	3 LEO	3 VIR	4 SCO	2 SAG	4 AQU	2 PIS	4 TAU
5 PIS	4 ARI	6 TAU	4 GEM	4 CAN	6 VIR	5 LIB	6 SAG	4 CAP	6 PIS	4 ARI	6 GEM
8 ARI	6 TAU	8 GEM	7 CAN	7 LEO	8 LIB	7 SCO	8 CAP	6 AQU	8 ARI	6 TAU	9 CAN
10 TAU	9 GEM	11 CAN	9 LEO	9 VIR	10 SCO	9 SAG	10 AQU	8 PIS	10 TAU	9 GEM	11 LEO
12 GEM	11 CAN	13 LEO	12 VIR	12 LIB	12 SAG	12 CAP	12 PIS	11 ARI	13 GEM	11 CAN	14 VIR
15 CAN	14 LEO	15 VIR	14 LIB	14 SCO	14 CAP	13 AQU	14 ARI	13 TAU	15 CAN	14 LEO	16 LIB
17 LEO	16 VIR	18 LIB	16 SCO	16 SAG	16 AQU	16 PIS	16 TAU	15 GEM	18 LEO	16 VIR	18 SCO
20 VIR	18 LIB	20 SCO	18 SAG	18 CAP	18 PIS	18 ARI	19 GEM	18 CAN	20 VIR	19 LIB	20 SAG
22 LIB	21 SCO	22 SAG	20 CAP	20 AQU	20 ARI	20 TAU	21 CAN	20 LEO	22 LIB	21 SCO	22 CAP
24 SCO	23 SAG	24 CAP	22 AQU	22 PIS	23 TAU	23 GEM	24 LEO	23 VIR	25 SCO	23 SAG	24 AQU
26 SAG	25 CAP	26 AQU	25 PIS	24 ARI	25 GEM	25 CAN	26 VIR	25 LIB	27 SAG	25 CAP	26 PIS
29 CAP	27 AQU	28 PIS	27 ARI	27 TAU	28 CAN	28 LEO	29 LIB	27 SCO	29 CAP	27 AQU	29 ARI
31 AQU	28 AQU	31 ARI	29 TAU	29 GEM	30 LEO	30 VIR	31 SCO	29 SAG	31 AQU	29 PIS	31 TAU
			30 TAU	31 GEM		31 VIR		30 SAG		30 PIS	

1890

JAN	FEB	MAR	APR	MAY	JUN	JUL	AUG	SEP	OCT	NOV	DEC
1 TAU	1 CAN	1 CAN	1 LEO	1 VIR	1 SCO	1 CAP	1 AQU	1 ARI	1 TAU	1 CAN	1 LEO
2 GEM	4 LEO	3 LEO	2 VIR	2 LIB	2 SAG	3 AQU	2 PIS	2 TAU	2 GEM	3 LEO	3 VIR
5 CAN	6 VIR	5 VIR	4 LIB	4 SCO	4 CAP	5 PIS	4 ARI	5 GEM	4 CAN	6 VIR	6 LIB
7 LEO	9 LIB	8 LIB	6 SCO	6 SAG	7 AQU	7 ARI	6 TAU	7 CAN	7 LEO	8 LIB	8 SCO
10 VIR	11 SCO	10 SCO	8 SAG	8 CAP	9 PIS	10 TAU	8 GEM	10 LEO	9 VIR	11 SCO	10 SAG
12 LIB	13 SAG	12 SAG	11 CAP	10 AQU	11 ARI	12 GEM	11 CAN	12 VIR	12 LIB	13 SAG	12 CAP
15 SCO	15 CAP	15 CAP	12 AQU	12 PIS	13 TAU	14 CAN	13 LEO	15 LIB	14 SCO	15 CAP	14 AQU
17 SAG	17 AQU	17 AQU	15 PIS	14 ARI	15 GEM	17 LEO	16 VIR	17 SCO	16 SAG	17 AQU	16 PIS
19 CAP	19 PIS	17 PIS	17 ARI	17 TAU	18 CAN	20 VIR	18 LIB	19 SAG	19 CAP	19 PIS	19 ARI
21 AQU	21 ARI	21 ARI	19 TAU	19 GEM	20 LEO	22 LIB	21 SCO	22 CAP	21 AQU	21 ARI	21 TAU
23 PIS	24 TAU	23 TAU	22 GEM	21 CAN	22 VIR	24 SCO	23 SAG	24 AQU	23 PIS	24 TAU	23 GEM
25 ARI	26 GEM	25 GEM	24 CAN	24 LEO	25 LIB	27 SAG	25 CAP	26 PIS	25 ARI	26 GEM	25 CAN
27 TAU	28 CAN	28 CAN	27 LEO	26 VIR	27 SCO	29 CAP	27 AQU	28 ARI	27 TAU	28 CAN	28 LEO
30 GEM		30 LEO	29 VIR	29 LIB	28 SAG	31 AQU	29 PIS	30 TAU	29 GEM	30 CAN	30 VIR
31 GEM		31 LEO	30 VIR	31 SCO	30 SAG		31 ARI		31 GEM		31 VIR

1891

JAN	FEB	MAR	APR	MAY	JUN	JUL	AUG	SEP	OCT	NOV	DEC
1 VIR	1 SCO	1 SCO	1 CAP	1 AQU	1 ARI	1 TAU	1 CAN	1 LEO	1 VIR	1 SCO	1 SAG
2 LIB	3 SAG	2 SAG	3 AQU	2 PIS	3 TAU	2 GEM	2 LEO	2 VIR	3 LIB	3 SAG	3 CAP
4 SCO	5 CAP	5 CAP	5 PIS	4 ARI	5 GEM	5 CAN	6 VIR	4 LIB	4 SCO	5 CAP	5 AQU
7 SAG	7 AQU	7 AQU	7 ARI	7 TAU	7 CAN	7 LEO	8 LIB	7 SCO	7 SAG	8 AQU	7 PIS
9 CAP	9 PIS	9 PIS	9 TAU	9 GEM	10 LEO	9 VIR	11 SCO	9 SAG	9 CAP	10 PIS	9 ARI
11 AQU	11 ARI	11 ARI	11 GEM	11 CAN	12 VIR	12 LIB	13 SAG	12 CAP	11 AQU	12 ARI	11 TAU
13 PIS	13 TAU	13 TAU	14 CAN	14 LEO	15 LIB	14 SCO	15 CAP	14 AQU	13 PIS	14 TAU	13 GEM
15 ARI	16 GEM	15 GEM	16 LEO	16 VIR	17 SCO	17 SAG	18 AQU	16 PIS	16 ARI	16 GEM	16 CAN
17 TAU	18 CAN	17 CAN	18 VIR	18 LIB	19 SAG	19 CAP	20 PIS	18 ARI	17 TAU	18 CAN	18 LEO
19 GEM	20 LEO	20 LEO	21 LIB	21 SCO	22 CAP	21 AQU	22 ARI	20 TAU	20 GEM	20 LEO	20 VIR
22 CAN	23 VIR	22 VIR	23 SCO	23 SAG	24 AQU	23 PIS	24 TAU	22 GEM	22 CAN	23 VIR	23 LIB
24 LEO	25 LIB	25 LIB	26 SAG	25 CAP	26 PIS	25 ARI	26 GEM	24 CAN	24 LEO	25 LIB	25 SCO
27 VIR	28 SCO	27 SCO	28 CAP	28 AQU	28 ARI	27 TAU	28 CAN	27 LEO	26 VIR	28 SCO	28 SAG
29 LIB		30 SAG	30 AQU	30 PIS	30 TAU	30 GEM	30 LEO	29 VIR	29 LIB	30 SAG	30 CAP
31 LIB		31 SAG		31 PIS		31 GEM	31 LEO	30 VIR	31 LIB	31 SAG	31 CAP

1892

JAN	FEB	MAR	APR	MAY	JUN	JUL	AUG	SEP	OCT	NOV	DEC
1 CAP	1 PIS	1 ARI	1 GEM	1 CAN	1 VIR	1 LIB	1 SCO	1 CAP	1 AQU	1 ARI	1 TAU
2 AQU	2 ARI	3 TAU	3 CAN	2 LEO	3 LIB	3 SCO	2 SAG	3 AQU	3 PIS	3 TAU	3 GEM
4 PIS	4 TAU	5 GEM	5 LEO	5 VIR	6 SCO	6 SAG	5 CAP	7 PIS	5 ARI	5 PIS	5 CAN
6 ARI	6 GEM	7 CAN	7 VIR	7 LIB	8 SAG	8 CAP	7 AQU	7 ARI	7 TAU	7 CAN	7 LEO
8 TAU	9 CAN	9 LEO	10 LIB	10 SCO	11 CAP	10 AQU	9 PIS	9 TAU	9 GEM	9 LEO	9 VIR
10 GEM	10 LEO	12 VIR	12 SCO	12 SAG	13 AQU	13 PIS	11 ARI	12 GEM	11 CAN	12 VIR	11 LIB
12 CAN	13 VIR	14 LIB	15 SAG	15 CAP	15 PIS	15 ARI	13 TAU	14 CAN	13 LEO	14 LIB	14 SCO
15 LEO	15 LIB	17 SCO	17 CAP	17 AQU	18 ARI	17 TAU	15 GEM	16 LEO	15 VIR	17 SCO	17 SAG
17 VIR	18 SCO	19 SAG	20 AQU	19 PIS	20 TAU	19 GEM	17 CAN	18 VIR	18 LIB	19 SAG	19 CAP
19 LIB	20 SAG	21 CAP	22 PIS	21 ARI	22 GEM	21 CAN	20 LEO	21 LIB	20 SCO	22 CAP	21 AQU
22 SCO	23 CAP	23 AQU	24 ARI	23 TAU	24 CAN	23 LEO	22 VIR	23 SCO	23 SAG	24 AQU	24 PIS
25 SAG	25 AQU	25 PIS	26 TAU	25 GEM	26 LEO	26 VIR	24 LIB	26 SAG	26 CAP	27 PIS	26 ARI
27 CAP	27 PIS	28 ARI	28 GEM	27 CAN	28 VIR	28 LIB	27 SCO	28 CAP	28 AQU	29 ARI	28 TAU
29 AQU	29 PIS	29 TAU	30 CAN	30 LEO	30 VIR	31 SCO	29 SAG	30 CAP	30 PIS	30 ARI	30 GEM
31 PIS		31 TAU		31 LEO			31 SAG		31 PIS		31 GEM

1893

JAN	FEB	MAR	APR	MAY	JUN	JUL	AUG	SEP	OCT	NOV	DEC
1 CAN	1 LEO	1 VIR	1 LIB	1 SCO	1 CAP	1 AQU	1 PIS	1 TAU	1 CAN	1 LEO	1 VIR
3 LEO	2 VIR	4 LIB	2 SCO	2 SAG	3 AQU	3 PIS	2 ARI	2 GEM	4 LEO	2 VIR	2 LIB
5 VIR	4 LIB	6 SCO	5 SAG	5 CAP	6 PIS	5 ARI	4 TAU	4 CAN	6 VIR	4 LIB	4 SCO
8 LIB	7 SCO	8 SAG	7 CAP	7 AQU	8 ARI	8 TAU	6 GEM	6 LEO	8 LIB	7 SCO	6 SAG
10 SCO	9 SAG	11 CAP	10 AQU	9 PIS	10 TAU	10 GEM	8 CAN	8 VIR	10 SCO	9 SAG	9 CAP
13 SAG	12 CAP	13 AQU	12 PIS	12 ARI	12 GEM	12 CAN	10 LEO	11 LIB	13 SAG	12 CAP	11 AQU
15 CAP	14 AQU	16 PIS	14 ARI	14 TAU	14 CAN	14 LEO	12 VIR	13 SCO	15 CAP	14 AQU	14 PIS
18 AQU	16 PIS	18 ARI	16 TAU	16 GEM	16 LEO	16 VIR	14 LIB	16 SAG	18 AQU	17 PIS	16 ARI
20 PIS	18 ARI	20 TAU	18 GEM	18 CAN	18 VIR	18 LIB	17 SCO	18 CAP	20 PIS	19 ARI	19 TAU
22 ARI	21 TAU	22 GEM	20 CAN	20 LEO	21 LIB	20 SCO	19 SAG	21 AQU	23 ARI	21 TAU	21 GEM
24 TAU	23 GEM	24 CAN	22 LEO	22 VIR	23 SCO	23 SAG	22 CAP	23 PIS	25 TAU	23 GEM	23 CAN
26 GEM	25 CAN	26 LEO	25 VIR	24 LIB	26 SAG	25 CAP	24 AQU	25 ARI	27 GEM	25 CAN	25 LEO
29 CAN	27 LEO	29 VIR	27 LIB	27 SCO	28 CAP	28 AQU	27 PIS	27 TAU	29 CAN	27 LEO	27 VIR
31 LEO	28 LEO	31 LIB	30 SCO	29 SAG	30 CAP	30 PIS	29 ARI	29 GEM	31 LEO	29 VIR	29 LIB
				31 SAG		31 PIS	31 TAU	30 GEM		30 VIR	30 SCO

1894

JAN	FEB	MAR	APR	MAY	JUN	JUL	AUG	SEP	OCT	NOV	DEC
1 SCO	1 CAP	1 CAP	1 AQU	1 PIS	1 TAU	1 GEM	1 LEO	1 LIB	1 SCO	1 SAG	1 AQU
3 SAG	4 AQU	3 AQU	2 PIS	2 ARI	3 GEM	2 CAN	2 VIR	3 SCO	3 SAG	2 CAP	4 PIS
5 CAP	6 PIS	6 PIS	4 ARI	4 TAU	5 CAN	4 LEO	4 LIB	5 SAG	5 CAP	4 AQU	6 ARI
8 AQU	9 ARI	8 ARI	7 TAU	6 GEM	7 LEO	6 VIR	7 SCO	8 CAP	8 AQU	7 PIS	9 TAU
10 PIS	11 TAU	10 TAU	9 GEM	8 CAN	9 VIR	8 LIB	9 SAG	10 AQU	10 PIS	9 ARI	11 GEM
13 ARI	13 GEM	13 GEM	11 CAN	10 LEO	11 LIB	10 SCO	12 CAP	13 PIS	13 ARI	11 TAU	13 CAN
15 TAU	15 CAN	15 CAN	13 LEO	12 VIR	13 SCO	13 SAG	14 AQU	15 ARI	15 TAU	13 GEM	15 LEO
17 GEM	17 LEO	17 LEO	15 VIR	15 LIB	16 SAG	16 CAP	17 PIS	18 TAU	17 GEM	16 CAN	17 VIR
19 CAN	19 VIR	19 VIR	17 LIB	17 SCO	18 CAP	18 AQU	19 ARI	20 GEM	19 CAN	18 LEO	19 LIB
21 LEO	22 LIB	21 LIB	20 SCO	19 SAG	21 AQU	20 PIS	21 TAU	22 CAN	21 LEO	20 VIR	21 SCO
23 VIR	24 SCO	23 SCO	22 SAG	22 CAP	23 PIS	23 ARI	24 GEM	24 LEO	24 VIR	22 LIB	24 SAG
25 LIB	26 SAG	26 SAG	24 CAP	24 AQU	26 ARI	25 TAU	26 CAN	26 VIR	26 LIB	24 SCO	26 CAP
27 SCO	28 SAG	28 CAP	27 AQU	27 PIS	28 TAU	27 GEM	28 LEO	28 LIB	28 SCO	26 SAG	29 AQU
30 SAG		31 AQU	29 PIS	29 ARI	30 GEM	29 CAN	30 VIR	30 SCO	30 SAG	29 CAP	31 PIS
31 SAG			30 PIS	31 TAU		31 LEO	31 VIR		31 SAG	30 CAP	

1895

JAN	FEB	MAR	APR	MAY	JUN	JUL	AUG	SEP	OCT	NOV	DEC
1 PIS	1 TAU	1 TAU	1 CAN	1 LEO	1 LIB	1 SCO	1 SAG	1 AQU	1 PIS	1 TAU	1 GEM
3 ARI	4 GEM	3 GEM	4 LEO	3 VIR	2 SCO	2 SAG	2 CAP	3 PIS	3 ARI	4 GEM	3 CAN
5 TAU	6 CAN	5 CAN	6 VIR	5 LIB	6 SAG	5 CAP	4 AQU	5 ARI	5 TAU	6 CAN	5 LEO
7 GEM	8 LEO	7 LEO	8 LIB	7 SCO	8 CAP	8 AQU	7 PIS	8 TAU	7 GEM	8 LEO	8 VIR
9 CAN	10 VIR	9 VIR	10 SCO	9 SAG	10 AQU	10 PIS	9 ARI	10 GEM	10 CAN	10 VIR	10 LIB
11 LEO	12 LIB	11 LIB	12 SAG	12 CAP	13 PIS	13 ARI	12 TAU	13 CAN	12 LEO	12 LIB	12 SCO
13 VIR	14 SCO	13 SCO	14 CAP	14 AQU	15 ARI	15 TAU	14 GEM	15 LEO	14 VIR	15 SCO	14 SAG
15 LIB	16 SAG	16 SAG	17 AQU	17 PIS	18 TAU	18 GEM	16 CAN	17 VIR	16 LIB	17 SAG	16 CAP
18 SCO	19 CAP	18 CAP	19 PIS	19 ARI	20 GEM	20 CAN	18 LEO	19 LIB	18 SCO	19 CAP	19 AQU
20 SAG	21 AQU	20 AQU	22 ARI	22 TAU	22 CAN	22 LEO	20 VIR	21 SCO	20 SAG	21 AQU	21 PIS
22 CAP	24 PIS	23 PIS	24 TAU	24 GEM	24 LEO	24 VIR	22 LIB	23 SAG	22 CAP	24 PIS	24 ARI
25 AQU	26 ARI	25 ARI	26 GEM	26 CAN	26 VIR	26 LIB	24 SCO	25 CAP	25 AQU	26 ARI	26 TAU
27 PIS	28 ARI	28 TAU	29 CAN	28 LEO	29 LIB	28 SCO	26 SAG	28 AQU	27 PIS	29 TAU	28 GEM
30 ARI		30 GEM	30 CAN	30 VIR	30 LIB	30 SAG	29 CAP	30 PIS	30 ARI	30 TAU	31 CAN
31 ARI		31 GEM		31 VIR			31 AQU		31 ARI		

1896

JAN	FEB	MAR	APR	MAY	JUN	JUL	AUG	SEP	OCT	NOV	DEC
1 CAN	1 VIR	1 LIB	1 SAG	1 CAP	1 AQU	1 PIS	1 TAU	1 GEM	1 LEO	1 VIR	1 SCO
2 LEO	2 LIB	3 SCO	3 CAP	3 AQU	2 PIS	2 ARI	3 GEM	2 CAN	3 VIR	2 LIB	3 SAG
4 VIR	4 SCO	5 SAG	6 AQU	5 PIS	4 ARI	4 TAU	5 CAN	4 LEO	5 LIB	4 SCO	5 CAP
6 LIB	6 SAG	7 CAP	8 PIS	8 ARI	7 TAU	7 GEM	7 LEO	6 VIR	7 SCO	6 SAG	8 AQU
8 SCO	9 CAP	9 AQU	11 ARI	10 TAU	9 GEM	9 CAN	10 VIR	8 LIB	9 SAG	8 CAP	10 PIS
10 SAG	11 AQU	12 PIS	13 TAU	13 GEM	12 CAN	11 LEO	12 LIB	10 SCO	12 CAP	10 AQU	12 ARI
13 CAP	14 PIS	14 ARI	16 GEM	15 CAN	14 LEO	13 VIR	14 SCO	12 SAG	14 AQU	13 PIS	15 TAU
15 AQU	16 ARI	17 TAU	18 CAN	18 LEO	16 VIR	15 LIB	16 SAG	14 CAP	16 PIS	15 ARI	17 GEM
17 PIS	19 TAU	19 GEM	20 LEO	20 VIR	18 LIB	17 SCO	18 CAP	17 AQU	19 ARI	18 TAU	20 CAN
20 ARI	21 GEM	22 CAN	23 VIR	22 LIB	20 SCO	20 SAG	20 AQU	19 PIS	21 TAU	20 GEM	22 LEO
22 TAU	23 CAN	24 LEO	25 LIB	24 SCO	22 SAG	22 CAP	23 PIS	22 ARI	24 GEM	22 CAN	24 VIR
25 GEM	26 LEO	26 VIR	27 SCO	26 SAG	24 CAP	24 AQU	25 ARI	24 TAU	26 CAN	25 LEO	27 LIB
27 CAN	28 VIR	28 LIB	29 SAG	28 CAP	27 AQU	26 PIS	28 TAU	27 GEM	29 LEO	27 VIR	29 SCO
29 LEO	29 VIR	30 SCO	30 SAG	30 AQU	29 PIS	29 ARI	30 GEM	29 CAN	31 VIR	29 LIB	31 SAG
31 VIR		31 SCO		31 AQU	30 PIS	31 TAU	31 GEM	30 CAN		30 LIB	

1897

JAN	FEB	MAR	APR	MAY	JUN	JUL	AUG	SEP	OCT	NOV	DEC
1 SAG	1 AQU	1 AQU	1 ARI	1 TAU	1 GEM	1 LEO	1 VIR	1 SCO	1 SAG	1 AQU	1 PIS
2 CAP	3 PIS	2 PIS	3 TAU	3 GEM	2 CAN	4 VIR	2 LIB	3 SAG	2 CAP	3 PIS	2 ARI
4 AQU	5 ARI	4 ARI	6 GEM	5 CAN	4 LEO	6 LIB	4 SCO	5 CAP	4 AQU	5 ARI	5 TAU
6 PIS	8 TAU	7 TAU	8 CAN	8 LEO	6 VIR	8 SCO	6 SAG	7 AQU	6 PIS	7 TAU	7 GEM
9 ARI	10 GEM	9 GEM	11 LEO	10 VIR	9 LIB	10 SAG	9 CAP	9 PIS	9 ARI	10 GEM	10 CAN
11 TAU	12 CAN	12 CAN	13 VIR	12 LIB	11 SCO	12 CAP	11 AQU	11 ARI	11 TAU	13 CAN	12 LEO
14 GEM	15 LEO	14 LEO	15 LIB	14 SCO	13 SAG	14 AQU	13 PIS	14 TAU	14 GEM	15 LEO	15 VIR
16 CAN	17 VIR	16 VIR	17 SCO	16 SAG	15 CAP	16 PIS	15 ARI	16 GEM	16 CAN	17 VIR	17 LIB
18 LEO	19 LIB	18 LIB	19 SAG	18 CAP	17 AQU	19 ARI	18 TAU	19 CAN	19 LEO	20 LIB	19 SCO
21 VIR	21 SCO	20 SCO	21 CAP	20 AQU	19 PIS	21 TAU	20 GEM	21 LEO	21 VIR	22 SCO	21 SAG
23 LIB	23 SAG	23 SAG	23 AQU	23 PIS	21 ARI	24 GEM	23 CAN	24 VIR	23 LIB	24 SAG	23 CAP
25 SCO	25 CAP	25 CAP	25 PIS	25 ARI	24 TAU	26 CAN	25 LEO	26 LIB	25 SCO	26 CAP	25 AQU
27 SAG	28 AQU	27 AQU	28 ARI	28 TAU	26 GEM	29 LEO	27 VIR	28 SCO	27 SAG	28 AQU	27 PIS
29 CAP		29 PIS	30 TAU	30 GEM	29 CAN	31 VIR	29 LIB	30 SAG	29 CAP	30 PIS	20 ARI
31 AQU					30 CAN		30 LIB		31 AQU		31 ARI

1898

JAN	FEB	MAR	APR	MAY	JUN	JUL	AUG	SEP	OCT	NOV	DEC
1 TAU	1 GEM	1 CAN	1 LEO	1 VIR	1 SCO	1 SAG	1 AQU	1 PIS	1 TAU	1 GEM	1 CAN
3 GEM	2 CAN	4 LEO	3 VIR	3 LIB	3 SAG	3 CAP	3 PIS	2 ARI	4 GEM	2 CAN	2 LEO
6 CAN	5 LEO	7 VIR	5 LIB	5 SCO	5 CAP	5 AQU	5 ARI	4 TAU	6 CAN	5 LEO	5 VIR
9 LEO	7 VIR	9 LIB	7 SCO	7 SAG	7 AQU	7 PIS	7 TAU	6 GEM	9 LEO	7 VIR	7 LIB
11 VIR	9 LIB	11 SCO	9 SAG	9 CAP	9 PIS	9 ARI	10 GEM	9 CAN	11 VIR	10 LIB	9 SCO
13 LIB	12 SCO	13 SAG	11 CAP	11 AQU	11 ARI	11 TAU	12 CAN	11 LEO	13 LIB	12 SCO	12 SAG
15 SCO	14 SAG	15 CAP	14 AQU	13 PIS	14 TAU	14 GEM	15 LEO	14 VIR	16 SCO	14 SAG	14 CAP
18 SAG	16 CAP	17 AQU	16 PIS	15 ARI	16 GEM	16 CAN	17 VIR	16 LIB	18 SAG	16 CAP	16 AQU
20 CAP	18 AQU	20 PIS	18 ARI	18 TAU	19 CAN	19 LEO	20 LIB	18 SCO	20 CAP	18 AQU	18 PIS
22 AQU	20 PIS	22 ARI	20 TAU	20 GEM	21 LEO	21 VIR	22 SCO	20 SAG	22 AQU	20 PIS	20 ARI
24 PIS	22 ARI	24 TAU	23 GEM	23 CAN	24 VIR	24 LIB	24 SAG	23 CAP	24 PIS	23 ARI	22 TAU
26 ARI	25 TAU	26 GEM	25 CAN	25 LEO	26 LIB	26 SCO	26 CAP	25 AQU	26 ARI	25 TAU	24 GEM
28 TAU	27 GEM	29 CAN	28 LEO	28 VIR	29 SCO	28 SAG	28 AQU	27 PIS	29 TAU	27 GEM	27 CAN
31 GEM	28 GEM	31 CAN	30 VIR	30 LIB	30 SCO	30 CAP	30 PIS	29 ARI	31 GEM	30 CAN	29 LEO
				31 LIB		31 CAP	31 PIS	30 ARI			31 LEO

1899

JAN	FEB	MAR	APR	MAY	JUN	JUL	AUG	SEP	OCT	NOV	DEC
1 VIR	1 LIB	1 SCO	1 SAG	1 AQU	1 PIS	1 TAU	1 GEM	1 LEO	1 VIR	1 LIB	1 SCO
3 LIB	2 SCO	4 SAG	2 CAP	4 PIS	2 ARI	4 GEM	2 CAN	4 VIR	3 LIB	2 SCO	2 SAG
6 SCO	4 SAG	6 CAP	4 AQU	6 ARI	4 TAU	6 CAN	5 LEO	6 LIB	6 SCO	4 SAG	4 CAP
8 SAG	6 CAP	8 AQU	6 PIS	8 TAU	6 GEM	9 LEO	7 VIR	9 SCO	8 SAG	7 CAP	6 AQU
10 CAP	8 AQU	10 PIS	8 ARI	10 GEM	9 CAN	11 VIR	10 LIB	11 SAG	10 CAP	9 AQU	8 PIS
12 AQU	10 PIS	12 ARI	10 TAU	12 CAN	11 LEO	14 LIB	12 SCO	13 CAP	13 AQU	11 PIS	10 ARI
14 PIS	12 ARI	14 TAU	13 GEM	15 LEO	14 VIR	16 SCO	15 SAG	15 AQU	15 PIS	13 ARI	12 TAU
16 ARI	15 TAU	16 GEM	15 CAN	18 VIR	16 LIB	18 SAG	17 CAP	17 PIS	17 ARI	15 TAU	15 GEM
18 TAU	17 GEM	19 CAN	18 LEO	20 LIB	19 SCO	20 CAP	19 AQU	19 ARI	19 TAU	17 GEM	17 CAN
21 GEM	19 CAN	21 LEO	20 VIR	22 SCO	21 SAG	22 AQU	21 PIS	21 TAU	21 GEM	20 CAN	19 LEO
23 CAN	22 LEO	24 VIR	23 LIB	24 SAG	23 CAP	24 PIS	23 ARI	24 GEM	23 CAN	22 LEO	22 VIR
26 LEO	25 VIR	26 LIB	25 SCO	27 CAP	25 AQU	26 ARI	25 TAU	26 CAN	26 LEO	25 VIR	24 LIB
28 VIR	27 LIB	29 SCO	27 SAG	29 AQU	27 PIS	29 TAU	27 GEM	28 LEO	29 VIR	27 LIB	27 SCO
31 LIB	28 LIB	31 SAG	29 CAP	31 PIS	29 ARI	31 GEM	30 CAN	30 LEO	31 LIB	29 SCO	24 SAG
			30 CAP		30 ARI		31 CAN			30 SCO	31 CAP

1900

JAN	FEB	MAR	APR	MAY	JUN	JUL	AUG	SEP	OCT	NOV	DEC
1 CAP	1 PIS	1 PIS	1 TAU	1 GEM	1 LEO	1 VIR	1 LIB	1 SAG	1 CAP	1 PIS	1 ARI
2 AQU	3 ARI	2 ARI	3 GEM	2 CAN	4 VIR	3 LIB	2 SCO	3 CAP	3 AQU	4 ARI	3 TAU
4 PIS	5 TAU	4 TAU	5 CAN	5 LEO	6 LIB	6 SCO	5 SAG	6 AQU	5 PIS	6 TAU	5 GEM
6 ARI	7 GEM	6 GEM	7 LEO	7 VIR	9 SCO	8 SAG	7 CAP	8 PIS	7 ARI	8 GEM	7 CAN
9 TAU	9 CAN	8 CAN	10 VIR	10 LIB	11 SAG	11 CAP	9 AQU	10 ARI	9 TAU	10 CAN	9 LEO
11 GEM	12 LEO	11 LEO	12 LIB	12 SCO	13 CAP	13 AQU	11 PIS	12 TAU	11 GEM	12 LEO	12 VIR
13 CAN	14 VIR	14 VIR	15 SCO	15 SAG	15 AQU	15 PIS	13 ARI	14 GEM	13 CAN	14 VIR	14 LIB
16 LEO	17 LIB	16 LIB	17 SAG	17 CAP	18 PIS	17 ARI	15 TAU	16 CAN	16 LEO	17 LIB	17 SCO
18 VIR	19 SCO	19 SCO	20 CAP	19 AQU	20 ARI	19 TAU	17 GEM	18 LEO	18 VIR	19 SCO	19 SAG
21 LIB	22 SAG	21 SAG	22 AQU	21 PIS	22 TAU	21 GEM	20 CAN	21 VIR	21 LIB	22 SAG	22 CAP
23 SCO	24 CAP	23 CAP	24 PIS	23 ARI	24 GEM	23 CAN	22 LEO	23 LIB	23 SCO	24 CAP	24 AQU
26 SAG	26 AQU	26 AQU	26 ARI	26 TAU	26 CAN	26 LEO	25 VIR	26 SCO	26 SAG	27 AQU	26 PIS
28 CAP	28 PIS	28 PIS	28 TAU	28 GEM	29 LEO	28 VIR	27 LIB	28 SAG	28 CAP	29 PIS	28 ARI
30 AQU	29 PIS	30 ARI	30 GEM	30 CAN	30 LEO	31 LIB	30 SCO	30 SAG	30 AQU	30 PIS	30 TAU
31 AQU		31 ARI		31 CAN			31 SCO		31 AQU		31 TAU

1901

JAN	FEB	MAR	APR	MAY	JUN	JUL	AUG	SEP	OCT	NOV	DEC
1 GEM	1 CAN	1 LEO	1 VIR	1 LIB	1 SAG	1 CAP	1 AQU	1 ARI	1 GEM	1 CAN	1 LEO
3 CAN	2 LEO	4 VIR	2 LIB	2 SCO	3 CAP	3 AQU	2 PIS	2 TAU	4 CAN	2 LEO	2 VIR
6 LEO	4 VIR	6 LIB	5 SCO	5 SAG	6 AQU	5 PIS	4 ARI	4 GEM	6 LEO	4 VIR	4 LIB
8 VIR	7 LIB	9 SCO	7 SAG	7 CAP	8 PIS	7 ARI	6 TAU	6 CAN	8 VIR	7 LIB	7 SCO
11 LIB	9 SCO	11 SAG	10 CAP	10 AQU	10 ARI	10 TAU	8 GEM	9 LEO	11 LIB	9 SCO	9 SAG
13 SCO	12 SAG	14 CAP	12 AQU	12 PIS	12 TAU	12 GEM	10 CAN	11 VIR	13 SCO	12 SAG	12 CAP
16 SAG	14 CAP	16 AQU	14 PIS	14 ARI	14 GEM	14 CAN	12 LEO	13 LIB	16 SAG	14 CAP	14 AQU
18 CAP	17 AQU	18 PIS	17 ARI	16 TAU	16 CAN	16 LEO	15 VIR	16 SCO	18 CAP	17 AQU	16 PIS
20 AQU	19 PIS	20 ARI	19 TAU	18 GEM	19 LEO	18 VIR	17 LIB	18 SAG	21 AQU	19 PIS	19 ARI
22 PIS	21 ARI	22 TAU	21 GEM	20 CAN	21 VIR	21 LIB	19 SCO	21 CAP	23 PIS	21 ARI	21 TAU
24 ARI	23 TAU	24 GEM	23 CAN	22 LEO	23 LIB	23 SCO	22 SAG	23 AQU	25 ARI	23 TAU	23 GEM
26 TAU	25 GEM	26 CAN	25 LEO	24 VIR	26 SCO	26 SAG	24 CAP	25 PIS	27 TAU	25 GEM	25 CAN
29 GEM	27 CAN	29 LEO	27 VIR	27 LIB	28 SAG	28 CAP	27 AQU	27 ARI	29 GEM	27 CAN	27 LEO
31 CAN	28 CAN	31 VIR	30 LIB	29 SCO	30 SAG	30 AQU	29 PIS	29 TAU	31 CAN	29 LEO	29 VIR
				31 SCO		31 AQU	31 ARI	30 TAU		30 LEO	31 LIB

1902

JAN	FEB	MAR	APR	MAY	JUN	JUL	AUG	SEP	OCT	NOV	DEC
1 LIB	1 SCO	1 SAG	1 CAP	1 AQU	1 ARI	1 TAU	1 CAN	1 VIR	1 LIB	1 SCO	1 SAG
3 SCO	2 SAG	4 CAP	2 AQU	2 PIS	3 TAU	2 GEM	3 LEO	3 LIB	3 SCO	2 SAG	2 CAP
5 SAG	4 CAP	6 AQU	5 PIS	4 ARI	5 GEM	4 CAN	5 VIR	6 SCO	5 SAG	4 CAP	4 AQU
8 CAP	7 AQU	8 PIS	7 ARI	6 TAU	7 CAN	6 LEO	7 LIB	8 SAG	8 CAP	7 AQU	7 PIS
10 AQU	9 PIS	10 ARI	9 TAU	8 GEM	9 LEO	8 VIR	9 SCO	11 CAP	10 AQU	9 PIS	9 ARI
13 PIS	11 ARI	13 TAU	11 GEM	10 CAN	11 VIR	11 LIB	12 SAG	13 AQU	13 PIS	12 ARI	11 TAU
15 ARI	13 TAU	15 GEM	13 CAN	12 LEO	13 LIB	13 SCO	14 CAP	15 PIS	15 ARI	14 TAU	13 GEM
17 TAU	15 GEM	17 CAN	15 LEO	15 VIR	16 SCO	15 SAG	17 AQU	18 ARI	17 TAU	16 GEM	15 CAN
19 GEM	18 CAN	19 LEO	17 VIR	17 LIB	18 SAG	18 CAP	19 PIS	20 TAU	19 GEM	18 CAN	17 LEO
21 CAN	20 LEO	21 VIR	20 LIB	19 SCO	21 CAP	20 AQU	21 ARI	22 GEM	21 CAN	20 LEO	19 VIR
23 LEO	22 VIR	23 LIB	22 SCO	22 SAG	23 AQU	23 PIS	24 TAU	24 CAN	23 LEO	22 VIR	21 LIB
25 VIR	24 LIB	26 SCO	25 SAG	24 CAP	26 PIS	25 ARI	26 GEM	26 LEO	26 VIR	24 LIB	24 SCO
28 LIB	27 SCO	28 SAG	27 CAP	27 AQU	28 ARI	27 TAU	28 CAN	28 VIR	28 LIB	27 SCO	26 SAG
30 SCO	28 SCO	31 CAP	30 AQU	29 PIS	30 TAU	30 GEM	30 LEO	30 VIR	30 SCO	29 SAG	29 CAP
31 SCO				31 PIS		31 GEM	31 LEO		31 SCO	30 SAG	31 AQU

1903

JAN	FEB	MAR	APR	MAY	JUN	JUL	AUG	SEP	OCT	NOV	DEC
1 AQU	1 ARI	1 ARI	1 GEM	1 CAN	1 VIR	1 LIB	1 SCO	1 CAP	1 AQU	1 PIS	1 TAU
3 PIS	4 TAU	3 TAU	4 CAN	3 LEO	3 LIB	3 SCO	2 SAG	3 AQU	3 PIS	2 ARI	3 GEM
5 ARI	6 GEM	5 GEM	6 LEO	5 VIR	6 SCO	5 SAG	4 CAP	5 PIS	5 ARI	4 TAU	6 CAN
8 TAU	8 CAN	7 CAN	8 VIR	7 LIB	8 SAG	8 CAP	7 AQU	8 ARI	8 TAU	6 GEM	8 LEO
10 GEM	10 LEO	9 LEO	10 LIB	10 SCO	11 CAP	10 AQU	9 PIS	10 TAU	10 GEM	8 CAN	10 VIR
12 CAN	12 VIR	11 VIR	12 SCO	12 SAG	13 AQU	13 PIS	12 ARI	13 GEM	12 CAN	10 LEO	12 LIB
14 LEO	14 LIB	14 LIB	15 SAG	14 CAP	16 PIS	15 ARI	14 TAU	15 CAN	14 LEO	12 VIR	14 SCO
16 VIR	16 SCO	16 SCO	17 CAP	17 AQU	18 ARI	18 TAU	16 GEM	17 LEO	16 VIR	15 LIB	16 SAG
18 LIB	19 SAG	18 SAG	20 AQU	19 PIS	20 TAU	20 GEM	18 CAN	19 VIR	18 LIB	17 SCO	19 CAP
20 SCO	21 CAP	21 CAP	22 PIS	22 ARI	23 GEM	22 CAN	20 LEO	21 LIB	20 SCO	19 SAG	21 AQU
23 SAG	24 AQU	23 AQU	24 ARI	24 TAU	25 CAN	24 LEO	22 VIR	22 SCO	23 SAG	21 CAP	24 PIS
25 CAP	26 PIS	26 PIS	27 TAU	26 GEM	27 LEO	26 VIR	24 LIB	25 SAG	25 CAP	24 AQU	26 ARI
28 AQU	28 PIS	28 ARI	29 GEM	28 CAN	29 VIR	28 LIB	27 SCO	28 CAP	28 AQU	26 PIS	29 TAU
30 PIS		30 TAU	30 GEM	30 LEO	30 VIR	30 SCO	29 SAG	30 AQU	30 PIS	29 ARI	31 GEM
31 PIS		31 TAU		31 LEO		31 SCO	31 CAP		31 PIS	30 ARI	

1904

JAN	FEB	MAR	APR	MAY	JUN	JUL	AUG	SEP	OCT	NOV	DEC
1 GEM	1 LEO	1 VIR	1 SCO	1 SAG	1 CAP	1 AQU	1 ARI	1 TAU	1 CAN	1 LEO	1 LIB
2 CAN	2 VIR	3 LIB	4 SAG	3 CAP	2 AQU	2 PIS	3 TAU	2 GEM	4 LEO	2 VIR	4 SCO
4 LEO	4 LIB	5 SCO	6 CAP	6 AQU	4 PIS	4 ARI	6 GEM	4 CAN	6 VIR	4 LIB	6 SAG
6 VIR	7 SCO	7 SAG	8 AQU	8 PIS	7 ARI	7 TAU	8 CAN	6 LEO	8 LIB	6 SCO	8 CAP
8 LIB	9 SAG	10 CAP	11 PIS	11 ARI	9 TAU	9 GEM	10 LEO	8 VIR	10 SCO	8 SAG	10 AQU
10 SCO	11 CAP	12 AQU	13 ARI	13 TAU	12 GEM	11 CAN	12 VIR	10 LIB	12 SAG	10 CAP	13 PIS
13 SAG	14 AQU	15 PIS	16 TAU	15 GEM	14 CAN	13 LEO	14 LIB	12 SCO	14 CAP	13 AQU	15 ARI
15 CAP	16 PIS	17 ARI	18 GEM	18 CAN	16 LEO	15 VIR	16 SCO	14 SAG	16 AQU	15 PIS	18 TAU
17 AQU	19 ARI	20 TAU	20 CAN	20 LEO	18 VIR	17 LIB	18 SAG	17 CAP	19 PIS	18 ARI	20 GEM
20 PIS	21 TAU	22 GEM	23 LEO	22 VIR	20 LIB	20 SCO	20 CAP	19 AQU	21 ARI	20 TAU	22 CAN
23 ARI	24 GEM	24 CAN	25 VIR	24 LIB	22 SCO	22 SAG	23 AQU	22 PIS	24 TAU	23 GEM	24 LEO
25 TAU	26 CAN	26 LEO	27 LIB	26 SCO	25 SAG	24 CAP	25 PIS	24 ARI	26 GEM	25 CAN	26 VIR
27 GEM	28 LEO	28 VIR	29 SCO	28 SAG	27 CAP	27 AQU	28 ARI	27 TAU	29 CAN	27 LEO	29 LIB
29 CAN	29 LEO	30 LIB	30 SCO	31 CAP	29 AQU	29 PIS	31 TAU	29 GEM	31 LEO	29 VIR	31 SCO
31 LEO		31 LIB			30 AQU	31 PIS		30 GEM		30 VIR	

1905

JAN	FEB	MAR	APR	MAY	JUN	JUL	AUG	SEP	OCT	NOV	DEC
1 SCO	1 CAP	1 CAP	1 PIS	1 ARI	1 TAU	1 CAN	1 LEO	1 LIB	1 SCO	1 CAP	1 AQU
2 SAG	3 AQU	2 AQU	3 ARI	3 TAU	2 GEM	4 LEO	2 VIR	3 SCO	2 SAG	3 AQU	2 PIS
4 CAP	5 PIS	4 PIS	6 TAU	6 GEM	4 CAN	6 VIR	4 LIB	5 SAG	4 CAP	5 PIS	5 ARI
6 AQU	8 ARI	7 ARI	8 GEM	8 CAN	6 LEO	8 LIB	6 SCO	7 CAP	6 AQU	8 ARI	7 TAU
9 PIS	10 TAU	10 TAU	11 CAN	10 LEO	9 VIR	10 SCO	9 SAG	9 AQU	9 PIS	10 TAU	10 GEM
11 ARI	13 GEM	12 GEM	13 LEO	12 VIR	11 LIB	12 SAG	11 CAP	12 PIS	11 ARI	13 GEM	12 CAN
14 TAU	15 CAN	14 CAN	15 VIR	15 LIB	13 SCO	14 CAP	13 AQU	14 ARI	14 TAU	15 CAN	15 LEO
16 GEM	17 LEO	17 LEO	17 LIB	17 SCO	15 SAG	17 AQU	15 PIS	17 TAU	16 GEM	17 LEO	17 VIR
19 CAN	19 VIR	19 VIR	19 SCO	19 SAG	17 CAP	19 PIS	18 ARI	19 GEM	19 CAN	20 VIR	19 LIB
21 LEO	21 LIB	21 LIB	21 SAG	21 CAP	19 AQU	21 ARI	20 TAU	22 CAN	21 LEO	22 LIB	21 SCO
23 VIR	23 SCO	23 SCO	23 CAP	23 AQU	22 PIS	24 TAU	23 GEM	24 LEO	23 VIR	24 SCO	23 SAG
25 LIB	25 SAG	25 SAG	26 AQU	25 PIS	24 ARI	26 GEM	25 CAN	26 VIR	26 LIB	26 SAG	25 CAP
27 SCO	28 CAP	27 CAP	28 PIS	28 ARI	27 TAU	29 CAN	27 LEO	28 LIB	28 SCO	28 CAP	28 AQU
29 SAG		29 AQU	30 PIS	30 TAU	29 GEM	31 LEO	30 VIR	30 SCO	29 SAG	30 AQU	30 PIS
31 CAP		31 AQU		31 TAU	30 GEM		31 VIR		31 SAG		31 PIS

1906

JAN	FEB	MAR	APR	MAY	JUN	JUL	AUG	SEP	OCT	NOV	DEC
1 ARI	1 TAU	1 TAU	1 CAN	1 LEO	1 LIB	1 SCO	1 CAP	1 AQU	1 ARI	1 TAU	1 GEM
4 TAU	3 GEM	2 GEM	3 LEO	3 VIR	3 SCO	3 SAG	3 AQU	2 PIS	4 TAU	3 GEM	2 CAN
6 GEM	5 CAN	4 CAN	5 VIR	5 LIB	5 SAG	5 CAP	5 PIS	4 ARI	6 GEM	5 CAN	5 LEO
9 CAN	7 LEO	7 LEO	8 LIB	7 SCO	7 CAP	7 AQU	8 ARI	6 TAU	9 CAN	8 LEO	7 VIR
11 LEO	10 VIR	9 VIR	10 SCO	9 SAG	9 AQU	9 PIS	10 TAU	9 GEM	11 LEO	10 VIR	10 LIB
13 VIR	12 LIB	11 LIB	12 SAG	11 CAP	12 PIS	11 ARI	13 GEM	11 CAN	14 VIR	12 LIB	12 SCO
15 LIB	14 SCO	13 SCO	14 CAP	13 AQU	14 ARI	14 TAU	15 CAN	14 LEO	16 LIB	14 SCO	14 SAG
18 SCO	16 SAG	15 SAG	16 AQU	15 PIS	16 TAU	16 GEM	18 LEO	16 VIR	18 SCO	16 SAG	16 CAP
20 SAG	18 CAP	17 CAP	18 PIS	18 ARI	19 GEM	19 CAN	20 VIR	18 LIB	20 SAG	18 CAP	18 AQU
22 CAP	20 AQU	20 AQU	20 ARI	20 TAU	21 CAN	21 LEO	22 LIB	20 SCO	22 CAP	20 AQU	20 PIS
24 AQU	23 PIS	22 PIS	23 TAU	23 GEM	24 LEO	24 VIR	24 SCO	23 SAG	24 AQU	23 PIS	22 ARI
26 PIS	25 ARI	24 ARI	25 GEM	25 CAN	26 VIR	26 LIB	26 SAG	25 CAP	26 PIS	25 ARI	25 TAU
29 ARI	27 TAU	27 TAU	28 CAN	28 LEO	29 LIB	28 SCO	28 CAP	27 AQU	29 ARI	27 TAU	27 GEM
31 TAU	28 TAU	29 GEM	30 LEO	30 VIR	30 LIB	30 SAG	31 AQU	29 PIS	31 TAU	30 GEM	30 CAN
		31 GEM		31 VIR		31 SAG		30 PIS			31 CAN

1907

JAN	FEB	MAR	APR	MAY	JUN	JUL	AUG	SEP	OCT	NOV	DEC
1 LEO	1 VIR	1 LIB	1 SCO	1 CAP	1 AQU	1 ARI	1 TAU	1 CAN	1 LEO	1 VIR	1 LIB
4 VIR	2 LIB	4 SCO	2 SAG	3 AQU	2 PIS	4 TAU	2 GEM	4 LEO	4 VIR	2 LIB	2 SCO
6 LIB	4 SCO	6 SAG	4 CAP	6 PIS	4 ARI	6 GEM	5 CAN	6 VIR	6 LIB	5 SCO	4 SAG
8 SCO	7 SAG	8 CAP	6 AQU	8 ARI	6 TAU	9 CAN	7 LEO	9 LIB	8 SCO	7 SAG	6 CAP
10 SAG	9 CAP	10 AQU	8 PIS	10 TAU	9 GEM	11 LEO	10 VIR	11 SCO	10 SAG	9 CAP	8 AQU
12 CAP	11 AQU	12 PIS	11 ARI	13 GEM	11 CAN	14 VIR	12 LIB	13 SAG	13 CAP	11 AQU	10 PIS
14 AQU	13 PIS	14 ARI	13 TAU	15 CAN	14 LEO	16 LIB	15 SCO	15 CAP	15 AQU	13 PIS	12 ARI
16 PIS	15 ARI	17 TAU	15 GEM	18 LEO	16 VIR	18 SCO	17 SAG	17 AQU	17 PIS	15 ARI	15 TAU
18 ARI	17 TAU	19 GEM	18 CAN	20 VIR	19 LIB	21 SAG	19 CAP	19 PIS	19 ARI	17 TAU	17 GEM
21 TAU	20 GEM	22 CAN	20 LEO	23 LIB	21 SCO	23 CAP	21 AQU	22 ARI	21 TAU	20 GEM	20 CAN
23 GEM	22 CAN	24 LEO	23 VIR	25 SCO	23 SAG	25 AQU	23 PIS	24 TAU	23 GEM	22 CAN	22 LEO
26 CAN	25 LEO	26 VIR	25 LIB	27 SAG	25 CAP	27 PIS	25 ARI	26 GEM	26 CAN	25 LEO	25 VIR
28 LEO	27 VIR	29 LIB	27 SCO	29 CAP	27 AQU	29 ARI	27 TAU	29 CAN	28 LEO	27 VIR	27 LIB
31 VIR	28 VIR	31 SCO	29 SAG	31 AQU	29 PIS	31 TAU	30 GEM	30 CAN	31 VIR	30 LIB	29 SCO
			30 SAG		30 PIS		31 GEM				31 SCO

1908

JAN	FEB	MAR	APR	MAY	JUN	JUL	AUG	SEP	OCT	NOV	DEC
1 SAG	1 AQU	1 AQU	1 ARI	1 TAU	1 CAN	1 LEO	1 LIB	1 SCO	1 SAG	1 AQU	1 PIS
3 CAP	3 PIS	2 PIS	2 TAU	2 GEM	3 LEO	3 VIR	4 SCO	3 SAG	2 CAP	3 PIS	2 ARI
5 AQU	5 ARI	4 ARI	4 GEM	4 CAN	5 VIR	5 LIB	6 SAG	5 CAP	4 AQU	5 ARI	4 TAU
7 PIS	7 TAU	6 TAU	7 CAN	7 LEO	8 LIB	8 SCO	8 CAP	7 AQU	6 PIS	7 TAU	6 GEM
9 ARI	10 GEM	8 GEM	9 LEO	9 VIR	10 SCO	10 SAG	10 AQU	9 PIS	8 ARI	9 GEM	9 CAN
11 TAU	12 CAN	10 CAN	12 VIR	11 LIB	12 SAG	12 CAP	12 PIS	11 ARI	10 TAU	11 CAN	11 LEO
13 GEM	15 LEO	13 LEO	14 LIB	14 SCO	15 CAP	14 AQU	14 ARI	13 TAU	12 GEM	14 LEO	13 VIR
16 CAN	17 VIR	15 VIR	16 SCO	16 SAG	17 AQU	16 PIS	16 TAU	15 GEM	15 CAN	16 VIR	16 LIB
18 LEO	20 LIB	18 LIB	19 SAG	18 CAP	19 PIS	18 ARI	19 GEM	17 CAN	17 LEO	19 LIB	18 SCO
21 VIR	22 SCO	20 SCO	21 CAP	20 AQU	21 ARI	20 TAU	21 CAN	20 LEO	20 VIR	21 SCO	21 SAG
23 LIB	24 SAG	22 SAG	23 AQU	22 PIS	23 TAU	22 GEM	24 LEO	22 VIR	22 LIB	23 SAG	23 CAP
26 SCO	26 CAP	25 CAP	25 PIS	25 ARI	25 GEM	25 CAN	26 VIR	25 LIB	25 SCO	26 CAP	25 AQU
28 SAG	29 AQU	27 AQU	27 ARI	27 TAU	28 CAN	27 LEO	29 LIB	27 SCO	27 SAG	28 AQU	27 PIS
30 CAP		29 PIS	29 TAU	29 GEM	30 LEO	30 VIR	31 SCO	30 SAG	29 CAP	30 PIS	29 ARI
31 CAP		31 ARI	30 TAU	31 CAN		31 VIR			31 AQU		31 TAU

1909

JAN	FEB	MAR	APR	MAY	JUN	JUL	AUG	SEP	OCT	NOV	DEC
1 TAU	1 CAN	1 CAN	1 LEO	1 LIB	1 SCO	1 SAG	1 AQU	1 ARI	1 TAU	1 CAN	1 LEO
3 GEM	4 LEO	3 LEO	2 VIR	4 SCO	3 SAG	2 CAP	3 PIS	3 TAU	3 GEM	3 LEO	3 VIR
5 CAN	6 VIR	5 VIR	4 LIB	6 SAG	5 CAP	4 AQU	5 ARI	5 GEM	5 CAN	6 VIR	6 LIB
7 LEO	9 LIB	8 LIB	7 SCO	9 CAP	7 AQU	6 PIS	7 TAU	8 CAN	7 LEO	8 LIB	8 SCO
10 VIR	11 SCO	10 SCO	9 SAG	11 AQU	9 PIS	9 ARI	9 GEM	10 LEO	10 VIR	11 SCO	11 SAG
12 LIB	13 SAG	13 SAG	11 CAP	13 PIS	11 ARI	11 TAU	11 CAN	12 VIR	12 LIB	13 SAG	13 CAP
15 SCO	16 CAP	15 CAP	14 AQU	15 ARI	13 TAU	13 GEM	14 LEO	15 LIB	15 SCO	16 CAP	15 AQU
17 SAG	18 AQU	17 AQU	16 PIS	17 TAU	16 GEM	15 CAN	16 VIR	17 SCO	17 SAG	18 AQU	18 PIS
19 CAP	20 PIS	19 PIS	18 ARI	19 GEM	18 CAN	17 LEO	19 LIB	20 SAG	20 CAP	20 PIS	20 ARI
21 AQU	22 ARI	21 ARI	20 TAU	21 CAN	20 LEO	20 VIR	21 SCO	22 CAP	22 AQU	23 ARI	22 TAU
23 PIS	24 TAU	23 TAU	22 GEM	24 LEO	22 VIR	22 LIB	24 SAG	25 AQU	24 PIS	25 TAU	24 GEM
25 ARI	26 GEM	25 GEM	24 CAN	26 VIR	25 LIB	25 SCO	26 CAP	27 PIS	26 ARI	27 GEM	26 CAN
28 TAU	28 CAN	28 CAN	26 LEO	29 LIB	27 SCO	27 SAG	28 AQU	29 ARI	28 TAU	29 CAN	28 LEO
30 GEM		30 LEO	29 VIR	31 SCO	30 SAG	30 CAP	30 PIS	30 ARI	30 GEM	30 CAN	31 VIR
31 GEM		31 LEO	30 VIR			31 CAP	31 PIS		31 GEM		

1910

JAN	FEB	MAR	APR	MAY	JUN	JUL	AUG	SEP	OCT	NOV	DEC
1 VIR	1 SCO	1 SCO	1 SAG	1 AQU	1 PIS	1 TAU	1 GEM	1 LEO	1 VIR	1 SCO	1 SAG
2 LIB	2 SAG	3 SAG	2 CAP	3 PIS	2 ARI	3 GEM	2 CAN	2 VIR	2 LIB	3 SAG	3 CAP
5 SCO	6 CAP	5 CAP	4 AQU	6 ARI	4 TAU	5 CAN	4 LEO	5 LIB	5 SCO	6 CAP	6 AQU
7 SAG	8 AQU	8 AQU	6 PIS	8 TAU	6 GEM	8 LEO	6 VIR	7 SCO	7 SAG	8 AQU	8 PIS
9 CAP	10 PIS	10 PIS	8 ARI	10 GEM	8 CAN	10 VIR	8 LIB	10 SAG	10 CAP	11 PIS	10 ARI
12 AQU	12 ARI	12 ARI	10 TAU	12 CAN	10 LEO	12 LIB	11 SCO	12 CAP	12 AQU	13 ARI	12 TAU
14 PIS	14 TAU	14 TAU	12 GEM	14 LEO	12 VIR	15 SCO	13 SAG	15 AQU	14 PIS	15 TAU	14 GEM
16 ARI	16 GEM	16 GEM	14 CAN	16 VIR	15 LIB	17 SAG	16 CAP	17 PIS	16 ARI	17 GEM	16 CAN
18 TAU	19 CAN	18 CAN	16 LEO	18 LIB	17 SCO	20 CAP	18 AQU	19 ARI	18 TAU	19 CAN	18 LEO
20 GEM	21 LEO	20 LEO	19 VIR	21 SCO	20 SAG	22 AQU	21 PIS	21 TAU	20 GEM	21 LEO	21 VIR
22 CAN	23 VIR	23 VIR	21 LIB	24 SAG	22 CAP	24 PIS	23 ARI	23 GEM	23 CAN	23 VIR	23 LIB
25 LEO	26 LIB	25 LIB	24 SCO	26 CAP	25 AQU	26 ARI	25 TAU	25 CAN	25 LEO	26 LIB	25 SCO
27 VIR	28 SCO	28 SCO	26 SAG	28 AQU	27 PIS	29 TAU	27 GEM	27 LEO	27 VIR	28 SCO	28 SAG
29 LIB		30 SAG	29 CAP	31 PIS	29 AQU	31 GEM	29 CAN	30 VIR	29 LIB	30 SCO	30 CAP
31 LIB		31 SAG	30 CAP		30 ARI		31 LEO		31 LIB		31 CAP

1911

JAN	FEB	MAR	APR	MAY	JUN	JUL	AUG	SEP	OCT	NOV	DEC
1 AQU	1 TAU	1 GEM	1 VIR	1 SAG	1 PIS	1 TAU	1 LEO	1 SCO	1 CAP	1 ARI	1 CAN
3 PIS	4 GEM	3 CAN	2 LIB	3 CAP	4 ARI	3 GEM	2 VIR	3 SAG	3 AQU	2 TAU	4 LEO
5 ARI	6 CAN	5 LEO	4 SCO	5 AQU	6 TAU	5 CAN	4 LIB	6 CAP	5 PIS	4 GEM	6 VIR
8 TAU	8 LEO	7 VIR	6 SAG	7 PIS	8 GEM	8 LEO	7 SCO	8 AQU	8 ARI	6 CAN	8 LIB
10 GEM	10 VIR	9 LIB	8 CAP	10 ARI	11 CAN	11 VIR	9 SAG	10 PIS	10 TAU	8 LEO	10 SCO
12 CAN	12 LIB	12 SCO	10 AQU	12 TAU	13 LEO	13 LIB	12 CAP	13 ARI	12 GEM	10 VIR	12 SAG
14 LEO	14 SCO	14 SAG	12 PIS	14 GEM	16 VIR	15 SCO	14 AQU	15 TAU	14 CAN	12 LIB	14 CAP
16 VIR	17 SAG	16 CAP	15 ARI	17 CAN	18 LIB	18 SAG	16 PIS	17 GEM	16 LEO	15 SCO	16 AQU
18 LIB	19 CAP	18 AQU	17 TAU	20 LEO	21 SCO	20 CAP	18 ARI	19 CAN	18 VIR	17 SAG	19 PIS
20 SCO	22 AQU	21 PIS	20 GEM	22 VIR	23 SAG	22 AQU	21 TAU	21 LEO	21 LIB	19 CAP	21 ARI
23 SAG	24 PIS	23 ARI	22 CAN	24 LIB	25 CAP	24 PIS	23 GEM	23 VIR	23 SCO	22 AQU	24 TAU
25 CAP	27 ARI	26 TAU	25 LEO	26 SCO	27 AQU	26 ARI	25 CAN	26 LIB	25 SAG	24 PIS	26 GEM
28 AQU	28 TAU	28 GEM	27 VIR	28 SAG	29 PIS	28 TAU	27 LEO	28 SCO	28 CAP	27 ARI	29 CAN
30 PIS		30 CAN	29 LIB	30 CAP	30 ARI	30 GEM	29 VIR	30 SAG	30 AQU	29 TAU	31 LEO
31 ARI		31 LEO	30 SCO	31 AQU		31 CAN	31 LIB		31 PIS	30 GEM	

1912

JAN	FEB	MAR	APR	MAY	JUN	JUL	AUG	SEP	OCT	NOV	DEC
1 TAU	1 CAN	1 LEO	1 VIR	1 SCO	1 SAG	1 CAP	1 PIS	1 ARI	1 GEM	1 CAN	1 VIR
2 GEM	3 LEO	3 VIR	2 LIB	3 SAG	2 CAP	2 AQU	3 ARI	2 TAU	4 CAN	2 LEO	3 LIB
4 CAN	5 VIR	5 LIB	4 SCO	6 CAP	5 AQU	4 PIS	6 TAU	4 GEM	6 LEO	4 VIR	6 SCO
6 LEO	7 LIB	7 SCO	6 SAG	8 AQU	7 PIS	7 ARI	8 GEM	6 CAN	8 VIR	6 LIB	8 SAG
8 VIR	9 SCO	10 SAG	9 CAP	11 PIS	10 ARI	9 TAU	10 CAN	8 LEO	10 LIB	8 SCO	10 CAP
10 LIB	11 SAG	12 CAP	11 AQU	13 ARI	12 TAU	12 GEM	12 LEO	10 VIR	12 SCO	11 SAG	13 AQU
13 SCO	14 CAP	15 AQU	14 PIS	16 TAU	14 GEM	14 CAN	14 VIR	12 LIB	14 SAG	13 CAP	15 PIS
15 SAG	16 AQU	17 PIS	16 ARI	18 GEM	16 CAN	16 LEO	16 LIB	15 SCO	17 CAP	15 AQU	18 ARI
18 CAP	19 PIS	20 ARI	18 TAU	20 CAN	18 LEO	18 VIR	18 SCO	17 SAG	19 AQU	18 PIS	20 TAU
20 AQU	21 ARI	22 TAU	20 GEM	22 LEO	20 VIR	20 LIB	20 SAG	19 CAP	22 PIS	20 ARI	22 GEM
23 PIS	24 TAU	24 GEM	22 CAN	24 VIR	22 LIB	22 SCO	23 CAP	22 AQU	24 ARI	23 TAU	25 CAN
25 ARI	26 GEM	26 CAN	25 LEO	26 LIB	25 SCO	24 SAG	25 AQU	24 PIS	26 TAU	25 GEM	27 LEO
27 TAU	28 CAN	28 LEO	27 VIR	28 SCO	27 SAG	27 CAP	28 PIS	27 ARI	29 GEM	27 CAN	29 VIR
30 GEM	29 CAN	30 VIR	29 LIB	31 SAG	29 CAP	29 AQU	30 ARI	29 TAU	31 CAN	29 LEO	31 LIB
31 GEM		31 VIR	30 LIB		30 CAP	31 AQU	31 ARI	30 TAU		30 LEO	

1913

JAN	FEB	MAR	APR	MAY	JUN	JUL	AUG	SEP	OCT	NOV	DEC
1 LIB	1 SAG	1 SAG	1 AQU	1 PIS	1 ARI	1 TAU	1 CAN	1 VIR	1 LIB	1 SAG	1 CAP
2 SCO	3 CAP	2 CAP	3 PIS	3 ARI	2 TAU	2 GEM	2 LEO	3 LIB	2 SCO	3 CAP	3 AQU
4 SAG	5 AQU	5 AQU	6 ARI	6 TAU	4 GEM	4 CAN	4 VIR	5 SCO	4 SAG	5 AQU	5 PIS
7 CAP	8 PIS	7 PIS	8 TAU	8 GEM	7 CAN	6 LEO	6 LIB	7 SAG	7 CAP	8 PIS	8 ARI
9 AQU	10 ARI	10 ARI	11 GEM	10 CAN	9 LEO	8 VIR	9 SCO	9 CAP	9 AQU	10 ARI	10 TAU
12 PIS	13 TAU	12 TAU	13 CAN	12 LEO	11 VIR	10 LIB	11 SAG	12 AQU	11 PIS	13 TAU	13 GEM
14 ARI	15 GEM	14 GEM	15 LEO	15 VIR	13 LIB	12 SCO	13 CAP	14 PIS	14 ARI	15 GEM	15 CAN
17 TAU	17 CAN	17 CAN	17 VIR	17 LIB	15 SCO	14 SAG	15 AQU	17 ARI	16 TAU	18 CAN	17 LEO
19 GEM	19 LEO	19 LEO	19 LIB	19 SCO	17 SAG	17 CAP	18 PIS	19 TAU	19 GEM	20 LEO	19 VIR
21 CAN	21 VIR	21 VIR	21 SCO	21 SAG	19 CAP	19 AQU	20 ARI	22 GEM	21 CAN	22 VIR	21 LIB
23 LEO	23 LIB	23 LIB	24 SAG	23 CAP	22 AQU	22 PIS	23 TAU	24 CAN	24 LEO	24 LIB	23 SCO
25 VIR	26 SCO	25 SCO	26 CAP	25 AQU	24 PIS	24 ARI	25 GEM	26 LEO	26 VIR	26 SCO	26 SAG
27 LIB	28 SAG	27 SAG	28 AQU	28 PIS	27 ARI	27 TAU	28 CAN	28 VIR	28 LIB	28 SAG	28 CAP
29 SCO		29 CAP	30 AQU	31 ARI	29 TAU	29 GEM	30 LEO	30 LIB	30 SCO	30 CAP	30 AQU
31 SAG		31 CAP			30 TAU	31 CAN	31 LEO		31 SCO		31 AQU

1914

JAN	FEB	MAR	APR	MAY	JUN	JUL	AUG	SEP	OCT	NOV	DEC
1 PIS	1 ARI	1 ARI	1 GEM	1 CAN	1 VIR	1 LIB	1 SAG	1 CAP	1 PIS	1 ARI	1 TAU
4 ARI	3 TAU	2 TAU	3 CAN	3 LEO	3 LIB	3 SCO	3 CAP	2 AQU	4 ARI	3 TAU	2 GEM
6 TAU	5 GEM	5 GEM	6 LEO	5 VIR	6 SCO	5 SAG	6 AQU	4 PIS	6 TAU	5 GEM	5 CAN
9 GEM	8 CAN	7 CAN	8 VIR	7 LIB	8 SAG	7 CAP	8 PIS	7 ARI	9 GEM	8 CAN	7 LEO
11 CAN	10 LEO	9 LEO	10 LIB	9 SCO	10 CAP	9 AQU	10 ARI	9 TAU	11 CAN	10 LEO	10 VIR
13 LEO	12 VIR	11 VIR	12 SCO	11 SAG	12 AQU	12 PIS	13 TAU	12 GEM	14 LEO	12 VIR	12 LIB
15 VIR	14 LIB	13 LIB	14 SAG	13 CAP	14 PIS	14 ARI	15 GEM	14 CAN	16 VIR	15 LIB	14 SCO
18 LIB	16 SCO	15 SCO	16 CAP	15 AQU	17 ARI	16 TAU	18 CAN	16 LEO	18 LIB	17 SCO	16 SAG
20 SCO	18 SAG	17 SAG	18 AQU	18 PIS	19 TAU	19 GEM	20 LEO	19 VIR	20 SCO	19 SAG	18 CAP
22 SAG	20 CAP	20 CAP	21 PIS	20 ARI	22 GEM	21 CAN	22 VIR	21 LIB	22 SAG	21 CAP	20 AQU
24 CAP	23 AQU	22 AQU	23 ARI	23 TAU	24 CAN	24 LEO	24 LIB	23 SCO	24 CAP	23 AQU	22 PIS
26 AQU	25 PIS	24 PIS	26 TAU	25 GEM	26 LEO	26 VIR	26 SCO	25 SAG	26 AQU	25 PIS	25 ARI
29 PIS	28 ARI	27 ARI	28 GEM	28 CAN	29 VIR	28 LIB	28 SAG	27 CAP	29 PIS	27 ARI	27 TAU
31 ARI		29 TAU	30 GEM	30 LEO	30 VIR	30 SCO	31 CAP	29 AQU	31 ARI	30 TAU	30 GEM
		31 TAU		31 LEO		31 SCO		30 AQU			31 GEM

1915

JAN	FEB	MAR	APR	MAY	JUN	JUL	AUG	SEP	OCT	NOV	DEC
1 CAN	1 LEO	1 LEO	1 LIB	1 SCO	1 CAP	1 AQU	1 ARI	1 GEM	1 CAN	1 LEO	1 VIR
4 LEO	2 VIR	2 VIR	2 SCO	2 SAG	2 AQU	2 PIS	3 TAU	4 CAN	4 LEO	3 VIR	2 LIB
6 VIR	4 LIB	4 LIB	4 SAG	4 TAU	4 PIS	4 ARI	5 GEM	6 LEO	6 VIR	5 LIB	4 SCO
8 LIB	6 SCO	6 SCO	6 CAP	6 AQU	7 ARI	6 TAU	8 CAN	9 VIR	8 LIB	7 SCO	6 SAG
10 SCO	9 SAG	8 SAG	8 AQU	8 PIS	9 TAU	9 GEM	10 LEO	11 LIB	10 SCO	9 SAG	8 CAP
12 SAG	11 CAP	10 CAP	11 PIS	10 ARI	12 GEM	11 CAN	12 VIR	13 SCO	13 SAG	11 CAP	10 AQU
14 CAP	13 AQU	12 AQU	13 ARI	13 TAU	14 CAN	14 LEO	15 LIB	15 SAG	15 CAP	13 AQU	12 PIS
17 AQU	15 PIS	14 PIS	16 TAU	15 GEM	17 LEO	16 VIR	17 SCO	17 CAP	17 AQU	15 PIS	15 ARI
19 PIS	17 ARI	17 ARI	18 GEM	18 CAN	19 VIR	18 LIB	19 SAG	19 AQU	19 PIS	17 ARI	17 TAU
21 ARI	20 TAU	19 TAU	21 CAN	20 LEO	21 LIB	21 SCO	21 CAP	22 PIS	21 ARI	20 TAU	20 GEM
24 TAU	22 GEM	22 GEM	23 LEO	23 VIR	23 SCO	23 SAG	23 AQU	24 ARI	24 TAU	22 GEM	22 CAN
26 GEM	25 CAN	24 CAN	25 VIR	25 LIB	25 SAG	25 CAP	25 PIS	26 TAU	26 GEM	25 CAN	25 LEO
29 CAN	27 LEO	27 LEO	28 LIB	27 SCO	27 CAP	27 AQU	28 ARI	29 GEM	29 CAN	27 LEO	27 VIR
31 LEO	28 LEO	29 VIR	30 SCO	29 SAG	29 AQU	29 PIS	30 TAU	30 GEM	31 LEO	30 VIR	30 LIB
		31 LIB		31 CAP	30 AQU	31 ARI	31 TAU				31 LIB

1916

JAN	FEB	MAR	APR	MAY	JUN	JUL	AUG	SEP	OCT	NOV	DEC
1 SCO	1 CAP	1 CAP	1 PIS	1 ARI	1 GEM	1 CAN	1 LEO	1 LIB	1 SCO	1 CAP	1 AQU
3 SAG	3 AQU	2 AQU	2 ARI	2 TAU	3 CAN	3 LEO	2 VIR	3 SCO	2 SAG	3 AQU	2 PIS
5 CAP	5 PIS	4 PIS	5 TAU	4 GEM	6 LEO	5 VIR	4 LIB	5 SAG	4 CAP	5 PIS	4 ARI
7 AQU	7 ARI	6 ARI	7 GEM	7 CAN	8 VIR	8 LIB	6 SCO	7 CAP	6 AQU	7 ARI	6 TAU
9 PIS	10 TAU	8 TAU	9 CAN	9 LEO	10 LIB	10 SCO	9 SAG	9 AQU	8 PIS	9 TAU	9 GEM
11 ARI	12 GEM	11 GEM	12 LEO	12 VIR	13 SCO	12 SAG	11 CAP	11 PIS	11 ARI	11 GEM	11 CAN
13 TAU	15 CAN	13 CAN	14 VIR	14 LIB	15 SAG	14 CAP	13 AQU	13 ARI	13 TAU	14 CAN	14 LEO
16 GEM	17 LEO	16 LEO	17 LIB	16 SCO	17 CAP	16 AQU	15 PIS	15 TAU	15 GEM	16 LEO	16 VIR
18 CAN	20 VIR	18 VIR	19 SCO	18 SAG	19 AQU	18 PIS	17 ARI	18 GEM	17 CAN	19 VIR	19 LIB
21 LEO	22 LIB	20 LIB	21 SAG	20 CAP	21 PIS	20 ARI	19 TAU	20 CAN	20 LEO	21 LIB	21 SCO
23 VIR	24 SCO	23 SCO	23 CAP	22 AQU	23 ARI	23 TAU	21 GEM	23 LEO	22 VIR	24 SCO	23 SAG
26 LIB	26 SAG	25 SAG	25 AQU	25 PIS	25 TAU	25 GEM	24 CAN	25 VIR	25 LIB	26 SAG	25 CAP
28 SCO	29 CAP	27 CAP	27 PIS	27 ARI	28 GEM	27 CAN	26 LEO	28 LIB	27 SCO	28 CAP	27 AQU
30 SAG		29 AQU	30 ARI	29 TAU	30 CAN	30 LEO	29 VIR	30 SCO	29 SAG	30 AQU	29 PIS
31 SAG		31 PIS		31 GEM		31 LEO	31 LIB		31 CAP		31 ARI

1917

JAN	FEB	MAR	APR	MAY	JUN	JUL	AUG	SEP	OCT	NOV	DEC
1 ARI	1 GEM	1 GEM	1 CAN	1 LEO	1 LIB	1 SCO	1 CAP	1 PIS	1 ARI	1 GEM	1 CAN
3 TAU	4 CAN	3 CAN	2 LEO	2 VIR	3 SCO	2 SAG	3 AQU	3 ARI	3 TAU	4 CAN	3 LEO
5 GEM	6 LEO	5 LEO	4 VIR	4 LIB	5 SAG	5 CAP	5 PIS	5 TAU	5 GEM	6 LEO	6 VIR
7 CAN	9 VIR	8 VIR	7 LIB	6 SCO	7 CAP	7 AQU	7 ARI	8 GEM	7 CAN	9 VIR	8 LIB
10 LEO	11 LIB	10 LIB	9 SCO	9 SAG	9 AQU	9 PIS	9 TAU	10 CAN	10 LEO	11 LIB	11 SCO
12 VIR	14 SCO	13 SCO	11 SAG	11 CAP	11 PIS	11 ARI	11 GEM	12 LEO	12 VIR	14 SCO	13 SAG
15 LIB	16 SAG	15 SAG	14 CAP	13 AQU	13 ARI	13 TAU	14 CAN	15 VIR	15 LIB	16 SAG	15 CAP
17 SCO	18 CAP	17 CAP	16 AQU	15 PIS	16 TAU	15 GEM	16 LEO	18 LIB	17 SCO	18 CAP	18 AQU
20 SAG	20 AQU	19 AQU	18 PIS	17 ARI	18 GEM	17 CAN	19 VIR	20 SCO	20 SAG	20 AQU	20 PIS
22 CAP	22 PIS	22 PIS	20 ARI	19 TAU	20 CAN	20 LEO	21 LIB	22 SAG	22 CAP	23 PIS	22 ARI
24 AQU	24 ARI	24 ARI	22 TAU	22 GEM	23 LEO	22 VIR	24 SCO	25 CAP	24 AQU	25 ARI	24 TAU
26 PIS	26 TAU	26 TAU	24 GEM	24 CAN	25 VIR	25 LIB	26 SAG	27 AQU	26 PIS	27 TAU	26 GEM
28 ARI	28 GEM	28 GEM	27 CAN	26 LEO	28 LIB	27 SCO	28 CAP	29 PIS	28 ARI	29 GEM	28 CAN
30 TAU		30 CAN	29 LEO	29 VIR	30 SCO	30 SAG	30 AQU	30 PIS	30 TAU	30 GEM	31 LEO
31 TAU		31 CAN	30 LEO	31 LIB		31 SAG	31 AQU		31 TAU		

1918

JAN	FEB	MAR	APR	MAY	JUN	JUL	AUG	SEP	OCT	NOV	DEC
1 LEO	1 LIB	1 LIB	1 SCO	1 CAP	1 AQU	1 ARI	1 TAU	1 CAN	1 LEO	1 LIB	1 SCO
2 VIR	4 SCO	3 SCO	2 SAG	4 AQU	2 PIS	3 TAU	2 GEM	3 LEO	2 VIR	3 SCO	3 SAG
5 LIB	6 SAG	5 SAG	4 CAP	6 PIS	4 ARI	6 GEM	4 CAN	5 VIR	5 LIB	6 SAG	6 CAP
7 SCO	8 CAP	8 CAP	6 AQU	8 ARI	6 TAU	8 CAN	6 LEO	7 LIB	7 SCO	8 CAP	8 AQU
10 SAG	10 AQU	10 AQU	8 PIS	10 TAU	8 GEM	10 LEO	9 VIR	10 SCO	10 SAG	11 AQU	10 PIS
12 CAP	12 PIS	12 PIS	10 ARI	12 GEM	10 CAN	12 VIR	11 LIB	12 SAG	12 CAP	13 PIS	12 ARI
14 AQU	14 ARI	14 ARI	12 TAU	14 CAN	13 LEO	15 LIB	14 SCO	15 CAP	15 AQU	15 ARI	15 TAU
16 PIS	16 TAU	16 TAU	14 GEM	16 LEO	15 VIR	17 SCO	16 SAG	17 AQU	17 PIS	17 TAU	17 GEM
18 ARI	19 GEM	18 GEM	17 CAN	19 VIR	18 LIB	20 SAG	19 CAP	19 PIS	19 ARI	19 GEM	19 CAN
20 TAU	21 CAN	20 CAN	19 LEO	21 LIB	20 SCO	22 CAP	21 AQU	21 TAU	21 TAU	21 CAN	21 LEO
22 GEM	23 LEO	23 LEO	21 VIR	24 SCO	22 SAG	24 AQU	23 PIS	23 TAU	23 GEM	23 LEO	23 VIR
25 CAN	26 VIR	25 VIR	24 LIB	26 SAG	25 CAP	26 PIS	25 ARI	25 GEM	25 CAN	26 VIR	26 LIB
27 LEO	28 LIB	28 LIB	26 SCO	28 CAP	27 AQU	28 ARI	27 TAU	27 CAN	27 LEO	28 LIB	28 SCO
30 VIR		30 SCO	29 SAG	31 AQU	29 PIS	31 TAU	29 GEM	30 LEO	29 VIR	30 LIB	31 SAG
31 VIR		31 SCO	30 SAG		30 PIS		31 CAN		31 VIR		

1919

JAN	FEB	MAR	APR	MAY	JUN	JUL	AUG	SEP	OCT	NOV	DEC
1 SAG	1 AQU	1 AQU	1 ARI	1 TAU	1 CAN	1 LEO	1 LIB	1 SCO	1 SAG	1 AQU	1 PIS
2 CAP	3 PIS	2 PIS	3 TAU	2 GEM	3 LEO	2 VIR	3 SCO	2 SAG	2 CAP	3 PIS	3 ARI
4 AQU	5 ARI	4 ARI	5 GEM	4 CAN	5 VIR	5 LIB	6 SAG	5 CAP	5 AQU	5 ARI	5 TAU
7 PIS	7 TAU	6 TAU	7 CAN	6 LEO	7 LIB	7 SCO	8 CAP	7 AQU	7 PIS	8 TAU	7 GEM
9 ARI	9 GEM	8 GEM	9 LEO	9 VIR	10 SCO	10 SAG	11 AQU	9 PIS	9 ARI	10 GEM	9 CAN
11 TAU	11 CAN	11 CAN	11 VIR	11 LIB	12 SAG	12 CAP	13 PIS	12 ARI	11 TAU	12 CAN	11 LEO
13 GEM	14 LEO	13 LEO	14 LIB	14 SCO	15 CAP	15 AQU	15 ARI	14 TAU	13 GEM	14 LEO	13 VIR
15 CAN	16 VIR	15 VIR	16 SCO	16 SAG	17 AQU	17 PIS	17 TAU	16 GEM	15 CAN	16 VIR	15 LIB
17 LEO	18 LIB	18 LIB	19 SAG	19 CAP	20 PIS	19 ARI	20 GEM	18 CAN	17 LEO	18 LIB	18 SCO
19 VIR	21 SCO	20 SCO	21 CAP	21 AQU	22 ARI	21 TAU	22 CAN	20 LEO	20 VIR	21 SCO	20 SAG
22 LIB	23 SAG	23 SAG	24 AQU	23 PIS	24 TAU	23 GEM	24 LEO	22 VIR	22 LIB	23 SAG	23 CAP
24 SCO	26 CAP	25 CAP	26 PIS	26 ARI	26 GEM	25 CAN	26 VIR	25 LIB	24 SCO	26 CAP	25 AQU
27 SAG	28 AQU	27 AQU	28 ARI	28 TAU	28 CAN	27 LEO	28 LIB	27 SCO	27 SAG	28 AQU	28 PIS
29 CAP		30 PIS	30 TAU	30 GEM	30 LEO	30 VIR	31 SCO	30 SAG	29 CAP	30 AQU	30 ARI
31 CAP		31 PIS		31 GEM		31 VIR			31 CAP		31 ARI

1920

JAN	FEB	MAR	APR	MAY	JUN	JUL	AUG	SEP	OCT	NOV	DEC
1 TAU	1 GEM	1 CAN	1 VIR	1 LIB	1 SAG	1 CAP	1 AQU	1 ARI	1 TAU	1 CAN	1 LEO
3 GEM	2 CAN	2 LEO	3 LIB	3 SCO	4 CAP	4 AQU	2 PIS	3 TAU	3 GEM	3 LEO	2 VIR
5 CAN	4 LEO	4 VIR	5 SCO	5 SAG	6 AQU	6 PIS	5 ARI	5 GEM	5 CAN	5 VIR	5 LIB
7 LEO	6 VIR	7 LIB	8 SAG	8 CAP	9 PIS	8 ARI	7 TAU	8 CAN	7 LEO	7 LIB	7 SCO
10 VIR	8 LIB	9 SCO	10 CAP	10 AQU	11 ARI	11 TAU	9 GEM	10 LEO	9 VIR	10 SCO	9 SAG
12 LIB	11 SCO	11 SAG	13 AQU	13 PIS	13 TAU	13 GEM	11 CAN	12 VIR	11 LIB	12 SAG	12 CAP
14 SCO	13 SAG	14 CAP	15 PIS	15 ARI	15 GEM	15 CAN	13 LEO	14 LIB	13 SCO	15 CAP	14 AQU
17 SAG	16 CAP	16 AQU	17 ARI	17 TAU	17 CAN	17 LEO	15 VIR	16 SCO	16 SAG	17 AQU	17 PIS
19 CAP	18 AQU	19 PIS	20 TAU	19 GEM	19 LEO	19 VIR	17 LIB	18 SAG	18 CAP	20 PIS	19 ARI
22 AQU	20 PIS	21 ARI	22 GEM	21 CAN	21 VIR	21 LIB	20 SCO	21 CAP	21 AQU	22 ARI	22 TAU
24 PIS	23 ARI	23 TAU	24 CAN	23 LEO	24 LIB	23 SCO	22 SAG	23 AQU	23 PIS	24 TAU	24 GEM
26 ARI	25 TAU	25 GEM	26 LEO	25 VIR	26 SCO	26 SAG	25 CAP	26 PIS	26 ARI	26 GEM	26 CAN
29 TAU	27 GEM	27 CAN	28 VIR	27 LIB	29 SAG	28 CAP	27 AQU	28 ARI	28 TAU	28 CAN	28 LEO
31 GEM	29 CAN	29 LEO	30 LIB	30 SCO	30 SAG	31 AQU	30 PIS	30 TAU	30 GEM	30 LEO	30 VIR
		31 LEO		31 SCO			31 PIS		31 GEM		31 VIR

1921

JAN	FEB	MAR	APR	MAY	JUN	JUL	AUG	SEP	OCT	NOV	DEC
1 LIB	1 SCO	1 SAG	1 CAP	1 AQU	1 ARI	1 TAU	1 GEM	1 LEO	1 LIB	1 SCO	1 SAG
3 SCO	2 SAG	4 CAP	3 AQU	2 PIS	4 TAU	3 GEM	2 CAN	2 VIR	4 SCO	2 SAG	2 CAP
6 SAG	4 CAP	6 AQU	5 PIS	5 ARI	6 GEM	5 CAN	4 LEO	4 LIB	6 SAG	4 CAP	4 AQU
8 CAP	7 AQU	9 PIS	7 ARI	7 TAU	8 CAN	7 LEO	6 VIR	6 SCO	8 CAP	7 AQU	7 PIS
11 AQU	9 PIS	11 ARI	10 TAU	9 GEM	10 LEO	9 VIR	8 LIB	8 SAG	11 AQU	9 PIS	9 ARI
13 PIS	12 ARI	14 TAU	12 GEM	11 CAN	12 VIR	11 LIB	10 SCO	11 CAP	13 PIS	12 ARI	12 TAU
16 ARI	14 TAU	16 GEM	14 CAN	14 LEO	14 LIB	13 SCO	12 SAG	13 AQU	16 ARI	14 TAU	14 GEM
18 TAU	17 GEM	18 CAN	16 LEO	16 VIR	16 SCO	16 SAG	15 CAP	16 PIS	18 TAU	17 GEM	16 CAN
20 GEM	19 CAN	20 LEO	18 VIR	18 LIB	19 SAG	18 CAP	17 AQU	18 ARI	20 GEM	19 CAN	18 LEO
22 CAN	21 LEO	22 VIR	21 LIB	20 SCO	21 CAP	21 AQU	20 PIS	21 TAU	23 CAN	21 LEO	20 VIR
24 LEO	23 VIR	24 LIB	23 SCO	22 SAG	24 AQU	23 PIS	22 ARI	23 GEM	25 LEO	23 VIR	22 LIB
26 VIR	25 LIB	26 SCO	25 SAG	25 CAP	26 PIS	26 ARI	25 TAU	25 CAN	27 VIR	25 LIB	25 SCO
28 LIB	27 SCO	29 SAG	27 CAP	27 AQU	29 ARI	28 TAU	27 GEM	27 LEO	29 LIB	27 SCO	27 SAG
31 SCO	28 SCO	31 CAP	30 AQU	30 PIS	30 ARI	31 GEM	29 CAN	29 VIR	31 SCO	30 SAG	29 CAP
				31 PIS			31 CAN	30 VIR			31 CAP

1922

JAN	FEB	MAR	APR	MAY	JUN	JUL	AUG	SEP	OCT	NOV	DEC
1 AQU	1 PIS	1 ARI	1 TAU	1 GEM	1 LEO	1 VIR	1 SCO	1 CAP	1 AQU	1 PIS	1 ARI
3 PIS	2 ARI	4 TAU	2 GEM	2 CAN	2 VIR	2 LIB	2 SAG	3 AQU	3 PIS	2 ARI	2 TAU
6 ARI	4 TAU	6 GEM	5 CAN	4 LEO	5 LIB	4 SCO	5 CAP	6 PIS	6 ARI	4 TAU	4 GEM
8 TAU	7 GEM	8 CAN	7 LEO	6 VIR	7 SCO	6 SAG	6 AQU	8 ARI	8 TAU	7 GEM	6 CAN
10 GEM	9 CAN	11 LEO	9 VIR	8 LIB	9 SAG	8 CAP	9 PIS	11 TAU	11 GEM	9 CAN	9 LEO
13 CAN	11 LEO	13 VIR	11 LIB	10 SCO	11 CAP	11 AQU	12 ARI	13 GEM	13 CAN	11 LEO	11 VIR
15 LEO	13 VIR	14 LIB	13 SCO	12 SAG	13 AQU	13 PIS	15 TAU	16 CAN	15 LEO	14 VIR	13 LIB
17 VIR	15 LIB	17 SCO	15 SAG	15 CAP	16 PIS	16 ARI	17 GEM	18 LEO	17 VIR	16 LIB	15 SCO
19 LIB	17 SCO	19 SAG	17 CAP	17 AQU	18 ARI	18 TAU	19 CAN	20 VIR	19 LIB	18 SCO	17 SAG
21 SCO	19 SAG	21 CAP	20 AQU	20 PIS	21 TAU	21 GEM	21 LEO	22 LIB	21 SCO	20 SAG	19 CAP
23 SAG	22 CAP	23 AQU	22 PIS	22 ARI	23 GEM	23 CAN	23 VIR	24 SCO	23 SAG	22 CAP	22 AQU
25 CAP	24 AQU	26 PIS	25 ARI	25 TAU	25 CAN	25 LEO	25 LIB	26 SAG	25 CAP	24 AQU	24 PIS
28 AQU	27 PIS	28 ARI	27 TAU	27 GEM	28 LEO	27 VIR	27 SCO	28 CAP	28 AQU	27 PIS	26 ARI
30 PIS	28 PIS	31 TAU	30 GEM	29 CAN	30 VIR	29 LIB	30 SAG	30 CAP	30 PIS	29 ARI	29 TAU
31 PIS				31 LEO		31 SCO	31 SAG		31 PIS	30 ARI	31 GEM

1923

JAN	FEB	MAR	APR	MAY	JUN	JUL	AUG	SEP	OCT	NOV	DEC
1 GEM	1 LEO	1 LEO	1 LIB	1 SCO	1 CAP	1 AQU	1 PIS	1 TAU	1 GEM	1 CAN	1 VIR
3 CAN	3 VIR	3 VIR	3 SCO	3 SAG	3 AQU	3 PIS	2 ARI	3 GEM	3 CAN	2 LEO	4 LIB
5 LEO	5 LIB	5 LIB	5 SAG	5 CAP	6 PIS	5 ARI	4 TAU	6 CAN	5 LEO	4 VIR	6 SCO
7 VIR	8 SCO	7 SCO	7 CAP	7 AQU	8 ARI	8 TAU	7 GEM	8 LEO	8 VIR	6 LIB	8 SAG
9 LIB	10 SAG	9 SAG	10 AQU	9 PIS	11 TAU	11 GEM	9 CAN	10 VIR	10 LIB	10 SCO	10 CAP
11 SCO	12 CAP	11 CAP	12 PIS	12 ARI	13 GEM	13 CAN	12 LEO	12 LIB	12 SCO	10 SAG	12 AQU
13 SAG	14 AQU	13 AQU	15 ARI	14 TAU	16 CAN	15 LEO	14 VIR	14 SCO	14 SAG	12 CAP	14 PIS
16 CAP	17 PIS	16 PIS	17 TAU	17 GEM	18 LEO	17 VIR	16 LIB	16 SAG	16 CAP	14 AQU	16 ARI
18 AQU	19 ARI	18 ARI	20 GEM	19 CAN	20 VIR	20 LIB	18 SCO	18 CAP	18 AQU	17 PIS	19 TAU
20 PIS	22 TAU	21 TAU	22 CAN	22 LEO	22 LIB	22 SCO	20 SAG	21 AQU	20 PIS	19 ARI	21 GEM
23 ARI	24 GEM	23 GEM	24 LEO	24 VIR	25 SCO	24 SAG	22 CAP	23 PIS	23 ARI	21 TAU	24 CAN
25 TAU	27 CAN	26 CAN	27 VIR	26 LIB	27 SAG	26 CAP	24 AQU	25 ARI	25 TAU	24 GEM	26 LEO
28 GEM	28 CAN	28 LEO	29 LIB	28 SCO	29 CAP	28 AQU	27 PIS	28 TAU	28 GEM	27 CAN	29 VIR
30 CAN		30 VIR	30 LIB	30 SAG	30 CAP	30 PIS	29 ARI	30 TAU	30 CAN	29 LEO	31 LIB
31 CAN		31 VIR		31 SAG		31 PIS	31 ARI		31 CAN	30 LEO	

1924

JAN	FEB	MAR	APR	MAY	JUN	JUL	AUG	SEP	OCT	NOV	DEC
1 LIB	1 SAG	1 CAP	1 PIS	1 ARI	1 TAU	1 GEM	1 LEO	1 VIR	1 SCO	1 SAG	1 AQU
2 SCO	2 CAP	3 AQU	4 ARI	3 TAU	2 GEM	2 CAN	3 VIR	2 LIB	3 SAG	2 CAP	3 PIS
4 SAG	4 AQU	5 PIS	6 TAU	6 GEM	5 CAN	4 LEO	5 LIB	4 SCO	5 CAP	4 AQU	5 ARI
6 CAP	7 PIS	7 ARI	9 GEM	8 CAN	7 LEO	7 VIR	8 SCO	6 SAG	7 AQU	6 PIS	8 TAU
8 AQU	9 ARI	10 TAU	11 CAN	11 LEO	10 VIR	9 LIB	10 SAG	8 CAP	10 PIS	8 ARI	10 GEM
10 PIS	11 TAU	12 GEM	14 LEO	13 VIR	12 LIB	11 SCO	12 CAP	10 AQU	12 ARI	10 TAU	13 CAN
13 ARI	14 GEM	15 CAN	16 VIR	16 LIB	14 SCO	13 SAG	14 AQU	12 PIS	14 TAU	13 GEM	15 LEO
15 TAU	16 CAN	17 LEO	18 LIB	18 SCO	16 SAG	15 CAP	16 PIS	15 ARI	17 GEM	15 CAN	18 VIR
18 GEM	19 LEO	20 VIR	20 SCO	20 SAG	18 CAP	17 AQU	18 ARI	17 TAU	19 CAN	18 LEO	20 LIB
20 CAN	21 VIR	22 LIB	22 SAG	22 CAP	20 AQU	20 PIS	20 TAU	19 GEM	22 LEO	20 VIR	22 SCO
22 LEO	23 LIB	24 SCO	24 CAP	24 AQU	22 PIS	22 ARI	23 GEM	22 CAN	24 VIR	23 LIB	24 SAG
25 VIR	25 SCO	26 SAG	26 AQU	26 PIS	24 ARI	24 TAU	25 CAN	24 LEO	26 LIB	25 SCO	26 CAP
27 LIB	28 SAG	28 CAP	29 PIS	28 ARI	27 TAU	27 GEM	28 LEO	27 VIR	28 SCO	27 SAG	28 AQU
29 SCO	29 SAG	30 AQU	30 PIS	31 TAU	29 GEM	29 CAN	30 VIR	29 LIB	31 SAG	29 CAP	30 PIS
31 AQU		31 AQU			30 GEM	31 CAN	31 VIR	30 LIB		30 CAP	31 PIS

1925

JAN	FEB	MAR	APR	MAY	JUN	JUL	AUG	SEP	OCT	NOV	DEC
1 PIS	1 TAU	1 TAU	1 CAN	1 LEO	1 VIR	1 LIB	1 SAG	1 AQU	1 PIS	1 TAU	1 GEM
2 ARI	3 GEM	2 GEM	3 LEO	3 VIR	2 LIB	2 SCO	2 CAP	3 PIS	2 ARI	3 GEM	3 CAN
4 TAU	5 CAN	5 CAN	6 VIR	6 LIB	4 SCO	4 SAG	4 AQU	5 ARI	4 TAU	5 CAN	5 LEO
6 GEM	8 LEO	7 LEO	8 LIB	8 SCO	6 SAG	6 CAP	6 PIS	7 TAU	7 GEM	8 LEO	8 VIR
9 CAN	10 VIR	10 VIR	10 SCO	10 SAG	8 CAP	8 AQU	8 ARI	9 GEM	9 CAN	10 VIR	10 LIB
12 LEO	13 LIB	12 LIB	13 SAG	12 CAP	10 AQU	10 PIS	10 TAU	12 CAN	11 LEO	13 LIB	13 SCO
14 VIR	15 SCO	14 SCO	15 CAP	14 AQU	12 PIS	12 ARI	13 GEM	14 LEO	14 VIR	15 SCO	15 SAG
16 LIB	17 SAG	16 SAG	17 AQU	16 PIS	15 ARI	14 TAU	15 CAN	17 VIR	16 LIB	17 SAG	17 CAP
19 SCO	19 CAP	18 CAP	19 PIS	18 ARI	17 TAU	17 GEM	18 LEO	19 LIB	19 SCO	19 CAP	19 AQU
21 SAG	21 AQU	21 AQU	21 ARI	21 TAU	19 GEM	19 CAN	20 VIR	21 SCO	21 SAG	21 AQU	21 PIS
23 CAP	23 PIS	23 PIS	23 TAU	23 GEM	22 CAN	22 LEO	23 LIB	24 SAG	23 CAP	24 PIS	23 ARI
25 AQU	25 ARI	25 PIS	26 GEM	26 CAN	24 LEO	24 VIR	25 SCO	26 CAP	25 AQU	26 ARI	25 TAU
27 PIS	28 TAU	27 TAU	28 CAN	28 LEO	27 VIR	27 LIB	27 SAG	28 AQU	27 PIS	28 TAU	28 GEM
29 ARI		29 GEM	30 CAN	31 VIR	29 LIB	29 SCO	30 CAP	30 PIS	29 ARI	30 GEM	30 CAN
31 TAU		31 GEM			30 LIB	31 SAG	31 CAP		31 ARI		31 CAN

1926

JAN	FEB	MAR	APR	MAY	JUN	JUL	AUG	SEP	OCT	NOV	DEC
1 LEO	1 VIR	1 VIR	1 SCO	1 SAG	1 AQU	1 PIS	1 TAU	1 GEM	1 LEO	1 VIR	1 LIB
4 VIR	3 LIB	2 LIB	3 SAG	2 CAP	3 PIS	2 ARI	3 GEM	2 CAN	4 VIR	3 LIB	2 SCO
6 LIB	5 SCO	4 SCO	5 CAP	5 AQU	5 ARI	4 TAU	5 CAN	4 LEO	6 LIB	5 SCO	5 SAG
9 SCO	8 SAG	7 SAG	7 AQU	7 PIS	7 TAU	7 GEM	8 LEO	7 VIR	9 SCO	7 SAG	7 CAP
11 SAG	10 CAP	9 CAP	10 PIS	9 ARI	9 GEM	9 CAN	10 VIR	9 LIB	11 SAG	10 CAP	9 AQU
13 CAP	12 AQU	11 AQU	12 ARI	11 TAU	12 CAN	12 LEO	13 LIB	12 SCO	14 CAP	12 AQU	11 PIS
15 AQU	14 PIS	13 PIS	14 TAU	13 GEM	14 LEO	14 VIR	15 SCO	14 SAG	16 AQU	14 PIS	14 ARI
17 PIS	16 ARI	15 ARI	16 GEM	15 CAN	17 VIR	17 LIB	18 SAG	16 CAP	18 PIS	16 ARI	16 TAU
19 ARI	18 TAU	17 TAU	18 CAN	18 LEO	19 LIB	19 SCO	20 CAP	18 AQU	20 ARI	18 TAU	18 GEM
21 TAU	20 GEM	19 GEM	21 LEO	20 VIR	22 SCO	21 SAG	22 AQU	21 PIS	22 TAU	20 GEM	20 CAN
24 GEM	22 CAN	22 CAN	23 VIR	23 LIB	24 SAG	24 CAP	24 PIS	22 ARI	24 GEM	23 CAN	22 LEO
26 CAN	25 LEO	24 LEO	26 LIB	25 SCO	26 CAP	26 AQU	26 ARI	24 TAU	26 CAN	25 LEO	25 VIR
29 LEO	27 VIR	27 VIR	28 SCO	28 SAG	28 AQU	28 PIS	28 TAU	27 GEM	29 LEO	27 VIR	27 LIB
31 VIR	28 VIR	29 LIB	30 SAG	30 CAP	30 PIS	30 ARI	30 GEM	29 CAN	31 VIR	30 LIB	30 SCO
		31 LIB		31 CAP		31 ARI	31 GEM	30 CAN			31 SCO

1927

JAN	FEB	MAR	APR	MAY	JUN	JUL	AUG	SEP	OCT	NOV	DEC
1 SAG	1 CAP	1 AQU	1 PIS	1 TAU	1 GEM	1 CAN	1 VIR	1 LIB	1 SAG	1 CAP	1 AQU
3 CAP	2 AQU	4 PIS	2 ARI	3 GEM	2 CAN	2 LEO	3 LIB	2 SCO	4 CAP	2 AQU	2 PIS
6 AQU	4 PIS	5 ARI	4 TAU	5 CAN	4 LEO	4 VIR	5 SCO	4 SAG	6 AQU	5 PIS	4 ARI
8 PIS	6 ARI	7 TAU	6 GEM	8 LEO	7 VIR	6 LIB	8 SAG	6 CAP	8 PIS	7 ARI	6 TAU
10 ARI	8 TAU	10 GEM	8 CAN	10 VIR	9 LIB	9 SCO	10 CAP	9 AQU	10 ARI	9 TAU	8 GEM
12 TAU	10 GEM	12 CAN	10 LEO	13 LIB	12 SCO	11 SAG	12 AQU	11 PIS	12 TAU	11 GEM	10 CAN
14 GEM	13 CAN	14 LEO	13 VIR	15 SCO	14 SAG	14 CAP	14 PIS	13 ARI	14 GEM	13 CAN	12 LEO
16 CAN	15 LEO	17 VIR	15 LIB	18 SAG	16 CAP	16 AQU	16 ARI	15 TAU	16 CAN	15 LEO	15 VIR
19 LEO	17 VIR	19 LIB	18 SCO	20 CAP	19 AQU	18 PIS	19 TAU	17 GEM	19 LEO	17 VIR	17 LIB
21 VIR	20 LIB	22 SCO	20 SAG	22 AQU	21 PIS	20 ARI	21 GEM	19 CAN	21 VIR	20 LIB	20 SCO
24 LIB	22 SCO	24 SAG	23 CAP	25 PIS	23 ARI	22 TAU	23 CAN	21 LEO	24 LIB	22 SCO	22 SAG
26 SCO	25 SAG	27 CAP	25 AQU	27 ARI	25 TAU	24 GEM	25 LEO	24 VIR	26 SCO	25 SAG	25 CAP
29 SAG	27 CAP	29 AQU	27 PIS	29 TAU	27 GEM	27 CAN	28 VIR	26 LIB	29 SAG	27 CAP	27 AQU
31 CAP	28 CAP	31 PIS	29 ARI	31 GEM	29 CAN	29 LEO	30 LIB	29 SCO	31 CAP	30 AQU	29 PIS
			30 ARI		30 CAN	31 VIR	31 LIB	30 SCO			31 ARI

1928

JAN	FEB	MAR	APR	MAY	JUN	JUL	AUG	SEP	OCT	NOV	DEC
1 ARI	1 GEM	1 CAN	1 LEO	1 VIR	1 SCO	1 SAG	1 AQU	1 PIS	1 ARI	1 GEM	1 CAN
2 TAU	3 CAN	3 LEO	2 VIR	2 LIB	3 SAG	3 CAP	4 PIS	2 ARI	2 TAU	2 CAN	2 LEO
5 GEM	5 LEO	6 VIR	4 LIB	4 SCO	5 CAP	5 AQU	6 ARI	4 TAU	4 GEM	4 LEO	4 VIR
7 CAN	7 VIR	8 LIB	7 SCO	7 SAG	8 AQU	7 PIS	8 TAU	6 GEM	6 CAN	6 VIR	6 LIB
9 LEO	10 LIB	11 SCO	9 SAG	9 CAP	10 PIS	10 ARI	10 GEM	9 CAN	8 LEO	9 LIB	8 SCO
11 VIR	12 SCO	13 SAG	12 CAP	12 AQU	12 ARI	12 TAU	12 CAN	11 LEO	10 VIR	11 SCO	11 SAG
13 LIB	15 SAG	16 CAP	14 AQU	14 PIS	15 TAU	14 GEM	14 LEO	13 VIR	13 LIB	14 SAG	14 CAP
16 SCO	17 CAP	18 AQU	17 PIS	16 ARI	17 GEM	16 CAN	17 VIR	15 LIB	15 SCO	16 CAP	16 AQU
18 SAG	20 AQU	20 PIS	19 ARI	18 TAU	19 CAN	18 LEO	19 LIB	18 SCO	17 SAG	19 AQU	18 PIS
21 CAP	22 PIS	22 ARI	21 TAU	20 GEM	21 LEO	20 VIR	20 SCO	20 SAG	20 CAP	21 PIS	21 ARI
23 AQU	24 ARI	24 TAU	23 GEM	22 CAN	23 VIR	23 LIB	24 SAG	23 CAP	23 AQU	23 ARI	23 TAU
25 PIS	26 TAU	26 GEM	25 CAN	24 LEO	25 LIB	25 SCO	26 CAP	25 AQU	25 PIS	26 TAU	25 GEM
28 ARI	28 GEM	28 CAN	27 LEO	27 VIR	28 SCO	28 SAG	29 AQU	27 PIS	27 ARI	28 GEM	27 CAN
30 TAU	29 GEM	31 LEO	29 VIR	29 LIB	30 SAG	30 CAP	31 PIS	30 ARI	29 TAU	30 CAN	29 LEO
31 TAU			30 VIR	31 SCO		31 CAP			31 GEM		31 VIR

1929

JAN	FEB	MAR	APR	MAY	JUN	JUL	AUG	SEP	OCT	NOV	DEC
1 VIR	1 SCO	1 SCO	1 SAG	1 CAP	1 PIS	1 ARI	1 GEM	1 LEO	1 VIR	1 SCO	1 SAG
2 LIB	4 SAG	3 SAG	2 CAP	2 AQU	3 ARI	2 TAU	3 CAN	3 VIR	3 LIB	4 SAG	3 CAP
5 SCO	6 CAP	5 CAP	4 AQU	4 PIS	5 TAU	4 GEM	5 LEO	5 LIB	5 SCO	6 CAP	6 AQU
7 SAG	9 AQU	8 AQU	7 PIS	6 ARI	7 GEM	6 CAN	7 VIR	8 SCO	7 SAG	9 AQU	9 PIS
10 CAP	11 PIS	10 PIS	9 ARI	9 TAU	9 CAN	8 LEO	9 LIB	10 SAG	10 CAP	11 PIS	11 ARI
12 AQU	13 ARI	12 ARI	11 TAU	11 GEM	11 LEO	10 VIR	11 SCO	12 CAP	12 AQU	14 ARI	13 TAU
15 PIS	16 TAU	15 TAU	13 GEM	13 CAN	13 VIR	13 LIB	14 SAG	15 AQU	15 PIS	16 TAU	15 GEM
17 ARI	18 GEM	17 GEM	15 CAN	15 LEO	15 LIB	15 SCO	16 CAP	17 PIS	17 ARI	18 GEM	17 CAN
19 TAU	20 CAN	19 CAN	17 LEO	17 VIR	18 SCO	17 SAG	19 AQU	20 ARI	19 TAU	20 CAN	19 LEO
21 GEM	22 LEO	21 LEO	20 VIR	19 LIB	20 SAG	20 CAP	21 PIS	22 TAU	22 GEM	22 LEO	21 VIR
23 CAN	24 VIR	23 VIR	22 LIB	21 SCO	23 CAP	22 AQU	24 ARI	24 GEM	24 CAN	24 VIR	24 LIB
25 LEO	26 LIB	26 LIB	24 SCO	24 SAG	25 AQU	25 PIS	26 TAU	26 CAN	26 LEO	26 LIB	26 SCO
28 VIR	28 SCO	28 SCO	27 SAG	26 CAP	28 PIS	27 ARI	28 GEM	29 LEO	28 VIR	29 SCO	28 SAG
30 LIB		30 SAG	29 CAP	29 AQU	30 ARI	30 TAU	30 CAN	30 LEO	30 LIB	30 SCO	31 CAP
31 LIB		31 SAG	30 CAP	31 PIS		31 TAU	31 CAN		31 LIB		

1930

JAN	FEB	MAR	APR	MAY	JUN	JUL	AUG	SEP	OCT	NOV	DEC
1 CAP	1 PIS	1 PIS	1 TAU	1 GEM	1 LEO	1 VIR	1 SCO	1 SAG	1 CAP	1 PIS	1 ARI
2 AQU	4 ARI	3 ARI	4 GEM	3 CAN	4 VIR	3 LIB	4 SAG	2 CAP	2 AQU	3 ARI	3 TAU
5 PIS	6 TAU	5 TAU	6 CAN	5 LEO	6 LIB	5 SCO	6 CAP	5 AQU	5 PIS	6 TAU	6 GEM
7 ARI	8 GEM	7 GEM	8 LEO	7 VIR	8 SCO	7 SAG	9 AQU	7 PIS	7 ARI	8 GEM	8 CAN
10 TAU	10 CAN	10 CAN	10 VIR	9 LIB	10 SAG	10 CAP	11 PIS	10 ARI	10 TAU	10 CAN	10 LEO
12 GEM	12 LEO	12 LEO	12 LIB	12 SCO	13 CAP	12 AQU	14 ARI	12 TAU	12 GEM	13 LEO	12 VIR
14 CAN	14 VIR	14 VIR	14 SCO	14 SAG	15 AQU	15 PIS	16 TAU	15 GEM	14 CAN	15 VIR	14 LIB
16 LEO	16 LIB	16 LIB	17 SAG	16 CAP	18 PIS	17 ARI	18 GEM	17 CAN	16 LEO	17 LIB	16 SCO
18 VIR	18 SCO	18 SCO	19 CAP	19 AQU	20 ARI	20 TAU	21 CAN	19 LEO	18 VIR	19 SCO	18 SAG
20 LIB	21 SAG	20 SAG	21 AQU	21 PIS	22 TAU	22 GEM	23 LEO	21 VIR	20 LIB	21 SAG	21 CAP
22 SCO	23 CAP	23 CAP	24 PIS	24 ARI	25 GEM	24 CAN	25 VIR	23 LIB	23 SCO	23 CAP	23 AQU
24 SAG	26 AQU	25 AQU	26 ARI	26 TAU	27 CAN	26 LEO	27 LIB	25 SCO	15 SAG	26 AQU	26 PIS
27 CAP	28 PIS	28 PIS	29 TAU	28 GEM	29 LEO	28 VIR	29 SCO	27 SAG	27 CAP	28 PIS	28 ARI
30 AQU		30 ARI	30 TAU	30 CAN	30 LEO	30 LIB	31 SAG	29 CAP	29 AQU	30 PIS	31 TAU
31 AQU		31 ARI		31 CAN		31 LIB		30 CAP	31 AQU		

1931

JAN	FEB	MAR	APR	MAY	JUN	JUL	AUG	SEP	OCT	NOV	DEC
1 TAU	1 CAN	1 CAN	1 VIR	1 LIB	1 SAG	1 CAP	1 PIS	1 ARI	1 TAU	1 CAN	1 LEO
2 GEM	3 LEO	2 LEO	3 LIB	2 SCO	3 CAP	2 AQU	4 ARI	2 TAU	2 GEM	3 LEO	3 VIR
4 CAN	5 VIR	4 VIR	5 SCO	4 SAG	5 AQU	5 PIS	6 TAU	5 GEM	5 CAN	5 VIR	5 LIB
6 LEO	7 LIB	6 LIB	7 SAG	6 CAP	7 PIS	7 ARI	9 GEM	7 CAN	7 LEO	7 LIB	7 SCO
8 VIR	9 SCO	8 SCO	9 CAP	9 AQU	10 ARI	10 TAU	11 CAN	9 LEO	9 VIR	9 SCO	9 SAG
10 LIB	11 SAG	10 SAG	11 AQU	11 PIS	12 TAU	12 GEM	13 LEO	11 VIR	11 LIB	11 SAG	11 SCO
12 SCO	13 CAP	13 CAP	14 PIS	14 ARI	15 GEM	14 CAN	15 VIR	13 LIB	13 SCO	13 CAP	13 AQU
15 SAG	16 AQU	15 AQU	16 ARI	16 TAU	17 CAN	17 LEO	17 LIB	15 SCO	15 SAG	16 AQU	15 PIS
17 CAP	18 PIS	17 PIS	19 TAU	18 GEM	19 LEO	19 VIR	19 SCO	18 SAG	17 CAP	18 PIS	18 ARI
19 AQU	21 ARI	20 ARI	21 GEM	21 CAN	21 VIR	21 LIB	21 SAG	20 CAP	19 AQU	21 ARI	20 TAU
22 PIS	23 TAU	23 TAU	24 CAN	23 LEO	23 LIB	23 SCO	23 CAP	22 AQU	22 PIS	23 TAU	23 GEM
24 ARI	26 GEM	25 GEM	26 LEO	25 VIR	26 SCO	25 SAG	26 AQU	25 PIS	24 ARI	26 GEM	25 CAN
27 TAU	28 CAN	27 CAN	28 VIR	27 LIB	28 SAG	27 CAP	28 PIS	27 ARI	27 TAU	28 CAN	28 LEO
29 GEM		29 LEO	30 LIB	29 SCO	30 CAP	30 AQU	31 ARI	30 TAU	29 GEM	30 LEO	30 VIR
31 GEM		31 LEO		31 SAG		31 AQU			31 GEM		31 VIR

1932

JAN	FEB	MAR	APR	MAY	JUN	JUL	AUG	SEP	OCT	NOV	DEC
1 LIB	1 SAG	1 SAG	1 AQU	1 PIS	1 TAU	1 GEM	1 CAN	1 VIR	1 LIB	1 SAG	1 CAP
3 SCO	4 CAP	2 CAP	3 PIS	2 ARI	4 GEM	4 CAN	2 LEO	3 LIB	2 SCO	3 CAP	2 AQU
5 SAG	6 AQU	4 AQU	5 ARI	5 TAU	6 CAN	6 LEO	4 VIR	5 SCO	4 SAG	5 AQU	4 PIS
7 SCO	8 PIS	6 PIS	8 TAU	8 GEM	9 LEO	8 VIR	7 LIB	7 SAG	6 CAP	7 PIS	7 ARI
9 AQU	11 ARI	9 ARI	10 GEM	10 CAN	11 VIR	10 LIB	9 SCO	9 SCO	9 AQU	10 ARI	9 TAU
12 PIS	13 TAU	11 TAU	13 CAN	12 LEO	13 LIB	12 SCO	11 SAG	11 AQU	11 PIS	12 TAU	12 GEM
14 ARI	16 GEM	14 GEM	15 LEO	15 VIR	15 SCO	15 SAG	13 CAP	14 PIS	13 ARI	15 GEM	14 CAN
17 TAU	18 CAN	16 CAN	17 VIR	17 LIB	17 SAG	17 CAP	15 AQU	16 ARI	16 TAU	17 CAN	17 LEO
19 GEM	20 LEO	19 LEO	19 LIB	19 SCO	19 CAP	19 AQU	17 PIS	19 TAU	18 GEM	20 LEO	19 VIR
22 CAN	22 VIR	21 VIR	21 SCO	21 SAG	21 AQU	21 PIS	20 ARI	21 GEM	21 CAN	22 VIR	21 LIB
24 LEO	24 LIB	23 LIB	23 SAG	23 CAP	24 PIS	23 ARI	22 TAU	24 CAN	23 LEO	24 LIB	24 SCO
26 VIR	27 SCO	25 SCO	25 CAP	25 AQU	26 ARI	26 TAU	25 GEM	26 LEO	26 VIR	26 SCO	26 SAG
28 LIB	29 SAG	27 SAG	28 AQU	27 PIS	29 TAU	28 GEM	27 CAN	28 VIR	28 LIB	28 SAG	28 CAP
30 SCO		29 CAP	30 PIS	30 ARI	30 TAU	31 CAN	30 LEO	30 LIB	30 SCO	30 CAP	30 AQU
31 SCO		31 AQU		31 ARI			31 LEO		31 SCO		31 AQU

1933

JAN	FEB	MAR	APR	MAY	JUN	JUL	AUG	SEP	OCT	NOV	DEC
1 PIS	1 ARI	1 TAU	1 GEM	1 CAN	1 VIR	1 LIB	1 SAG	1 CAP	1 PIS	1 ARI	1 TAU
3 ARI	2 TAU	4 GEM	3 CAN	2 LEO	3 LIB	3 SCO	3 CAP	2 AQU	3 ARI	2 TAU	2 GEM
6 TAU	4 GEM	6 CAN	5 LEO	5 VIR	6 SCO	5 SAG	5 AQU	4 PIS	6 TAU	5 GEM	4 CAN
8 GEM	7 CAN	9 LEO	7 VIR	7 LIB	8 SAG	7 CAP	8 PIS	6 ARI	8 GEM	7 CAN	7 LEO
11 CAN	9 LEO	11 VIR	10 LIB	9 SCO	10 CAP	9 AQU	10 ARI	8 TAU	11 CAN	10 LEO	9 VIR
13 LEO	12 VIR	13 LIB	12 SCO	11 SAG	12 AQU	11 PIS	12 TAU	11 GEM	13 LEO	12 VIR	12 LIB
15 VIR	14 LIB	15 SCO	14 SAG	13 CAP	14 PIS	13 ARI	14 GEM	13 CAN	16 VIR	14 LIB	14 SCO
18 LIB	16 SCO	17 SAG	16 CAP	15 AQU	16 ARI	16 TAU	17 CAN	16 LEO	18 LIB	16 SCO	16 SAG
20 SCO	18 SAG	20 CAP	18 AQU	17 PIS	18 TAU	18 GEM	20 LEO	18 VIR	20 SCO	19 SAG	18 SCO
22 SAG	20 CAP	22 AQU	20 PIS	20 ARI	21 GEM	21 CAN	22 VIR	21 LIB	22 SAG	21 CAP	20 AQU
24 CAP	22 AQU	24 PIS	23 ARI	22 TAU	23 CAN	23 LEO	24 LIB	23 SCO	24 CAP	23 AQU	22 PIS
26 AQU	25 PIS	26 ARI	25 TAU	25 GEM	26 LEO	26 VIR	26 SCO	25 SAG	26 AQU	25 PIS	24 ARI
28 PIS	27 ARI	29 TAU	27 GEM	27 CAN	28 VIR	28 LIB	29 SAG	27 CAP	28 PIS	27 ARI	27 TAU
31 ARI	28 ARI	31 GEM	30 CAN	30 LEO	30 VIR	30 SCO	31 CAP	29 AQU	31 ARI	29 TAU	29 GEM
				31 LEO		31 SCO		30 AQU		30 TAU	31 GEM

1934

JAN	FEB	MAR	APR	MAY	JUN	JUL	AUG	SEP	OCT	NOV	DEC
1 CAN	1LEO	1 VIR	1 LIB	1 SCO	1 CAP	1 PIS	1 ARI	1 GEM	1 CAN	1 LEO	1 VIR
3 LEO	2 VIR	4 LIB	2 SCO	2 SAG	2 AQU	4 ARI	2 TAU	3 CAN	3 LEO	2 VIR	2 LIB
6 VIR	4 LIB	6 SCO	4 SAG	4 CAP	4 PIS	6 TAU	4 GEM	6 LEO	6 VIR	4 LIB	4 SCO
8 LIB	7 SCO	8 SAG	6 CAP	6 AQU	6 ARI	8 GEM	7 CAN	8 VIR	8 LIB	7 SCO	6 SAG
10 SCO	9 SAG	10 CAP	8 AQU	8 PIS	9 TAU	11 CAN	9 LEO	11 LIB	10 SCO	9 SAG	8 CAP
12 SAG	11 CAP	12 AQU	11 PIS	10 ARI	11 GEM	13 LEO	12 VIR	13 SCO	13 SAG	11 CAP	10 AQU
14 CAP	13 AQU	14 PIS	13 ARI	12 TAU	13 CAN	16 VIR	14 LIB	15 SAG	15 CAP	13 AQU	12 PIS
16 AQU	15 PIS	16 ARI	15 TAU	15 GEM	16 LEO	18 LIB	17 SCO	18 CAP	17 AQU	15 PIS	15 ARI
18 PIS	17 ARI	19 TAU	17 GEM	17 CAN	18 VIR	21 SCO	19 SAG	20 AQU	19 PIS	17 ARI	17 TAU
21 ARI	19 TAU	21 GEM	20 CAN	20 LEO	21 LIB	23 SAG	21 CAP	22 PIS	21 ARI	20 TAU	19 GEM
23 TAU	22 GEM	23 CAN	22 LEO	22 VIR	23 SCO	25 CAP	23 AQU	24 ARI	23 TAU	22 GEM	22 CAN
25 GEM	24 CAN	26 LEO	25 VIR	25 LIB	25 SAG	27 AQU	25 PIS	26 TAU	25 GEM	24 CAN	24 LEO
28 CAN	27 LEO	28 VIR	27 LIB	27 SCO	27 CAP	29 PIS	27 ARI	28 GEM	28 CAN	27 LEO	27 VIR
30 LEO	28 LEO	31 LIB	29 SCO	29 SAG	29 AQU	31 ARI	29 TAU	30 CAN	30 LEO	29 VIR	29 LIB
21 LEO			30 SCO	31 CAP	30 AQU		31 TAU		31 LEO	30 VIR	31 SCO

1935

JAN	FEB	MAR	APR	MAY	JUN	JUL	AUG	SEP	OCT	NOV	DEC
1 SCO	1 CAP	1 CAP	1 PIS	1 ARI	1 GEM	1 CAN	1 LEO	1 LIB	1 SCO	1 CAP	1 AQU
3 SAG	3 AQU	3 AQU	3 ARI	3 TAU	3 CAN	3 LEO	2 VIR	3 SCO	3 SAG	4 AQU	3 PIS
5 CAP	5 PIS	5 PIS	5 TAU	5 GEM	6 LEO	6 VIR	4 LIB	6 SAG	5 CAP	6 PIS	5 ARI
7 AQU	7 ARI	7 ARI	7 GEM	7 CAN	8 VIR	8 LIB	7 SCO	8 CAP	7 AQU	8 ARI	7 TAU
9 PIS	9 TAU	9 TAU	10 CAN	9 LEO	11 LIB	11 SCO	9 SAG	10 AQU	10 PIS	10 TAU	9 GEM
11 ARI	12 GEM	11 GEM	12 LEO	12 VIR	13 SCO	13 SAG	12 CAP	12 PIS	12 ARI	12 GEM	12 CAN
13 TAU	14 CAN	13 CAN	15 VIR	14 LIB	16 SAG	15 CAP	14 AQU	14 ARI	13 TAU	14 CAN	14 LEO
15 GEM	17 LEO	16 LEO	17 LIB	17 SCO	18 CAP	17 AQU	16 PIS	16 TAU	16 GEM	16 LEO	16 VIR
18 CAN	19 VIR	18 VIR	20 SCO	19 SAG	20 AQU	19 ARI	18 ARI	18 GEM	18 CAN	19 VIR	19 LIB
20 LEO	22 LIB	21 LIB	22 SAG	21 AQU	22 PIS	21 TAU	20 TAU	20 CAN	20 LEO	21 LIB	21 SCO
23 VIR	24 SCO	23 SCO	24 CAP	24 PIS	24 ARI	23 GEM	22 GEM	23 LEO	23 VIR	24 SCO	24 SAG
25 LIB	26 SAG	26 SAG	26 AQU	26 ARI	26 TAU	26 CAN	24 CAN	25 VIR	25 LIB	26 SAG	26 CAP
28 SCO	28 SAG	28 CAP	28 PIS	28 TAU	28 GEM	28 LEO	27 LEO	28 LIB	28 SCO	29 CAP	28 AQU
30 SAG		30 AQU	30 PIS	30 TAU	30 GEM	30 LEO	29 VIR	30 SCO	30 SAG	30 CAP	30 PIS
31 SAG		31 AQU					31 VIR		31 SAG		31 PIS

1936

JAN	FEB	MAR	APR	MAY	JUN	JUL	AUG	SEP	OCT	NOV	DEC
1 ARI	1 TAU	1 GEM	1 LEO	1 VIR	1 LIB	1 SCO	1 CAP	1 PIS	1 ARI	1 GEM	1 CAN
4 TAU	2 GEM	2 CAN	4 VIR	3 LIB	2 SCO	2 SAG	3 AQU	3 ARI	3 TAU	3 CAN	3 LEO
6 GEM	4 CAN	5 LEO	6 LIB	6 SCO	5 SAG	4 CAP	5 PIS	5 TAU	5 GEM	6 LEO	5 VIR
8 CAN	7 LEO	7 VIR	9 SCO	8 SAG	7 CAP	7 AQU	7 ARI	8 GEM	7 CAN	8 VIR	8 LIB
10 LEO	9 VIR	10 LIB	11 SAG	11 CAP	9 AQU	9 PIS	9 TAU	10 CAN	9 LEO	10 LIB	10 SCO
13 VIR	11 LIB	12 SCO	13 CAP	13 AQU	11 PIS	11 ARI	11 GEM	12 LEO	12 VIR	13 SCO	13 SAG
15 LIB	14 SCO	15 SAG	16 AQU	15 PIS	14 ARI	13 TAU	13 CAN	14 VIR	14 LIB	15 SAG	15 CAP
18 SCO	16 SAG	17 CAP	18 PIS	17 ARI	16 TAU	15 GEM	16 LEO	17 LIB	17 SCO	18 CAP	18 AQU
20 SAG	19 CAP	19 AQU	20 ARI	19 TAU	18 GEM	17 CAN	18 VIR	19 SCO	19 SAG	20 AQU	20 PIS
22 SCO	21 AQU	22 PIS	22 TAU	21 GEM	20 CAN	19 LEO	21 LIB	22 SAG	22 CAP	23 PIS	22 ARI
25 AQU	23 PIS	24 ARI	24 GEM	23 CAN	22 LIB	22 VIR	23 SCO	24 CAP	24 AQU	25 ARI	24 TAU
27 PIS	25 ARI	25 TAU	26 CAN	26 LEO	24 SCO	24 LIB	26 SAG	27 AQU	26 PIS	27 TAU	26 GEM
29 ARI	27 TAU	28 GEM	28 LEO	28 VIR	27 LIB	27 SCO	28 CAP	29 PIS	28 ARI	29 GEM	28 CAN
31 TAU	29 GEM	30 CAN	30 LEO	31 SAG	29 SCO	29 SAG	30 AQU	30 PIS	30 TAU	30 GEM	30 LEO
		31 CAN			30 SCO	31 SAG	31 AQU		31 TAU		31 LEO

1937

JAN	FEB	MAR	APR	MAY	JUN	JUL	AUG	SEP	OCT	NOV	DEC
1 LEO	1 LIB	1 LIB	1 SAG	1 CAP	1 AQU	1 ARI	1 TAU	1 CAN	1 LEO	1 LIB	1 SCO
2 VIR	3 SCO	2 SCO	4 CAP	3 AQU	2 PIS	4 TAU	2 GEM	2 LEO	2 VIR	3 SCO	3 SAG
4 LIB	5 SAG	5 SAG	6 AQU	6 PIS	4 ARI	6 GEM	4 CAN	5 VIR	4 LIB	5 SAG	5 CAP
6 SCO	8 CAP	7 CAP	8 PIS	8 ARI	6 TAU	8 CAN	6 LEO	7 LIB	7 SCO	8 CAP	8 AQU
9 SAG	10 AQU	10 AQU	10 ARI	10 TAU	8 GEM	10 LEO	8 VIR	9 SCO	9 SAG	10 SCO	10 PIS
11 CAP	12 PIS	12 PIS	12 TAU	12 GEM	10 CAN	12 VIR	10 LIB	12 SAG	12 CAP	13 AQU	12 ARI
14 AQU	15 ARI	14 ARI	14 GEM	14 CAN	12 LEO	14 LIB	13 SCO	14 CAP	14 AQU	15 PIS	15 TAU
16 PIS	17 TAU	16 TAU	16 CAN	16 LEO	14 VIR	17 SCO	15 SAG	17 AQU	16 PIS	17 ARI	17 GEM
18 ARI	19 GEM	18 GEM	19 LEO	18 VIR	17 LIB	19 SAG	18 CAP	19 PIS	19 ARI	19 TAU	19 CAN
20 TAU	21 CAN	20 CAN	21 VIR	20 LIB	19 SCO	22 CAP	20 AQU	21 ARI	21 TAU	21 GEM	21 LEO
22 GEM	23 LEO	22 LEO	23 LIB	23 SCO	22 SAG	24 AQU	23 PIS	23 TAU	23 GEM	23 CAN	23 VIR
25 CAN	25 VIR	25 VIR	26 SCO	26 SAG	24 CAP	26 PIS	25 ARI	25 GEM	25 CAN	25 LEO	25 LIB
27 LEO	28 LIB	27 LIB	28 SAG	28 CAP	27 AQU	29 ARI	27 TAU	27 CAN	27 LEO	28 VIR	27 SCO
29 VIR		29 SCO	30 SAG	31 AQU	29 PIS	31 TAU	29 GEM	30 LEO	29 VIR	30 SCO	30 SAG
31 LIB		31 SCO			30 PIS		31 CAN		31 LIB		31 SAG

1938

JAN	FEB	MAR	APR	MAY	JUN	JUL	AUG	SEP	OCT	NOV	DEC
1 CAP	1 AQU	1 AQU	1 ARI	1 TAU	1 CAN	1 LEO	1 LIB	1 SCO	1 CAP	1 AQU	1 PIS
4 AQU	3 PIS	2 PIS	3 TAU	2 GEM	3 LEO	2 VIR	3 SCO	2 SAG	4 AQU	3 PIS	3 ARI
6 PIS	5 ARI	4 ARI	5 GEM	4 CAN	5 VIR	4 LIB	5 SAG	4 CAP	6 PIS	5 ARI	5 TAU
9 ARI	7 TAU	6 TAU	7 CAN	6 LEO	7 LIB	6 SCO	8 CAP	7 AQU	9 ARI	7 TAU	7 GEM
11 TAU	9 GEM	9 GEM	9 LEO	8 VIR	9 SCO	9 SAG	10 AQU	9 PIS	11 TAU	10 GEM	9 CAN
13 GEM	11 CAN	11 CAN	11 VIR	11 LIB	12 SAG	11 CAP	13 PIS	11 ARI	13 GEM	12 CAN	11 LEO
15 CAN	13 LEO	13 LEO	13 LIB	13 SCO	14 CAP	14 AQU	15 ARI	14 TAU	15 CAN	14 LEO	13 VIR
17 LEO	16 VIR	15 VIR	16 SCO	15 SAG	17 AQU	16 PIS	17 TAU	16 GEM	17 LEO	16 VIR	15 LIB
19 VIR	18 LIB	17 LIB	18 SAG	18 CAP	19 PIS	19 ARI	20 GEM	18 CAN	20 VIR	18 LIB	17 SCO
21 LIB	20 SCO	19 SCO	21 CAP	20 AQU	22 ARI	21 TAU	22 CAN	20 LEO	22 LIB	20 SCO	20 SAG
24 SCO	22 SAG	22 SAG	23 AQU	23 PIS	24 TAU	23 GEM	24 LEO	22 VIR	24 SCO	23 SAG	22 CAP
26 SAG	25 CAP	24 CAP	26 PIS	25 ARI	26 GEM	25 CAN	26 VIR	24 LIB	26 SAG	25 CAP	25 AQU
29 CAP	27 AQU	27 AQU	28 ARI	28 TAU	28 CAN	27 LEO	28 LIB	27 SCO	29 CAP	28 AQU	27 PIS
31 AQU	28 AQU	29 PIS	30 TAU	30 GEM	30 LEO	29 VIR	30 SCO	29 SAG	31 AQU	30 PIS	30 ARI
		31 PIS		31 GEM		31 VIR	31 SCO	30 SAG			31 ARI

1939

JAN	FEB	MAR	APR	MAY	JUN	JUL	AUG	SEP	OCT	NOV	DEC
1 TAU	1 GEM	1 CAN	1 LEO	1 LIB	1 SCO	1 CAP	1 AQU	1 ARI	1 TAU	1 GEM	1 LEO
3 GEM	2 CAN	3 LEO	2 VIR	3 SCO	2 SAG	4 AQU	3 PIS	4 TAU	4 GEM	2 CAN	4 VIR
5 CAN	4 LEO	5 VIR	4 LIB	5 SAG	4 CAP	6 PIS	5 ARI	6 GEM	6 CAN	4 LEO	6 LIB
7 LEO	6 VIR	7 LIB	6 SCO	8 CAP	7 AQU	9 ARI	8 TAU	9 CAN	8 LEO	6 VIR	8 SCO
9 VIR	8 LIB	9 SCO	8 SAG	10 AQU	9 PIS	11 TAU	10 GEM	11 LEO	10 VIR	8 LIB	10 SAG
11 LIB	10 SCO	12 SAG	10 CAP	13 PIS	12 ARI	14 GEM	12 CAN	13 VIR	12 LIB	11 SCO	12 CAP
14 VIR	12 SAG	14 CAP	13 AQU	15 ARI	14 TAU	16 CAN	14 LEO	15 LIB	14 SCO	13 SAG	15 AQU
16 SAG	15 CAP	17 AQU	15 PIS	18 TAU	16 GEM	18 LEO	16 VIR	17 SCO	16 SAG	15 CAP	17 PIS
19 CAP	17 AQU	19 PIS	18 ARI	20 GEM	18 CAN	20 VIR	18 LIB	19 SAG	19 CAP	17 AQU	20 ARI
21 AQU	20 PIS	22 ARI	20 TAU	22 CAN	20 LEO	22 LIB	20 SCO	21 CAP	21 AQU	20 PIS	22 TAU
24 PIS	22 ARI	24 TAU	23 GEM	24 LEO	22 VIR	24 SCO	23 SAG	24 AQU	24 PIS	22 ARI	25 GEM
26 ARI	25 TAU	26 GEM	25 CAN	26 VIR	25 LIB	26 SAG	25 CAP	26 PIS	26 ARI	25 TAU	27 CAN
29 TAU	27 GEM	29 CAN	27 LEO	28 LIB	27 SCO	29 CAP	27 AQU	29 ARI	28 TAU	27 GEM	29 LIB
31 GEM	28 GEM	31 LEO	29 VIR	31 SCO	29 SAG	31 AQU	30 PIS	30 ARI	31 GEM	29 CAN	31 SCO
			30 VIR		30 SAG		31 PIS			30 CAN	

1940

JAN	FEB	MAR	APR	MAY	JUN	JUL	AUG	SEP	OCT	NOV	DEC
1 VIR	1 SCO	1 SAG	1 CAP	1 AQU	1 ARI	1 TAU	1 CAN	1 LEO	1 LIB	1 SCO	1 CAP
2 LIB	3 SAG	3 CAP	2 AQU	2 PIS	3 TAU	3 GEM	4 LEO	2 VIR	3 SCO	2 SAG	4 AQU
4 SCO	5 CAP	6 AQU	4 PIS	4 ARI	5 GEM	5 CAN	6 VIR	4 LIB	5 SAG	4 CAP	6 PIS
6 SAG	7 AQU	8 PIS	7 ARI	7 TAU	8 CAN	7 LEO	8 LIB	6 SCO	8 CAP	6 AQU	8 ARI
9 CAP	10 PIS	11 ARI	9 TAU	9 GEM	10 LEO	9 VIR	10 SCO	8 SAG	10 AQU	9 PIS	11 TAU
11 AQU	12 ARI	13 TAU	12 GEM	11 CAN	12 VIR	11 LIB	12 SAG	10 CAP	12 PIS	11 ARI	14 GEM
14 PIS	15 TAU	16 GEM	14 CAN	14 LEO	14 LIB	14 SCO	14 CAP	13 AQU	15 ARI	14 TAU	16 CAN
16 ARI	17 GEM	18 CAN	16 LEO	16 VIR	16 SCO	16 SAG	16 AQU	15 PIS	17 TAU	16 GEM	18 LEO
19 TAU	20 CAN	20 LEO	19 VIR	18 LIB	18 SAG	18 CAP	19 PIS	18 ARI	20 GEM	19 CAN	20 VIR
21 GEM	22 LEO	22 VIR	21 LIB	20 SCO	21 CAP	20 AQU	21 ARI	20 TAU	22 CAN	21 LEO	23 LIB
23 CAN	24 VIR	24 LIB	23 SCO	22 SAG	23 AQU	23 PIS	24 TAU	23 GEM	25 LEO	23 VIR	25 SCO
25 LEO	26 LIB	26 SCO	25 SAG	24 CAP	25 PIS	25 ARI	26 GEM	25 CAN	27 VIR	25 LIB	27 SAG
27 VIR	28 SCO	28 SAG	27 CAP	26 AQU	28 ARI	28 TAU	29 CAN	27 LEO	29 LIB	27 SCO	29 CAP
29 LIB	29 SCO	30 CAP	29 AQU	29 PIS	30 TAU	30 GEM	31 LEO	29 VIR	31 SCO	29 SAG	31 AQU
31 SCO		31 CAP	30 AQU	31 ARI		31 GEM		30 VIR		30 SAG	

1941

JAN	FEB	MAR	APR	MAY	JUN	JUL	AUG	SEP	OCT	NOV	DEC
1 AQU	1 ARI	1 ARI	1 TAU	1 GEM	1 LEO	1 VIR	1 SCO	1 CAP	1 AQU	1 ARI	1 TAU
2 PIS	4 TAU	3 TAU	2 GEM	2 CAN	3 VIR	2 LIB	2 SAG	3 AQU	3 PIS	4 TAU	3 GEM
5 ARI	6 GEM	6 GEM	4 CAN	4 LEO	5 LIB	4 SCO	5 CAP	5 PIS	5 ARI	6 GEM	6 CAN
7 TAU	9 CAN	8 CAN	7 LEO	6 VIR	7 SCO	6 SAG	7 AQU	8 ARI	7 TAU	9 CAN	8 LEO
10 GEM	11 LEO	10 LEO	9 VIR	8 LIB	9 SAG	8 CAP	9 PIS	10 TAU	10 GEM	11 LEO	11 VIR
12 CAN	13 VIR	12 VIR	11 LIB	10 SCO	11 CAP	10 AQU	11 ARI	13 GEM	12 CAN	14 VIR	13 LIB
14 LEO	15 LIB	14 LIB	13 SCO	12 SAG	13 AQU	13 PIS	14 TAU	15 CAN	15 LEO	16 LIB	15 SCO
17 VIR	17 SCO	17 SCO	15 SAG	14 CAP	15 PIS	15 ARI	16 GEM	17 LEO	17 VIR	18 SCO	17 SAG
19 LIB	19 SAG	19 SAG	17 CAP	17 AQU	18 ARI	17 TAU	19 CAN	20 VIR	19 LIB	20 SAG	19 CAP
21 SCO	21 CAP	21 CAP	19 AQU	19 PIS	20 TAU	20 GEM	21 LIB	22 LIB	21 SCO	22 CAP	21 AQU
23 SAG	24 AQU	23 AQU	22 PIS	21 ARI	23 GEM	22 CAN	23 SCO	24 SCO	23 SAG	24 AQU	23 PIS
25 CAP	26 PIS	25 PIS	24 ARI	24 TAU	25 CAN	25 LEO	25 SAG	26 SAG	25 CAP	26 PIS	26 ARI
27 AQU	28 ARI	28 ARI	27 TAU	26 GEM	27 LEO	27 VIR	28 CAP	28 CAP	27 AQU	28 ARI	28 TAU
30 PIS		30 TAU	29 GEM	29 CAN	30 VIR	29 LIB	30 AQU	30 AQU	30 PIS	30 ARI	31 GEM
31 PIS		31 TAU	30 GEM	31 LEO		31 SCO	31 SAG		31 PIS		

1942

JAN	FEB	MAR	APR	MAY	JUN	JUL	AUG	SEP	OCT	NOV	DEC
1 GEM	1 LEO	1 LEO	1 LIB	1 SCO	1 CAP	1 AQU	1 ARI	1 ARI	1 GEM	1 LEO	1 VIR
2 CAN	3 VIR	3 VIR	3 SCO	3 SAG	3 AQU	3 PIS	4 TAU	2 GEM	2 CAN	4 VIR	3 LIB
5 LEO	6 LIB	5 LIB	5 SAG	5 CAP	5 PIS	5 ARI	6 GEM	5 CAN	5 LEO	6 LIB	6 SCO
7 VIR	8 SCO	7 SCO	7 CAP	7 AQU	8 ARI	7 TAU	9 CAN	7 LEO	7 VIR	8 SCO	8 SAG
9 LIB	10 SAG	9 SAG	10 AQU	9 PIS	10 TAU	10 GEM	11 LEO	10 VIR	9 LIB	10 SAG	10 CAP
12 SCO	12 CAP	11 CAP	12 PIS	11 ARI	13 GEM	12 CAN	14 VIR	12 LIB	12 SCO	12 CAP	12 AQU
14 SAG	14 AQU	13 AQU	14 ARI	14 TAU	15 CAN	15 LEO	16 LIB	14 SCO	14 SAG	14 AQU	14 PIS
16 CAP	16 PIS	16 PIS	17 TAU	16 GEM	18 LEO	17 VIR	18 SCO	16 SAG	16 CAP	16 PIS	16 ARI
18 AQU	18 ARI	18 ARI	19 GEM	19 CAN	20 VIR	20 LIB	20 SAG	19 CAP	18 AQU	19 ARI	18 TAU
20 PIS	21 TAU	20 TAU	22 CAN	21 LEO	22 LIB	22 SCO	22 CAP	21 AQU	20 PIS	21 TAU	21 GEM
22 ARI	23 GEM	23 GEM	24 LEO	24 VIR	25 SCO	24 SAG	24 AQU	23 PIS	22 ARI	23 GEM	23 CAN
24 TAU	26 CAN	25 CAN	26 VIR	26 LIB	27 SAG	26 CAP	26 PIS	25 ARI	25 TAU	26 CAN	26 LEO
27 GEM	28 LEO	28 LEO	29 LIB	28 SCO	29 CAP	28 ARI	29 ARI	27 TAU	27 GEM	28 LEO	28 VIR
30 CAN		30 VIR	30 LIB	30 SAG	30 CAP	30 PIS	31 TAU	30 GEM	30 CAN	30 LEO	31 LIB
31 CAN		31 VIR		31 SAG		31 PIS			31 CAN		

1943

JAN	FEB	MAR	APR	MAY	JUN	JUL	AUG	SEP	OCT	NOV	DEC
1 LIB	1 SAG	1 SAG	1 AQU	1 PIS	1 TAU	1 GEM	1 LEO	1 VIR	1 LIB	1 SAG	1 CAP
2 SCO	2 CAP	2 CAP	2 PIS	2 ARI	3 GEM	2 CAN	4 VIR	2 LIB	2 SCO	3 CAP	2 AQU
4 SAG	4 AQU	4 AQU	4 ARI	4 TAU	5 CAN	5 LEO	6 LIB	5 SCO	4 SAG	5 AQU	4 PIS
6 CAP	6 PIS	6 PIS	7 TAU	6 GEM	7 LEO	7 VIR	8 SCO	7 SAG	6 CAP	7 PIS	6 ARI
8 AQU	9 ARI	8 ARI	9 GEM	9 CAN	10 VIR	10 LIB	11 SAG	9 CAP	9 AQU	9 ARI	8 TAU
10 PIS	11 TAU	10 TAU	11 CAN	11 LEO	12 LIB	12 SCO	13 CAP	11 AQU	11 PIS	11 TAU	11 GEM
12 ARI	13 GEM	12 GEM	14 LEO	14 VIR	15 SCO	14 SAG	15 AQU	13 PIS	13 ARI	13 GEM	13 CAN
14 TAU	16 CAN	15 CAN	16 VIR	16 LIB	17 SAG	16 CAP	17 PIS	15 ARI	15 TAU	16 CAN	16 LEO
17 GEM	18 LEO	17 LEO	19 LIB	18 SCO	19 CAP	18 AQU	19 ARI	17 TAU	17 GEM	18 LEO	18 VIR
19 CAN	21 VIR	20 VIR	21 SCO	21 SAG	21 AQU	20 PIS	21 TAU	20 GEM	19 CAN	21 VIR	21 LIB
22 LEO	23 LIB	22 LIB	23 SAG	23 CAP	23 PIS	22 ARI	23 GEM	22 CAN	22 LEO	23 LIB	23 SCO
24 VIR	25 SCO	25 SCO	25 CAP	25 AQU	25 ARI	25 TAU	26 CAN	25 LEO	24 VIR	26 SCO	25 SAG
27 LIB	28 SAG	27 SAG	27 AQU	27 PIS	27 TAU	27 GEM	28 LEO	27 VIR	27 LIB	28 SAG	27 CAP
29 SCO		29 CAP	30 PIS	29 ARI	30 GEM	29 CAN	31 VIR	30 LIB	29 SCO	30 CAP	29 AQU
31 SAG		31 AQU		31 TAU		31 CAN			31 SAG		31 PIS

1944

JAN	FEB	MAR	APR	MAY	JUN	JUL	AUG	SEP	OCT	NOV	DEC
1 PIS	1 TAU	1 TAU	1 CAN	1 LEO	1 LIB	1 SCO	1 SAG	1 AQU	1 PIS	1 TAU	1 GEM
3 ARI	3 GEM	2 GEM	3 LEO	2 VIR	4 SCO	3 SAG	2 CAP	3 PIS	2 ARI	3 GEM	2 CAN
5 TAU	6 CAN	4 CAN	5 VIR	5 LIB	6 SAG	6 CAP	4 AQU	5 ARI	4 TAU	5 CAN	4 LEO
7 GEM	8 LEO	6 LEO	8 LIB	7 SCO	8 CAP	8 AQU	6 PIS	7 TAU	6 GEM	7 LEO	7 VIR
9 CAN	11 VIR	9 VIR	10 SCO	10 SAG	10 AQU	10 PIS	8 ARI	9 GEM	8 CAN	9 VIR	9 LIB
12 LEO	13 LIB	11 LIB	13 SAG	12 CAP	13 PIS	12 ARI	10 TAU	11 CAN	11 LEO	12 LIB	12 SCO
14 VIR	16 SCO	14 SCO	15 CAP	14 AQU	15 ARI	14 TAU	12 GEM	13 LEO	13 VIR	15 SCO	14 SAG
17 LIB	18 SAG	16 SAG	17 AQU	16 PIS	17 TAU	16 GEM	15 CAN	16 VIR	16 LIB	17 SAG	17 CAP
19 SCO	20 CAP	19 CAP	19 PIS	18 ARI	19 GEM	19 CAN	17 LEO	18 LIB	18 SCO	19 CAP	19 AQU
22 SAG	22 AQU	21 AQU	21 ARI	21 TAU	21 CAN	21 LEO	20 VIR	21 SCO	21 SAG	22 AQU	21 PIS
24 CAP	24 PIS	23 PIS	23 TAU	23 GEM	24 LEO	23 VIR	22 LIB	23 SAG	23 CAP	24 PIS	23 ARI
26 AQU	26 ARI	25 ARI	25 GEM	25 CAN	26 VIR	26 LIB	25 SCO	26 CAP	25 AQU	26 ARI	25 TAU
28 PIS	28 TAU	27 TAU	28 CAN	27 LEO	29 LIB	28 SCO	29 SAG	28 AQU	27 PIS	28 TAU	27 GEM
30 ARI	29 TAU	29 GEM	30 LEO	30 VIR	30 LIB	31 SAG	30 CAP	30 PIS	30 ARI	30 GEM	30 CAN
31 ARI		31 CAN		31 VIR			31 CAP		31 ARI		31 CAN

1945

JAN	FEB	MAR	APR	MAY	JUN	JUL	AUG	SEP	OCT	NOV	DEC
1 LEO	1 VIR	1 LIB	1 SCO	1 SAG	1 AQU	1 PIS	1 TAU	1 CAN	1 LEO	1 VIR	1 LIB
3 VIR	2 LIB	4 SCO	3 SAG	2 CAP	3 PIS	3 ARI	3 GEM	4 LEO	3 VIR	2 LIB	2 SCO
6 LIB	5 SCO	6 SAG	5 CAP	5 AQU	5 ARI	5 TAU	5 CAN	6 VIR	6 LIB	4 SCO	4 SAG
8 SCO	7 SAG	9 CAP	7 AQU	7 PIS	7 TAU	7 GEM	7 LEO	8 LIB	8 SCO	7 SAG	7 CAP
11 SAG	9 CAP	11 AQU	10 PIS	9 ARI	9 GEM	9 CAN	10 VIR	11 SCO	11 SAG	9 CAP	9 AQU
13 CAP	12 AQU	13 PIS	12 ARI	11 TAU	11 CAN	11 LEO	12 LIB	13 SAG	13 CAP	12 AQU	11 PIS
15 AQU	14 PIS	15 ARI	14 TAU	13 GEM	14 LEO	13 VIR	15 SCO	16 CAP	16 AQU	14 PIS	14 ARI
17 PIS	16 ARI	17 TAU	16 GEM	15 CAN	16 VIR	16 LIB	17 SAG	18 AQU	18 PIS	16 ARI	16 TAU
19 ARI	18 TAU	19 GEM	18 CAN	17 LEO	18 LIB	18 SCO	20 CAP	20 PIS	20 ARI	18 TAU	18 GEM
21 TAU	20 GEM	21 CAN	20 LEO	20 VIR	21 SCO	21 SAG	22 AQU	22 ARI	22 TAU	20 GEM	20 CAN
24 GEM	22 CAN	24 LEO	22 VIR	22 LIB	23 SAG	23 CAP	24 PIS	24 TAU	24 GEM	22 CAN	22 LEO
26 CAN	24 LEO	26 VIR	25 LIB	25 SCO	26 CAP	25 AQU	26 ARI	26 GEM	26 CAN	24 LEO	24 VIR
28 LEO	27 VIR	29 LIB	27 SCO	27 SAG	28 AQU	28 PIS	28 TAU	29 CAN	28 LEO	27 VIR	26 LIB
31 VIR	28 VIR	31 SCO	30 SAG	30 CAP	30 PIS	30 ARI	30 GEM	30 CAN	30 VIR	29 LIB	29 SCO
				31 CAP		31 ARI	31 GEM		31 VIR	30 LIB	31 SCO

1946

JAN	FEB	MAR	APR	MAY	JUN	JUL	AUG	SEP	OCT	NOV	DEC
1 SAG	1 CAP	1 AQU	1 PIS	1 TAU	1 GEM	1 LEO	1 VIR	1 SCO	1 SAG	1 CAP	1 AQU
3 CAP	2 AQU	3 PIS	2 ARI	3 GEM	2 CAN	3 VIR	2 LIB	3 SAG	3 CAP	2 AQU	2 PIS
5 AQU	4 PIS	5 ARI	4 TAU	5 CAN	4 LEO	6 LIB	4 SCO	6 CAP	6 AQU	4 PIS	4 ARI
8 PIS	6 ARI	8 TAU	6 GEM	7 LEO	6 VIR	8 SCO	7 SAG	8 AQU	8 PIS	7 ARI	6 TAU
10 ARI	8 TAU	10 GEM	8 CAN	10 VIR	8 LIB	11 SAG	9 CAP	11 PIS	10 ARI	9 TAU	8 GEM
12 TAU	10 GEM	12 CAN	10 LEO	12 LIB	11 SCO	13 CAP	12 AQU	13 ARI	12 TAU	11 GEM	10 CAN
14 GEM	13 CAN	14 LEO	12 VIR	15 SCO	13 SAG	16 AQU	14 PIS	15 TAU	14 GEM	13 CAN	12 LEO
16 CAN	15 LEO	16 VIR	15 LIB	17 SAG	16 CAP	18 PIS	16 ARI	17 GEM	16 CAN	15 LEO	14 VIR
18 LEO	17 VIR	19 LIB	17 SCO	20 CAP	18 AQU	20 ARI	19 TAU	19 CAN	19 LEO	17 VIR	17 LIB
21 VIR	19 LIB	21 SCO	20 SAG	22 AQU	21 PIS	22 TAU	21 GEM	21 LEO	21 VIR	19 LIB	19 SCO
23 LIB	22 SCO	24 SAG	22 CAP	24 PIS	23 ARI	25 GEM	23 CAN	23 VIR	23 LIB	22 SCO	21 SAG
25 SCO	24 SAG	26 CAP	25 AQU	27 ARI	25 TAU	27 CAN	25 LEO	26 LIB	25 SCO	24 SAG	24 CAP
28 SAG	27 CAP	28 AQU	27 PIS	29 TAU	27 GEM	29 LEO	27 VIR	28 SCO	28 SAG	27 CAP	26 AQU
30 CAP	28 CAP	31 PIS	29 ARI	31 GEM	29 CAN	31 VIR	29 LIB	30 SCO	30 CAP	29 AQU	29 PIS
31 CAP			30 ARI		30 CAN		31 LIB		31 CAP	30 AQU	31 ARI

1947

JAN	FEB	MAR	APR	MAY	JUN	JUL	AUG	SEP	OCT	NOV	DEC
1 ARI	1 GEM	1 GEM	1 LEO	1 VIR	1 SCO	1 SAG	1 CAP	1 PIS	1 ARI	1 GEM	1 CAN
3 TAU	3 CAN	2 CAN	3 VIR	2 LIB	3 SAG	3 CAP	2 AQU	3 ARI	3 TAU	3 CAN	3 LEO
5 GEM	5 LEO	4 LEO	5 LIB	5 SCO	6 CAP	6 AQU	4 PIS	5 TAU	5 GEM	5 LEO	5 VIR
7 CAN	7 VIR	7 VIR	7 SCO	7 SAG	8 AQU	8 PIS	7 ARI	8 GEM	7 CAN	7 VIR	7 LIB
9 LEO	9 LIB	9 LIB	10 SAG	9 CAP	11 PIS	11 ARI	9 TAU	10 CAN	9 LEO	10 LIB	9 SCO
11 VIR	12 SCO	11 SCO	12 CAP	12 AQU	13 ARI	13 TAU	11 GEM	12 LEO	11 VIR	12 SCO	11 SAG
13 LIB	14 SAG	13 SAG	15 AQU	15 PIS	15 TAU	15 GEM	13 CAN	14 VIR	13 LIB	14 SAG	14 CAP
15 SCO	17 CAP	16 CAP	17 PIS	17 ARI	18 GEM	17 CAN	15 LEO	16 LIB	15 SCO	17 CAP	16 AQU
18 SAG	19 AQU	18 AQU	19 ARI	19 TAU	20 CAN	19 LEO	17 VIR	18 SCO	18 SAG	19 AQU	19 PIS
20 CAP	21 PIS	21 PIS	22 TAU	21 GEM	22 LEO	21 VIR	20 LIB	20 SAG	20 CAP	22 PIS	21 ARI
23 AQU	24 ARI	23 ARI	24 GEM	23 CAN	24 VIR	23 LIB	22 SCO	23 CAP	23 AQU	24 ARI	24 TAU
25 PIS	26 TAU	25 TAU	26 CAN	25 LEO	26 LIB	25 SCO	24 SAG	25 AQU	25 PIS	26 TAU	26 GEM
28 ARI	28 GEM	27 GEM	28 LEO	27 VIR	28 SCO	28 SAG	27 CAP	28 PIS	28 ARI	28 GEM	28 CAN
30 TAU		30 CAN	30 VIR	30 LIB	30 SCO	30 CAP	29 AQU	30 ARI	30 TAU	30 GEM	30 LEO
31 TAU		31 CAN		31 LIB		31 CAP	31 AQU		31 TAU		31 LEO

1948

JAN	FEB	MAR	APR	MAY	JUN	JUL	AUG	SEP	OCT	NOV	DEC
1 VIR	1 LIB	1 SCO	1 CAP	1 AQU	1 PIS	1 ARI	1 GEM	1 LEO	1 VIR	1 SCO	1 SAG
3 LIB	2 SCO	2 SAG	3 AQU	3 PIS	2 ARI	2 TAU	3 CAN	3 VIR	3 LIB	3 SAG	3 CAP
5 SCO	4 SAG	5 CAP	6 PIS	6 ARI	5 TAU	4 GEM	5 LEO	5 LIB	5 SCO	5 CAP	5 AQU
8 SAG	6 CAP	7 AQU	8 ARI	8 TAU	7 GEM	6 CAN	7 VIR	7 SCO	7 SAG	8 AQU	8 PIS
10 CAP	9 AQU	10 PIS	11 TAU	10 GEM	9 CAN	8 LEO	9 LIB	9 SAG	9 CAP	10 PIS	10 ARI
13 AQU	11 PIS	12 ARI	13 GEM	13 CAN	11 LEO	10 VIR	11 SCO	12 CAP	12 AQU	13 ARI	13 TAU
15 PIS	14 ARI	15 TAU	15 CAN	15 LEO	13 VIR	12 LIB	13 SAG	14 AQU	14 PIS	15 TAU	15 GEM
18 ARI	16 TAU	17 GEM	18 LEO	17 VIR	15 LIB	15 SCO	16 CAP	17 PIS	17 ARI	18 GEM	17 CAN
20 TAU	19 GEM	19 CAN	20 VIR	19 LIB	17 SCO	17 SAG	18 AQU	19 ARI	19 TAU	20 CAN	19 LEO
22 GEM	21 CAN	21 LEO	22 LIB	21 SCO	20 SAG	19 CAP	21 PIS	22 TAU	21 GEM	22 LEO	22 VIR
24 CAN	23 LEO	23 VIR	24 SCO	23 SAG	22 CAP	22 AQU	23 ARI	24 GEM	24 CAN	24 VIR	24 LIB
26 LEO	25 VIR	25 LIB	26 SAG	26 CAP	24 AQU	24 PIS	26 TAU	26 CAN	26 LEO	26 LIB	26 SCO
28 VIR	27 LIB	27 SCO	28 CAP	28 AQU	27 PIS	27 ARI	28 GEM	29 LEO	28 VIR	29 SCO	28 SAG
30 LIB	29 SCO	30 SAG	30 CAP	31 PIS	29 ARI	29 TAU	30 CAN	30 LEO	30 LIB	30 SCO	30 CAP
31 LIB		31 SAG			30 ARI	31 TAU	31 CAN		31 LIB		30 CAP

1949

JAN	FEB	MAR	APR	MAY	JUN	JUL	AUG	SEP	OCT	NOV	DEC
1 CAP	1 PIS	1 PIS	1 TAU	1 GEM	1 CAN	1 VIR	1 SCO	1 SAG	1 CAP	1 PIS	1 ARI
2 AQU	3 ARI	2 ARI	3 GEM	3 CAN	2 LEO	3 LIB	4 SAG	2 CAP	2 AQU	3 ARI	3 TAU
4 PIS	5 TAU	5 TAU	6 CAN	5 LEO	4 VIR	5 SCO	6 CAP	4 AQU	4 PIS	5 TAU	5 GEM
7 ARI	8 GEM	7 GEM	8 LEO	7 VIR	6 LIB	7 SAG	8 AQU	7 PIS	6 ARI	8 GEM	7 CAN
9 TAU	10 CAN	10 CAN	10 VIR	10 LIB	8 SCO	10 CAP	10 PIS	9 ARI	9 TAU	10 CAN	10 LEO
11 GEM	12 LEO	12 LEO	12 LIB	12 SCO	10 SAG	12 AQU	13 ARI	12 TAU	12 GEM	13 LEO	12 VIR
14 CAN	14 VIR	14 VIR	14 SCO	14 SAG	12 CAP	14 PIS	15 TAU	14 GEM	14 CAN	15 VIR	14 LIB
16 LEO	16 LIB	16 LIB	16 SAG	16 CAP	14 AQU	17 ARI	18 GEM	17 CAN	16 LEO	17 LIB	16 SCO
18 VIR	18 SCO	18 SCO	18 CAP	18 AQU	17 PIS	19 TAU	20 CAN	19 LEO	18 VIR	19 SCO	18 SAG
20 LIB	20 SAG	20 SAG	21 AQU	20 PIS	19 ARI	22 GEM	23 LEO	21 VIR	21 LIB	21 SAG	20 CAP
22 SCO	23 CAP	22 CAP	23 PIS	23 ARI	22 TAU	24 CAN	25 VIR	23 LIB	23 SCO	23 CAP	23 AQU
24 SAG	25 AQU	24 AQU	26 ARI	25 TAU	24 GEM	26 LEO	27 LIB	25 SCO	25 SAG	25 AQU	25 PIS
27 CAP	28 PIS	27 PIS	28 TAU	28 GEM	27 CAN	28 VIR	29 SCO	27 SAG	27 CAP	28 PIS	27 ARI
29 AQU		29 ARI	30 TAU	30 CAN	29 LEO	30 LIB	31 SAG	29 CAP	29 AQU	30 ARI	30 TAU
31 PIS		31 ARI		31 CAN	30 LEO	31 LIB		30 CAP	31 PIS		31 TAU

1950

JAN	FEB	MAR	APR	MAY	JUN	JUL	AUG	SEP	OCT	NOV	DEC
1 GEM	1 CAN	1 CAN	1 VIR	1 LIB	1 SAG	1 CAP	1 PIS	1 ARI	1 GEM	1 CAN	1 LEO
4 CAN	2 LEO	2 LEO	3 LIB	2 SCO	2 CAP	2 AQU	3 ARI	2 TAU	4 CAN	3 LEO	2 VIR
6 LEO	5 VIR	4 VIR	5 SCO	4 SAG	4 AQU	4 PIS	5 TAU	4 GEM	6 LEO	5 VIR	5 LIB
8 VIR	7 LIB	6 LIB	7 SAG	6 CAP	7 PIS	6 ARI	8 GEM	7 CAN	9 VIR	7 LIB	7 SCO
10 LIB	9 SCO	8 SCO	9 CAP	8 AQU	9 ARI	9 TAU	10 CAN	9 LEO	11 LIB	9 SCO	9 SAG
13 SCO	11 SAG	10 SAG	11 AQU	10 PIS	12 TAU	11 GEM	13 LEO	11 VIR	13 SCO	11 SAG	11 CAP
15 SAG	13 CAP	12 CAP	13 PIS	13 ARI	14 GEM	14 CAN	15 VIR	13 LIB	15 SAG	13 CAP	13 AQU
17 CAP	15 AQU	15 AQU	16 ARI	15 TAU	17 CAN	16 LEO	17 LIB	16 SCO	17 CAP	15 AQU	15 PIS
19 AQU	18 PIS	17 PIS	18 TAU	18 GEM	19 LEO	19 VIR	19 SCO	18 SAG	19 AQU	18 PIS	17 ARI
21 PIS	20 ARI	19 ARI	21 GEM	20 CAN	21 VIR	21 LIB	21 SAG	20 CAP	21 PIS	20 ARI	20 TAU
24 ARI	23 TAU	22 TAU	23 CAN	23 LEO	24 LIB	23 SCO	23 CAP	22 AQU	24 ARI	22 TAU	22 GEM
26 TAU	25 GEM	24 GEM	26 LEO	25 VIR	26 SCO	25 SAG	26 AQU	24 PIS	26 TAU	25 GEM	25 CAN
29 GEM	28 CAN	27 CAN	28 VIR	27 LIB	28 SAG	27 CAP	28 PIS	26 ARI	29 GEM	28 CAN	27 LEO
31 CAN		29 LEO	30 LIB	29 SCO	30 CAP	29 AQU	30 ARI	29 TAU	31 CAN	30 LEO	30 VIR
		31 VIR		31 SAG		31 PIS	31 ARI	30 TAU			31 VIR

1951

JAN	FEB	MAR	APR	MAY	JUN	JUL	AUG	SEP	OCT	NOV	DEC
1 LIB	1 SCO	1 SAG	1 AQU	1 PIS	1 ARI	1 GEM	1 CAN	1 VIR	1 LIB	1 SCO	1 CAP
3 SCO	2 SAG	3 CAP	3 PIS	3 ARI	2 TAU	4 CAN	3 LEO	4 LIB	3 SCO	2 SAG	3 AQU
5 SAG	4 CAP	5 AQU	6 ARI	5 TAU	4 GEM	6 LEO	5 VIR	6 SCO	5 SAG	4 CAP	5 PIS
7 CAP	6 AQU	7 PIS	8 TAU	8 GEM	7 CAN	9 VIR	7 LIB	8 SAG	8 CAP	6 AQU	7 ARI
9 AQU	8 PIS	9 ARI	11 GEM	10 CAN	9 LEO	11 LIB	10 SCO	10 CAP	10 AQU	8 PIS	10 TAU
11 PIS	10 ARI	12 TAU	13 CAN	13 LEO	12 VIR	14 SCO	12 SAG	12 AQU	12 PIS	10 ARI	12 GEM
14 ARI	12 TAU	14 GEM	16 LEO	15 VIR	14 LIB	16 SAG	14 CAP	14 PIS	14 ARI	13 TAU	15 CAN
16 TAU	15 GEM	17 CAN	18 VIR	18 LIB	16 SCO	18 CAP	16 AQU	17 ARI	16 TAU	15 GEM	17 LEO
19 GEM	17 CAN	19 LEO	20 LIB	20 SCO	18 SAG	20 AQU	18 PIS	19 TAU	19 GEM	17 CAN	20 VIR
21 CAN	20 LEO	22 VIR	22 SCO	22 SAG	20 CAP	22 PIS	20 ARI	21 GEM	21 CAN	20 LEO	22 LIB
24 LEO	22 VIR	24 LIB	24 SAG	24 CAP	22 AQU	24 ARI	22 TAU	24 CAN	24 LEO	22 VIR	24 SCO
26 VIR	24 LIB	26 SCO	26 CAP	26 AQU	24 PIS	26 TAU	25 GEM	26 LEO	26 VIR	25 LIB	27 SAG
28 LIB	27 SCO	28 SAG	28 AQU	28 PIS	26 ARI	29 GEM	27 CAN	29 VIR	28 LIB	27 SCO	29 CAP
30 SCO	28 SCO	30 CAP	30 AQU	30 ARI	29 TAU	31 CAN	30 LEO	30 VIR	31 SCO	29 SAG	31 AQU
31 SCO		31 CAP		31 ARI	30 TAU		31 LEO			30 SAG	

1952

JAN	FEB	MAR	APR	MAY	JUN	JUL	AUG	SEP	OCT	NOV	DEC
1 AQU	1 ARI	1 TAU	1 GEM	1 CAN	1 VIR	1 LIB	1 SAG	1 CAP	1 PIS	1 ARI	1 GEM
2 PIS	2 TAU	3 GEM	2 CAN	2 LEO	3 LIB	3 SCO	3 CAP	2 AQU	3 ARI	2 TAU	4 CAN
4 ARI	5 GEM	5 CAN	4 LEO	4 VIR	5 SCO	5 SAG	5 AQU	4 PIS	5 TAU	4 GEM	6 LEO
6 TAU	7 CAN	8 LEO	7 VIR	7 LIB	8 SAG	7 CAP	7 PIS	6 ARI	8 GEM	6 CAN	9 VIR
8 GEM	10 LEO	11 VIR	9 LIB	9 SCO	10 CAP	9 AQU	9 ARI	8 TAU	10 CAN	9 LEO	11 LIB
11 CAN	12 VIR	13 LIB	12 SCO	11 SAG	12 AQU	11 PIS	12 TAU	10 GEM	12 LEO	11 VIR	14 SCO
13 LEO	15 LIB	15 SCO	14 SAG	13 CAP	14 PIS	13 ARI	14 GEM	13 CAN	15 VIR	14 LIB	16 SAG
16 VIR	17 SCO	18 SAG	16 CAP	15 AQU	16 ARI	15 TAU	16 CAN	15 LEO	17 LIB	16 SCO	18 CAP
18 LIB	19 SAG	20 CAP	18 AQU	17 PIS	18 TAU	18 GEM	19 LEO	18 VIR	20 SCO	18 SAG	20 AQU
21 SCO	21 CAP	22 AQU	20 PIS	20 ARI	20 GEM	20 CAN	21 VIR	20 LIB	22 SAG	21 CAP	22 PIS
23 SAG	23 AQU	24 PIS	22 ARI	22 TAU	23 CAN	23 LEO	24 LIB	23 SCO	24 CAP	23 AQU	24 ARI
25 CAP	26 PIS	26 ARI	25 TAU	24 GEM	25 LEO	25 VIR	26 SCO	25 SAG	26 AQU	25 PIS	26 TAU
27 AQU	28 ARI	28 TAU	27 GEM	27 CAN	28 VIR	28 LIB	29 SAG	27 CAP	29 PIS	27 ARI	29 GEM
29 PIS	29 ARI	30 GEM	29 CAN	29 LEO	30 LIB	30 SCO	31 CAP	29 AQU	31 ARI	29 TAU	31 CAN
31 ARI		31 GEM	30 CAN	31 LEO		31 SCO		30 AQU		30 TAU	

1953

JAN	FEB	MAR	APR	MAY	JUN	JUL	AUG	SEP	OCT	NOV	DEC
1 CAN	1 VIR	1 VIR	1 LIB	1 SAG	1 CAP	1 AQU	1 ARI	1 GEM	1 CAN	1 VIR	1 LIB
2 LEO	4 LIB	3 LIB	2 SCO	4 CAP	2 AQU	2 PIS	2 TAU	3 CAN	2 LEO	4 LIB	3 SCO
5 VIR	6 SCO	5 SCO	4 SAG	6 AQU	4 PIS	4 ARI	4 GEM	5 LEO	5 VIR	6 SCO	6 SAG
7 LIB	9 SAG	8 SAG	6 CAP	8 PIS	6 ARI	6 TAU	6 CAN	8 VIR	7 LIB	9 SAG	8 CAP
10 SCO	11 CAP	10 CAP	9 AQU	10 ARI	8 TAU	8 GEM	9 LEO	10 LIB	10 SCO	11 CAP	10 AQU
12 SAG	13 AQU	12 AQU	11 PIS	12 TAU	11 GEM	10 CAN	11 VIR	13 SCO	12 SAG	13 AQU	13 PIS
14 CAP	15 PIS	14 PIS	13 ARI	14 GEM	13 CAN	13 LEO	14 LIB	15 SAG	15 CAP	15 PIS	15 ARI
16 AQU	17 ARI	16 ARI	15 TAU	16 CAN	15 LEO	15 VIR	16 SCO	17 CAP	17 AQU	18 ARI	17 TAU
18 PIS	19 TAU	18 TAU	17 GEM	19 LEO	18 VIR	18 LIB	19 SAG	20 AQU	19 PIS	20 TAU	19 GEM
20 ARI	21 GEM	20 GEM	19 CAN	21 VIR	20 LIB	20 SCO	21 CAP	22 PIS	21 ARI	22 GEM	21 CAN
23 TAU	23 CAN	23 CAN	21 LEO	24 LIB	23 SCO	22 SAG	23 AQU	24 ARI	23 TAU	24 CAN	23 LEO
25 GEM	26 LEO	25 LEO	24 VIR	26 SCO	25 SAG	25 CAP	25 PIS	26 TAU	25 GEM	26 LEO	26 VIR
27 CAN	28 VIR	28 VIR	27 LIB	29 SAG	27 CAP	27 AQU	27 ARI	28 GEM	27 CAN	28 VIR	28 LIB
30 LEO		30 LIB	29 SCO	31 CAP	29 AQU	29 PIS	29 TAU	30 CAN	30 LEO	30 VIR	31 SCO
31 LEO		31 LIB	30 SCO		30 AQU	31 ARI	31 GEM		31 LEO		

1954

JAN	FEB	MAR	APR	MAY	JUN	JUL	AUG	SEP	OCT	NOV	DEC
1 SCO	1 CAP	1 CAP	1 PIS	1 ARI	1 GEM	1 CAN	1 VIR	1 LIB	1 SCO	1 CAP	1 AQU
2 SAG	3 AQU	3 AQU	3 ARI	3 TAU	3 CAN	3 LEO	4 LIB	2 SCO	2 SAG	4 AQU	3 PIS
5 CAP	5 PIS	5 PIS	5 TAU	5 GEM	5 LEO	5 VIR	6 SCO	5 SAG	5 CAP	6 PIS	5 ARI
7 AQU	7 ARI	7 ARI	7 GEM	7 CAN	8 VIR	7 LIB	9 SAG	7 CAP	7 AQU	8 ARI	7 TAU
9 PIS	9 TAU	9 TAU	9 CAN	9 LEO	10 LIB	10 SCO	11 CAP	10 AQU	9 PIS	10 TAU	9 GEM
11 ARI	11 GEM	11 GEM	12 LEO	11 VIR	12 SCO	12 SAG	13 AQU	12 PIS	11 ARI	12 GEM	11 CAN
13 TAU	14 CAN	13 CAN	14 VIR	14 LIB	15 SAG	15 CAP	16 PIS	14 TAU	13 TAU	14 CAN	13 LEO
15 GEM	16 LEO	15 LEO	16 LIB	16 SCO	17 CAP	17 AQU	18 ARI	16 GEM	15 GEM	16 LEO	16 VIR
17 CAN	18 VIR	18 VIR	19 SCO	19 SAG	20 AQU	19 PIS	20 TAU	18 CAN	18 CAN	18 VIR	18 LIB
20 LEO	21 LIB	20 LIB	21 SAG	21 CAP	22 PIS	21 ARI	22 GEM	20 LEO	20 LEO	21 LIB	21 SCO
22 VIR	23 SCO	23 SCO	24 CAP	24 AQU	24 ARI	24 TAU	24 CAN	23 VIR	22 VIR	23 SCO	23 SAG
25 LIB	26 SAG	25 SAG	26 AQU	26 PIS	26 TAU	26 GEM	26 LEO	25 LIB	25 LIB	26 SAG	26 CAP
27 SCO	28 CAP	28 CAP	29 PIS	28 ARI	28 GEM	28 CAN	29 VIR	27 SCO	27 SCO	28 CAP	28 AQU
30 SAG		30 AQU	30 PIS	30 TAU	30 CAN	30 LEO	31 LIB	30 SCO	30 SAG	30 CAP	30 PIS
31 SAG				31 TAU		31 LEO			31 SAG		31 PIS

1955

JAN	FEB	MAR	APR	MAY	JUN	JUL	AUG	SEP	OCT	NOV	DEC
1 PIS	1 TAU	1 GEM	1 CAN	1 VIR	1 LIB	1 SCO	1 CAP	1 AQU	1 PIS	1 TAU	1 GEM
2 ARI	2 GEM	3 CAN	2 LEO	4 LIB	2 SCO	2 SAG	3 AQU	2 PIS	2 ARI	2 GEM	2 CAN
4 TAU	4 CAN	6 LEO	4 VIR	6 SCO	5 SAG	5 CAP	6 PIS	4 ARI	4 TAU	4 CAN	4 LEO
6 GEM	6 LEO	8 VIR	6 LIB	9 SAG	7 CAP	7 AQU	8 ARI	7 TAU	6 GEM	6 LEO	6 VIR
8 CAN	8 VIR	10 LIB	9 SCO	11 CAP	10 AQU	10 PIS	10 TAU	9 GEM	8 CAN	9 VIR	8 LIB
10 LEO	11 LIB	13 SCO	11 SAG	14 AQU	12 PIS	12 ARI	12 GEM	11 CAN	10 LEO	11 LIB	10 SCO
12 VIR	13 SCO	15 SAG	14 CAP	16 PIS	15 ARI	14 TAU	15 CAN	13 LEO	12 VIR	13 SCO	13 SAG
14 LIB	16 SAG	18 CAP	16 AQU	18 ARI	17 TAU	16 GEM	17 LEO	15 VIR	15 LIB	16 SAG	16 CAP
17 SCO	18 CAP	20 AQU	19 PIS	20 TAU	19 GEM	18 CAN	19 VIR	17 LIB	17 SCO	18 CAP	18 AQU
19 SAG	21 AQU	22 PIS	21 ARI	22 GEM	21 CAN	20 LEO	21 LIB	20 SCO	19 SAG	21 AQU	21 PIS
22 CAP	23 PIS	24 ARI	23 TAU	24 CAN	23 LEO	22 VIR	23 SCO	22 SAG	22 CAP	23 PIS	23 ARI
24 AQU	25 ARI	27 TAU	25 GEM	26 LEO	25 VIR	25 LIB	26 SAG	25 CAP	24 AQU	26 ARI	25 TAU
27 PIS	27 TAU	29 GEM	27 CAN	29 VIR	27 LIB	27 SCO	28 CAP	27 AQU	27 PIS	28 TAU	27 GEM
29 ARI	28 TAU	31 CAN	29 LEO	31 LIB	30 SCO	29 SAG	31 AQU	30 PIS	29 ARI	30 GEM	29 CAN
31 TAU			30 LEO			31 SAG			31 TAU		31 LEO

1956

JAN	FEB	MAR	APR	MAY	JUN	JUL	AUG	SEP	OCT	NOV	DEC
1 LEO	1 LIB	1 SCO	1 SAG	1 CAP	1 PIS	1 ARI	1 TAU	1 CAN	1 LEO	1 LIB	1 SCO
2 VIR	3 SCO	4 SAG	3 CAP	3 AQU	4 ARI	3 TAU	2 GEM	2 LEO	2 VIR	2 SCO	2 SAG
4 LIB	6 SAG	6 CAP	5 AQU	5 PIS	6 TAU	6 GEM	4 CAN	4 VIR	4 LIB	5 SAG	4 CAP
7 SCO	8 CAP	9 AQU	8 PIS	7 ARI	8 GEM	8 CAN	6 LEO	7 LIB	6 SCO	7 CAP	7 AQU
9 SAG	11 AQU	11 PIS	10 ARI	10 TAU	10 CAN	10 LEO	8 VIR	9 SCO	8 SAG	10 AQU	9 PIS
12 CAP	13 PIS	14 ARI	12 TAU	12 GEM	12 LEO	12 VIR	10 LIB	11 SAG	11 CAP	12 PIS	12 ARI
14 AQU	15 ARI	16 TAU	14 GEM	14 CAN	14 VIR	14 LIB	12 SCO	13 CAP	13 AQU	15 ARI	14 TAU
17 PIS	18 TAU	18 GEM	17 CAN	16 LEO	16 LIB	16 SCO	15 SAG	16 AQU	16 PIS	17 TAU	17 GEM
19 ARI	20 GEM	20 CAN	19 LEO	18 VIR	19 SCO	18 SAG	17 CAP	18 PIS	18 ARI	19 GEM	19 CAN
21 TAU	22 CAN	22 LEO	21 VIR	20 LIB	21 SAG	21 CAP	20 AQU	21 ARI	21 TAU	21 CAN	21 LEO
24 GEM	24 LEO	24 VIR	23 LIB	22 SCO	24 CAP	23 AQU	22 PIS	23 TAU	23 GEM	23 LEO	23 VIR
26 CAN	26 VIR	27 LIB	25 SCO	25 SAG	26 AQU	26 PIS	25 ARI	25 GEM	25 CAN	25 VIR	25 LIB
28 LEO	28 LIB	29 SCO	28 SAG	27 CAP	29 PIS	28 ARI	27 TAU	28 CAN	27 LEO	28 LIB	27 SCO
30 VIR	29 LIB	31 SAG	30 CAP	30 AQU	30 PIS	31 TAU	29 GEM	30 LEO	29 VIR	30 SCO	29 SAG
31 VIR				31 AQU			31 CAN		31 LIB		31 SAG

1957

JAN	FEB	MAR	APR	MAY	JUN	JUL	AUG	SEP	OCT	NOV	DEC
1 CAP	1 AQU	1 PIS	1 ARI	1 TAU	1 CAN	1 LEO	1 LIB	1 SAG	1 CAP	1 AQU	1 PIS
3 AQU	2 PIS	4 ARI	2 TAU	2 GEM	3 LEO	2 VIR	3 SCO	3 CAP	3 AQU	2 PIS	2 ARI
6 PIS	5 ARI	6 TAU	5 GEM	4 CAN	5 VIR	4 LIB	5 SAG	6 AQU	6 PIS	4 ARI	4 TAU
8 ARI	7 TAU	9 GEM	7 CAN	6 LEO	7 LIB	6 SCO	7 CAP	8 PIS	8 ARI	7 TAU	7 GEM
11 TAU	9 GEM	11 CAN	9 LEO	9 VIR	9 SCO	9 SAG	10 AQU	11 ARI	11 TAU	9 GEM	9 CAN
13 GEM	11 CAN	13 LEO	11 VIR	11 LIB	11 SAG	11 CAP	12 PIS	13 TAU	13 GEM	12 CAN	11 LEO
15 CAN	14 LEO	15 VIR	13 LIB	13 SCO	14 CAP	13 AQU	15 ARI	16 GEM	15 CAN	14 LEO	13 VIR
17 LEO	15 VIR	17 LIB	15 SCO	15 SAG	16 AQU	16 PIS	17 TAU	18 CAN	18 LEO	16 VIR	15 LIB
19 VIR	17 LIB	19 SCO	18 SAG	17 CAP	19 PIS	18 ARI	20 GEM	20 LEO	20 VIR	18 LIB	17 SCO
21 LIB	20 SCO	21 SAG	20 CAP	20 AQU	21 ARI	21 TAU	22 CAN	22 VIR	22 LIB	20 SCO	20 SAG
23 SCO	22 SAG	24 CAP	22 AQU	22 PIS	23 TAU	23 GEM	24 LEO	24 LIB	24 SCO	22 SAG	22 CAP
26 SAG	24 CAP	26 AQU	25 PIS	25 ARI	26 GEM	25 CAN	26 VIR	26 SCO	26 SAG	24 CAP	24 AQU
28 CAP	27 AQU	29 PIS	27 ARI	27 TAU	28 CAN	27 LEO	28 LIB	28 SAG	28 CAP	27 AQU	27 PIS
30 AQU	28 AQU	31 ARI	30 TAU	29 GEM	30 LEO	29 VIR	30 SCO	30 SAG	30 AQU	29 PIS	29 ARI
31 AQU				31 GEM		31 LIB	31 SCO		31 AQU	30 PIS	31 ARI

1958

JAN	FEB	MAR	APR	MAY	JUN	JUL	AUG	SEP	OCT	NOV	DEC
1 TAU	1 GEM	1 CAN	1 LEO	1 LIB	1 SCO	1 CAP	1 AQU	1 ARI	1 TAU	1 GEM	1 LEO
3 GEM	2 CAN	3 LEO	2 VIR	3 SCO	2 SAG	3 AQU	2 PIS	3 TAU	3 GEM	2 CAN	4 VIR
5 CAN	4 LEO	5 VIR	4 LIB	5 SAG	4 CAP	6 PIS	4 ARI	6 GEM	6 CAN	4 LEO	6 LIB
7 LEO	6 VIR	7 LIB	6 SCO	7 CAP	6 AQU	8 ARI	7 TAU	8 CAN	8 LEO	6 VIR	8 SCO
9 VIR	8 LIB	9 SCO	8 SAG	10 AQU	8 PIS	11 TAU	10 GEM	11 LEO	10 VIR	9 LIB	10 SAG
12 LIB	10 SCO	11 SAG	10 CAP	12 PIS	11 ARI	13 GEM	12 CAN	13 VIR	12 LIB	11 SCO	12 CAP
14 SCO	12 SAG	14 CAP	12 AQU	14 ARI	13 TAU	16 CAN	14 LEO	15 LIB	14 SCO	13 SAG	14 AQU
16 SAG	14 CAP	16 AQU	15 PIS	17 TAU	16 GEM	18 LEO	16 VIR	17 SCO	16 SAG	15 CAP	16 PIS
18 CAP	17 AQU	18 PIS	17 ARI	20 GEM	18 CAN	20 VIR	18 LIB	19 SAG	18 CAP	17 AQU	19 ARI
20 AQU	19 PIS	21 ARI	20 TAU	22 CAN	20 LEO	22 LIB	20 SCO	21 CAP	20 AQU	19 PIS	21 TAU
23 PIS	22 ARI	24 TAU	22 GEM	24 LEO	23 VIR	24 SCO	22 SAG	23 AQU	23 PIS	22 ARI	24 GEM
25 ARI	24 TAU	26 GEM	25 CAN	26 VIR	25 LIB	26 SAG	25 CAP	26 PIS	25 ARI	24 TAU	26 CAN
28 TAU	27 GEM	28 CAN	27 LEO	28 LIB	27 SCO	28 CAP	27 AQU	28 ARI	28 TAU	27 GEM	29 LEO
30 GEM	28 GEM	31 LEO	29 VIR	31 SCO	29 SAG	31 AQU	29 PIS	30 ARI	30 GEM	29 CAN	31 VIR
31 GEM			30 VIR		30 SAG		31 PIS		31 GEM	30 CAN	

1959

JAN	FEB	MAR	APR	MAY	JUN	JUL	AUG	SEP	OCT	NOV	DEC
1 VIR	1 SCO	1 SCO	1 CAP	1 AQU	1 ARI	1 TAU	1 GEM	1 LEO	1 VIR	1 SCO	1 SAG
2 LIB	3 SAG	2 SAG	2 AQU	2 PIS	3 TAU	3 GEM	2 CAN	3 VIR	2 LIB	3 SAG	2 CAP
4 SCO	5 CAP	4 CAP	5 PIS	4 ARI	6 GEM	6 CAN	4 LEO	5 LIB	4 SCO	5 CAP	4 AQU
6 SAG	7 AQU	6 AQU	7 ARI	7 TAU	8 CAN	8 LEO	7 VIR	7 SCO	7 SAG	7 AQU	7 PIS
8 CAP	9 PIS	9 PIS	10 TAU	9 GEM	11 LEO	10 VIR	9 LIB	9 SAG	9 CAP	9 PIS	9 ARI
11 AQU	12 ARI	11 ARI	12 GEM	12 CAN	13 VIR	13 LIB	11 SCO	11 CAP	11 AQU	12 ARI	11 TAU
13 PIS	14 TAU	13 TAU	15 CAN	14 LEO	15 LIB	15 SCO	13 SAG	14 AQU	13 PIS	14 TAU	14 GEM
15 ARI	17 GEM	16 GEM	17 LEO	17 VIR	17 SCO	17 SAG	15 CAP	16 PIS	15 ARI	17 GEM	16 CAN
18 TAU	19 CAN	18 CAN	19 VIR	19 LIB	19 SAG	19 CAP	17 AQU	18 ARI	18 TAU	19 CAN	19 LEO
20 GEM	21 LEO	21 LEO	22 LIB	21 SCO	21 CAP	21 AQU	19 PIS	20 TAU	20 GEM	22 LEO	21 VIR
23 CAN	24 VIR	23 VIR	24 SCO	23 SAG	23 AQU	23 PIS	22 ARI	23 GEM	23 CAN	24 VIR	24 LIB
25 LEO	26 LIB	25 LIB	26 SAG	25 CAP	26 PIS	25 ARI	24 TAU	25 CAN	25 LEO	26 LIB	26 SCO
27 VIR	28 SCO	27 SCO	28 CAP	27 AQU	28 ARI	28 TAU	27 GEM	28 LEO	28 VIR	28 SCO	28 SAG
29 LIB		29 SAG	30 AQU	29 PIS	30 TAU	30 GEM	29 CAN	30 VIR	30 LIB	30 SAG	30 CAP
31 LIB		31 CAP		31 PIS		31 GEM	31 CAN		31 LIB		31 CAP

1960

JAN	FEB	MAR	APR	MAY	JUN	JUL	AUG	SEP	OCT	NOV	DEC
1 AQU	1 PIS	1 ARI	1 GEM	1 CAN	1 LEO	1 VIR	1 SCO	1 CAP	1 AQU	1 ARI	1 TAU
3 PIS	2 ARI	2 TAU	4 CAN	3 LEO	2 VIR	2 LIB	3 SAG	3 AQU	2 PIS	3 TAU	3 GEM
5 ARI	4 TAU	5 GEM	6 LEO	6 VIR	5 LIB	4 SCO	5 CAP	5 PIS	5 ARI	5 GEM	5 CAN
8 TAU	6 GEM	7 CAN	9 VIR	8 LIB	7 SCO	6 SAG	7 AQU	7 ARI	7 TAU	8 CAN	8 LEO
10 GEM	9 CAN	10 LEO	11 LIB	10 SCO	9 SAG	8 CAP	9 PIS	9 TAU	9 GEM	10 LEO	10 VIR
13 CAN	11 LEO	12 VIR	13 SCO	12 SAG	11 CAP	10 AQU	11 ARI	12 GEM	12 CAN	13 VIR	13 LIB
15 LEO	14 VIR	14 LIB	15 SAG	14 CAP	13 AQU	12 PIS	13 TAU	14 CAN	14 LEO	15 LIB	15 SCO
18 VIR	16 LIB	17 SCO	17 CAP	16 AQU	15 PIS	14 ARI	15 GEM	17 LEO	17 VIR	18 SCO	17 SAG
20 LIB	18 SCO	19 SAG	19 AQU	19 PIS	17 ARI	17 TAU	18 CAN	19 VIR	19 LIB	20 SAG	19 CAP
22 SCO	20 SAG	21 CAP	21 PIS	21 ARI	19 TAU	19 GEM	20 LEO	22 LIB	21 SCO	22 CAP	21 AQU
24 SAG	23 CAP	23 AQU	24 ARI	23 TAU	22 GEM	22 CAN	23 VIR	24 SCO	23 SAG	24 AQU	23 PIS
26 CAP	25 AQU	25 PIS	26 TAU	26 GEM	24 CAN	24 LEO	25 LIB	26 SAG	25 CAP	26 PIS	25 ARI
28 AQU	27 PIS	27 ARI	28 GEM	28 CAN	27 LEO	27 VIR	28 SCO	28 CAP	28 AQU	28 ARI	28 TAU
30 PIS	29 ARI	30 TAU	30 GEM	31 LEO	29 VIR	29 LIB	30 SAG	30 AQU	30 PIS	30 TAU	30 GEM
31 PIS		31 TAU			30 VIR	31 SCO	31 SAG		31 PIS		31 GEM

1961

JAN	FEB	MAR	APR	MAY	JUN	JUL	AUG	SEP	OCT	NOV	DEC
1 GEM	1 LEO	1 LEO	1 LIB	1 SCO	1 CAP	1 AQU	1 ARI	1 TAU	1 CAN	1 LEO	1 VIR
2 CAN	3 VIR	2 VIR	3 SCO	3 SAG	3 AQU	3 PIS	3 TAU	2 GEM	4 LEO	3 VIR	3 LIB
4 LEO	5 LIB	5 LIB	5 SAG	5 CAP	5 PIS	5 ARI	5 GEM	4 CAN	6 VIR	5 LIB	5 SCO
7 VIR	8 SCO	7 SCO	8 CAP	7 AQU	7 ARI	7 TAU	8 CAN	7 LEO	9 LIB	8 SCO	7 SAG
9 LIB	10 SAG	9 SAG	10 AQU	9 PIS	10 TAU	9 GEM	10 LEO	9 VIR	11 SCO	10 SAG	10 CAP
11 SCO	12 CAP	11 CAP	12 PIS	11 ARI	12 GEM	12 CAN	13 VIR	12 LIB	14 SAG	12 CAP	12 AQU
14 SAG	14 AQU	13 AQU	14 ARI	13 TAU	14 CAN	14 LEO	15 LIB	14 SCO	16 CAP	14 AQU	14 PIS
16 CAP	16 PIS	16 PIS	16 TAU	16 GEM	17 LEO	17 VIR	18 SCO	16 SAG	18 AQU	17 PIS	16 ARI
18 AQU	18 ARI	18 ARI	18 GEM	18 CAN	19 VIR	19 LIB	20 SAG	19 CAP	20 PIS	19 ARI	18 TAU
20 PIS	20 TAU	20 TAU	21 CAN	21 LEO	22 LIB	22 SCO	22 CAP	21 AQU	22 ARI	21 TAU	20 GEM
22 ARI	23 GEM	22 GEM	23 LEO	23 VIR	24 SCO	24 SAG	24 AQU	23 PIS	24 TAU	23 GEM	23 CAN
24 TAU	25 CAN	24 CAN	26 VIR	26 LIB	27 SAG	26 CAP	26 PIS	25 ARI	27 GEM	25 CAN	25 LEO
26 GEM	28 LEO	27 LEO	28 LIB	28 SCO	29 CAP	28 AQU	28 ARI	27 TAU	29 CAN	28 LEO	27 VIR
29 CAN		29 VIR	30 LIB	30 SAG	30 CAP	30 PIS	31 TAU	29 GEM	31 LEO	30 VIR	30 LIB
31 LEO		31 VIR		31 SAG		31 PIS		30 GEM			31 LIB

1962

JAN	FEB	MAR	APR	MAY	JUN	JUL	AUG	SEP	OCT	NOV	DEC
1 SCO	1 SAG	1 SAG	1 AQU	1 PIS	1 TAU	1 GEM	1 LEO	1 VIR	1 SCO	1 SAG	1 CAP
4 SAG	2 CAP	2 CAP	2 PIS	2 AQU	2 GEM	2 CAN	3 VIR	2 LIB	4 SAG	3 CAP	2 AQU
6 CAP	4 AQU	4 AQU	4 ARI	4 TAU	4 CAN	4 LEO	5 LIB	4 SCO	6 CAP	5 AQU	4 PIS
8 AQU	6 PIS	6 PIS	6 TAU	6 GEM	7 LEO	7 VIR	8 SCO	7 SAG	9 AQU	7 PIS	6 ARI
10 PIS	8 ARI	8 ARI	8 GEM	8 CAN	9 VIR	9 LIB	10 SAG	9 CAP	11 PIS	9 ARI	9 TAU
12 ARI	11 TAU	10 TAU	11 CAN	10 LEO	12 LIB	12 SCO	13 CAP	11 AQU	13 ARI	11 TAU	11 GEM
14 TAU	13 GEM	12 GEM	13 LEO	13 VIR	14 SCO	14 SAG	15 AQU	13 PIS	15 TAU	13 GEM	13 CAN
16 GEM	15 CAN	14 CAN	16 VIR	15 LIB	17 SAG	16 CAP	17 PIS	15 ARI	17 GEM	15 CAN	15 LEO
19 CAN	18 LEO	17 LEO	18 LIB	18 SCO	19 CAP	18 AQU	19 ARI	17 TAU	19 CAN	17 LEO	17 VIR
21 LEO	20 VIR	19 VIR	21 SCO	20 SAG	21 AQU	20 PIS	21 TAU	19 GEM	21 LEO	20 VIR	20 LIB
24 VIR	23 LIB	22 LIB	23 SAG	23 CAP	23 PIS	23 ARI	23 GEM	22 CAN	24 VIR	22 LIB	22 SCO
26 LIB	25 SCO	24 SCO	25 CAP	25 AQU	25 ARI	25 TAU	25 CAN	24 LEO	26 LIB	25 SCO	25 SAG
29 SCO	27 SAG	27 SAG	28 AQU	27 PIS	27 TAU	27 GEM	28 LEO	26 VIR	29 SCO	27 SAG	27 CAP
31 SAG	28 SAG	29 CAP	30 PIS	29 ARI	30 GEM	29 CAN	30 VIR	29 LIB	31 SAG	30 CAP	29 AQU
		31 AQU		31 TAU		31 LEO	31 VIR	30 LIB			31 AQU

1963

JAN	FEB	MAR	APR	MAY	JUN	JUL	AUG	SEP	OCT	NOV	DEC
1 PIS	1 TAU	1 TAU	1 CAN	1 LEO	1 VIR	1 SCO	1 SAG	1 AQU	1 PIS	1 ARI	1 GEM
3 ARI	3 GEM	2 GEM	3 LEO	3 VIR	2 LIB	4 SAG	3 CAP	4 PIS	3 ARI	2 TAU	3 CAN
5 TAU	5 CAN	5 CAN	6 VIR	5 LIB	4 SCO	6 CAP	5 AQU	6 ARI	5 TAU	3 GEM	5 LEO
7 GEM	8 LEO	7 LEO	8 LIB	8 SCO	7 SAG	9 AQU	7 PIS	8 TAU	7 GEM	6 CAN	7 VIR
9 CAN	10 VIR	9 VIR	11 SCO	10 SAG	9 CAP	11 PIS	9 ARI	10 GEM	9 CAN	8 LEO	10 LIB
11 LEO	12 LIB	12 LIB	13 SAG	13 CAP	11 AQU	13 ARI	11 TAU	12 CAN	11 LEO	10 VIR	12 SCO
14 VIR	15 SCO	14 SCO	16 CAP	15 AQU	14 PIS	15 TAU	14 GEM	14 LEO	14 VIR	12 LIB	15 SAG
16 LIB	17 SAG	17 SAG	18 AQU	17 PIS	16 ARI	17 GEM	16 CAN	16 VIR	16 LIB	15 SCO	17 CAP
19 SCO	20 CAP	19 CAP	20 PIS	20 ARI	18 TAU	19 CAN	18 LEO	19 LIB	19 SCO	17 SAG	20 AQU
21 SAG	22 AQU	22 AQU	22 ARI	22 TAU	20 GEM	22 LEO	20 VIR	21 SCO	21 SAG	20 CAP	22 PIS
23 CAP	24 PIS	24 PIS	24 TAU	24 GEM	22 CAN	24 VIR	23 LIB	24 SAG	24 CAP	22 AQU	24 ARI
26 AQU	26 ARI	26 ARI	26 GEM	26 CAN	24 LEO	26 LIB	25 SCO	26 CAP	26 AQU	25 PIS	26 TAU
28 PIS	28 TAU	28 TAU	28 CAN	28 LEO	26 VIR	29 SCO	28 SAG	29 AQU	28 PIS	27 ARI	28 GEM
30 ARI		30 GEM	30 LEO	30 VIR	29 LIB	31 SAG	30 CAP	30 AQU	31 ARI	29 TAU	30 CAN
31 ARI		31 GEM		31 VIR	30 LIB		31 CAP			30 TAU	31 CAN

1964

JAN	FEB	MAR	APR	MAY	JUN	JUL	AUG	SEP	OCT	NOV	DEC
1 LEO	1 VIR	1 LIB	1 SCO	1 SAG	1 AQU	1 PIS	1 TAU	1 GEM	1 LEO	1 VIR	1 SCO
4 VIR	2 LIB	3 SCO	2 SAG	2 CAP	3 PIS	3 ARI	3 GEM	2 CAN	3 VIR	2 LIB	4 SAG
6 LIB	5 SCO	6 SAG	4 CAP	4 AQU	5 ARI	5 TAU	5 CAN	4 LEO	5 LIB	4 SCO	6 CAP
8 SCO	7 SAG	8 CAP	7 AQU	7 PIS	7 TAU	7 GEM	7 LEO	6 VIR	8 SCO	6 SAG	9 AQU
11 SAG	10 CAP	11 AQU	9 PIS	9 ARI	9 GEM	9 CAN	9 VIR	8 LIB	10 SAG	9 CAP	11 PIS
13 CAP	12 AQU	13 PIS	11 ARI	11 TAU	11 CAN	11 LEO	11 LIB	10 SCO	12 CAP	11 AQU	14 ARI
16 AQU	15 PIS	15 ARI	14 TAU	13 GEM	13 LEO	13 VIR	14 SCO	13 SAG	15 AQU	14 PIS	16 TAU
18 PIS	17 ARI	17 TAU	16 GEM	15 CAN	16 VIR	15 LIB	16 SAG	15 CAP	17 PIS	16 ARI	18 GEM
20 ARI	19 TAU	19 GEM	18 CAN	17 LEO	18 LIB	17 SCO	19 CAP	18 AQU	20 ARI	18 TAU	20 CAN
23 TAU	21 GEM	21 CAN	20 LEO	19 VIR	20 SCO	20 SAG	21 AQU	20 PIS	22 TAU	20 GEM	22 LEO
25 GEM	23 CAN	24 LEO	22 VIR	22 LIB	23 SAG	23 CAP	24 PIS	22 ARI	24 GEM	22 CAN	24 VIR
27 CAN	25 LEO	26 VIR	24 LIB	24 SCO	25 CAP	25 AQU	26 ARI	24 TAU	26 CAN	24 LEO	26 LIB
29 LEO	27 VIR	28 LIB	27 SCO	26 SAG	28 AQU	27 PIS	28 TAU	27 GEM	28 LEO	27 VIR	28 SCO
31 VIR	29 VIR	30 SCO	29 SAG	29 CAP	30 PIS	30 ARI	30 GEM	29 CAN	30 VIR	29 LIB	31 SAG
		31 SCO	30 SAG	31 CAP		31 ARI	31 GEM	30 CAN	31 VIR	30 LIB	

1965

JAN	FEB	MAR	APR	MAY	JUN	JUL	AUG	SEP	OCT	NOV	DEC
1 SAG	1 AQU	1 AQU	1 PIS	1 TAU	1 GEM	1 LEO	1 VIR	1 SCO	1 SAG	1 AQU	1 PIS
2 CAP	4 PIS	3 PIS	2 ARI	3 GEM	2 CAN	3 VIR	2 LIB	2 SAG	2 CAP	4 PIS	3 ARI
5 AQU	6 ARI	5 ARI	4 TAU	5 CAN	4 LEO	5 LIB	4 SCO	5 CAP	5 AQU	6 ARI	6 TAU
7 PIS	8 TAU	8 TAU	6 GEM	8 LEO	6 VIR	8 SCO	6 SAG	7 AQU	7 PIS	8 TAU	8 GEM
10 ARI	11 GEM	10 GEM	8 CAN	10 VIR	8 LIB	10 SAG	9 CAP	10 PIS	10 ARI	11 GEM	10 CAN
12 TAU	13 CAN	12 CAN	10 LEO	12 LIB	10 SCO	12 CAP	11 AQU	12 ARI	12 TAU	13 CAN	12 LEO
14 GEM	15 LEO	14 LEO	12 VIR	14 SCO	13 SAG	15 AQU	14 PIS	15 TAU	14 GEM	15 LEO	14 VIR
16 CAN	17 VIR	16 VIR	15 LIB	16 SAG	15 CAP	17 PIS	16 ARI	17 GEM	17 CAN	17 VIR	16 LIB
18 LEO	19 LIB	18 LIB	17 SCO	19 CAP	18 AQU	20 ARI	19 TAU	19 CAN	19 LEO	19 LIB	19 SCO
20 VIR	21 SCO	20 SCO	19 SAG	21 AQU	20 PIS	22 TAU	21 GEM	21 LEO	21 VIR	21 SCO	21 SAG
22 LIB	23 SAG	23 SAG	22 CAP	24 PIS	23 ARI	25 GEM	23 CAN	23 VIR	23 LIB	24 SAG	23 CAP
25 SCO	26 CAP	25 CAP	24 AQU	26 ARI	25 TAU	27 CAN	25 LEO	26 LIB	25 SCO	26 CAP	26 AQU
27 SAG	28 AQU	28 AQU	27 PIS	29 TAU	27 GEM	29 LEO	27 VIR	28 SCO	27 SAG	28 AQU	28 PIS
30 CAP		30 PIS	29 ARI	31 GEM	29 CAN	31 VIR	29 LIB	30 SAG	30 CAP	30 AQU	31 ARI
31 CAP		31 PIS	30 ARI		30 CAN		31 SCO		31 CAP		

1966

JAN	FEB	MAR	APR	MAY	JUN	JUL	AUG	SEP	OCT	NOV	DEC
1 ARI	1 GEM	1 GEM	1 LEO	1 VIR	1 SCO	1 SAG	1 AQU	1 PIS	1 ARI	1 GEM	1 CAN
2 TAU	3 CAN	2 CAN	3 VIR	2 LIB	3 SAG	2 CAP	4 PIS	2 ARI	2 TAU	3 CAN	3 LEO
5 GEM	5 LEO	5 LEO	5 LIB	4 SCO	5 CAP	5 AQU	6 ARI	5 TAU	5 GEM	5 LEO	5 VIR
7 CAN	7 VIR	7 VIR	7 SCO	7 SAG	8 AQU	7 PIS	9 TAU	7 GEM	7 CAN	8 VIR	7 LIB
9 LEO	9 LIB	8 LIB	9 SAG	9 CAP	10 PIS	10 ARI	11 GEM	10 CAN	9 LEO	10 LIB	9 SCO
11 VIR	11 SCO	11 SCO	11 CAP	11 AQU	13 ARI	12 TAU	13 CAN	12 LEO	11 VIR	12 SCO	11 SAG
13 LIB	13 SAG	13 SAG	14 AQU	14 PIS	15 TAU	15 GEM	15 LEO	14 VIR	13 LIB	14 SAG	13 CAP
15 SCO	16 CAP	15 CAP	16 PIS	16 ARI	17 GEM	17 CAN	17 VIR	16 LIB	15 SCO	16 CAP	16 AQU
17 SAG	18 AQU	18 AQU	19 ARI	19 TAU	20 CAN	19 LEO	19 LIB	18 SCO	17 SAG	18 AQU	18 PIS
20 CAP	21 PIS	20 PIS	21 TAU	21 GEM	22 LEO	21 VIR	21 SCO	20 SAG	20 CAP	21 PIS	21 ARI
22 AQU	23 ARI	23 ARI	24 GEM	23 CAN	24 VIR	23 LIB	24 SAG	22 CAP	22 AQU	23 ARI	23 TAU
25 PIS	26 TAU	25 TAU	26 CAN	25 LEO	26 LIB	25 SCO	26 CAP	25 AQU	24 PIS	26 TAU	26 GEM
27 ARI	28 GEM	27 GEM	28 LEO	27 VIR	28 SCO	27 SAG	28 AQU	27 PIS	27 ARI	28 GEM	28 CAN
30 TAU		30 CAN	30 VIR	30 LIB	30 SAG	30 CAP	31 PIS	30 ARI	29 TAU	30 CAN	30 LEO
31 TAU		31 CAN		31 LIB		31 CAP			31 TAU		31 LEO

1967

JAN	FEB	MAR	APR	MAY	JUN	JUL	AUG	SEP	OCT	NOV	DEC
1 VIR	1 LIB	1 SCO	1 SAG	1 AQU	1 PIS	1 ARI	1 GEM	1 CAN	1 LEO	1 LIB	1 SCO
3 LIB	2 SCO	3 SAG	2 CAP	4 PIS	2 ARI	2 TAU	3 CAN	2 LEO	2 VIR	2 SCO	2 SAG
5 SCO	4 SAG	5 CAP	4 AQU	6 ARI	5 TAU	5 GEM	6 LEO	4 VIR	4 LIB	4 SAG	4 CAP
8 SAG	6 CAP	8 AQU	6 PIS	9 TAU	7 GEM	7 CAN	8 VIR	6 LIB	6 SCO	6 CAP	6 AQU
10 CAP	8 AQU	10 PIS	9 ARI	11 GEM	10 CAN	9 LEO	10 LIB	8 SCO	8 SAG	8 AQU	8 PIS
12 AQU	11 PIS	13 ARI	11 TAU	14 CAN	12 LEO	12 VIR	12 SCO	10 SAG	10 CAP	11 PIS	10 ARI
14 PIS	13 ARI	15 TAU	14 GEM	16 LEO	14 VIR	14 LIB	14 SAG	13 CAP	12 AQU	13 ARI	13 TAU
17 ARI	16 TAU	18 GEM	16 CAN	18 VIR	16 LIB	16 SCO	16 CAP	15 AQU	14 PIS	16 TAU	15 GEM
19 TAU	18 GEM	20 CAN	19 LEO	20 LIB	19 SCO	18 SAG	19 AQU	17 PIS	17 ARI	18 GEM	18 CAN
22 GEM	21 CAN	22 LEO	21 VIR	22 SCO	21 SAG	20 CAP	21 PIS	20 ARI	19 TAU	21 CAN	20 LEO
24 CAN	23 LEO	24 VIR	23 LIB	24 SAG	23 CAP	22 AQU	23 ARI	22 TAU	22 GEM	23 LEO	23 VIR
26 LEO	25 VIR	26 LIB	25 SCO	26 CAP	25 AQU	25 PIS	26 TAU	25 GEM	24 CAN	25 VIR	25 LIB
28 VIR	27 LIB	28 SCO	27 SAG	28 AQU	27 PIS	27 ARI	28 GEM	27 CAN	27 LEO	28 LIB	27 SCO
30 LIB	28 LIB	30 SAG	29 CAP	31 PIS	30 ARI	30 TAU	31 CAN	29 LEO	29 VIR	30 SCO	29 SAG
31 LIB		31 SAG	30 CAP			31 TAU		30 LEO	31 LIB		31 CAP

1968

JAN	FEB	MAR	APR	MAY	JUN	JUL	AUG	SEP	OCT	NOV	DEC
1 CAP	1 PIS	1 ARI	1 TAU	1 GEM	1 LEO	1 VIR	1 LIB	1 SAG	1 AQU	1 PIS	1 ARI
2 AQU	3 ARI	4 TAU	3 GEM	3 CAN	4 VIR	3 LIB	2 SCO	2 CAP	4 PIS	2 ARI	2 TAU
4 PIS	6 TAU	6 GEM	5 CAN	5 LEO	6 LIB	5 SCO	4 SAG	4 AQU	6 ARI	5 TAU	4 GEM
7 ARI	8 GEM	9 CAN	8 LEO	7 VIR	8 SCO	7 SAG	6 CAP	6 PIS	8 TAU	7 GEM	7 CAN
9 TAU	11 CAN	11 LEO	10 VIR	10 LIB	10 SAG	9 CAP	8 AQU	9 ARI	11 GEM	10 CAN	9 LEO
12 GEM	13 LEO	14 VIR	12 LIB	12 SCO	12 CAP	11 AQU	10 PIS	11 TAU	13 CAN	12 LEO	12 VIR
14 CAN	15 VIR	16 LIB	14 SCO	14 SAG	14 AQU	14 PIS	12 ARI	13 GEM	16 LEO	15 VIR	14 LIB
17 LEO	17 LIB	18 SCO	16 SAG	16 CAP	16 PIS	16 ARI	15 TAU	16 CAN	18 VIR	17 LIB	16 SCO
19 VIR	19 SCO	20 SAG	18 SCO	18 AQU	19 ARI	18 TAU	17 GEM	18 LEO	20 LIB	19 SCO	18 SAG
21 LIB	22 SAG	22 CAP	20 AQU	20 PIS	21 TAU	21 GEM	20 CAN	21 VIR	23 SCO	21 SAG	20 CAP
23 SCO	24 CAP	24 AQU	23 PIS	22 ARI	24 GEM	23 CAN	22 LEO	23 LIB	25 SAG	23 CAP	22 AQU
25 SAG	26 AQU	26 PIS	25 ARI	25 TAU	26 CAN	26 LEO	24 VIR	25 SCO	27 CAP	25 AQU	24 PIS
27 CAP	28 PIS	29 ARI	28 TAU	27 GEM	29 LEO	28 VIR	27 LIB	27 SAG	29 AQU	27 PIS	27 ARI
30 AQU	29 PIS	31 TAU	30 GEM	30 CAN	30 LEO	30 LIB	29 SCO	29 CAP	31 PIS	29 ARI	29 TAU
31 AQU				31 CAN		31 LIB	31 SAG	30 CAP		30 ARI	31 TAU

1969

JAN	FEB	MAR	APR	MAY	JUN	JUL	AUG	SEP	OCT	NOV	DEC
1 GEM	1 CAN	1 LEO	1 VIR	1 LIB	1 SAG	1 CAP	1 PIS	1 TAU	1 GEM	1 CAN	1 LEO
3 CAN	2 LEO	4 VIR	2 LIB	2 SCO	2 CAP	2 AQU	2 ARI	3 GEM	3 CAN	2 LEO	2 VIR
6 LEO	4 VIR	6 LIB	5 SCO	4 SAG	4 AQU	4 PIS	4 TAU	6 CAN	6 LEO	5 VIR	4 LIB
8 VIR	7 LIB	8 SCO	7 SAG	6 CAP	6 PIS	6 ARI	6 GEM	8 LEO	8 VIR	7 LIB	7 SCO
10 LIB	9 SCO	10 SAG	9 CAP	8 AQU	9 ARI	8 TAU	9 CAN	11 VIR	11 LIB	9 SCO	9 SAG
13 SCO	11 SAG	12 CAP	11 AQU	10 PIS	11 TAU	11 GEM	12 LEO	13 LIB	13 SCO	11 SAG	11 CAP
15 SAG	13 CAP	15 AQU	13 PIS	12 ARI	13 GEM	13 CAN	15 VIR	16 SCO	15 SAG	13 CAP	13 AQU
17 CAP	15 AQU	17 PIS	15 ARI	15 TAU	16 CAN	16 LEO	17 LIB	18 SAG	17 CAP	15 AQU	15 PIS
19 AQU	17 PIS	19 ARI	18 TAU	17 GEM	19 LEO	18 VIR	19 SCO	20 CAP	19 AQU	18 PIS	17 ARI
21 PIS	19 ARI	21 TAU	20 GEM	20 CAN	21 VIR	21 LIB	22 SAG	22 AQU	21 PIS	20 ARI	19 TAU
23 ARI	22 TAU	24 GEM	22 CAN	22 LEO	23 LIB	23 SCO	24 CAP	24 PIS	24 ARI	22 TAU	22 GEM
25 TAU	24 GEM	26 CAN	25 LEO	25 VIR	26 SCO	25 SAG	26 AQU	26 ARI	26 TAU	24 GEM	24 CAN
28 GEM	27 CAN	29 LEO	27 VIR	27 LIB	28 SAG	27 CAP	28 PIS	28 TAU	28 GEM	27 CAN	27 LEO
30 CAN	28 CAN	31 VIR	30 LIB	29 SCO	30 CAP	29 AQU	30 ARI	30 TAU	30 CAN	29 LEO	29 VIR
31 CAN				31 SAG		31 PIS	31 ARI		31 CAN	30 LEO	31 VIR

1970

JAN	FEB	MAR	APR	MAY	JUN	JUL	AUG	SEP	OCT	NOV	DEC
1 LIB	1 SCO	1 SAG	1 AQU	1 PIS	1 TAU	1 GEM	1 CAN	1 VIR	1 LIB	1 SCO	1 CAP
3 SCO	2 SAG	3 CAP	4 PIS	3 ARI	4 GEM	3 CAN	2 LEO	3 LIB	3 SCO	2 SAG	3 AQU
5 SAG	4 CAP	5 AQU	6 ARI	5 TAU	6 CAN	6 LEO	4 VIR	6 SCO	5 SAG	4 CAP	5 PIS
7 CAP	6 AQU	7 PIS	8 TAU	7 GEM	8 LEO	8 VIR	7 LIB	8 SAG	8 CAP	6 AQU	8 ARI
9 AQU	8 PIS	9 ARI	10 GEM	10 CAN	11 VIR	11 LIB	9 SCO	10 CAP	10 AQU	8 PIS	10 TAU
11 PIS	10 ARI	11 TAU	12 CAN	12 LEO	13 LIB	13 SCO	12 SAG	12 AQU	12 PIS	10 ARI	12 GEM
13 ARI	12 TAU	13 GEM	15 LEO	15 VIR	16 SCO	15 SAG	14 CAP	14 PIS	14 ARI	12 TAU	14 CAN
16 TAU	14 GEM	16 CAN	17 VIR	17 LIB	18 SAG	18 CAP	16 AQU	16 ARI	16 TAU	14 GEM	16 LEO
18 GEM	17 CAN	18 LEO	20 LIB	19 SCO	20 CAP	20 AQU	18 PIS	19 TAU	18 GEM	17 CAN	19 VIR
20 CAN	19 LEO	21 VIR	22 SCO	22 SAG	22 AQU	22 PIS	20 ARI	21 GEM	20 CAN	19 LEO	22 LIB
23 LEO	22 VIR	23 LIB	24 SAG	24 CAP	24 PIS	24 ARI	22 TAU	23 CAN	23 LEO	22 VIR	24 SCO
25 VIR	24 LIB	26 SCO	27 CAP	26 AQU	26 ARI	26 TAU	24 GEM	25 LEO	25 VIR	24 LIB	26 SAG
28 LIB	27 SCO	28 SAG	29 AQU	28 PIS	29 TAU	28 GEM	27 CAN	28 VIR	28 LIB	27 SCO	29 CAP
30 SCO	28 SCO	30 CAP	31 AQU	30 ARI	30 TAU	30 CAN	29 LEO	30 VIR	30 SCO	29 SAG	31 AQU
31 SCO		31 CAP		31 ARI		31 CAN	31 LEO		31 SCO	30 SAG	

1971

JAN	FEB	MAR	APR	MAY	JUN	JUL	AUG	SEP	OCT	NOV	DEC
1 AQU	1 ARI	1 TAU	1 GEM	1 CAN	1 VIR	1 LIB	1 SCO	1 CAP	1 AQU	1 ARI	1 TAU
2 PIS	2 TAU	4 GEM	2 CAN	2 LEO	3 LIB	3 SCO	2 SAG	3 AQU	2 PIS	3 TAU	2 GEM
4 ARI	4 GEM	6 CAN	5 LEO	4 VIR	6 SCO	5 SAG	4 CAP	5 PIS	4 ARI	5 GEM	4 CAN
6 TAU	7 CAN	8 LEO	7 VIR	7 LIB	8 SAG	8 CAP	6 AQU	7 ARI	6 TAU	7 CAN	6 LEO
8 GEM	9 LEO	11 VIR	10 LIB	9 SCO	10 CAP	10 AQU	8 PIS	9 TAU	8 GEM	9 LEO	9 VIR
10 CAN	12 VIR	13 LIB	12 SCO	12 SAG	13 AQU	12 PIS	10 ARI	11 GEM	10 CAN	11 VIR	11 LIB
13 LEO	14 LIB	16 SCO	15 SAG	14 CAP	15 PIS	14 ARI	13 TAU	13 CAN	13 LEO	14 LIB	14 SCO
15 VIR	17 SCO	18 SAG	17 CAP	16 AQU	17 ARI	16 TAU	15 GEM	15 LEO	15 VIR	16 SCO	16 SAG
18 LIB	19 SAG	21 CAP	19 AQU	19 PIS	19 TAU	18 GEM	17 CAN	18 VIR	18 LIB	19 SAG	19 CAP
20 SCO	21 CAP	23 AQU	21 PIS	21 ARI	21 GEM	21 CAN	19 LEO	20 LIB	20 SCO	21 CAP	21 AQU
23 SAG	23 AQU	25 PIS	23 ARI	23 TAU	23 CAN	23 LEO	22 VIR	23 SCO	23 SAG	24 AQU	23 PIS
25 CAP	26 PIS	27 ARI	25 TAU	25 GEM	26 LEO	25 VIR	24 LIB	25 SAG	25 CAP	26 PIS	25 ARI
27 AQU	27 ARI	29 TAU	27 GEM	27 CAN	28 VIR	28 LIB	27 SCO	28 CAP	28 AQU	28 ARI	27 TAU
29 PIS	28 ARI	31 GEM	30 CAN	29 LEO	30 VIR	30 SCO	29 SAG	30 AQU	30 PIS	30 TAU	30 GEM
31 ARI				31 LEO		31 SCO	31 SAG		31 PIS		31 GEM

1972

JAN	FEB	MAR	APR	MAY	JUN	JUL	AUG	SEP	OCT	NOV	DEC
1 CAN	1 LEO	1 VIR	1 SCO	1 SAG	1 CAP	1 AQU	1 ARI	1 GEM	1 CAN	1 VIR	1 LIB
3 LEO	2 VIR	2 LIB	4 SAG	3 CAP	2 AQU	2 PIS	2 TAU	3 CAN	2 LEO	3 LIB	3 SCO
5 VIR	4 LIB	5 SCO	6 CAP	6 AQU	4 PIS	4 ARI	4 GEM	5 LEO	4 VIR	5 SCO	5 SAG
8 LIB	6 SCO	7 SAG	8 AQU	8 PIS	7 ARI	6 TAU	6 CAN	7 VIR	7 LIB	8 SAG	8 CAP
10 SCO	9 SAG	10 CAP	11 PIS	10 ARI	9 TAU	8 GEM	8 LEO	9 LIB	9 SCO	10 CAP	10 AQU
13 SAG	11 CAP	12 AQU	13 ARI	12 TAU	11 GEM	10 CAN	11 VIR	12 SCO	12 SAG	13 AQU	13 PIS
15 CAP	14 AQU	14 PIS	15 TAU	14 GEM	13 CAN	12 LEO	13 LIB	14 SAG	14 CAP	15 PIS	15 ARI
17 AQU	16 PIS	16 ARI	17 GEM	16 CAN	15 LEO	14 VIR	16 SCO	17 CAP	17 AQU	18 ARI	17 TAU
19 PIS	18 ARI	18 TAU	19 CAN	18 LEO	17 VIR	17 LIB	18 SAG	19 AQU	19 PIS	20 TAU	19 GEM
22 ARI	20 TAU	20 GEM	21 LEO	21 VIR	19 LIB	19 SCO	21 CAP	22 PIS	21 ARI	22 GEM	21 CAN
24 TAU	22 GEM	22 CAN	23 VIR	23 LIB	22 SCO	22 SAG	23 AQU	24 ARI	23 TAU	24 CAN	23 LEO
26 GEM	24 CAN	25 LEO	26 LIB	26 SCO	24 SAG	24 CAP	25 PIS	26 TAU	25 GEM	26 LEO	25 VIR
28 CAN	27 LEO	27 VIR	28 SCO	28 SAG	27 CAP	27 AQU	27 ARI	28 GEM	27 CAN	28 VIR	27 LIB
30 LEO	29 VIR	30 LIB	30 SCO	31 CAP	29 AQU	29 PIS	29 TAU	30 CAN	29 LEO	30 LIB	30 SCO
31 LEO		31 LIB			30 AQU	31 ARI	31 GEM		31 LEO		31 SCO

1973

JAN	FEB	MAR	APR	MAY	JUN	JUL	AUG	SEP	OCT	NOV	DEC
1 SAG	1 CAP	1 CAP	1 PIS	1 ARI	1 GEM	1 CAN	1 VIR	1 LIB	1 SAG	1 CAP	1 AQU
4 CAP	3 AQU	2 AQU	3 ARI	3 TAU	3 CAN	2 LEO	3 LIB	2 SCO	4 CAP	3 AQU	3 PIS
6 AQU	5 PIS	4 PIS	5 TAU	5 GEM	5 LEO	4 VIR	5 SCO	4 SAG	7 AQU	5 PIS	5 ARI
9 PIS	7 ARI	7 ARI	7 GEM	7 CAN	7 VIR	7 LIB	8 SAG	7 CAP	9 PIS	8 ARI	7 TAU
11 ARI	10 TAU	9 TAU	9 CAN	9 LEO	9 LIB	9 SCO	10 CAP	9 AQU	11 ARI	10 TAU	9 GEM
13 TAU	12 GEM	11 GEM	11 LEO	11 VIR	12 SCO	12 SAG	13 AQU	12 PIS	13 TAU	12 GEM	11 CAN
15 GEM	14 CAN	13 CAN	14 VIR	13 LIB	14 SAG	14 CAP	15 PIS	14 ARI	16 GEM	14 CAN	13 LEO
17 CAN	16 LEO	15 LEO	16 LIB	16 SCO	17 CAP	17 AQU	18 ARI	16 TAU	18 CAN	16 LEO	15 VIR
19 LEO	18 VIR	17 VIR	18 SCO	18 SAG	19 AQU	19 PIS	20 TAU	18 GEM	20 LEO	18 VIR	18 LIB
22 VIR	20 LIB	20 LIB	21 SAG	21 CAP	22 PIS	21 ARI	22 GEM	20 CAN	22 VIR	20 LIB	20 SCO
24 LIB	23 SCO	22 SCO	23 CAP	23 AQU	24 ARI	24 TAU	24 CAN	23 LEO	24 LIB	23 SCO	22 SAG
26 SCO	25 SAG	24 SAG	26 AQU	26 PIS	26 TAU	26 GEM	26 LEO	25 VIR	26 SCO	25 SAG	25 CAP
29 SAG	28 CAP	27 CAP	28 PIS	28 ARI	28 GEM	28 CAN	28 VIR	27 LIB	29 SAG	28 CAP	27 AQU
31 CAP		29 AQU	30 ARI	30 TAU	30 CAN	30 LEO	30 LIB	29 SCO	31 CAP	30 AQU	30 PIS
		31 AQU		31 TAU		31 LEO	31 LIB	30 SCO			31 PIS

1974

JAN	FEB	MAR	APR	MAY	JUN	JUL	AUG	SEP	OCT	NOV	DEC
1 ARI	1 TAU	1 GEM	1 CAN	1 VIR	1 LIB	1 CAP	1 CAP	1 AQU	1 ARI	1 TAU	1 GEM
4 TAU	2 GEM	4 CAN	2 LEO	3 LIB	3 SCO	2 SAG	3 AQU	2 PIS	4 TAU	2 GEM	2 CAN
6 GEM	4 CAN	6 LEO	4 VIR	6 SCO	5 SAG	4 CAP	5 PIS	4 ARI	6 GEM	4 CAN	4 LEO
8 CAN	6 LEO	8 VIR	6 LIB	8 SAG	7 CAP	7 AQU	8 ARI	6 TAU	8 CAN	7 LEO	6 VIR
10 LEO	8 VIR	10 LIB	8 SCO	10 CAP	9 AQU	9 PIS	10 TAU	9 GEM	10 LEO	9 VIR	8 LIB
12 VIR	10 LIB	12 SCO	11 SAG	13 AQU	12 PIS	12 ARI	13 GEM	11 CAN	12 VIR	11 LIB	10 SCO
14 LIB	13 SCO	14 SAG	13 CAP	15 PIS	14 ARI	14 TAU	15 CAN	13 LEO	15 LIB	13 SCO	13 SAG
16 SCO	15 SAG	17 CAP	16 AQU	18 ARI	17 TAU	16 GEM	17 LEO	15 VIR	17 SCO	15 SAG	15 CAP
19 SAG	17 CAP	19 AQU	18 PIS	20 TAU	19 GEM	18 CAN	19 VIR	17 LIB	19 SAG	18 CAP	17 AQU
21 CAP	20 AQU	22 PIS	21 ARI	22 GEM	21 CAN	20 LEO	21 LIB	19 SCO	21 CAP	20 AQU	20 PIS
24 AQU	22 PIS	24 ARI	23 TAU	24 CAN	23 LEO	22 VIR	23 SCO	21 SAG	24 AQU	23 PIS	22 ARI
26 PIS	25 ARI	26 TAU	25 GEM	26 LEO	25 VIR	24 LIB	25 SAG	24 CAP	26 PIS	25 ARI	25 TAU
29 ARI	27 TAU	29 GEM	27 CAN	29 VIR	27 LIB	26 SCO	28 CAP	26 AQU	29 ARI	27 TAU	27 GEM
31 TAU	28 TAU	31 CAN	29 LEO	31 LIB	29 SCO	29 SAG	30 AQU	29 PIS	31 TAU	30 GEM	29 CAN
			30 LEO		30 SCO	31 CAP	31 AQU	30 PIS			30 LEO

1975

JAN	FEB	MAR	APR	MAY	JUN	JUL	AUG	SEP	OCT	NOV	DEC
1 LEO	1 LIB	1 LIB	1 SAG	1 CAP	1 AQU	1 ARI	1 TAU	1 CAN	1 LEO	1 LIB	1 SCO
2 VIR	3 SCO	2 SCO	3 CAP	3 AQU	2 PIS	4 TAU	3 GEM	3 LEO	3 VIR	3 SCO	3 SAG
4 LIB	5 SAG	4 SAG	5 AQU	5 PIS	4 ARI	6 GEM	5 CAN	5 VIR	5 LIB	5 SAG	5 CAP
6 SCO	7 CAP	7 CAP	8 PIS	8 ARI	7 TAU	9 CAN	7 LEO	7 LIB	7 SCO	8 CAP	7 AQU
9 SAG	10 AQU	9 AQU	10 ARI	10 GEM	9 GEM	11 LEO	9 VIR	9 SCO	9 SAG	10 AQU	10 PIS
11 CAP	12 PIS	12 PIS	13 TAU	13 CAN	11 CAN	13 VIR	11 LIB	12 SAG	11 CAP	12 PIS	12 ARI
14 AQU	15 ARI	14 ARI	15 GEM	15 LEO	13 LEO	15 LIB	13 SCO	14 CAP	14 AQU	15 ARI	15 TAU
16 PIS	17 TAU	17 TAU	18 CAN	17 VIR	15 VIR	17 SCO	15 SAG	16 AQU	16 PIS	17 TAU	17 GEM
19 ARI	20 GEM	19 GEM	20 LEO	19 LIB	17 LIB	19 SAG	18 CAP	19 PIS	19 ARI	20 GEM	19 CAN
21 TAU	22 CAN	21 CAN	22 VIR	21 SCO	20 SCO	21 CAP	20 AQU	21 ARI	21 TAU	22 CAN	22 LEO
23 GEM	24 LEO	24 LEO	24 LIB	23 SAG	22 SAG	24 AQU	22 PIS	24 TAU	23 GEM	24 LEO	24 VIR
26 CAN	26 VIR	26 VIR	26 SCO	25 CAP	24 CAP	26 PIS	25 ARI	26 GEM	26 CAN	27 VIR	26 LIB
28 LEO	28 LIB	28 LIB	28 SAG	28 AQU	26 AQU	29 ARI	28 TAU	29 CAN	28 LEO	29 LIB	28 SCO
30 VIR		30 SCO	30 CAP	30 AQU	29 PIS	31 TAU	30 GEM	30 CAN	30 VIR	30 LIB	30 SAG
31 VIR		31 SCO		31 AQU	30 PIS		31 GEM		31 VIR		31 SAG

1976

JAN	FEB	MAR	APR	MAY	JUN	JUL	AUG	SEP	OCT	NOV	DEC
1 CAP	1 AQU	1 PIS	1 ARI	1 TAU	1 CAN	1 LEO	1 LIB	1 SAG	1 CAP	1 PIS	1 ARI
4 AQU	2 PIS	3 ARI	2 TAU	2 GEM	3 LEO	2 VIR	3 SCO	3 CAP	3 AQU	4 ARI	3 TAU
6 PIS	5 ARI	6 TAU	4 GEM	4 CAN	5 VIR	4 LIB	5 SAG	5 AQU	5 PIS	6 TAU	6 GEM
8 ARI	7 TAU	8 GEM	7 CAN	6 LEO	7 LIB	6 SCO	7 CAP	8 PIS	7 ARI	9 GEM	9 CAN
11 TAU	10 GEM	11 CAN	9 LEO	9 VIR	9 SCO	9 SAG	9 AQU	10 ARI	10 TAU	11 CAN	11 LEO
13 GEM	12 CAN	13 LEO	11 VIR	11 LIB	11 SAG	11 CAP	11 PIS	13 TAU	13 GEM	14 LEO	13 VIR
16 CAN	14 LEO	15 VIR	13 LIB	13 SCO	13 CAP	13 AQU	14 ARI	15 GEM	15 CAN	16 VIR	15 LIB
18 LEO	16 VIR	17 LIB	15 SCO	15 SAG	15 AQU	15 PIS	16 TAU	18 CAN	17 LEO	18 LIB	18 SCO
20 VIR	18 LIB	19 SCO	17 SAG	17 CAP	18 PIS	18 ARI	19 GEM	20 LEO	20 VIR	20 SCO	20 SAG
22 LIB	21 SCO	21 SAG	19 CAP	19 AQU	20 ARI	20 TAU	21 CAN	22 VIR	22 LIB	22 SAG	22 CAP
24 SCO	23 SAG	23 CAP	22 AQU	21 PIS	23 TAU	23 GEM	24 LEO	24 LIB	24 SCO	24 CAP	24 AQU
26 SAG	25 CAP	25 AQU	24 PIS	24 ARI	25 GEM	25 CAN	26 VIR	26 SCO	26 SAG	26 AQU	26 PIS
29 CAP	27 AQU	28 PIS	27 ARI	26 TAU	28 CAN	27 LEO	28 LIB	28 SAG	28 CAP	29 PIS	28 ARI
31 AQU	29 AQU	30 ARI	29 TAU	29 GEM	30 LEO	29 VIR	30 SCO	30 CAP	30 AQU	30 PIS	31 TAU
		31 ARI	30 TAU	31 CAN		31 VIR	31 SCO		31 AQU		

1977

JAN	FEB	MAR	APR	MAY	JUN	JUL	AUG	SEP	OCT	NOV	DEC
1 TAU	1 CAN	1 CAN	1 LEO	1 LIB	1 SCO	1 CAP	1 AQU	1 ARI	1 TAU	1 CAN	1 LEO
2 GEM	4 LEO	3 LEO	2 VIR	3 SCO	2 SAG	3 AQU	2 PIS	3 TAU	2 GEM	4 LEO	3 VIR
5 CAN	6 VIR	5 VIR	4 LIB	5 SAG	4 CAP	5 PIS	4 ARI	5 GEM	5 CAN	6 VIR	6 LIB
7 LEO	8 LIB	7 LIB	6 SCO	7 CAP	6 AQU	7 ARI	6 TAU	8 CAN	7 LEO	8 LIB	8 SCO
9 VIR	10 SCO	9 SCO	8 SAG	9 AQU	8 PIS	10 TAU	9 GEM	10 LEO	10 VIR	11 SCO	10 SAG
12 LIB	12 SAG	11 SAG	10 CAP	11 PIS	10 ARI	12 GEM	11 CAN	12 VIR	12 LIB	13 SAG	12 CAP
14 SCO	14 CAP	14 CAP	12 AQU	14 ARI	13 TAU	15 CAN	14 LEO	15 LIB	14 SCO	15 CAP	14 AQU
16 SAG	16 AQU	16 AQU	14 PIS	16 TAU	15 GEM	17 LEO	16 VIR	17 SCO	16 SAG	17 AQU	16 PIS
18 CAP	19 PIS	18 PIS	17 ARI	19 GEM	18 CAN	20 VIR	18 LIB	19 SAG	18 CAP	19 PIS	18 ARI
20 AQU	21 ARI	20 ARI	19 TAU	21 CAN	20 LEO	22 LIB	20 SCO	21 CAP	20 AQU	21 ARI	21 TAU
22 PIS	23 TAU	23 TAU	21 GEM	24 LEO	23 VIR	24 SCO	23 SAG	23 AQU	23 PIS	23 TAU	23 GEM
25 ARI	26 GEM	25 GEM	24 CAN	26 VIR	25 LIB	26 SAG	25 CAP	25 PIS	25 ARI	26 GEM	26 CAN
27 TAU	28 GEM	28 CAN	27 LEO	29 LIB	27 SCO	28 CAP	27 AQU	28 ARI	27 TAU	28 CAN	28 LEO
30 GEM		30 LEO	29 VIR	31 SCO	29 SAG	30 AQU	29 PIS	30 TAU	30 GEM	30 CAN	31 VIR
31 GEM		31 LEO	30 VIR		30 SAG	31 AQU	31 ARI		31 GEM		

1978

JAN	FEB	MAR	APR	MAY	JUN	JUL	AUG	SEP	OCT	NOV	DEC
1 VIR	1 SCO	1 SCO	1 CAP	1 AQU	1 ARI	1 TAU	1 CAN	1 LEO	1 VIR	1 SCO	1 SAG
2 LIB	3 SAG	2 SAG	3 AQU	2 PIS	3 TAU	2 GEM	4 LEO	2 VIR	2 LIB	3 SAG	2 CAP
4 SCO	5 CAP	4 CAP	5 PIS	4 ARI	5 GEM	5 CAN	6 VIR	5 LIB	4 SCO	5 CAP	4 AQU
6 SAG	7 AQU	6 AQU	7 ARI	6 TAU	8 CAN	7 LEO	9 LIB	7 SCO	7 SAG	7 AQU	6 PIS
8 CAP	9 PIS	8 PIS	9 TAU	9 GEM	10 LEO	10 VIR	11 SCO	9 SAG	9 CAP	9 PIS	9 ARI
10 AQU	11 ARI	10 ARI	11 GEM	11 CAN	13 VIR	12 LIB	13 SAG	12 CAP	11 AQU	11 ARI	11 TAU
12 PIS	13 TAU	13 TAU	14 CAN	14 LEO	15 LIB	15 SCO	15 CAP	14 AQU	13 PIS	14 TAU	13 GEM
15 ARI	16 GEM	15 GEM	16 LEO	16 VIR	17 SCO	17 SAG	17 AQU	16 PIS	15 ARI	16 GEM	16 CAN
17 TAU	18 CAN	18 CAN	19 VIR	19 LIB	19 SAG	19 CAP	19 PIS	18 ARI	17 TAU	18 CAN	18 LEO
19 GEM	21 LEO	20 LEO	21 LIB	21 SCO	21 CAP	21 AQU	21 ARI	20 TAU	20 GEM	21 LEO	21 VIR
22 CAN	23 VIR	23 VIR	23 SCO	23 SAG	23 AQU	23 PIS	24 TAU	22 GEM	22 CAN	23 VIR	23 LIB
25 LEO	26 LIB	25 LIB	26 SAG	25 CAP	25 PIS	25 ARI	26 GEM	25 CAN	25 LEO	26 LIB	26 SCO
27 VIR	28 SCO	27 SCO	28 CAP	27 AQU	28 ARI	27 TAU	28 CAN	27 LEO	27 VIR	28 SCO	28 SAG
29 LIB		29 SAG	30 AQU	29 PIS	30 TAU	30 GEM	31 LEO	30 VIR	29 LIB	30 SAG	30 CAP
31 LIB		31 CAP		31 ARI		31 GEM			31 LIB		31 CAP

1979

JAN	FEB	MAR	APR	MAY	JUN	JUL	AUG	SEP	OCT	NOV	DEC
1 AQU	1 ARI	1 ARI	1 GEM	1 CAN	1 LEO	1 VIR	1 SCO	1 SAG	1 AQU	1 PIS	1 TAU
3 PIS	3 TAU	3 TAU	4 CAN	4 LEO	2 VIR	2 LIB	3 SAG	2 CAP	4 PIS	2 ARI	3 GEM
5 ARI	6 GEM	5 GEM	6 LEO	6 VIR	5 LIB	5 SCO	6 CAP	4 AQU	6 ARI	4 TAU	6 CAN
7 TAU	8 CAN	7 CAN	9 VIR	9 LIB	7 SCO	7 SAG	8 AQU	6 PIS	8 TAU	6 GEM	8 LEO
9 GEM	11 LEO	10 LEO	11 LIB	11 SCO	10 SAG	9 CAP	10 PIS	8 ARI	10 GEM	8 CAN	10 VIR
12 CAN	13 VIR	12 VIR	14 SCO	13 SAG	12 CAP	11 AQU	12 ARI	10 TAU	12 CAN	11 LEO	13 LIB
14 LEO	16 LIB	15 LIB	16 SAG	15 CAP	14 AQU	13 PIS	14 TAU	12 GEM	14 LEO	13 VIR	16 SCO
17 VIR	18 SCO	17 SCO	18 CAP	18 AQU	16 GEM	15 ARI	16 GEM	15 CAN	17 VIR	16 LIB	18 SAG
19 LIB	20 SAG	20 SAG	20 AQU	20 PIS	18 CAN	17 TAU	18 CAN	17 LEO	19 LIB	18 SCO	20 CAP
22 SCO	23 CAP	22 CAP	22 PIS	22 ARI	20 LEO	20 GEM	21 LEO	20 VIR	22 SCO	20 SAG	22 AQU
24 SAG	25 AQU	24 AQU	25 ARI	24 TAU	22 VIR	22 CAN	23 VIR	22 LIB	24 SAG	23 CAP	24 PIS
26 CAP	27 PIS	26 PIS	27 TAU	26 GEM	25 LIB	25 LEO	26 LIB	25 SCO	27 CAP	25 AQU	26 ARI
28 AQU	28 PIS	28 ARI	29 GEM	28 CAN	27 SCO	27 VIR	28 SCO	27 SAG	29 AQU	27 PIS	29 TAU
30 PIS		30 TAU	30 GEM	31 LEO	30 SAG	30 LIB	31 SAG	29 CAP	31 PIS	29 ARI	31 GEM
31 PIS		31 TAU				31 LIB		30 CAP		30 ARI	

1980

JAN	FEB	MAR	APR	MAY	JUN	JUL	AUG	SEP	OCT	NOV	DEC
1 GEM	1 LEO	1 VIR	1 LIB	1 SCO	1 CAP	1 AQU	1 ARI	1 TAU	1 CAN	1 LEO	1 VIR
2 CAN	3 VIR	4 LIB	3 SCO	2 SAG	3 AQU	3 PIS	3 TAU	2 GEM	3 LEO	2 VIR	2 LIB
4 LEO	6 LIB	6 SCO	5 SAG	5 CAP	6 PIS	5 ARI	5 GEM	4 CAN	6 VIR	5 LIB	4 SCO
7 VIR	8 SCO	9 SAG	8 CAP	7 AQU	8 ARI	7 TAU	8 CAN	6 LEO	8 LIB	7 SCO	7 SAG
9 LIB	11 SAG	11 CAP	10 AQU	9 PIS	10 TAU	9 GEM	10 LEO	9 VIR	11 SCO	10 SAG	9 CAP
12 SCO	13 CAP	13 AQU	12 PIS	11 ARI	12 GEM	11 CAN	12 VIR	11 LIB	13 SAG	12 CAP	12 AQU
14 SAG	15 AQU	16 PIS	14 ARI	13 TAU	14 CAN	14 LEO	15 LIB	14 SCO	16 CAP	14 AQU	14 PIS
16 CAP	17 PIS	18 ARI	16 TAU	15 GEM	16 LEO	16 VIR	17 SCO	16 SAG	18 AQU	17 PIS	16 ARI
19 AQU	19 ARI	20 TAU	18 GEM	18 CAN	19 VIR	18 LIB	20 SAG	18 CAP	20 PIS	19 ARI	18 TAU
21 PIS	21 TAU	22 GEM	20 CAN	20 LEO	21 LIB	21 SCO	22 CAP	21 AQU	22 ARI	21 TAU	20 GEM
23 ARI	23 GEM	24 CAN	22 LEO	22 VIR	24 SCO	23 SAG	24 AQU	23 PIS	24 TAU	23 GEM	22 CAN
25 TAU	26 CAN	26 LEO	25 VIR	25 LIB	26 SAG	26 CAP	26 PIS	25 ARI	26 GEM	25 CAN	24 LEO
27 GEM	28 LEO	29 VIR	27 LIB	27 SCO	28 CAP	28 AQU	28 ARI	27 TAU	28 CAN	27 LEO	27 VIR
29 CAN	29 LEO	31 LIB	30 SCO	30 SAG	30 CAP	30 PIS	30 TAU	29 GEM	31 LEO	29 VIR	29 LIB
31 CAN				31 SAG		31 PIS	31 TAU	30 GEM		30 VIR	31 LIB

1981

JAN	FEB	MAR	APR	MAY	JUN	JUL	AUG	SEP	OCT	NOV	DEC
1 SCO	1 SAG	1 CAP	1 AQU	1 PIS	1 TAU	1 GEM	1 LEO	1 LIB	1 SCO	1 SAG	1 CAP
3 SAG	2 CAP	4 AQU	2 PIS	2 ARI	2 GEM	2 CAN	2 VIR	3 SCO	3 SAG	2 CAP	2 AQU
6 CAP	4 AQU	6 PIS	4 ARI	4 TAU	4 CAN	4 LEO	5 LIB	6 SAG	6 CAP	5 AQU	4 PIS
8 AQU	6 PIS	8 ARI	6 TAU	6 GEM	6 LEO	6 VIR	7 SCO	8 CAP	8 AQU	7 PIS	6 ARI
10 PIS	9 ARI	10 TAU	8 GEM	8 CAN	9 VIR	8 LIB	10 SAG	11 AQU	11 PIS	9 ARI	9 TAU
12 ARI	11 TAU	12 GEM	10 CAN	10 LEO	11 LIB	11 SCO	12 CAP	13 PIS	13 ARI	11 TAU	11 GEM
14 TAU	13 GEM	14 CAN	13 LEO	12 VIR	13 SCO	13 SAG	14 AQU	15 ARI	15 TAU	13 GEM	13 CAN
17 GEM	15 CAN	16 LEO	15 VIR	15 LIB	16 SAG	16 CAP	17 PIS	17 TAU	17 GEM	15 CAN	15 LEO
19 CAN	17 LEO	19 VIR	17 LIB	17 SCO	18 CAP	18 AQU	19 ARI	19 GEM	19 CAN	17 LEO	17 VIR
21 LEO	19 VIR	21 LIB	20 SCO	20 SAG	21 AQU	20 PIS	21 TAU	21 CAN	21 LEO	19 VIR	19 LIB
23 VIR	22 LIB	24 SCO	22 SAG	22 CAP	23 PIS	23 ARI	23 GEM	24 LEO	23 VIR	22 LIB	21 SCO
25 LIB	24 SCO	26 SAG	25 CAP	25 AQU	25 ARI	25 TAU	25 CAN	26 VIR	26 LIB	24 SCO	24 SAG
28 SCO	27 SAG	29 CAP	27 AQU	27 PIS	28 TAU	27 GEM	27 LEO	28 LIB	28 SCO	27 SAG	27 CAP
31 SAG	28 SAG	31 AQU	30 PIS	29 ARI	30 GEM	29 CAN	30 VIR	30 LIB	30 SAG	29 CAP	29 AQU
				31 TAU		31 LEO	31 VIR		31 SAG	30 CAP	31 PIS

1982

JAN	FEB	MAR	APR	MAY	JUN	JUL	AUG	SEP	OCT	NOV	DEC
1 PIS	1 TAU	1 TAU	1 CAN	1 LEO	1 LIB	1 SCO	1 SAG	1 AQU	1 PIS	1 TAU	1 GEM
3 ARI	3 GEM	3 GEM	3 LEO	2 VIR	3 SCO	3 SAG	2 CAP	3 PIS	3 ARI	4 GEM	3 CAN
5 TAU	5 CAN	5 CAN	5 VIR	5 LIB	6 SAG	6 CAP	4 AQU	6 ARI	5 TAU	6 CAN	5 LEO
7 GEM	7 LEO	7 LEO	8 LIB	7 SCO	8 CAP	8 AQU	7 PIS	8 TAU	7 GEM	8 LEO	7 VIR
9 CAN	10 VIR	9 VIR	10 SCO	10 SAG	11 AQU	11 PIS	9 ARI	10 GEM	9 CAN	10 VIR	9 LIB
11 LEO	12 LIB	11 LIB	12 SAG	12 CAP	13 PIS	13 ARI	12 TAU	12 CAN	11 LEO	12 LIB	12 SCO
13 VIR	14 SCO	14 SCO	15 CAP	15 AQU	16 ARI	15 TAU	14 GEM	14 LEO	14 VIR	14 SCO	14 SAG
15 LIB	17 SAG	16 SAG	17 AQU	17 PIS	18 TAU	17 GEM	16 CAN	16 VIR	16 LIB	17 SAG	16 CAP
18 SCO	19 CAP	18 CAP	20 PIS	19 ARI	20 GEM	19 CAN	18 LEO	18 LIB	18 SCO	19 CAP	19 AQU
20 SAG	22 AQU	21 AQU	22 ARI	22 TAU	22 CAN	21 LEO	20 VIR	21 SCO	20 SAG	22 AQU	22 PIS
23 CAP	24 PIS	23 PIS	24 TAU	24 GEM	24 LEO	23 VIR	22 LIB	23 SAG	23 CAP	24 PIS	24 ARI
25 AQU	26 ARI	26 ARI	26 GEM	26 CAN	26 VIR	26 LIB	24 SCO	26 CAP	25 AQU	27 ARI	26 TAU
28 PIS	28 TAU	28 TAU	28 CAN	28 LEO	28 LIB	28 SCO	27 SAG	28 AQU	28 PIS	29 TAU	28 GEM
30 ARI		30 GEM	30 LEO	30 VIR	30 LIB	30 SAG	29 CAP	30 AQU	30 ARI	30 TAU	30 CAN
31 ARI		31 GEM		31 VIR		31 SAG	31 CAP		31 ARI		31 CAN

1983

JAN	FEB	MAR	APR	MAY	JUN	JUL	AUG	SEP	OCT	NOV	DEC
1 LEO	1 VIR	1 LIB	1 SCO	1 SAG	1 AQU	1 PIS	1 ARI	1 GEM	1 CAN	1 VIR	1 LIB
3 VIR	2 LIB	3 SCO	2 SAG	2 CAP	3 PIS	3 ARI	2 TAU	3 CAN	2 LEO	2 LIB	2 SCO
6 LIB	4 SCO	6 SAG	5 CAP	4 AQU	6 ARI	6 TAU	4 GEM	5 LEO	4 VIR	5 SCO	4 SAG
8 SCO	6 SAG	8 CAP	7 AQU	7 PIS	8 TAU	8 GEM	6 CAN	7 VIR	6 LIB	7 SAG	6 CAP
10 SAG	9 CAP	11 AQU	10 PIS	9 ARI	10 GEM	10 CAN	8 LEO	9 LIB	8 SCO	9 CAP	9 AQU
13 CAP	12 AQU	13 PIS	12 ARI	12 TAU	12 CAN	12 LEO	10 VIR	11 SCO	10 SAG	12 AQU	11 PIS
15 AQU	14 PIS	16 ARI	14 TAU	14 GEM	14 LEO	14 VIR	12 LIB	13 SAG	13 CAP	14 PIS	14 ARI
18 PIS	16 ARI	18 TAU	17 GEM	16 CAN	16 VIR	16 LIB	14 SCO	15 CAP	15 AQU	17 ARI	16 TAU
20 ARI	19 TAU	20 GEM	19 CAN	18 LEO	19 LIB	18 SCO	17 SAG	18 AQU	18 PIS	19 TAU	19 GEM
23 TAU	21 GEM	23 CAN	21 LEO	20 VIR	21 SCO	20 SAG	19 CAP	20 PIS	20 ARI	21 GEM	21 CAN
25 GEM	23 CAN	25 LEO	23 VIR	22 LIB	23 SAG	23 CAP	22 AQU	23 ARI	23 TAU	23 CAN	23 LEO
27 CAN	25 LEO	27 VIR	25 LIB	25 SCO	26 CAP	25 AQU	24 PIS	25 TAU	25 GEM	26 LEO	25 VIR
29 LEO	27 VIR	29 LIB	27 SCO	27 SAG	28 AQU	28 PIS	27 ARI	28 GEM	27 CAN	28 VIR	27 LIB
31 VIR	28 VIR	31 SCO	30 SAG	29 CAP	30 AQU	30 ARI	29 TAU	30 CAN	29 LEO	30 LIB	29 SCO
				31 CAP		31 ARI	31 GEM		31 VIR		31 SAG

1984

JAN	FEB	MAR	APR	MAY	JUN	JUL	AUG	SEP	OCT	NOV	DEC
1 SAG	1 AQU	1 AQU	1 ARI	1 TAU	1 GEM	1 LEO	1 VIR	1 SCO	1 SAG	1 AQU	1 PIS
3 CAP	4 PIS	2 PIS	3 TAU	3 GEM	2 CAN	3 VIR	2 LIB	2 SAG	2 CAP	3 PIS	3 ARI
5 AQU	7 ARI	5 ARI	6 GEM	5 CAN	4 LEO	5 LIB	4 SCO	4 CAP	4 AQU	5 ARI	5 TAU
8 PIS	9 TAU	7 TAU	8 CAN	8 LEO	6 VIR	8 SCO	6 SAG	7 AQU	7 PIS	8 TAU	8 GEM
10 ARI	11 GEM	10 GEM	10 LEO	10 VIR	8 LIB	10 SAG	8 CAP	9 PIS	9 ARI	10 GEM	10 CAN
13 TAU	14 CAN	12 CAN	13 VIR	12 LIB	10 SCO	12 CAP	11 AQU	12 ARI	12 TAU	13 CAN	12 LEO
15 GEM	16 LEO	14 LEO	15 LIB	14 SCO	12 SAG	14 AQU	13 PIS	14 TAU	14 GEM	15 LEO	14 VIR
17 CAN	18 VIR	16 VIR	17 SCO	16 SAG	15 CAP	17 PIS	16 ARI	17 GEM	17 CAN	17 VIR	17 LIB
19 LEO	20 LIB	18 LIB	19 SAG	18 CAP	17 AQU	19 ARI	18 TAU	19 CAN	19 LEO	19 LIB	19 SCO
21 VIR	22 SCO	20 SCO	21 CAP	21 AQU	19 PIS	22 TAU	21 GEM	21 LEO	21 VIR	21 SCO	21 SAG
23 LIB	24 SAG	22 SAG	23 AQU	23 PIS	22 ARI	24 GEM	23 CAN	24 VIR	23 LIB	23 SAG	23 CAP
25 SCO	26 CAP	25 CAP	26 PIS	26 ARI	24 TAU	26 CAN	25 LEO	25 LIB	25 SCO	26 CAP	25 AQU
28 SAG	29 AQU	27 AQU	28 ARI	28 TAU	27 GEM	29 LEO	27 VIR	27 SCO	27 SAG	28 AQU	28 PIS
30 CAP		29 PIS	30 ARI	30 GEM	29 CAN	31 VIR	29 LIB	30 SAG	29 CAP	30 PIS	30 ARI
31 CAP		31 PIS		31 GEM	30 CAN		31 SCO		31 AQU		31 ARI

1985

JAN	FEB	MAR	APR	MAY	JUN	JUL	AUG	SEP	OCT	NOV	DEC
1 ARI	1 GEM	1 GEM	1 LEO	1 VIR	1 SCO	1 SAG	1 AQU	1 PIS	1 ARI	1 GEM	1 CAN
2 TAU	3 CAN	2 CAN	3 VIR	2 LIB	3 SAG	2 CAP	3 PIS	2 ARI	2 TAU	3 CAN	3 LEO
4 GEM	5 LEO	4 LEO	5 LIB	4 SCO	5 CAP	4 AQU	5 ARI	4 TAU	4 GEM	5 LEO	5 VIR
6 CAN	7 VIR	6 VIR	7 SCO	6 SAG	7 AQU	7 PIS	8 TAU	7 GEM	7 CAN	8 VIR	7 LIB
9 LEO	9 LIB	8 LIB	9 SAG	8 CAP	9 PIS	9 ARI	10 GEM	9 CAN	9 LEO	10 LIB	9 SCO
11 VIR	11 SCO	10 SCO	11 CAP	11 AQU	12 ARI	12 TAU	13 CAN	12 LEO	11 VIR	12 SCO	11 SAG
13 LIB	13 SAG	13 SAG	13 AQU	13 PIS	14 TAU	14 GEM	15 LEO	14 VIR	13 LIB	14 SAG	13 CAP
15 SCO	16 CAP	15 CAP	16 PIS	15 ARI	17 GEM	17 CAN	17 VIR	16 LIB	15 SCO	16 CAP	15 AQU
17 SAG	18 AQU	17 AQU	18 ARI	18 TAU	19 CAN	19 LEO	19 LIB	18 SCO	17 SAG	18 AQU	17 PIS
19 CAP	20 PIS	19 PIS	21 TAU	21 GEM	22 LEO	21 VIR	22 SCO	20 SAG	19 CAP	20 PIS	20 ARI
22 AQU	23 ARI	22 ARI	23 GEM	23 CAN	24 VIR	23 LIB	24 SAG	22 CAP	22 AQU	23 ARI	22 TAU
24 PIS	25 TAU	24 TAU	26 CAN	25 LEO	26 LIB	25 SCO	26 CAP	24 AQU	24 PIS	25 TAU	25 GEM
26 ARI	28 GEM	27 GEM	28 LEO	28 VIR	28 SCO	27 SAG	28 AQU	27 PIS	26 ARI	28 GEM	27 CAN
29 TAU		29 CAN	30 VIR	30 LIB	30 SAG	30 CAP	30 PIS	29 ARI	29 TAU	30 CAN	30 LEO
31 GEM		31 CAN		31 LIB		31 CAP	31 PIS	30 ARI	31 GEM		31 LEO

1986

JAN	FEB	MAR	APR	MAY	JUN	JUL	AUG	SEP	OCT	NOV	DEC
1 VIR	1 LIB	1 SCO	1 CAP	1 AQU	1 PIS	1 TAU	1 GEM	1 CAN	1 VIR	1 LIB	1 SCO
3 LIB	2 SCO	3 SAG	4 AQU	3 PIS	2 ARI	4 GEM	3 CAN	2 LEO	4 LIB	2 SCO	2 SAG
6 SCO	4 SAG	5 CAP	6 PIS	5 ARI	4 TAU	6 CAN	5 LEO	4 VIR	6 SCO	4 SAG	4 CAP
8 SAG	6 CAP	7 AQU	8 ARI	8 TAU	7 GEM	9 LEO	8 VIR	6 LIB	8 SAG	6 CAP	6 AQU
10 CAP	8 AQU	10 PIS	11 TAU	10 GEM	9 CAN	11 VIR	10 LIB	8 SCO	10 CAP	8 AQU	8 PIS
12 AQU	10 PIS	12 ARI	13 GEM	13 CAN	12 LEO	14 LIB	12 SCO	11 SAG	12 AQU	10 PIS	10 ARI
14 PIS	13 ARI	14 TAU	16 CAN	15 LEO	14 VIR	16 SCO	14 SAG	13 CAP	14 PIS	13 ARI	12 TAU
16 ARI	15 TAU	17 GEM	18 LEO	18 VIR	16 LIB	18 SAG	16 CAP	15 AQU	16 ARI	15 TAU	15 GEM
19 TAU	18 GEM	19 CAN	21 VIR	20 LIB	19 SCO	20 CAP	18 AQU	17 PIS	19 TAU	18 GEM	17 CAN
21 GEM	20 CAN	22 LEO	23 LIB	22 SCO	21 SAG	22 AQU	21 PIS	19 ARI	21 GEM	20 CAN	20 LEO
24 CAN	22 LEO	24 VIR	25 SCO	24 SAG	23 CAP	24 PIS	23 ARI	21 TAU	24 CAN	23 LEO	22 VIR
26 LEO	25 VIR	26 LIB	27 SAG	26 CAP	25 AQU	26 ARI	25 TAU	24 GEM	26 LEO	25 VIR	25 LIB
28 VIR	27 LIB	28 SCO	29 CAP	28 AQU	27 PIS	29 TAU	28 GEM	26 CAN	29 VIR	27 LIB	27 SCO
31 LIB	28 LIB	30 SAG	30 CAP	30 PIS	29 ARI	31 GEM	30 CAN	29 LEO	31 LIB	30 SCO	29 SAG
		31 SAG		31 PIS	30 ARI		31 CAN	30 LEO			31 CAP

1987

JAN	FEB	MAR	APR	MAY	JUN	JUL	AUG	SEP	OCT	NOV	DEC
1 CAP	1 PIS	1 PIS	1 TAU	1 GEM	1 CAN	1 VIR	1 LIB	1 SAG	1 CAP	1 PIS	1 ARI
2 AQU	3 ARI	2 ARI	3 GEM	3 CAN	2 LEO	4 LIB	3 SCO	3 CAP	3 AQU	3 ARI	3 TAU
4 PIS	5 TAU	4 TAU	5 CAN	5 LEO	4 VIR	6 SCO	5 SAG	5 AQU	5 PIS	5 TAU	5 GEM
6 ARI	7 GEM	7 GEM	8 LEO	8 VIR	7 LIB	8 SAG	7 CAP	7 PIS	7 ARI	8 GEM	7 CAN
9 TAU	10 CAN	9 CAN	10 VIR	10 LIB	9 SCO	10 CAP	9 AQU	9 ARI	9 TAU	10 CAN	10 LEO
11 GEM	12 LEO	12 LEO	13 LIB	12 SCO	11 SAG	12 AQU	11 PIS	11 TAU	11 GEM	12 LEO	12 VIR
14 CAN	15 VIR	14 VIR	15 SCO	15 SAG	13 CAP	14 PIS	13 ARI	14 GEM	14 CAN	15 VIR	15 LIB
16 LEO	17 LIB	16 LIB	17 SAG	17 CAP	15 AQU	17 ARI	15 TAU	16 CAN	16 LEO	17 LIB	17 SCO
19 VIR	20 SCO	19 SCO	19 CAP	19 AQU	17 PIS	19 TAU	17 GEM	19 LEO	19 VIR	20 SCO	19 SAG
21 LIB	22 SAG	21 SAG	21 AQU	21 PIS	19 ARI	21 GEM	20 CAN	21 VIR	21 LIB	22 SAG	21 CAP
23 SCO	24 CAP	23 CAP	24 PIS	23 ARI	22 TAU	24 CAN	22 LEO	24 LIB	23 SCO	24 CAP	23 AQU
25 SAG.	26 AQU	25 AQU	26 ARI	25 TAU	24 GEM	26 LEO	25 VIR	26 SCO	26 SAG	26 AQU	25 PIS
27 CAP	28 PIS	27 PIS	28 TAU	28 GEM	26 CAN	29 VIR	27 LIB	28 SAG	28 CAP	28 PIS	28 ARI
29 AQU		29 ARI	30 GEM	30 CAN	29 LEO	31 LIB	30 SCO	30 CAP	30 AQU	30 ARI	30 TAU
31 PIS		31 ARI		31 CAN	30 LEO		31 SCO		31 AQU		31 TAU

1988

JAN	FEB	MAR	APR	MAY	JUN	JUL	AUG	SEP	OCT	NOV	DEC
1 GEM	1 CAN	1 LEO	1 VIR	1 LIB	1 SAG	1 CAP	1 PIS	1 TAU	1 GEM	1 LEO	1 VIR
4 CAN	2 LEO	3 VIR	2 LIB	2 SCO	2 CAP	2 AQU	2 ARI	3 GEM	2 CAN	4 VIR	4 LIB
6 LEO	5 VIR	6 LIB	4 SCO	4 SAG	4 AQU	4 PIS	4 TAU	5 CAN	5 LEO	6 LIB	6 SCO
9 VIR	7 LIB	8 SCO	7 SAG	6 CAP	7 PIS	6 ARI	7 GEM	8 LEO	7 VIR	9 SCO	8 SAG
11 LIB	10 SCO	10 SAG	9 CAP	8 AQU	9 ARI	8 TAU	9 CAN	10 VIR	10 LIB	11 SAG	11 CAP
13 SCO	12 SAG	13 CAP	11 AQU	10 PIS	11 TAU	10 GEM	11 LEO	13 LIB	12 SCO	13 CAP	13 AQU
16 SAG	14 CAP	15 AQU	13 PIS	12 ARI	13 GEM	13 CAN	14 VIR	15 SCO	15 SAG	16 AQU	15 PIS
18 CAP	16 AQU	17 PIS	15 ARI	15 TAU	15 CAN	15 LEO	16 LIB	18 SAG	17 CAP	18 PIS	17 ARI
20 AQU	18 PIS	19 ARI	17 TAU	17 GEM	18 LEO	18 VIR	19 SCO	20 CAP	19 AQU	20 ARI	19 TAU
22 PIS	20 ARI	21 TAU	19 GEM	19 CAN	20 VIR	20 LIB	21 SAG	22 AQU	21 PIS	22 TAU	21 GEM
24 ARI	22 TAU	23 GEM	22 CAN	21 LEO	23 LIB	23 SCO	24 CAP	24 PIS	24 ARI	24 GEM	24 CAN
26 TAU	25 GEM	25 CAN	24 LEO	24 VIR	25 SCO	25 SAG	26 AQU	26 ARI	26 TAU	26 CAN	26 LEO
28 GEM	27 CAN	28 LEO	27 VIR	26 LIB	28 SAG	27 CAP	28 PIS	28 TAU	28 GEM	29 LEO	28 VIR
31 CAN	29 CAN	30 VIR	29 LIB	29 SCO	30 CAP	29 AQU	30 ARI	30 GEM	30 CAN	30 LEO	31 LIB
		31 VIR	30 LIB	31 SAG		31 PIS	31 ARI		31 CAN		

1989

JAN	FEB	MAR	APR	MAY	JUN	JUL	AUG	SEP	OCT	NOV	DEC
1 LIB	1 SAG	1 SAG	1 AQU	1 PIS	1 TAU	1 GEM	1 LEO	1 VIR	1 LIB	1 SAG	1 CAP
2 SCO	3 CAP	3 CAP	4 PIS	3 ARI	3 GEM	3 CAN	4 VIR	3 LIB	2 SCO	4 CAP	3 AQU
5 SAG	6 AQU	5 AQU	6 ARI	5 TAU	6 CAN	5 LEO	6 LIB	5 SCO	5 SAG	6 AQU	6 PIS
7 CAP	8 PIS	7 PIS	8 TAU	7 GEM	8 LEO	7 VIR	9 SCO	8 SAG	7 CAP	8 PIS	8 ARI
9 AQU	10 ARI	9 ARI	10 GEM	9 CAN	10 VIR	10 LIB	11 SAG	10 CAP	10 AQU	10 ARI	10 TAU
11 PIS	12 TAU	11 TAU	12 CAN	11 LEO	13 LIB	12 SCO	14 CAP	12 AQU	12 PIS	12 TAU	12 GEM
13 ARI	14 GEM	13 GEM	14 LEO	14 VIR	15 SCO	15 SAG	16 AQU	14 PIS	14 ARI	14 GEM	14 CAN
15 TAU	16 CAN	15 CAN	16 VIR	16 LIB	18 SAG	17 CAP	18 PIS	16 ARI	16 TAU	16 CAN	16 LEO
18 GEM	19 LEO	18 LEO	19 LIB	19 SCO	20 CAP	20 AQU	20 ARI	18 TAU	18 GEM	19 LEO	18 VIR
20 CAN	21 VIR	20 VIR	22 SCO	21 SAG	22 AQU	22 PIS	22 TAU	21 GEM	20 CAN	21 VIR	21 LIB
22 LEO	24 LIB	23 LIB	24 SAG	24 CAP	24 PIS	24 ARI	24 GEM	23 CAN	22 LEO	23 LIB	23 SCO
25 VIR	26 SCO	25 SCO	26 CAP	26 AQU	27 ARI	26 TAU	26 CAN	25 LEO	25 VIR	26 SCO	26 SAG
27 LIB	28 SCO	28 SAG	29 AQU	28 PIS	29 TAU	28 GEM	29 LEO	27 VIR	27 LIB	28 SAG	28 CAP
30 SCO		30 CAP	30 AQU	30 ARI	30 TAU	30 CAN	31 VIR	30 LIB	30 SCO	30 SAG	30 AQU
31 SCO		31 CAP		31 ARI		31 CAN			31 SCO		31 AQU

1990

JAN	FEB	MAR	APR	MAY	JUN	JUL	AUG	SEP	OCT	NOV	DEC
1 AQU	1 ARI	1 ARI	1 GEM	1 CAN	1 VIR	1 LIB	1 SAG	1 CAP	1 AQU	1 ARI	1 TAU
2 PIS	2 TAU	2 TAU	2 CAN	2 LEO	2 LIB	2 SCO	4 CAP	2 AQU	2 PIS	3 TAU	2 GEM
4 ARI	4 GEM	4 GEM	4 LEO	4 VIR	5 SCO	5 SAG	6 AQU	5 PIS	4 ARI	5 GEM	4 CAN
6 TAU	7 CAN	6 CAN	7 VIR	6 LIB	7 SAG	7 CAP	8 PIS	7 ARI	6 TAU	7 CAN	6 LEO
8 GEM	9 LEO	8 LEO	9 LIB	9 SCO	10 CAP	10 AQU	11 ARI	9 TAU	8 GEM	9 LEO	8 VIR
10 CAN	11 VIR	10 VIR	11 SCO	11 SAG	12 AQU	12 PIS	13 TAU	11 GEM	10 CAN	11 VIR	11 LIB
12 LEO	13 LIB	13 LIB	14 SAG	14 CAP	15 PIS	14 ARI	15 GEM	13 CAN	13 LEO	13 LIB	13 SCO
15 VIR	16 SCO	15 SCO	17 CAP	16 AQU	17 ARI	16 TAU	17 CAN	15 LEO	15 VIR	16 SCO	16 SAG
17 LIB	18 SAG	18 SAG	19 AQU	19 PIS	19 TAU	19 GEM	19 LEO	18 VIR	17 LIB	18 SAG	18 CAP
20 SCO	21 CAP	20 CAP	21 PIS	21 ARI	21 GEM	21 CAN	21 VIR	20 LIB	20 SCO	21 CAP	21 AQU
22 SAG	23 AQU	23 AQU	23 ARI	23 TAU	23 CAN	23 LEO	24 LIB	22 SCO	22 SAG	23 AQU	23 PIS
24 CAP	25 PIS	25 PIS	25 TAU	25 GEM	25 LEO	25 VIR	26 SCO	25 SAG	25 CAP	26 PIS	25 ARI
27 AQU	28 ARI	27 ARI	27 GEM	27 CAN	27 VIR	27 LIB	28 SAG	27 CAP	27 AQU	28 ARI	28 TAU
29 PIS		29 TAU	29 CAN	29 LEO	30 LIB	30 SCO	31 CAP	30 AQU	29 PIS	30 TAU	30 GEM
31 ARI		31 GEM	30 CAN	31 VIR		31 SCO			31 PIS		31 GEM

1991

JAN	FEB	MAR	APR	MAY	JUN	JUL	AUG	SEP	OCT	NOV	DEC
1 CAN	1 VIR	1 VIR	1 SCO	1 SAG	1 CAP	1 AQU	1 ARI	1 TAU	1 CAN	1 VIR	1 LIB
3 LEO	3 LIB	3 LIB	4 SAG	4 CAP	2 AQU	2 PIS	3 TAU	2 GEM	3 LEO	4 LIB	3 SCO
5 VIR	6 SCO	5 SCO	6 CAP	6 AQU	5 PIS	5 ARI	5 GEM	4 CAN	5 VIR	6 SCO	6 SAG
7 LIB	8 SAG	7 SAG	9 AQU	9 PIS	7 ARI	7 TAU	7 CAN	6 LEO	7 LIB	8 SAG	8 CAP
9 SCO	11 CAP	10 CAP	11 PIS	11 ARI	10 TAU	9 GEM	9 LEO	8 VIR	10 SCO	11 CAP	11 AQU
12 SAG	13 AQU	13 AQU	14 ARI	13 TAU	12 GEM	11 CAN	11 VIR	10 LIB	12 SAG	13 AQU	13 PIS
14 CAP	16 PIS	15 PIS	16 TAU	15 GEM	14 CAN	13 LEO	14 LIB	12 SCO	14 CAP	16 PIS	16 ARI
17 AQU	18 ARI	17 ARI	18 GEM	17 CAN	16 LEO	15 VIR	16 SCO	15 SAG	17 AQU	18 ARI	18 TAU
19 PIS	20 TAU	19 TAU	20 CAN	19 LEO	18 VIR	17 LIB	18 SAG	17 CAP	19 PIS	20 TAU	20 GEM
22 ARI	22 GEM	21 GEM	22 LEO	21 VIR	20 LIB	19 SCO	21 CAP	20 AQU	22 ARI	23 GEM	22 CAN
24 TAU	24 CAN	24 CAN	24 VIR	24 LIB	22 SCO	22 SAG	23 AQU	22 PIS	24 TAU	25 CAN	24 LEO
26 GEM	26 LEO	26 LEO	26 LIB	26 SCO	25 SAG	24 CAP	26 PIS	24 ARI	26 GEM	27 LEO	26 VIR
28 CAN	28 LEO	28 VIR	29 SCO	28 SAG	27 CAP	27 AQU	28 ARI	27 TAU	28 CAN	29 VIR	28 LIB
30 LEO		30 LIB	30 SCO	31 CAP	30 AQU	29 PIS	30 TAU	29 GEM	30 LEO	30 VIR	30 SCO
31 LEO		31 LIB				31 PIS	31 TAU	30 GEM	31 LEO		31 SCO

1992

JAN	FEB	MAR	APR	MAY	JUN	JUL	AUG	SEP	OCT	NOV	DEC
1 SCO	1 CAP	1 AQU	1 PIS	1 ARI	1 GEM	1 CAN	1 VIR	1 SCO	1 SAG	1 CAP	1 AQU
2 SAG	3 AQU	4 PIS	3 ARI	2 TAU	3 CAN	2 LEO	3 LIB	4 SAG	3 CAP	2 AQU	2 PIS
4 CAP	6 PIS	6 ARI	5 TAU	5 GEM	5 LEO	4 VIR	5 SCO	6 CAP	6 AQU	5 PIS	4 ARI
7 AQU	8 ARI	9 TAU	7 GEM	7 CAN	7 VIR	7 LIB	7 SAG	8 AQU	8 PIS	7 ARI	7 TAU
9 PIS	10 TAU	11 GEM	9 CAN	9 LEO	9 LIB	9 SCO	10 CAP	11 PIS	11 ARI	9 TAU	9 GEM
12 ARI	13 GEM	13 CAN	12 LEO	11 VIR	11 SCO	11 SAG	12 AQU	13 ARI	13 TAU	12 GEM	11 CAN
14 TAU	15 CAN	15 LEO	14 VIR	13 LIB	13 SAG	13 CAP	15 PIS	16 TAU	16 GEM	14 CAN	13 LEO
16 GEM	17 LEO	17 VIR	16 LIB	15 SCO	16 CAP	16 AQU	17 ARI	18 GEM	18 CAN	16 LEO	16 VIR
18 CAN	19 VIR	19 LIB	18 SCO	17 SAG	19 AQU	18 PIS	20 TAU	21 CAN	20 LEO	18 VIR	18 LIB
20 LEO	21 LIB	21 SCO	20 SAG	20 CAP	21 PIS	21 ARI	22 GEM	23 LEO	22 VIR	20 LIB	20 SCO
22 VIR	23 SCO	24 SAG	22 CAP	22 AQU	24 ARI	23 TAU	24 CAN	25 VIR	24 LIB	23 SCO	22 SAG
24 LIB	25 SAG	26 CAP	25 AQU	25 PIS	26 TAU	26 GEM	26 LEO	27 LIB	26 SCO	25 SAG	24 CAP
27 SCO	28 CAP	29 AQU	28 PIS	27 ARI	28 GEM	28 CAN	28 VIR	29 SCO	28 SAG	27 CAP	27 AQU
29 SAG	29 CAP	31 PIS	30 ARI	30 TAU	30 CAN	30 LEO	30 LIB	30 SCO	31 CAP	29 AQU	29 PIS
31 SAG				31 TAU		31 LEO	31 LIB			30 AQU	31 PIS

1993

JAN	FEB	MAR	APR	MAY	JUN	JUL	AUG	SEP	OCT	NOV	DEC
1 ARI	1 TAU	1 GEM	1 CAN	1 VIR	1 LIB	1 SAG	1 CAP	1 PIS	1 ARI	1 TAU	1 GEM
3 TAU	2 GEM	4 CAN	2 LEO	4 LIB	2 SCO	4 CAP	2 AQU	3 ARI	3 TAU	2 GEM	2 CAN
6 GEM	4 CAN	6 LEO	4 VIR	6 SCO	4 SAG	6 AQU	5 PIS	6 TAU	6 GEM	4 CAN	4 LEO
8 CAN	6 LEO	8 VIR	6 LIB	8 SAG	6 CAP	8 PIS	7 ARI	8 GEM	8 CAN	7 LEO	6 VIR
10 LEO	8 VIR	10 LIB	8 SCO	10 CAP	9 AQU	11 ARI	10 TAU	11 CAN	10 LEO	9 VIR	8 LIB
12 VIR	10 LIB	12 SCO	10 SAG	12 AQU	11 PIS	13 TAU	12 GEM	13 LEO	13 VIR	11 LIB	10 SCO
14 LIB	12 SCO	14 SAG	12 CAP	15 PIS	13 ARI	16 GEM	14 CAN	15 VIR	15 LIB	13 SCO	12 SAG
16 SCO	15 SAG	16 CAP	15 AQU	17 ARI	16 TAU	18 CAN	17 LEO	17 LIB	17 SCO	15 SAG	15 CAP
18 SAG	17 CAP	19 AQU	17 PIS	20 TAU	18 GEM	20 LEO	19 VIR	19 SCO	19 SAG	17 CAP	17 AQU
21 CAP	19 AQU	21 PIS	20 ARI	22 GEM	21 CAN	22 VIR	21 LIB	21 SAG	21 CAP	19 AQU	19 PIS
23 AQU	22 PIS	24 ARI	22 TAU	24 CAN	23 LEO	24 LIB	23 SCO	23 CAP	23 AQU	22 PIS	22 ARI
26 PIS	24 ARI	26 TAU	25 GEM	27 LEO	25 VIR	26 SCO	25 SAG	26 AQU	25 PIS	24 ARI	24 TAU
28 ARI	27 TAU	29 GEM	27 CAN	29 VIR	27 LIB	29 SAG	27 CAP	28 PIS	28 ARI	27 TAU	27 GEM
31 TAU	28 TAU	31 CAN	29 LEO	31 LIB	29 SCO	31 CAP	29 AQU	30 PIS	30 TAU	29 GEM	29 CAN
			30 LEO		30 SCO		31 AQU		31 TAU	30 GEM	31 LEO

1994

JAN	FEB	MAR	APR	MAY	JUN	JUL	AUG	SEP	OCT	NOV	DEC
1 LEO	1 LIB	1 LIB	1 SAG	1 CAP	1 PIS	1 ARI	1 TAU	1 CAN	1 LEO	1 LIB	1 SCO
2 VIR	3 SCO	2 SCO	3 CAP	2 AQU	3 ARI	3 TAU	2 GEM	3 LEO	3 VIR	3 SCO	3 SAG
4 LIB	5 SAG	4 SAG	5 AQU	5 PIS	6 TAU	6 GEM	4 CAN	5 VIR	5 LIB	5 SAG	5 CAP
7 SCO	7 CAP	6 CAP	7 PIS	7 ARI	8 GEM	8 CAN	7 LEO	7 LIB	7 SCO	7 CAP	7 AQU
9 SAG	9 AQU	9 AQU	10 ARI	10 TAU	11 CAN	10 LEO	9 VIR	10 SCO	9 SAG	9 AQU	9 PIS
11 CAP	12 PIS	11 PIS	12 TAU	12 GEM	13 LEO	13 VIR	11 LIB	12 SAG	11 CAP	12 PIS	11 ARI
13 AQU	14 ARI	13 ARI	15 GEM	15 CAN	15 VIR	15 LIB	13 SCO	14 CAP	13 AQU	14 ARI	14 TAU
15 PIS	17 TAU	16 TAU	17 CAN	17 LEO	18 LIB	17 SCO	15 SAG	16 AQU	15 PIS	17 TAU	16 GEM
18 ARI	19 GEM	19 GEM	20 LEO	19 VIR	20 SCO	19 SAG	18 CAP	18 PIS	18 ARI	19 GEM	19 CAN
20 TAU	22 CAN	21 CAN	22 VIR	21 LIB	22 SAG	21 CAP	20 AQU	21 ARI	20 TAU	22 CAN	21 LEO
23 GEM	24 LEO	23 LEO	24 LIB	23 SCO	24 CAP	23 AQU	22 PIS	23 TAU	23 GEM	24 LEO	24 VIR
25 CAN	26 VIR	26 VIR	26 SCO	25 SAG	26 AQU	26 PIS	24 ARI	26 GEM	25 CAN	27 VIR	26 LIB
28 LEO	28 LIB	28 LIB	28 SAG	27 CAP	28 PIS	28 ARI	27 TAU	28 CAN	28 LEO	29 LIB	28 SCO
30 VIR		30 SCO	30 CAP	30 AQU	30 PIS	30 TAU	29 GEM	30 CAN	30 VIR	30 LIB	30 SAG
31 VIR		31 SCO		31 AQU		31 TAU	31 GEM		31 VIR		31 SAG

1995

JAN	FEB	MAR	APR	MAY	JUN	JUL	AUG	SEP	OCT	NOV	DEC
1 CAP	1 AQU	1 PIS	1 ARI	1 TAU	1 CAN	1 LEO	1 VIR	1 SCO	1 SAG	1 AQU	1 PIS
3 AQU	2 PIS	3 ARI	2 TAU	2 GEM	3 LEO	3 VIR	2 LIB	2 SAG	2 CAP	2 PIS	2 ARI
5 PIS	4 ARI	6 TAU	5 GEM	5 CAN	6 VIR	5 LIB	4 SCO	4 CAP	4 AQU	4 ARI	4 TAU
8 ARI	7 TAU	8 GEM	7 CAN	7 LEO	8 LIB	8 SCO	6 SAG	6 AQU	6 PIS	7 TAU	6 GEM
10 TAU	9 GEM	11 CAN	10 LEO	9 VIR	10 SCO	10 SAG	8 CAP	9 PIS	8 ARI	9 GEM	9 CAN
13 GEM	12 CAN	13 LEO	12 VIR	12 LIB	12 SAG	12 CAP	10 AQU	11 ARI	10 TAU	12 CAN	11 LEO
15 CAN	14 LEO	16 VIR	14 LIB	14 SCO	14 CAP	14 AQU	12 PIS	13 TAU	13 GEM	14 LEO	14 VIR
18 LEO	16 VIR	18 LIB	16 SCO	16 SAG	16 AQU	16 PIS	14 ARI	15 GEM	15 CAN	17 VIR	16 LIB
20 VIR	19 LIB	20 SCO	18 SAG	18 CAP	18 PIS	18 ARI	17 TAU	18 CAN	18 LEO	19 LIB	19 SCO
22 LIB	21 SCO	22 SAG	20 CAP	20 AQU	21 ARI	20 TAU	19 GEM	20 LEO	20 VIR	21 SCO	21 SAG
24 SCO	23 SAG	24 CAP	23 AQU	22 PIS	23 TAU	23 GEM	22 CAN	23 VIR	23 LIB	23 SAG	23 CAP
27 SAG	25 CAP	26 AQU	25 PIS	24 ARI	26 GEM	25 CAN	24 LEO	25 LIB	25 SCO	25 CAP	25 AQU
29 CAP	27 AQU	29 PIS	27 ARI	27 TAU	28 CAN	28 LEO	26 VIR	27 SCO	27 SAG	27 AQU	27 PIS
31 AQU	28 AQU	31 ARI	29 TAU	29 GEM	30 CAN	30 VIR	29 LIB	29 SAG	29 CAP	29 PIS	29 ARI
			30 TAU	31 GEM		31 VIR	31 SCO	30 SAG	31 AQU	30 PIS	31 TAU

1996

JAN	FEB	MAR	APR	MAY	JUN	JUL	AUG	SEP	OCT	NOV	DEC
1 TAU	1 CAN	1 CAN	1 VIR	1 LIB	1 SCO	1 CAP	1 PIS	1 ARI	1 TAU	1 CAN	1 LEO
3 GEM	4 LEO	2 LEO	3 LIB	3 SCO	2 SAG	3 AQU	3 ARI	2 TAU	2 GEM	3 LEO	3 VIR
5 CAN	6 VIR	5 VIR	6 SCO	5 SAG	4 CAP	5 PIS	6 TAU	4 GEM	4 CAN	5 VIR	5 LIB
8 LEO	9 LIB	7 LIB	8 SAG	7 CAP	6 AQU	7 ARI	8 GEM	7 CAN	7 LEO	8 LIB	8 SCO
10 VIR	11 SCO	9 SCO	10 CAP	9 AQU	8 PIS	9 TAU	10 CAN	9 LEO	9 VIR	10 SCO	10 SAG
13 LIB	13 SAG	12 SAG	12 AQU	11 PIS	10 ARI	12 GEM	13 LEO	12 VIR	12 LIB	12 SAG	12 CAP
15 SCO	15 CAP	14 CAP	14 PIS	14 ARI	12 TAU	14 CAN	16 VIR	14 LIB	14 SCO	15 CAP	14 AQU
17 SAG	17 AQU	16 AQU	16 ARI	16 TAU	15 GEM	17 LEO	18 LIB	17 SCO	16 SAG	17 AQU	16 PIS
19 CAP	20 PIS	18 PIS	19 TAU	18 GEM	17 CAN	19 VIR	20 SCO	19 SAG	18 CAP	19 PIS	18 ARI
21 AQU	22 ARI	20 ARI	21 GEM	21 CAN	19 LEO	22 LIB	23 SAG	21 CAP	20 AQU	21 ARI	20 TAU
23 PIS	24 TAU	22 TAU	23 CAN	23 LEO	22 VIR	24 SCO	25 CAP	23 AQU	23 PIS	23 TAU	23 GEM
25 ARI	26 GEM	25 GEM	26 LEO	26 VIR	24 LIB	26 SAG	27 AQU	25 PIS	25 ARI	25 GEM	25 CAN
27 TAU	29 CAN	27 CAN	28 VIR	28 LIB	27 SCO	28 CAP	29 PIS	27 ARI	27 TAU	28 CAN	28 LEO
30 GEM		30 LEO	30 VIR	30 SCO	29 SAG	30 AQU	31 ARI	29 TAU	29 GEM	30 LEO	30 VIR
31 GEM		31 LEO		31 SCO	30 SAG	31 AQU		30 TAU	31 CAN		31 VIR

1997

JAN	FEB	MAR	APR	MAY	JUN	JUL	AUG	SEP	OCT	NOV	DEC
1 VIR	1 SCO	1 SCO	1 CAP	1 AQU	1 ARI	1 TAU	1 CAN	1 LEO	1 LIB	1 SCO	1 SAG
2 LIB	3 SAG	2 SAG	3 AQU	2 PIS	3 TAU	2 GEM	3 LEO	2 VIR	4 SCO	3 SAG	2 CAP
4 SCO	5 CAP	4 CAP	5 PIS	4 ARI	5 GEM	4 CAN	5 VIR	4 LIB	6 SAG	5 CAP	4 AQU
6 SAG	7 AQU	6 AQU	7 ARI	6 TAU	7 CAN	7 LEO	8 LIB	7 SCO	9 CAP	7 AQU	7 PIS
8 CAP	9 PIS	8 PIS	9 TAU	8 GEM	9 LEO	9 VIR	10 SCO	9 SAG	11 AQU	9 PIS	9 ARI
10 AQU	11 ARI	10 ARI	11 GEM	11 CAN	12 VIR	12 LIB	13 SAG	12 CAP	13 PIS	12 ARI	11 TAU
12 PIS	13 TAU	12 TAU	13 CAN	13 LEO	14 LIB	14 SCO	15 CAP	14 AQU	15 ARI	14 TAU	13 GEM
14 ARI	15 GEM	15 GEM	16 LEO	15 VIR	17 SCO	17 SAG	17 AQU	16 PIS	17 TAU	16 GEM	15 CAN
17 TAU	18 CAN	17 CAN	18 VIR	18 LIB	19 SAG	19 CAP	19 PIS	18 ARI	19 GEM	18 CAN	17 LEO
19 GEM	20 LEO	19 LEO	21 LIB	20 SCO	21 CAP	21 AQU	21 ARI	20 TAU	21 CAN	20 LEO	20 VIR
21 CAN	23 VIR	22 VIR	23 SCO	23 SAG	23 AQU	23 PIS	23 TAU	22 GEM	24 LEO	23 VIR	22 LIB
24 LEO	25 LIB	24 LIB	25 SAG	25 CAP	26 PIS	25 ARI	25 GEM	24 CAN	26 VIR	25 LIB	25 SCO
26 VIR	28 SCO	27 SCO	28 CAP	27 AQU	28 ARI	27 TAU	28 CAN	26 LEO	29 LIB	28 SCO	27 SAG
29 LIB		29 SAG	30 AQU	29 PIS	30 TAU	29 GEM	30 LEO	29 VIR	31 SCO	30 SAG	30 CAP
31 SCO		31 SAG		31 ARI		31 GEM	31 LEO	30 VIR			31 CAP

1998

JAN	FEB	MAR	APR	MAY	JUN	JUL	AUG	SEP	OCT	NOV	DEC
1 AQU	1 ARI	1 ARI	1 GEM	1 CAN	1 LEO	1 LIB	1 SCO	1 SAG	1 AQU	1 PIS	1 TAU
3 PIS	3 TAU	3 TAU	3 CAN	3 LEO	2 VIR	4 SCO	3 SAG	2 CAP	3 PIS	2 ARI	3 GEM
5 ARI	6 GEM	5 GEM	6 LEO	5 VIR	4 LIB	6 SAG	5 CAP	4 AQU	6 ARI	4 TAU	5 CAN
7 TAU	8 CAN	7 CAN	8 VIR	8 LIB	7 SCO	9 CAP	7 AQU	6 PIS	7 TAU	6 GEM	7 LEO
9 GEM	10 LEO	9 LEO	11 LIB	10 SCO	9 SAG	11 AQU	10 PIS	8 ARI	9 GEM	8 CAN	10 VIR
12 CAN	13 VIR	12 VIR	13 SCO	13 SAG	12 CAP	13 PIS	12 ARI	10 TAU	12 CAN	10 LEO	12 LIB
14 LEO	15 LIB	14 LIB	16 SAG	15 CAP	14 AQU	15 ARI	14 TAU	12 GEM	14 LEO	12 VIR	15 SCO
16 VIR	18 SCO	17 SCO	18 CAP	18 AQU	16 PIS	18 TAU	16 GEM	14 CAN	16 VIR	15 LIB	17 SAG
19 LIB	20 SAG	19 SAG	20 AQU	20 PIS	18 ARI	20 GEM	18 CAN	17 LEO	19 LIB	17 SCO	20 CAP
21 SCO	22 CAP	22 CAP	23 PIS	22 ARI	20 TAU	22 CAN	20 LEO	19 VIR	21 SCO	20 SAG	22 AQU
24 SAG	25 AQU	24 AQU	25 ARI	24 TAU	22 GEM	24 LEO	23 VIR	21 LIB	24 SAG	22 CAP	24 PIS
26 CAP	27 PIS	26 PIS	27 TAU	26 GEM	24 CAN	26 VIR	25 LIB	24 SCO	26 CAP	25 AQU	27 ARI
28 AQU	28 PIS	28 ARI	29 GEM	28 CAN	27 LEO	29 LIB	28 SCO	26 SAG	29 AQU	27 PIS	29 TAU
30 PIS		30 TAU	30 GEM	30 LEO	29 VIR	31 SCO	30 SAG	29 CAP	31 PIS	29 ARI	31 GEM
31 PIS		31 TAU		31 LEO	30 VIR		31 SAG	30 CAP		30 ARI	

1999

JAN	FEB	MAR	APR	MAY	JUN	JUL	AUG	SEP	OCT	NOV	DEC
1 GEM	1 LEO	1 LEO	1 LIB	1 SCO	1 SAG	1 AQU	1 PIS	1 TAU	1 GEM	1 LEO	1 VIR
2 CAN	3 VIR	2 VIR	3 SCO	3 SAG	2 CAP	4 PIS	2 ARI	3 GEM	2 CAN	3 VIR	2 LIB
4 LEO	5 LIB	4 LIB	6 SAG	5 CAP	4 AQU	6 ARI	4 TAU	5 CAN	4 LEO	5 LIB	5 SCO
6 VIR	7 SCO	7 SCO	8 CAP	8 AQU	6 PIS	8 TAU	6 GEM	7 LEO	6 VIR	7 SCO	7 SAG
9 LIB	10 SAG	9 SAG	11 AQU	10 PIS	9 ARI	10 GEM	9 CAN	9 VIR	9 LIB	10 SAG	10 CAP
11 SCO	12 CAP	12 CAP	13 PIS	12 ARI	11 TAU	12 CAN	11 LEO	11 LIB	11 SCO	12 CAP	12 AQU
14 SAG	15 AQU	14 AQU	15 ARI	14 TAU	13 GEM	14 LEO	13 VIR	14 SCO	14 SAG	15 AQU	15 PIS
16 CAP	17 PIS	16 PIS	17 TAU	16 GEM	15 CAN	16 VIR	15 LIB	16 SAG	16 CAP	17 PIS	17 ARI
18 AQU	19 ARI	19 ARI	19 GEM	18 CAN	17 LEO	19 LIB	17 SCO	19 CAP	19 AQU	20 ARI	19 TAU
21 PIS	21 TAU	21 TAU	21 CAN	20 LEO	19 VIR	21 SCO	20 SAG	21 AQU	21 PIS	22 TAU	21 GEM
23 ARI	23 GEM	23 GEM	23 LEO	23 VIR	21 LIB	24 SAG	22 CAP	24 PIS	23 ARI	24 GEM	23 CAN
25 TAU	25 CAN	25 CAN	25 VIR	25 LIB	24 SCO	26 CAP	25 AQU	26 ARI	25 TAU	26 CAN	25 LEO
27 GEM	28 LEO	27 LEO	28 LIB	28 SCO	26 SAG	29 AQU	27 PIS	28 TAU	27 GEM	28 LEO	27 VIR
29 CAN		29 VIR	30 SCO	30 SAG	29 CAP	31 PIS	29 ARI	30 GEM	29 CAN	30 VIR	30 LIB
31 LEO		31 VIR		31 SAG	30 CAP		31 ARI		31 LEO		31 LIB

2000

JAN	FEB	MAR	APR	MAY	JUN	JUL	AUG	SEP	OCT	NOV	DEC
1 SCO	1 SAG	1 CAP	1 AQU	1 PIS	1 TAU	1 GEM	1 LEO	1 LIB	1 SCO	1 CAP	1 AQU
3 SAG	2 CAP	3 AQU	2 PIS	2 ARI	2 GEM	2 CAN	2 VIR	3 SCO	2 SAG	4 AQU	4 PIS
6 CAP	5 AQU	5 PIS	4 ARI	4 TAU	4 CAN	4 LEO	4 LIB	5 SAG	5 CAP	6 PIS	6 ARI
8 AQU	7 PIS	8 ARI	6 TAU	6 GEM	6 LEO	6 VIR	6 SCO	8 CAP	7 AQU	9 ARI	8 TAU
11 PIS	10 ARI	10 TAU	8 GEM	8 CAN	8 VIR	8 LIB	9 SAG	10 AQU	10 PIS	11 TAU	11 GEM
13 ARI	12 TAU	12 GEM	11 CAN	10 LEO	10 LIB	10 SCO	11 CAP	13 PIS	12 ARI	13 GEM	13 CAN
16 TAU	14 GEM	14 CAN	13 LEO	12 VIR	13 SCO	13 SAG	14 AQU	15 ARI	15 TAU	15 CAN	15 LEO
18 GEM	16 CAN	16 LEO	15 VIR	14 LIB	15 SAG	15 CAP	16 PIS	17 TAU	17 GEM	17 LEO	17 VIR
20 CAN	18 LEO	19 VIR	17 LIB	17 SCO	18 CAP	18 AQU	19 ARI	20 GEM	19 CAN	19 VIR	19 LIB
22 LEO	20 VIR	21 LIB	19 SCO	19 SAG	20 AQU	20 PIS	21 TAU	22 CAN	21 LEO	22 LIB	21 SCO
24 VIR	22 LIB	23 SCO	22 SAG	22 CAP	23 PIS	23 ARI	23 GEM	24 LEO	23 VIR	24 SCO	23 SAG
26 LIB	25 SCO	25 SAG	24 CAP	24 AQU	25 ARI	25 TAU	25 CAN	26 VIR	25 LIB	26 SAG	26 CAP
28 SCO	27 SAG	28 CAP	27 AQU	27 PIS	28 TAU	27 GEM	27 LEO	28 LIB	28 SCO	29 CAP	28 AQU
31 SAG	29 SAG	30 AQU	29 PIS	29 ARI	30 GEM	29 CAN	29 VIR	30 SCO	30 SAG	30 CAP	31 PIS
		31 AQU	30 PIS	31 TAU		31 LEO	31 VIR		31 SAG		

ARIES MOON

Your Moon in Aries makes you impulsive, impatient, impetuous, temperamental, impractical and affectionate. You love challenges and you tend to be secretive in your business dealings, which is detrimental when carried to an extreme, and you often do this. You have a great need to be told how wonderful you are and how much you are loved, and so far as you're concerned, you can't hear this enough. You love new adventures, you love romance, and with the right partner, you'll keep the love light burning, but until you find the right one, your love life will be unstable. You're a big talker, full of exciting plans of all the things you're going to do, but when it comes time to put up or shut up, your plans usually fizzle out. You tend to try to make people think you're smarter than you are. You dazzle at first, and waste a lot of energy on time-consuming projects that probably will never happen. But your enthusiasm is contagious, and if you could *only* get some determination and stick-to-it-iveness in your life, (which you could if you really worked at it), you could be a real winner.

TAURUS MOON

Your Moon in Taurus makes you practical and methodical. You're loaded with common sense and love to be married. You are monogamous and won't stray, and are a devoted and loving mate. You are honest with your feelings, so one always knows where you're at emotionally. You love luxury and are romantic, and love expensive presents. Family ties are very important to you. You love your home and your greatest pleasure-time is spent there. Others may want and need to gallivant, but not you. And music often plays an important part in your life in some way. You need harmony in your domestic life and you have a great need for emotional and material security, and until you find that special someone with whom you can share your life, you will not be happy.

GEMINI MOON

Your Moon in Gemini makes you restless and always seeking "Mr. or Ms. Right," that perfect love that exists only in your mind. You are dual-natured and never really satisfied with the person you're with.

You tend to flirt a lot, which is not too flattering to your companion. You're easily bored and treat romance lightly, never really taking it seriously. You're very impatient, and although you're terribly bright, it's very superficial and you don't have the patience to delve deeply into anything. Also, you tend to start plans and projects with a lot of enthusiasm, but give up quickly and rarely finish any of them. You have a very active imagination and truth is not a fetish with you. In fact, you bend it quite a bit. You have plenty of charm, which gets you out of a lot of scrapes and lets you manipulate, balancing several affairs at one time. It's almost impossible for you to be faithful to one person, but as I said, your incredible charm and sparkling personality lets you get away with a lot.

CANCER MOON

Your Moon in Cancer makes you super-sensitive, sentimental and devoted to your home. You are a very emotional and vulnerable person, easily hurt but rarely showing the hurt, keeping it inside instead. You are a faithful partner and very affectionate, full of hugs and kisses. You tend to be possessive, which you should try to control, and you also tend to make those closest to you feel guilty whenever you're hurt, which is often. Instead of expressing your anger in a healthy, open way, you keep it inside and sulk a lot, which of course *would* provoke guilt. You're moody and have frequent ups and downs. You're very intuitive to your mate's needs and can feel when he or she wants something, and because of your loving nature, you're always there to be sure that those wants and needs are taken care of.

LEO MOON

Your Moon in Leo makes you romantic, passionate and conventional in your passions. You love beautiful things and place a high value on money and status. What you need more than anything else is attention—the spotlight must be on you or you're unhappy. You love flattery and don't really care if it's sincere or not. You're very generous, but you're also domineering and can be extremely jealous. You care too much about what others think of you, and this tends to give you far too much pride. You're very aware of externals and overlook all the really important qualities that make for a good relationship. You want your mate to make you look good, and sometimes you will miss a good and positive relationship because you only judged the outside and never even looked inside.

VIRGO MOON

Your Moon in Virgo makes you critical, reserved and cautious. You are not a feeling person, and if you are not a highly developed Moon in Virgo, you are a cold and unresponsive person who tends to be picky, hard-to-please and a fuss-budget in romantic affairs. You are usually more successful in business than you are in love, because you can control business to a certain extent (and you *do* like to control things), but you sure can't control people, and people make romance. You are very logical, not emotional, and not above disregarding others' feelings as you criticize. You're a perfectionist, and also very conscientious, analytical, and have a way with details. You are quite perceptive, a good conversationalist, and because of your sharp mind, very quick at picking up on things.

LIBRA MOON

Your Moon in Libra makes you *very* romantic and always looking for love. But not a true, deep love. You love to flirt and you're satisfied with a surface love and are attracted to a good-looking body rather than a good character. You're a mental person rather than an emotional one and tend to be secretive. Your life will be full of promiscuous affairs, and it is very difficult for you to be faithful to one partner. You don't like to be alone and you have a need to share everything, so you like lots of parties and people. You also need to be the center of attention. If your first marriage doesn't work out, you'll try a second, a third, and a fourth, with lots of affairs in between.

SCORPIO MOON

Your Moon in Scorpio makes you extremely passionate, but also makes you extremely fearful of being vulnerable. You repress your feelings, and because of this, you have a hard time expressing love.

You are demanding, intense, domineering, jealous, strong-willed and a rebel. You have a temper which, when uncontrolled, can get you into a lot of trouble. Also, your sex drive is so strong that it too needs to be controlled. If you find a lover you feel you can really trust, then you let down your fearful guard and you can have an intensely satisfying love and sex life. But if you don't find your ideal, you will be happiest channeling all your sexual energy into your career or an all-consuming hobby.

SAGITTARIUS MOON

Your Moon in Sagittarius makes you full of enthusiasm and lots of fun to be around. You love good food, good drink and good times, mixed with lots of good people. You're sparkling as a person and as a conversationalist, and you have a great sense of humor. You know the right time to say something funny, and you always do. You love the adventure of travel and try to get away as often as you can (if you can't afford it, you'll talk about it a lot and wind up eating German or Spanish or Russian food and dream about each country as you're eating). You're very generous, optimistic, impulsive, changeable (and sometimes a little fickle), spontaneous and, with your terrific sense of humor (you can laugh at anything), you're a lot of fun to be around.

CAPRICORN MOON

Your Moon in Capricorn makes you tremendously ambitious, with a drive to succeed backed by enormous determination. You tend to be calculating and not demonstrative, and often marry for money. You are always striving for something, and many times when you get what you want, you find something else you feel you must have. You also tend to be a super-achiever who is capable of round-the-clock work. The lower, unevolved Moon in Capricorns tend to go into relationships thinking only of what you will get out of them, but the higher evolved you are, the more self-sacrificing you will be, and the more giving and dependable and helpful to your partner you will be, and once you find your ideal relationship (which is usually never early in life), you will be totally involved and satisfied with your mate.

AQUARIUS MOON

Your Moon in Aquarius makes you very friendly and a warm person to be around. You have an understanding nature, and people can sense this and they seek you out to help them with their problems, because you tend to be analytical about feelings, and can help them objectively solve their problems. In a romance, you're looking more for a close friend or a partner who can share your life, rather than an all-consuming passion who could dominate your feelings. You love the unusual—anything really different stimulates you because you need to see things in a different light more than the rest of us. You have a quirk about you that sometimes makes only an unavailable person attractive to you. If he or she is married or going with someone else, you decide you must have him or her. You love communication, and are very open and honest emotionally in your relationships.

PISCES MOON

Your Moon in Pisces makes you emotional, affectionate and receptive to everything around you. You love being married and having a family. You are basically a day-dreamer, making lots of plans which you rarely work out.

You're very sensitive, and this sensitivity gives you a poetic quality. You've also got a psychic ability, your ESP is acute, and often you'll have dreams that tell you what's going to happen in the future. Moon in Pisces has a dual quality which sometimes makes you itchy and restless, and this can lead to boredom, where drugs and booze are the palliatives, making life more exciting temporarily (and it's *always* only a temporary lift). Stick with your home and family, which will bring you all the joy and the security you need.

4

Your 12 Rising Signs (Ascendants), and Chart

Your Ascendant is determined by the sign that was rising on the Eastern horizon at the exact time (to the hour and minute) of your birth. Your Rising Sign (Ascendant) determines your personality, your approach to life, how you express your self, how you will start to find your own personal meaning in your life, how your self is manifested to the rest of the world, how everyone around you sees you—your body, the way you walk and talk, the way you move around, and your mental inclinations and quirks. Many times when you meet people, your Ascendant will be more obvious to them than your Sun Sign.

Your Ascendant draws you to what you need to learn in order to become in life what you want to become.

You Ascendant chart is on the following pages.

Your Ascendant

HOW TO FIND THE POSITION OF ASCENDANT
AT THE TIME OF YOUR BIRTH

January 1
Approximate Time of Birth

A.M.	P.M.
12:30 Libra	1:10 Taurus
3:05 Scorpio	2:50 Gemini
5:35 Sagittarius	5:05 Cancer
7:50 Capricorn	7:30 Leo
9:30 Aquarius	10:05 Virgo
10:45 Pisces	11:40 Libra
11:55 Aries	

January 15
Approximate Time of Birth

A.M.	P.M.
1:05 Scorpio	12:10 Taurus
4:35 Sagittarius	1:50 Gemini
6:50 Capricorn	4:05 Cancer
8:25 Aquarius	6:15 Leo
9:45 Pisces	9:05 Virgo
10:55 Aries	11:30 Libra

February 1
Approximate Time of Birth

A.M.	P.M.
1:05 Scorpio	12:50 Gemini
3:35 Sagittarius	3:05 Cancer
5:50 Capricorn	5:30 Leo
7:25 Aquarius	8:05 Virgo
8:40 Pisces	10:30 Libra
9:55 Aries	
11:10 Taurus	

February 15
Approximate Time of Birth

A.M.	P.M.
12:05 Scorpio	2:05 Cancer
2:40 Sagittarius	4:30 Leo
4:50 Capricorn	7:05 Virgo
6:25 Aquarius	9:30 Libra
7:45 Pisces	11:05 Scorpio
8:55 Aries	
10:10 Taurus	
11:50 Gemini	

March 1
Approximate Time of Birth

A.M.	P.M.
1:35 Sagittarius	1:05 Cancer
3:50 Capricorn	3:30 Leo
5:25 Aquarius	6:05 Virgo
6:45 Pisces	8:30 Libra
7:55 Aries	11:05 Scorpio
9:10 Taurus	
10:50 Gemini	

March 15
Approximate Time of Birth

A.M.	P.M.
12:35 Sagittarius	12:05 Cancer
2:50 Capricorn	2:30 Leo
4:25 Aquarius	5:05 Virgo
5:45 Pisces	7:30 Libra
6:55 Aries	10:05 Scorpio
8:10 Taurus	11:55 Sagittarius
9:50 Gemini	

April 1
Approximate Time of Birth

A.M.	P.M.
1:50 Capricorn	1:30 Leo
3:25 Aquarius	4:05 Virgo
4:45 Pisces	6:30 Libra
5:55 Aries	9:05 Scorpio
7:10 Taurus	11:35 Sagittarius
8:50 Gemini	
11:05 Cancer	

April 15
Approximate Time of Birth

A.M.	P.M.
12:30 Capricorn	12:30 Leo
2:55 Aquarius	3:05 Virgo
3:45 Pisces	5:30 Libra
4:55 Aries	8:05 Scorpio
6:10 Taurus	10:35 Sagittarius
7:50 Gemini	11:40 Capricorn
10:05 Cancer	

May 1
Approximate Time of Birth

A.M.	P.M.
1:25 Aquarius	2:05 Virgo
2:45 Pisces	4:30 Libra
3:55 Aries	7:05 Scorpio
5:10 Taurus	9:35 Sagittarius
6:50 Gemini	11:50 Capricorn
9:05 Cancer	
11:30 Leo	

May 15
Approximate Time of Birth

A.M.	P.M.
12:25 Aquarius	1:05 Virgo
1:45 Pisces	3:30 Libra
2:55 Aries	6:05 Scorpio
4:10 Taurus	8:35 Sagittarius
5:50 Gemini	10:50 Capricorn
8:05 Cancer	
10:30 Leo	

June 1
Approximate Time of Birth

A.M.	P.M.
12:45 Pisces	12:05 Virgo
1:55 Aries	2:30 Libra
3:10 Taurus	5:05 Scorpio
4:50 Gemini	7:35 Sagittarius
7:05 Cancer	9:50 Capricorn
9:35 Leo	11:25 Aquarius

June 15
Approximate Time of Birth

A.M.	P.M.
12:55 Aries	1:30 Libra
2:10 Taurus	4:05 Scorpio
3:50 Gemini	6:35 Sagittarius
6:05 Cancer	8:50 Capricorn
8:30 Leo	10:25 Aquarius
11:05 Virgo	11:45 Pisces

July 1
Approximate Time of Birth

A.M.	P.M.
1:10 Taurus	12:30 Libra
2:50 Gemini	3:05 Scorpio
5:05 Cancer	5:35 Sagittarius
7:30 Leo	7:50 Capricorn
10:05 Virgo	9:25 Aquarius
	10:45 Pisces
	11:35 Aries

July 15
Approximate Time of Birth

A.M.	P.M.
12:10 Taurus	2:05 Scorpio
1:50 Gemini	4:35 Sagittarius
4:05 Cancer	6:50 Capricorn
6:30 Leo	8:25 Aquarius
9:00 Virgo	9:45 Pisces
11:30 Libra	10:55 Aries

August 1
Approximate Time of Birth

A.M.	P.M.
12:50 Gemini	1:05 Scorpio
3:05 Cancer	3:35 Sagittarius
5:30 Leo	5:50 Capricorn
8:05 Virgo	7:25 Aquarius
10:30 Libra	8:45 Pisces
	9:55 Aries
	11:10 Taurus

August 15
Approximate Time of Birth

A.M.	P.M.
2:05 Cancer	12:05 Scorpio
4:30 Leo	2:35 Sagittarius
7:05 Virgo	4:50 Capricorn
9:30 Libra	6:25 Aquarius
	7:45 Pisces
	8:55 Aries
	10:10 Taurus
	11:50 Gemini

September 1
Approximate Time of Birth

A.M.	P.M.
1:05 Cancer	1:35 Sagittarius
3:30 Leo	3:50 Capricorn
6:10 Virgo	5:25 Aquarius
8:30 Libra	6:45 Pisces
11:05 Scorpio	7:55 Aries
	9:10 Taurus
	10:50 Gemini

September 15
Approximate Time of Birth

A.M.	P.M.
12:05 Cancer	12:35 Sagittarius
2:30 Leo	2:50 Capricorn
5:05 Virgo	4:25 Aquarius
7:30 Libra	5:45 Pisces
10:05 Scorpio	6:55 Aries
	8:10 Taurus
	9:50 Gemini

October 1
Approximate Time of Birth

A.M.	P.M.
1:30 Leo	1:50 Capricorn
4:05 Virgo	3:15 Aquarius
6:30 Libra	4:45 Pisces
9:05 Scorpio	5:55 Aries
11:35 Sagittarius	7:10 Taurus
	8:50 Gemini
	11:05 Cancer

October 15
Approximate Time of Birth

A.M.	P.M.
12:30 Leo	12:50 Capricorn
3:05 Virgo	2:25 Aquarius
5:30 Libra	3:45 Pisces
8:05 Scorpio	4:55 Aries
10:35 Sagittarius	6:10 Taurus
	7:50 Gemini
	10:05 Cancer

November 1
Approximate Time of Birth

A.M.	P.M.
2:05 Virgo	1:25 Aquarius
4:30 Libra	2:45 Pisces
7:05 Scorpio	3:55 Aries
9:35 Sagittarius	5:10 Taurus
11:50 Capricorn	6:50 Gemini
	9:05 Cancer
	11:30 Leo

November 15
Approximate Time of Birth

A.M.	P.M.
1:05 Virgo	12:25 Aquarius
3:30 Libra	1:45 Pisces
6:15 Scorpio	2:55 Aries
8:35 Sagittarius	4:10 Taurus
10:50 Capricorn	5:50 Gemini
	8:05 Cancer
	10:30 Leo

December 1
Approximate Time of Birth

A.M.	P.M.
12:05 Virgo	12:45 Pisces
2:30 Libra	1:55 Aries
5:05 Scorpio	3:10 Taurus
7:35 Sagittarius	4:50 Gemini
9:50 Capricorn	7:05 Cancer
11:25 Aquarius	9:30 Leo

December 15
Approximate Time of Birth

A.M.	P.M.
1:30 Libra	12:55 Aries
4:05 Scorpio	2:10 Taurus
6:35 Sagittarius	3:50 Gemini
8:50 Capricorn	6:00 Cancer
10:25 Aquarius	8:30 Leo
11:45 Pisces	11:05 Virgo

ARIES ASCENDANT

Your Aries Rising gives you your energy, and your impatience. You're bold, aggressive, and you have an enormous amount of egotism and pride. When it comes to refining and completing all the details of whatever you're working on, you lose interest, and you've probably got hundreds of uncompleted projects. You're ardent in your endeavors (as long as they last), quick in your actions and fiery in your ways.

TAURUS ASCENDANT

Your Taurus Rising gives you a mellow voice with melodious overtones and soft, rich undertones. You love music and have an artistic bent. You're not quick, but your slow plodding and bull-headedness keep you working toward your goals when everyone else has quit. Long-term planning is also a strength. You are a trifle hedonistic and your desires for rich, fattening foods can give you weight problems.

GEMINI ASCENDANT

Your Gemini Rising gives you a will-o-the-wisp quality that's fun to be around. You're not a doer, you're a thinker and fast talker, and one never knows really *where* you stand on anything. If you could only bring the two of you (the Twins) together and work in harmony as one instead of two, you could probably conquer the world! You're clever and versatile, and you've a quickness about you and a light airiness that makes it seem your feet never really touch the ground.

CANCER ASCENDANT

Your Cancer Rising gives you your sensitivity and your intuition. You are emotional and restless, ever searching for that special person to complete you. You're very affectionate and a toucher with those you feel close to and trust. You love your home and family and express your self best there, usually loving to cook (which will not help to keep your body gorgeous and trim).

LEO ASCENDANT

Leo Rising gives you your enthusiasm, your magnetism and your sunny smile and loving disposition. You're big-hearted, warm, open and carry your self like a monarch. You tend to think of yourself as royalty, and also tend to be insensitive to others. You have a magnetism about you and a flair for dramatic situations. The sun seems to shine right through you and gives you an outer glow.

VIRGO ASCENDANT

Your Virgo Rising gives you your ability to converse on any matter with anybody. You're very modest in your achievements and are critical of your self and others. You have a strong sense of responsibility, you're cooperative, but you also have bouts with stinginess. You rarely have a weight problem and are usually slender with a well-proportioned body.

LIBRA ASCENDANT

Your Libra Rising gives you your charm and great taste and artistic ability. Anything off-color (vulgar people, crude jokes) offends you, and anything off-balance (too much food or booze, too many people or too much solitude) upsets you. Staying on an even keel and keeping your scales always balanced is a must. You usually have a dimple somewhere on your well-curved body.

SCORPIO ASCENDANT

Your Scorpio Rising gives you your passion in everything you do—you eat and drink with a passion, you work with a passion and, of course, you love with a passion. You are very intense in all your endeavors—and you tend to be temperamental and domineering. But you're also clever and have a faculty for getting what you want. You have deep, piercing eyes that seem to see right through people.

SAGITTARIUS ASCENDANT

Your Sagittarius Rising gives you your outspokenness and your ability to embroider the truth. You tend to overstate facts. You're extroverted and peppy, and absolutely adore travel and conversation. You have humor and you don't waste time—you go right for what you want. You also have long, graceful thighs and are rarely fat.

CAPRICORN ASCENDANT

Your Capricorn Rising gives you your determination and great ambition, but usually your ambition will pay off later in life. You are very self-conscious and opinionated, but you are reliable and a super-organizer. Your body is angular and your eyes are penetrating. You are quietly a very sensual person (the world will never know it, but your lover will).

AQUARIUS ASCENDANT

Your Aquarius Rising gives you your uniqueness—you're really like no other. You're unconventional, unpredictable, with an originality about you that seems to be totally modern and even futuristic. You are fascinated by people and the world around you, and are a person of action—you don't just talk about doing things, you *do* them. You have imperfect features, but they're lovely.

PISCES ASCENDANT

Your Pisces Rising gives you your dreaminess and your dual nature (you can pick and become either one of the Two Fish swimming in opposite directions—one for your betterment and self-reliance, and the other not). You are a deeply-feeling person, *very* romantic and emotional, but you tend to be a clinger. As you mature, you have a propensity to overweight which is extremely difficult for you to control.

5

Your 12 Mercury Signs and Chart

Mercury is the agent through which your inner self makes contact with the outer world. Mercury is also your mind, and your communication with other people, so it's very important that your Mercury be compatible with your mate's.

Mercury rules the type of mentality you were born with, your practical reasoning, your sense perception, your mental processes, your way of working and also all the different forms of communication, and without communication we would never make friends—or lovers!

Your Mercury is found in either your own Sun Sign, the sign before your Sun Sign, or the sign right after it.

How to Find the Position of Mercury at the Time of Your Birth

Because Mercury changes signs as often as it does, it would take too many pages to chart it exactly, but this very small planet is located so close to the Sun that it is *never* more than 28° away from it. Now there are only 30° in each astro-logical sign, so Mercury is always either in your own Sun Sign (the date of your birth) or only one sign away. For instance, if you are a Virgo, born on August 28th, your Mercury would be either in Virgo (your Sun Sign) or in Leo (the sign before Virgo) or in Libra (the sign after Virgo). The way you can tell is to read the description of your Sun Sign, then read the sign just before it, and then the sign just after it, and figure out which one is you. They will each be very different, so it should be fairly easy to find the one which is you.

MERCURY IN ARIES

Your Mercury in Aries gives you a sharp, creative and inventive mind. You love being first in everything you do, you need to pioneer in all areas, and you're a beginner of projects. You're also a good speech writer, and are able to toss off beautiful love letters.

MERCURY IN TAURUS

Your Mercury in Taurus gives you a stubbornness that makes you very set in your ways—once you make up your mind, you hang in there. Your opinions are fixed, and rarely do you change them. You also have a terrific memory, which helps in everything you do.

MERCURY IN GEMINI

Your Mercury in Gemini gives you an alertness and intellectuality, which, when mixed with your wittiness, make you a clever person indeed. You're an incorrigible flirt, and your duality (the Twins) makes you moody, and keeps everyone around you on their toes, 'cause you're either on top of the world or in the pits. You love to gossip.

MERCURY IN CANCER

Your Mercury in Cancer gives you a sentimentality which is sweet to be around. You love to send little gifts to those you care for, like flowers for her or a plant for his office. You also like to send love notes via telegrams. But, alas, you're not constant in your loves.

MERCURY IN LEO

Your Mercury in Leo gives you a generosity of spirit that is hard to match. You have a warmth about you and a dynamic approach to everything you do. Your generosity spills over into your sex life, which is hot and heavy. You have a forceful will and strong powers of concentration.

MERCURY IN VIRGO

Your Mercury in Virgo makes you a bit inhibited in the way you express your self. You're a real perfectionist and want every little detail in your work to be perfect. You usually find others don't share your impeccability with details, and this drives you up the wall. If you would only realize most people *aren't* as conscientious as you, and then just do the best you can with those around you, you'd be a lot happier and more productive.

MERCURY IN LIBRA

Your Mercury in Libra gives you a balanced approach in most things. You are romantic and adore receiving little love notes. But you're not too keen on sending them. It's important to you to be the wooed, not the wooer. You love the chase, but only if you're the chasee.

MERCURY IN SCORPIO

Your Mercury in Scorpio gives an air of secrecy about you. You're not above sending unsigned notes of passion to one you secretly admire. You love mystery and mysterious things, and people sense an ESP about you. Sometimes you're able to read their minds.

MERCURY IN SAGITTARIUS

Your Mercury in Sagittarius gives you your directness in everything you do, your need for travel and your love of all forms of communication. Your thoughts go out like arrows, straight and fast and sure. You make a good newscaster because you strip everything down to the facts—no jazz, no fluff—jùst facts.

MERCURY IN CAPRICORN

Your Mercury in Capricorn gives you your organizational ability which will be a great help in realizing your tremendous ambitions. You're pragmatic and down-to-earth and always looking to better your self through your associations. Your mind is full of visions of success, dreams of money and fantasies of power.

MERCURY IN AQUARIUS

Your Mercury in Aquarius gives you your analytical ability mixed with your idealism, which makes you an ideal person to help others with problems. People sense this about you and are drawn to you. You truly do like to help, and would make a great "advice to the lovelorn" columnist, or social worker.

MERCURY IN PISCES

Your Mercury in Pisces gives you your talent in creating fantasies. You have a keen imagination, an inventive mind, and love to create and work with illusion. You thrive in advertising and films, which are *all* illusion. You're a good lecturer, and sometimes have talent in the spiritual field, with real psychic ability.

6

Your 12 Venus Signs and Chart

Venus is the planet that influences your love life and your sex life more than any other planet because it links you to all emotional stimuli and impressions you receive from outside your self. Whatever sign your Venus is in will define your attitude to these emotional stimuli and impressions, and how you'll react toward feelings of love and intimacy.

Venus has the strongest influence over romance and marriage, and when Venus is in a strong placement, you will almost always have a great capacity for love and a life full of affection. Venus rules everything to do with love—friendship, affection, courtship, romance, marriage, divorce and, of course, intimacy (which so many people are afraid of, and which I go into at great length in my last book, *Isle of View* (*Say It Out Loud*), which is *all* about love).

Your Venus Sign is determined by the year you were born. Your Venus Chart is on the following pages.

Your Venus Chart

VENUS IN ARIES

1850	MAR 17 – APR 10
1851	APR 30 – MAY 24
1852	FEB 17 – MAR 11
1853	APR 1 – APR 24
1854	MAY 7 – JUN 4
1855	MAR 2 – MAR 26
1856	APR 15 – MAY 9
1857	FEB 4 – MAR 3
1858	MAR 17 – APR 9
1859	APR 29 – MAY 24
1860	FEB 16 – MAR 11
1861	MAR 31 – APR 24
1862	MAY 7 – JUN 4
1863	MAR 2 – MAR 25
1864	APR 15 – MAY 8
1865	FEB 4 – MAR 3
1866	MAR 16 – APR 8
1867	APR 29 – MAY 23
1868	FEB 16 – MAR 11
1869	MAR 31 – APR 23
1870	MAY 7 – JUN 3
1871	MAR 1 – MAR 25
1872	APR 14 – MAY 8
1873	FEB 3 – MAR 3
1874	MAR 16 – APR 8
1875	APR 28 – MAY 23
1876	FEB 15 – MAR 10
1877	MAR 30 – APR 23
1878	MAY 7 – JUN 3
1879	MAR 1 – MAR 24
1880	APR 14 – MAY 7
1881	FEB 3 – MAR 3
1882	MAR 15 – APR 7
1883	APR 28 – MAY 22
1884	FEB 15 – MAR 10
1885	MAR 30 – APR 22
1886	MAY 7 – JUN 3
1887	FEB 28 – MAR 24
1888	APR 13 – MAY 7
1889	FEB 3 – MAR 4
1890	MAR 15 – APR 7
1891	APR 27 – MAY 22
1892	FEB 14 – MAR 9
1893	MAR 29 – APR 22
1894	MAY 6 – JUN 2
1895	FEB 28 – MAR 23
1896	APR 13 – MAY 6
1897	FEB 2 – MAR 4
1898	MAR 14 – APR 6
1899	APR 27 – MAY 21
1900	FEB 14 – MAR 10
1901	MAR 30 – APR 22
1902	MAY 8 – JUN 3
1903	MAR 1 – MAR 24
1904	APR 14 – MAY 7
1905	FEB 4 – MAR 6
	MAY 10 – MAY 28
1906	MAR 15 – APR 7
1907	APR 28 – MAY 22
1908	FEB 15 – MAR 10
1909	MAR 30 – APR 22
1910	MAR 8 – APR 3
1911	FEB 28 – MAR 23
1912	APR 13 – MAY 7
1913	FEB 3 – MAR 6
	MAY 3 – MAY 31
1914	MAR 15 – APR 7
1915	APR 28 – MAY 22
1916	FEB 14 – MAR 9
1917	MAR 29 – APR 21
1918	MAY 7 – JUN 3
1919	FEB 28 – MAR 23
1920	APR 13 – MAY 6
1921	FEB 3 – MAR 7
	APR 26 – JUN 2
1922	MAR 14 – APR 6

VENUS IN ARIES

1923	APR 27 – MAY 21
1924	FEB 14 – MAR 9
1925	MAR 29 – APR 21
1926	MAY 7 – JUN 2
1927	FEB 27 – MAR 22
1928	APR 12 – MAY 6
1929	FEB 3 – MAR 8
	APR 21 – JUN 2
1930	MAR 13 – APR 6
1931	APR 27 – MAY 21
1932	FEB 13 – MAR 9
1933	MAR 28 – APR 20
1934	MAY 7 – JUN 2
1935	FEB 27 – MAR 22
1936	APR 12 – MAY 5
1937	FEB 3 – MAR 9
	APR 15 – JUN 4
1938	MAR 13 – APR 5
1939	APR 26 – MAY 20
1940	FEB 13 – MAR 8
1941	MAR 28 – APR 20
1942	MAY 7 – JUN 2
1943	FEB 26 – MAR 21
1944	APR 11 – MAY 4
1945	FEB 3 – MAR 11
	APR 8 – JUN 4
1946	MAR 12 – APR 5
1947	APR 26 – MAY 20
1948	FEB 12 – MAR 8
1949	MAR 27 – APR 19
1950	MAY 6 – JUN 1
1951	FEB 25 – MAR 21
1952	APR 10 – MAY 4
1953	FEB 3 – MAR 14
	APR 1 – JUN 5
1954	MAR 12 – APR 4
1955	APR 25 – MAY 19
1956	FEB 12 – MAR 7
1957	MAR 26 – APR 19
1958	MAY 6 – JUN 1
1959	FEB 25 – MAR 20
1960	APR 10 – MAY 3
1961	FEB 3 – JUN 5
1962	MAR 11 – APR 3
1963	APR 25 – MAY 19
1964	FEB 11 – MAR 7
1965	MAR 26 – APR 18
1966	MAY 6 – MAY 31
1967	FEB 24 – MAR 20
1968	APR 9 – MAY 3
1969	FEB 3 – JUN 6
1970	MAR 11 – APR 3
1971	APR 24 – MAY 18
1972	FEB 11 – MAR 7
1973	MAR 25 – MAR 18
1974	MAY 5 – MAY 31
1975	FEB 24 – MAR 19
1976	APR 9 – MAY 2
1977	FEB 3 – JUN 6
1978	MAR 10 – APR 2
1979	APR 24 – MAY 18
1980	FEB 10 – MAR 6
1981	MAR 25 – APR 17
1982	MAY 5 – MAY 30
1983	FEB 23 – MAR 19
1984	APR 8 – MAY 2
1985	FEB 3 – MAY 6
1986	MAR 10 – APR 2
1987	APR 23 – MAY 17
1988	FEB 10 – MAR 6
1989	MAR 24 – APR 16
1990	MAY 5 – MAY 30
1991	FEB 23 – MAR 18
1992	APR 8 – MAY 1
1993	FEB 3 – JUN 6
1994	MAR 9 – APR 1
1995	APR 23 – MAY 16
1996	FEB 10 – MAR 6
1997	MAR 24 – APR 16
1998	MAY 4 – MAY 29
1999	FEB 22 – MAR 18
2000	APR 7 – MAY 1

VENUS IN TAURUS

1850	APR 11 – MAY 4
1851	MAY 25 – JUN 18
1852	MAR 12 – APR 6
1853	APR 25 – MAY 19
1854	JUN 5 – JUL 1
1855	MAR 27 – APR 19
1856	MAY 10 – JUN 2
1857	MAR 4 – JUL 6
1858	APR 10 – MAY 3
1859	MAY 25 – JUN 18
1860	MAR 12 – APR 6
1861	APR 25 – MAY 18
1862	JUN 5 – JUN 30
1863	MAR 26 – APR 19
1864	MAY 9 – JUN 2
1865	MAR 4 – JUL 6
1866	APR 9 – MAY 3
1867	MAY 24 – JUN 17
1868	MAR 12 – APR 6
1869	APR 24 – MAY 18
1870	JUN 4 – JUN 30
1871	MAR 26 – APR 18
1872	MAY 9 – JUN 1
1873	MAR 4 – JUL 7
1874	APR 9 – MAY 2
1875	MAY 24 – JUN 17
1876	MAR 11 – APR 5
1877	APR 24 – MAY 17
1878	JUN 4 – JUN 30
1879	MAR 25 – APR 18
1880	MAY 8 – JUN 1
1881	MAR 4 – JUL 7
1882	APR 8 – MAY 2
1883	MAY 23 – JUN 16
1884	MAR 11 – APR 5
1885	APR 23 – MAY 16
1886	JUN 4 – JUN 29
1887	MAR 25 – APR 17
1888	MAY 8 – MAY 21
1889	MAR 5 – JUL 7
1890	APR 8 – MAY 1
1891	MAY 23 – JUN 16
1892	MAR 10 – APR 4
1893	APR 23 – MAY 16
1894	JUN 3 – JUN 29
1895	MAR 24 – APR 17
1896	MAY 7 – MAY 31
1897	MAR 5 – JUL 7
1898	APR 7 – MAY 1
1899	MAY 22 – JUN 15
1900	MAR 11 – APR 6
1901	APR 23 – MAY 17
1902	JUN 4 – JUN 3
1903	MAR 25 – APR 18
1904	MAY 8 – JUN 1
1905	MAR 7 – MAY 9
	MAY 29 – JUL 8
1906	APR 8 – MAY 2
1907	MAY 23 – JUN 16
1908	MAR 11 – APR 5
1909	APR 23 – MAY 16
1910	JUN 4 – JUN 29
1911	MAR 24 – APR 17
1912	MAY 8 – MAY 31
1913	MAR 7 – MAY 2
	JUN 1 – JUL 8
1914	APR 8 – MAY 1
1915	MAY 23 – JUN 16
1916	MAR 10 – APR 5
1917	APR 22 – MAY 16
1918	JUN 4 – JUN 29
1919	MAR 24 – APR 17
1920	MAY 7 – MAY 31
1921	MAR 8 – APR 25
	JUN 3 – JUL 8
1922	APR 7 – MAY 1
1923	MAY 22 – JUN 15
1924	MAR 10 – APR 5
1925	APR 22 – MAY 15
1926	JUN 3 – JUN 28
1927	MAR 23 – APR 16
1928	MAY 7 – MAY 30

VENUS IN TAURUS

1929	MAR 9 – APR 20
	JUN 4 – JUL 8
1930	APR 7 – APR 30
1931	MAY 22 – JUN 14
1932	MAR 10 – APR 5
1933	APR 21 – MAY 15
1934	JUN 3 – JUN 28
1935	MAR 23 – APR 16
1936	MAY 6 – MAY 29
1937	MAR 10 – APR 14
	JUN 5 – JUL 7
1938	APR 6 – APR 29
1939	MAY 21 – JUN 14
1940	MAR 9 – APR 4
1941	APR 21 – MAY 14
1942	JUN 3 – JUN 27
1943	MAR 22 – APR 15
1944	MAY 5 – MAY 29
1945	MAR 12 – APR 7
	JUN 5 – JUL 7
1946	APR 6 – APR 29
1947	MAY 21 – JUN 13
1948	MAR 9 – APR 4
1949	APR 20 – MAY 14
1950	JUN 2 – JUN 27
1951	MAR 22 – APR 15
1952	MAY 5 – MAY 28
1953	MAR 15 – MAR 31
	JUN 6 – JUL 7
1954	APR 5 – APR 28
1955	MAY 20 – JUN 13
1956	MAR 8 – APR 4
1957	APR 20 – MAY 13
1958	JUN 2 – JUN 26
1959	MAR 21 – APR 14
1960	MAY 4 – MAY 28
1961	JUN 6 – JUL 7
1962	APR 4 – APR 28
1963	MAY 20 – JUN 12
1964	MAR 8 – APR 4
1965	APR 19 – MAY 12
1966	JUN 1 – JUN 26
1967	MAR 21 – APR 14
1968	MAY 4 – MAY 27
1969	JUN 7 – JUL 6
1970	APR 4 – APR 27
1971	MAY 19 – JUN 12
1972	MAR 8 – APR 3
1973	MAR 19 – MAY 12
1974	JUN 1 – JUN 25
1975	MAR 20 – APR 13
1976	MAY 3 – MAY 27
1977	JUN 7 – JUL 6
1978	APR 3 – APR 27
1979	MAY 19 – JUN 11
1980	MAR 7 – APR 3
1981	APR 18 – MAY 11
1982	MAY 31 – JUN 25
1983	MAR 20 – APR 13
1984	MAY 3 – MAY 26
1985	MAY 7 – JUL 6
1986	APR 3 – APR 26
1987	MAY 18 – JUN 11
1988	MAR 7 – APR 3
1989	APR 17 – MAY 11
1990	MAY 31 – JUN 25
1991	MAR 19 – APR 13
1992	MAY 2 – MAY 26
1993	JUN 7 – JUL 6
1994	APR 2 – APR 26
1995	MAY 17 – JUN 10
1996	MAR 7 – APR 3
1997	APR 17 – MAY 10
1998	MAY 30 – JUN 24
1999	MAR 19 – APR 12
2000	MAY 2 – MAY 25

VENUS IN GEMINI

1850	MAY 5 – MAY 28	1890	MAY 2 – MAY 26
1851	JUN 19 – JUL 13	1891	JUN 17 – JUL 10
1852	APR 7 – MAY 4	1892	APR 5 – MY 4
1853	MAY 20 – JUN 12	1893	MAY 17 – JUN 9
1854	JUL 2 – JUL 27	1894	JUN 30 – JUL 24
1855	APR 20 – MAY 14	1895	APR 18 – MAY 12
1856	JUN 3 – JUN 27	1896	JUN 1 – JUN 24
1857	JUL 7 – AUG 6	1897	JUL 8 – AUG 5
1858	MAY 4 – MAY 28	1898	MAY 2 – MAY 25
1859	JUN 19 – JUL 12	1899	JUN 16 – JUL 10
1860	APR 7 – MAY 4	1900	APR 7 – MAY 5
1861	MAY 19 – JUN 11	1901	MAY 18 – JUN 10
1862	JUL 1 – JUL 26	1902	JUL 1 – JUL 25
1863	APR 20 – MAY 14	1903	APR 19 – MAY 13
1864	JUN 3 – JUN 26	1904	JUN 2 – JUN 25
1865	JUL 7 – AUG 6	1905	JUL 9 – AUG 6
1866	MAY 4 – MAY 27	1906	MAY 3 – MAY 26
1867	JUN 18 – JUL 12	1907	JUN 17 – JUL 11
1868	APR 7 – MAY 4	1908	APR 6 – MAY 5
1869	MAY 19 – JUN 11	1909	MAY 17 – JUN 10
1870	JUL 1 – JUL 26	1910	JUN 30 – JUL 25
1871	APR 19 – MAY 14	1911	APR 18 – MAY 13
1872	JUN 2 – JUN 26	1912	JUN 1 – JUN 25
1873	JUL 8 – AUG 6	1913	JUL 9 – AUG 5
1874	MAY 3 – MAY 27	1914	MAY 2 – MAY 26
1875	JUN 18 – JUL 11	1915	JUN 17 – JUL 10
1876	APR 6 – MAY 4	1916	APR 6 – MAY 5
1877	MAY 18 – JUN 10	1917	MAY 17 – JUN 9
1878	JUL 1 – JUL 25	1918	JUN 30 – JUL 24
1879	APR 19 – MAY 13	1919	APR 18 – MAY 12
1880	JUN 2 – JUN 25	1920	JUN 1 – JUN 24
1881	JUL 8 – AUG 5	1921	JUL 9 – AUG 5
1882	MAY 3 – MAY 26	1922	MAY 2 – MAY 25
1883	JUN 17 – JUL 11	1923	JUN 16 – JUL 10
1884	APR 6 – MAY 4	1924	APR 6 – MAY 6
1885	MAY 17 – JUN 10	1925	MAY 16 – JUN 9
1886	JUN 30 – JUL 25	1926	JUN 29 – JUL 24
1887	APR 18 – MAY 13	1927	APR 17 – MAY 12
1888	MAY 22 – JUL 25	1928	MAY 31 – JUN 23
1889	JUL 8 – AUG 5	1929	JUL 9 – AUG 5

VENUS IN GEMINI

1930	MAY 1 – MAY 25
1931	JUN 15 – JUL 9
1932	APR 6 – MAY 6
	JUL 14 – JUL 28
1933	MAY 16 – JUN 8
1934	JUN 29 – JUL 23
1935	APR 17 – MAY 11
1936	MAY 30 – JUN 23
1937	JUL 8 – AUG 4
1938	APR 30 – MAY 24
1939	JUN 15 – JUL 9
1940	APR 5 – MAY 6
	JUL 6 – AUG 1
1941	MAY 15 – JUN 7
1942	JUN 28 – JUL 23
1943	APR 16 – MAY 11
1944	MAY 30 – JUN 22
1945	JUL 8 – AUG 4
1946	APR 30 – MAY 24
1947	JUN 14 – JUL 8
1948	APR 5 – MAY 7
1949	MAY 15 – JUN 7
1950	JUN 28 – JUL 22
1951	APR 16 – MAY 11
1952	MAY 29 – JUN 22
1953	JUL 8 – AUG 4
1954	APR 29 – MAY 23
1955	JUN 14 – JUL 8
1956	APR 5 – MAY 8
	JUN 24 – AUG 4
1957	MAY 14 – JUN 6
1958	JUN 27 – JUL 22
1959	APR 15 – MAY 10
1960	MAY 29 – JUN 21
1961	JUL 8 – AUG 3
1962	APR 29 – MAY 23
1963	JUN 13 – JUL 7
1964	APR 5 – MAY 9
	JUN 18 – AUG 5
1965	MAY 13 – JUN 6
1966	JUN 27 – JUL 21
1967	APR 15 – MAY 10
1968	MAY 28 – JUN 21
1969	JUL 7 – AUG 3
1970	APR 28 – MAY 22
1971	JUN 13 – JUL 6
1972	APR 4 – MAY 10
	JUN 12 – AUG 6
1973	MAY 13 – JUN 5
1974	JUN 26 – JUL 21
1975	APR 14 – MAY 9
1976	MAY 28 – JUN 20
1977	JUL 7 – AUG 2
1978	JUN 12 – JUL 6
1979	JUN 12 – JUL 6
1980	APR 4 – MAY 12
	JUN 6 – AUG 6
1981	MAY 12 – JUN 5
1982	JUN 26 – JUL 20
1983	APR 14 – MAY 9
1984	MAY 27 – JUN 20
1985	JUL 7 – AUG 2
1986	APR 27 – MAY 21
1987	JUN 12 – JUL 5
1988	APR 4 – MAY 17
	MAY 28 – AUG 6
1989	MAY 12 – JUN 4
1990	JUN 26 – JUL 20
1991	APR 14 – MAY 9
1992	MAY 27 – JUN 19
1993	JUL 7 – AUG 1
1994	APR 27 – MAY 21
1995	JUN 11 – JUL 5
1996	APR 4 – AUG 7
1997	MAY 11 – JUN 4
1998	JUN 25 – JUL 19
1999	APR 13 – MAY 8
2000	MAY 26 – JUN 18

VENUS IN CANCER

1850	MAY 29 – JUN 22
1851	JUL 14 – AUG 17
1852	MAY 5 – JUN 8
	JUL 19 – SEP 5
1853	JUN 13 – JUL 6
1854	JUL 28 – AUG 21
1855	MAY 15 – JUN 9
1856	JUN 28 – JUL 21
1857	AUG 7 – SEP 2
1858	MAY 29 – JUN 22
1859	JUL 13 – AUG 6
1860	MAY 5 – JUN 10
	JUL 13 – SEP 5
1861	JUN 12 – JUL 6
1862	JUL 27 – AUG 20
1863	MAY 15 – JUN 9
1864	JUN 27 – JUL 21
1865	AUG 7 – SEP 2
1866	MAY 28 – JUN 21
1867	JUL 13 – AUG 6
1868	MAY 5 – JUN 12
	JUL 7 – SEP 6
1869	JUN 12 – JUL 5
1870	JUL 27 – AUG 20
1871	MAY 15 – JUN 9
1872	JUN 27 – JUL 20
1873	AUG 7 – SEP 2
1874	MAY 28 – JUN 21
1875	JUL 12 – AUG 5
1876	MAY 5 – JUN 17
	JUN 28 – SEP 6
1877	JUN 11 – JUL 5
1878	JUL 26 – AUG 19
1879	MAY 14 – JUN 8
1880	JUN 26 – JUL 20
1881	AUG 6 – SEP 1
1882	MAY 27 – JUN 20
1883	JUL 12 – AUG 4
1884	MAY 5 – SEP 7
1885	JUN 11 – JUL 4
1886	JUL 26 – AUG 19
1887	MAY 14 – JUN 8
1888	JUN 26 – JUL 19
1889	AUG 6 – SEP 1
1890	MAY 27 – JUN 20
1891	JUL 11 – AUG 4
1892	MAY 5 – SEP 7
1893	JUN 10 – JUL 4
1894	JUL 25 – AUG 18
1895	MAY 13 – JUN 7
1896	JUN 25 – JUL 19
1897	AUG 6 – AUG 31
1898	MAY 26 – JUN 19
1899	JUL 11 – AUG 3
1900	MAY 6 – SEP 8
1901	JUN 11 – JUL 5
1902	JUL 26 – AUG 19
1903	MAY 14 – JUN 9
1904	JUN 26 – JUL 19
1905	AUG 7 – SEP 1
1906	MAY 27 – JUN 20
1907	JUL 12 – AUG 4
1908	MAY 6 – SEP 8
1909	JUN 11 – JUL 4
1910	JUL 26 – AUG 19
1911	MAY 14 – JUN 8
1912	JUN 26 – JUL 19
1913	AUG 6 – SEP 1
1914	MAY 27 – JUN 20
1915	JUL 11 – AUG 4
1916	MAY 6 – SEP 8
1917	JUN 10 – JUL 4
1918	JUL 25 – AUG 18
1919	MAY 13 – JUN 8
1920	JUN 25 – JUL 18
1921	AUG 6 – AUG 31
1922	MAY 26 – JUN 19
1923	JUL 11 – AUG 3
1924	MAY 7 – SEP 8
1925	JUN 10 – JUL 3

VENUS IN CANCER

1926	JUL 25 – AUG 18
1927	MAY 13 – JUN 8
1928	JUN 24 – JUL 18
1929	AUG 6 – AUG 31
1930	MAY 26 – JUN 19
1931	JUL 10 – AUG 3
1932	MAY 7 – JUL 13
	JUL 29 – SEP 8
1933	JUN 9 – JUL 3
1934	JUL 24 – AUG 17
1935	MAY 12 – JUN 7
1936	JUN 24 – JUL 17
1937	AUG 5 – AUG 30
1938	MAY 25 – JUN 18
1939	JUL 10 – AUG 2
1940	MAY 7 – JUL 5
	AUG – SEP 8
1941	JUN 8 – JUL 2
1942	JUL 24 – AUG 17
1943	MAY 12 – JUN 7
1944	JUN 23 – JUL 17
1945	AUG 5 – AUG 30
1946	MAY 25 – JUN 18
1947	JUL 9 – AUG 2
1948	MAY 8 – SEP 8
1949	JUN 8 – JUL 1
1950	JUL 23 – AUG 16
1951	MAY 12 – JUN 7
1952	JUN 23 – JUL 16
1953	AUG 5 – AUG 30
1954	MAY 24 – JUN 17
1955	JUL 9 – AUG 1
1956	MAY 9 – JUN 23
	AUG 5 – SEP 8
1957	JUN 7 – JUL 1
1958	JUL 23 – AUG 16
1959	MAY 11 – JUN 6
1960	JUN 22 – JUL 16
1961	AUG 4 – AUG 29
1962	MAY 24 – JUN 17
1963	JUL 8 – JUL 31
1964	MAY 10 – JUN 17
	AUG 6 – SEP 8
1965	JUN 7 – JUN 30
1966	JUL 22 – AUG 15
1967	MAY 11 – JUN 6
1968	JUN 22 – JUL 15
1969	AUG 4 – AUG 29
1970	MAY 23 – JUN 16
1971	JUL 7 – JUL 31
1972	MAY 11 – JUN 11
	AUG 7 – SEP 7
1973	JUN 6 – JUN 30
1974	JUL 22 – AUG 14
1975	MAY 10 – JUN 6
1976	JUN 21 – JUL 14
1977	AUG 3 – AUG 28
1978	MAY 12 – JUN 16
1979	JUL 7 – JUL 30
1980	MAY 13 – JUN 5
	AUG 7 – SEP 7
1981	JUN 6 – JUN 29
1982	JUL 21 – AUG 14
1983	MAY 16 – JUN 6
1984	JUN 21 – JUL 14
1985	AUG 3 – AUG 28
1986	MAY 22 – JUN 15
1987	JUL 6 – JUL 30
1988	MAY 18 – MAY 27
	AUG 7 – SEP 7
1989	JUN 5 – JUN 29
1990	JUL 21 – AUG 13
1991	MAY 10 – JUN 6
1992	JUN 20 – JUL 13
1993	AUG 2 – AUG 27
1994	MAY 22 – JUN 15
1995	JUL 6 – JUL 29
1996	AUG 8 – SEP 7
1997	JUN 5 – JUN 28
1998	JUL 20 – AUG 13
1999	MAY 9 – JUN 5
2000	JUN 19 – JUL 13

VENUS IN LEO

Year	From	To
1850	JUN 23	JUL 17
1851	AUG 8	AUG 31
1852	JUN 9	JUL 18
	SEP 6	OCT 8
1853	JUL 7	JUL 31
1854	AUG 22	SEP 15
1855	JUN 10	JUL 7
1856	JUL 22	AUG 15
1857	SEP 3	SEP 28
1858	JUN 23	JUL 17
1859	AUG 7	AUG 30
1860	JUN 11	JUL 12
	SEP 6	OCT 8
1861	JUL 7	JUL 30
1862	AUG 21	SEP 14
1863	JUN 10	JUL 7
1864	JUL 22	AUG 14
1865	SEP 3	SEP 28
1866	JUN 22	JUL 16
1867	AUG 7	AUG 30
1868	JUN 13	JUL 6
	SEP 7	OCT 8
1869	JUL 6	JUL 30
1870	AUG 21	SEP 13
1871	JUN 10	JUL 6
1872	JUL 21	AUG 13
1873	SEP 3	SEP 27
1874	JUN 22	JUL 16
1875	AUG 6	AUG 29
1876	JUN 18	JUN 27
	SEP 7	OCT 7
1877	JUL 6	JUL 29
1878	AUG 20	SEP 13
1879	JUN 9	JUL 6
1880	JUL 21	AUG 13
1881	SEP 2	SEP 27
1882	JUN 21	JUL 15
1883	AUG 5	AUG 29
1884	SEP 8	OCT 7
1885	JUL 5	JUL 29
1886	AUG 20	SEP 12
1887	JUN 9	JUL 6
1888	JUL 20	AUG 12
1889	SEP 2	SEP 26
1890	JUN 21	JUL 15
1891	AUG 5	AUG 28
1892	SEP 8	OCT 7
1893	JUL 5	JUL 28
1894	AUG 19	SEP 12
1895	JUN 8	JUL 6
1896	JUL 20	AUG 12
1897	SEP 1	SEP 26
1898	JUN 20	JUL 14
1899	AUG 4	AUG 28
1900	SEP 9	OCT 8
1901	JUL 6	JUL 29
1902	AUG 20	SEP 13
1903	JUN 10	JUL 7
1904	JUL 20	AUG 13
1905	SEP 2	SEP 27
1906	JUN 21	JUL 16
1907	AUG 5	AUG 29
1908	SEP 9	OCT 6
1909	JUL 5	JUL 29
1910	AUG 20	SEP 12
1911	JUN 9	JUL 7
1912	JUL 20	AUG 12
1913	SEP 2	SEP 26
1914	JUN 21	JUL 15
1915	AUG 5	AUG 28
1916	SEP 9	OCT 7
1917	JUL 5	JUL 28
1918	AUG 19	SEP 12
1919	JUN 9	JUL 7
1920	JUL 19	AUG 12
1921	SEP 1	SEP 26
1922	JUN 20	JUL 15
1923	AUG 4	AUG 27
1924	SEP 9	OCT 7
1925	JUL 4	JUL 28
1926	AUG 19	SEP 11
1927	JUN 9	JUL 7

VENUS IN LEO

1928	JUL 19	–	AUG 11
1929	SEP 1	–	SEP 25
1930	JUN 20	–	JUL 14
1931	AUG 4	–	AUG 27
1932	SEP 9	–	OCT 7
1933	JUL 4	–	JUL 27
1934	AUG 18	–	SEP 11
1935	JUN 8	–	JUL 7
1936	JUL 18	–	AUG 11
1937	AUG 31	–	SEP 25
1938	JUN 19	–	JUL 14
1939	AUG 3	–	AUG 26
1940	SEP 9	–	OCT 6
1941	JUL 3	–	JUL 27
1942	AUG 18	–	SEP 10
1943	JUN 8	–	JUL 7
1944	JUL 18	–	AUG 10
1945	AUG 31	–	SEP 24
1946	JUN 19	–	JUL 13
1947	AUG 3	–	AUG 26
1948	SEP 9	–	OCT 6
1949	JUL 2	–	JUL 26
1950	AUG 17	–	SEP 10
1951	JUN 8	–	JUL 8
1952	JUL 17	–	AUG 9
1953	AUG 31	–	SEP 24
1954	JUN 18	–	JUL 13
1955	AUG 2	–	AUG 25
1956	SEP 9	–	OCT 6
1957	JUL 2	–	JUL 26
1958	AUG 17	–	SEP 9
1959	JUN 7	–	JUL 8
	SEP 21	–	SEP 25
1960	JUL 17	–	AUG 9
1961	AUG 30	–	SEP 23
1962	JUN 18	–	JUL 12
1963	AUG 1	–	AUG 25
1964	SEP 9	–	OCT 5
1965	JUL 1	–	JUL 25
1966	AUG 16	–	SEP 8
1967	JUN 7	–	JUL 8
	SEP 10	–	OCT 1
1968	JUL 6	–	AUG 8
1969	AUG 30	–	SEP 23
1970	JUN 17	–	JUL 12
1971	AUG 1	–	AUG 24
1972	SEP 8	–	OCT 5
1973	JUL 1	–	JUL 25
1974	AUG 15	–	SEP 8
1975	JUN 7	–	JUL 9
	SEP 3	–	OCT 4
1976	JUL 15	–	AUG 8
1977	AUG 29	–	SEP 22
1978	JUN 17	–	JUL 12
1979	JUL 31	–	AUG 24
1980	SEP 8	–	OCT 4
1981	JUN 30	–	JUL 24
1982	AUG 15	–	SEP 7
1983	JUN 7	–	JUL 10
	AUG 28	–	OCT 5
1984	JUL 15	–	AUG 7
1985	AUG 29	–	SEP 22
1986	JUN 16	–	JUL 11
1987	JUL 31	–	AUG 23
1988	SEP 8	–	OCT 4
1989	JUN 30	–	JUL 24
1990	AUG 14	–	SEP 7
1991	JUN 7	–	JUL 11
1992	JUL 14	–	AUG 7
1993	AUG 28	–	SEP 21
1994	JUN 16	–	JUL 11
1995	JUL 30	–	AUG 23
1996	SEP 8	–	OCT 4
1997	JUN 29	–	JUL 23
1998	AUG 14	–	SEP 6
1999	JUN 6	–	JUL 12
	AUG 16	–	OCT 7
2000	JUL 14	–	AUG 6

VENUS IN VIRGO

1850	JUL 18 – AUG 12
1851	SEP 1 – SEP 24
1852	OCT 9 – NOV 4
1853	AUG 1 – AUG 25
1854	SEP 16 – OCT 9
1855	JUL 8 – AUG 8
1856	AUG 16 – SEP 8
1857	SEP 29 – OCT 23
1858	JUL 18 – AUG 12
1859	AUG 31 – SEP 24
1860	OCT 9 – NOV 4
1861	JUL 31 – AUG 24
1862	SEP 15 – OCT 8
1863	JUL 8 – AUG 8
	OCT 8 – NOV 1
1864	AUG 15 – SEP 7
1865	SEP 29 – OCT 22
1866	JUL 17 – AUG 11
1867	AUG 31 – SEP 23
1868	OCT 9 – NOV 4
1869	JUL 31 – AUG 24
1870	SEP 14 – OCT 8
1871	JUL 7 – AUG 9
1872	AUG 14 – SEP 7
1873	SEP 28 – OCT 22
1874	JUL 17 – AUG 11
1875	AUG 30 – SEP 22
1876	OCT 8 – NOV 3
1877	JUL 30 – AUG 23
1878	SEP 14 – OCT 8
1879	JUL 7 – AUG 10
	SEP 25 – NOV 4
1880	AUG 14 – SEP 6
1881	SEP 28 – OCT 21
1882	JUL 16 – AUG 10
1883	AUG 30 – SEP 22
1884	OCT 8 – NOV 4
1885	JUL 30 – AUG 23
1886	SEP 13 – OCT 7
1887	JUL 7 – AUG 11
	SEP 19 – NOV 5
1888	AUG 13 – SEP 6
1889	SEP 27 – OCT 21
1890	JUL 16 – AUG 10
1891	AUG 29 – SEP 21
1892	OCT 8 – NOV 2
1893	JUL 29 – AUG 22
1894	SEP 13 – OCT 6
1895	JUL 7 – AUG 13
	SEP 13 – NOV 6
1896	AUG 13 – SEP 5
1897	SEP 27 – OCT 20
1898	JUL 15 – AUG 10
1899	AUG 29 – SEP 21
1900	OCT 9 – NOV 3
1901	JUL 30 – AUG 23
1902	SEP 14 – OCT 7
1903	JUL 8 – AUG 17
	SEP 7 – NOV 8
1904	AUG 14 – SEP 6
1905	SEP 28 – OCT 21
1906	JUL 17 – AUG 11
1907	AUG 30 – SEP 22
1908	OCT 7 – NOV 3
1909	JUL 30 – AUG 23
1910	SEP 13 – OCT 6
1911	JUL 8 – NOV 9
1912	AUG 13 – SEP 6
1913	SEP 27 – OCT 21
1914	JUL 16 – AUG 10
1915	AUG 29 – SEP 22
1916	OCT 8 – NOV 3
1917	JUL 29 – AUG 22
1918	SEP 13 – OCT 6
1919	JUL 8 – NOV 9
1920	AUG 13 – SEP 5
1921	SEP 27 – OCT 20
1922	JUL 16 – AUG 10
1923	AUG 28 – SEP 21
1924	OCT 8 – NOV 2
1925	JUL 29 – AUG 30
1926	SEP 12 – OCT 5

VENUS IN VIRGO

Year	From		To
1927	JUL 8	–	NOV 9
1928	AUG 12	–	SEP 4
1929	SEP 26	–	OCT 20
1930	JUL 15	–	AUG 10
1931	AUG 28	–	SEP 20
1932	OCT 8	–	NOV 2
1933	JUL 28	–	AUG 21
1934	SEP 12	–	OCT 5
1935	JUL 8	–	NOV 9
1936	AUG 12	–	SEP 4
1937	SEP 26	–	OCT 19
1938	JUL 15	–	AUG 9
1939	AUG 27	–	SEP 20
1940	OCT 7	–	NOV 1
1941	JUL 28	–	AUG 21
1942	SEP 11	–	OCT 4
1943	JUL 8	–	NOV 9
1944	AUG 11	–	SEP 3
1945	SEP 25	–	OCT 19
1946	JUL 14	–	AUG 9
1947	AUG 27	–	SEP 19
1948	OCT 7	–	NOV 1
1949	JUL 27	–	AUG 20
1950	SEP 11	–	OCT 4
1951	JUL 9	–	NOV 9
1952	AUG 10	–	SEP 3
1953	SEP 25	–	OCT 18
1954	JUL 14	–	AUG 9
1955	AUG 26	–	SEP 18
1956	OCT 7	–	OCT 31
1957	JUL 27	–	AUG 20
1958	SEP 10	–	OCT 3
1959	JUL 9	–	SEP 20
	SEP 26	–	NOV 9
1960	AUG 10	–	SEP 2
1961	SEP 24	–	OCT 18
1962	JUL 13	–	AUG 8
1963	AUG 26	–	SEP 18
1964	OCT 6	–	OCT 31
1965	JUL 26	–	AUG 19
1966	SEP 9	–	OCT 3
1967	JUL 9	–	SEP 9
	OCT 7	–	NOV 9
1968	AUG 9	–	SEP 2
1969	SEP 24	–	OCT 17
1970	JUL 13	–	AUG 8
1971	AUG 25	–	SEP 17
1972	OCT 6	–	OCT 30
1973	JUL 26	–	AUG 19
1974	SEP 9	–	OCT 2
1975	JUL 10	–	SEP 2
	OCT 5	–	NOV 9
1976	AUG 9	–	SEP 1
1977	SEP 23	–	OCT 17
1978	JUL 13	–	AUG 8
1979	AUG 25	–	SEP 17
1980	OCT 5	–	OCT 30
1981	JUL 25	–	AUG 18
1982	SEP 8	–	OCT 2
1983	JUL 11	–	AUG 27
	OCT 6	–	NOV 9
1984	AUG 8	–	SEP 1
1985	SEP 23	–	OCT 16
1986	JUL 12	–	AUG 7
1987	AUG 24	–	SEP 16
1988	OCT 5	–	OCT 29
1989	JUL 25	–	AUG 18
1990	SEP 8	–	OCT 1
1991	JUL 12	–	AUG 21
	OCT 7	–	NOV 9
1992	AUG 8	–	AUG 31
1993	SEP 22	–	OCT 16
1994	JUL 12	–	AUG 7
1995	AUG 24	–	SEP 16
1996	OCT 5	–	OCT 29
1997	JUL 24	–	AUG 17
1998	SEP 7	–	SEP 30
1999	JUL 13	–	AUG 15
	OCT 8	–	NOV 9
2000	AUG 7	–	AUG 31

VENUS IN LIBRA

Year	Dates	Year	Dates
1850	AUG 13 – SEP 7	1886	OCT 8 – OCT 31
1851	SEP 25 – OCT 18	1887	AUG 12 – SEP 18
1852	NOV 5 – NOV 30		NOV 6 – DEC 8
1853	AUG 26 – SEP 18	1888	SEP 7 – SEP 30
1854	OCT 10 – NOV 2	1889	OCT 22 – NOV 14
1855	AUG 9 – OCT 16	1890	AUG 11 – SEP 6
	OCT 28 – DEC 8	1891	SEP 22 – OCT 15
1856	SEP 9 – OCT 2	1892	NOV 3 – NOV 27
1857	OCT 24 – NOV 16	1893	AUG 23 – SEP 16
1858	AUG 13 – SEP 7	1894	OCT 7 – OCT 30
1859	SEP 25 – OCT 18	1895	AUG 14 – SEP 12
1860	NOV 5 – NOV 29		NOV 7 – DEC 8
1861	AUG 25 – SEP 18	1896	SEP 6 – SEP 29
1862	OCT 9 – NOV 1	1897	OCT 21 – NOV 13
1863	AUG 9 – OCT 7	1898	AUG 11 – SEP 6
	NOV 2 – DEC 8	1899	SEP 22 – OCT 15
1864	SEP 8 – OCT 2	1900	NOV 4 – NOV 28
1865	OCT 23 – NOV 16	1901	AUG 24 – SEP 17
1866	AUG 12 – SEP 7	1902	OCT 8 – OCT 31
1867	SEP 24 – OCT 17	1903	AUG 18 – SEP 6
1868	NOV 5 – NOV 29		NOV 9 – DEC 9
1869	AUG 25 – SEP 18	1904	SEP 7 – SEP 30
1870	OCT 9 – NOV 1	1905	OCT 22 – NOV 14
1871	AUG 10 – SEP 30	1906	AUG 12 – SEP 7
	NOV 4 – DEC 8	1907	SEP 23 – OCT 16
1872	SEP 8 – OCT 1	1908	NOV 4 – NOV 28
1873	OCT 23 – NOV 15	1909	AUG 24 – SEP 17
1874	AUG 12 – SEP 7	1910	OCT 7 – OCT 30
1875	SEP 23 – OCT 16	1911	NOV 10 – DEC 9
1876	NOV 4 – NOV 28	1912	SEP 7 – SEP 29
1877	AUG 24 – SEP 17	1913	OCT 22 – NOV 14
1878	OCT 9 – OCT 31	1914	AUG 11 – SEP 7
1879	AUG 11 – SEP 24	1915	SEP 23 – OCT 15
	NOV 5 – DEC 8	1916	NOV 4 – NOV 27
1880	SEP 7 – SEP 30	1917	AUG 23 – SEP 16
1881	OCT 22 – NOV 14	1918	OCT 7 – OCT 30
1882	AUG 11 – SEP 6	1919	AUG 23 – AUG 27
1883	SEP 23 – OCT 16		NOV 10 – DEC 9
1884	NOV 4 – NOV 28	1920	SEP 6 – SEP 29
1885	AUG 24 – SEP 16	1921	OCT 21 – NOV 13

VENUS IN LIBRA

1922	AUG 11 – SEP 7
1923	SEP 22 – OCT 15
1924	NOV 3 – NOV 27
1925	AUG 31 – SEP 16
1926	OCT 6 – OCT 29
1927	NOV 10 – DEC 8
1928	SEP 5 – SEP 29
1929	OCT 21 – NOV 13
1930	AUG 11 – SEP 7
1931	SEP 21 – OCT 14
1932	NOV 3 – NOV 27
1933	AUG 22 – SEP 15
1934	OCT 6 – OCT 29
1935	NOV 10 – DEC 8
1936	SEP 5 – SEP 28
1937	OCT 20 – NOV 12
1938	AUG 10 – SEP 7
1939	SEP 21 – OCT 14
1940	NOV 2 – NOV 26
1941	AUG 22 – SEP 15
1942	OCT 5 – OCT 28
1943	NOV 10 – DEC 7
1944	SEP 4 – SEP 28
1945	OCT 20 – NOV 12
1946	AUG 10 – SEP 7
1947	SEP 20 – OCT 13
1948	NOV 2 – NOV 26
1949	AUG 21 – SEP 14
1950	OCT 5 – OCT 28
1951	NOV 10 – DEC 8
1952	SEP 4 – SEP 27
1953	OCT 19 – NOV 11
1954	AUG 10 – SEP 6
1955	SEP 19 – OCT 13
1956	NOV 1 – NOV 25
1957	AUG 21 – SEP 14
1958	OCT 4 – OCT 27
1959	NOV 10 – DEC 7
1960	SEP 3 – SEP 27
1961	OCT 19 – NOV 11
1962	AUG 9 – SEP 7
1963	SEP 19 – OCT 12
1964	NOV 1 – NOV 25
1965	AUG 20 – SEP 13
1966	OCT 4 – OCT 27
1967	NOV 10 – DEC 7
1968	SEP 3 – SEP 26
1969	OCT 18 – NOV 10
1970	AUG 9 – SEP 7
1971	SEP 18 – OCT 11
1972	OCT 31 – NOV 24
1973	AUG 20 – SEP 13
1974	OCT 3 – OCT 26
1975	NOV 10 – DEC 7
1976	SEP 2 – SEP 26
1977	OCT 18 – NOV 10
1978	AUG 9 – SEP 7
1979	SEP 18 – OCT 11
1980	OCT 31 – NOV 24
1981	AUG 19 – SEP 12
1982	OCT 3 – OCT 26
1983	NOV 10 – DEC 6
1984	SEP 2 – SEP 25
1985	OCT 17 – NOV 9
1986	AUG 8 – SEP 7
1987	SEP 17 – OCT 10
1988	OCT 30 – NOV 23
1989	AUG 19 – SEP 12
1990	OCT 2 – OCT 25
1991	AUG 22 – OCT 6
	NOV 10 – DEC 6
1992	SEP 1 – SEP 25
1993	OCT 17 – NOV 9
1994	AUG 8 – SEP 7
1995	SEP 17 – OCT 10
1996	OCT 30 – NOV 23
1997	AUG 18 – SEP 12
1998	OCT 1 – OCT 24
1999	NOV 10 – DEC 5
2000	SEP 1 – SEP 24

VENUS IN SCORPIO

1850	SEP 8 – OCT 6
1851	OCT 19 – NOV 11
1852	DEC 1 – DEC 24
1853	SEP 19 – OCT 13
1854	NOV 3 – NOV 26
1855	OCT 17 – OCT 27
	DEC 9 – DEC 31
1856	JAN 1 – JAN 5
	OCT 3 – OCT 26
1857	NOV 17 – DEC 10
1858	SEP 8 – OCT 6
1859	OCT 19 – NOV 11
1860	NOV 30 – DEC 24
1861	SEP 19 – OCT 13
1862	NOV 2 – NOV 25
1863	DEC 9 – DEC 31
1864	JAN 1 – JAN 5
	OCT 3 – OCT 26
1865	NOV 17 – DEC 10
1866	SEP 8 – OCT 6
1867	OCT 18 – NOV 10
1868	NOV 30 – DEC 23
1869	SEP 18 – OCT 13
1870	NOV 2 – NOV 25
1871	OCT 1 – NOV 3
	DEC 9 – DEC 31
1872	JAN 1 – JAN 5
	OCT 2 – OCT 25
1873	NOV 16 – DEC 9
1874	SEP 8 – OCT 6
1875	OCT 17 – NOV 9
1876	NOV 29 – DEC 23
1877	SEP 18 – OCT 12
1878	NOV 1 – NOV 24
1879	DEC 9 – DEC 31
1880	JAN 1 – JAN 4
	OCT 1 – OCT 25
1881	NOV 15 – DEC 8
1882	SEP 7 – OCT 6
1883	OCT 17 – NOV 9
1884	NOV 29 – DEC 22
1885	SEP 17 – OCT 12
1886	NOV 1 – NOV 23
1887	DEC 9 – DEC 31
1888	JAN 1 – JAN 4
	OCT 1 – OCT 24
1889	NOV 15 – DEC 8
1890	SEP 7 – OCT 7
1891	OCT 16 – NOV 8
1892	NOV 28 – DEC 22
1893	SEP 17 – OCT 11
1894	OCT 31 – NOV 23
1895	DEC 9 – DEC 31
1896	JAN 1 – JAN 3
	SEP 30 – OCT 24
1897	NOV 14 – DEC 7
1898	SEP 7 – OCT 7
1899	OCT 16 – NOV 8
1900	NOV 29 – DEC 23
1901	SEP 18 – OCT 12
1902	NOV 1 – NOV 24
1903	DEC 10 – DEC 31
1904	JAN 1 – JAN 5
	OCT 1 – OCT 25
1905	NOV 15 – DEC 8
1906	SEP 8 – OCT 9
	DEC 16 – DEC 25
1907	OCT 17 – NOV 9
1908	NOV 29 – DEC 22
1909	SEP 18 – OCT 12
1910	OCT 31 – NOV 23
1911	DEC 10 – DEC 31
1912	JAN 1 – JAN 4
	OCT 1 – OCT 24
1913	NOV 15 – DEC 8
1914	SEP 8 – OCT 10
	DEC 6 – DEC 31
1915	OCT 16 – NOV 8
1916	NOV 28 – DEC 22
1917	SEP 17 – OCT 11

VENUS IN SCORPIO

Year	From		To
1918	OCT 31	–	NOV 23
1919	DEC 10	–	DEC 31
1920	JAN 1	–	JAN 4
	SEP 30	–	OCT 24
1921	NOV 14	–	DEC 7
1922	SEP 8	–	OCT 10
	NOV 29	–	DEC 31
1923	JAN 1	–	JAN 2
	OCT 16	–	NOV 8
1924	NOV 28	–	DEC 21
1925	SEP 17	–	OCT 11
1926	OCT 30	–	NOV 22
1927	DEC 9	–	DEC 31
1928	JAN 1	–	JAN 4
	SEP 30	–	OCT 23
1929	NOV 14	–	DEC 7
1930	SEP 8	–	OCT 12
	NOV 23	–	DEC 31
1931	JAN 1	–	JAN 3
	OCT 15	–	NOV 7
1932	NOV 28	–	DEC 21
1933	SEP 16	–	OCT 11
1934	OCT 30	–	NOV 22
1935	DEC 9	–	DEC 31
1936	JAN 1	–	JAN 3
	SEP 29	–	OCT 23
1937	NOV 13	–	DEC 6
1938	SEP 8	–	OCT 13
	NOV 16	–	DEC 31
1939	JAN 1	–	JAN 4
	OCT 15	–	NOV 7
1940	NOV 27	–	DEC 20
1941	SEP 16	–	OCT 10
1942	OCT 29	–	NOV 21
1943	DEC 8	–	DEC 31
1944	JAN 1	–	JAN 3
	SEP 29	–	OCT 22
1945	NOV 13	–	DEC 6
1946	SEP 8	–	OCT 16
1947	OCT 14	–	NOV 6
1948	NOV 27	–	DEC 20
1949	SEP 15	–	OCT 10
1950	OCT 29	–	NOV 21
1951	DEC 9	–	DEC 31
1952	JAN 1	–	JAN 2
	SEP 28	–	OCT 22
1953	NOV 12	–	DEC 5
1954	SEP 7	–	OCT 23
	OCT 28	–	DEC 31
1955	JAN 1	–	JAN 6
	OCT 14	–	NOV 6
1956	NOV 26	–	DEC 19
1957	SEP 15	–	OCT 10
1958	OCT 28	–	NOV 20
1959	DEC 8	–	DEC 31
1960	JAN 1	–	JAN 2
	SEP 28	–	OCT 21
1961	NOV 12	–	DEC 5
1962	SEP 8	–	DEC 31
1963	JAN 1	–	JAN 6
	OCT 13	–	NOV 5
1964	NOV 26	–	DEC 19
1965	SEP 14	–	OCT 9
1966	OCT 28	–	NOV 20
1967	DEC 8	–	DEC 31
1968	JAN 1		
	SEP 27	–	OCT 21
1969	NOV 11	–	DEC 4
1970	SEP 8	–	DEC 31
1971	JAN 1	–	JAN 7
	OCT 12	–	NOV 5
1972	NOV 25	–	DEC 18
1973	SEP 14	–	OCT 9
1974	OCT 27	–	NOV 19
1975	DEC 8	–	DEC 31
1976	JAN 1		
	SEP 27	–	OCT 20
1977	NOV 11	–	DEC 4
1978	SEP 8	–	DEC 31
1979	JAN 1	–	JAN 7
	OCT 12	–	NOV 4
1980	NOV 25	–	DEC 18

VENUS IN SCORPIO

1981	SEP 13 – OCT 9
1982	OCT 27 – NOV 18
1983	DEC 7 – DEC 31
1984	JAN 1
	SEP 26 – OCT 20
1985	NOV 10 – DEC 3
1986	SEP 8 – DEC 31
1987	JAN 1 – JAN 7
	OCT 11 – NOV 3
1988	NOV 24 – DEC 17
1989	SEP 13 – OCT 8
1990	OCT 26 – NOV 18
1991	DEC 7 – DEC 31
1992	SEP 26 – OCT 19
1993	NOV 10 – DEC 2
1994	SEP 8 – DEC 31
1995	JAN 1 – JAN 7
	OCT 11 – NOV 3
1996	NOV 24 – DEC 17
1997	SEP 13 – OCT 8
1998	OCT 25 – NOV 17
1999	DEC 6 – DEC 31
2000	SEP 25 – OCT 19

VENUS IN SAGITTARIUS

1850	JAN 1 – JAN 4
	OCT 7 – NOV 15
	DEC 6 – DEC 31
1851	JAN 1 – FEB 3
	NOV 12 – DEC 5
1852	DEC 25 – DEC 31
1853	JAN 1 – JAN 18
	OCT 14 – NOV 8
1854	NOV 27 – DEC 19
1855	NO TRANSIT OF SIGN DURING 1855
1856	JAN 6 – JAN 31
	OCT 27 – NOV 20
1857	DEC 11 – DEC 31
1858	JAN 1 – JAN 3
	OCT 7 – DEC 31
1859	JAN 1 – FEB 3
	NOV 12 – DEC 4
1860	DEC 25 – DEC 31
1861	JAN 1 – JAN 17
	OCT 14 – NOV 7
1862	NOV 26 – DEC 19
1863	NO TRANSIT OF SIGN DURING 1863
1864	JAN 6 – JAN 31
	OCT 27 – NOV 19
1865	DEC 11 – DEC 31
1866	JAN 1 – JAN 2
	OCT 7 – DEC 31
1867	JAN 1 – FEB 4
	NOV 11 – DEC 4
1868	DEC 24 – DEC 31
1869	JAN 1 – JAN 17
	OCT 14 – NOV 7
1870	NOV 26 – DEC 18
1871	NO TRANSIT OF SIGN DURING 1871
1872	JAN 6 – JAN 30
	OCT 26 – NOV 19
1873	DEC 10 – DEC 31
1874	JAN 1 – JAN 2
	OCT 7 – DEC 31
1875	JAN 1 – FEB 4
	NOV 10 – DEC 3
1876	DEC 24 – DEC 31
1877	JAN 1 – JAN 16
	OCT 13 – NOV 7
1878	NOV 25 – DEC 18

VENUS IN SAGITTARIUS

1879	NO TRANSIT OF SIGN DURING 1879
1880	JAN 5 – JAN 30
	OCT 26 – NOV 18
1881	DEC 9 – DEC 31
1882	JAN 1
	OCT 7 – DEC 31
1883	JAN 1 – FEB 4
	NOV 10 – DEC 3
1884	DEC 23 – DEC 31
1885	JAN 1 – JAN 16
	OCT 13 – NOV 6
1886	NOV 24 – DEC 17
1887	NO TRANSIT OF SIGN DURING 1887
1888	JAN 5 – JAN 29
	OCT 25 – NOV 18
1889	DEC 9 – DEC 31
1890	JAN 1
	OCT 8 – DEC 31
1891	JAN 1 – FEB 5
	NOV 9 – DEC 2
1892	DEC 23 – DEC 31
1893	JAN 1 – JAN 15
	OCT 12 – NOV 6
1894	NOV 24 – DEC 17
1895	NO TRANSIT OF SIGN DURING 1895
1896	JAN 4 – JAN 29
	OCT 25 – NOV 17
1897	DEC 8 – DEC 31
1898	OCT 8 – DEC 31
1899	JAN 1 – FEB 5
	NOV 9 – DEC 2
1900	DEC 24 – JAN 16
1901	JAN 1 – JAN 17
	OCT 13 – NOV 7
1902	NOV 25 – DEC 18
1903	NO TRANSIT OF SIGN DURING 1903
1904	JAN 6 – JAN 30
	OCT 26 – NOV 18
1905	DEC 9 – DEC 31
1906	JAN 1
	OCT 10 – DEC 15
	DEC 26 – DEC 31
1907	JAN 1 – FEB 6
	NOV 10 – DEC 3
1908	DEC 23 – DEC 31
1909	JAN 1 – JAN 15
	OCT 13 – NOV 7
1910	NOV 24 – DEC 17
1911	NO TRANSIT OF SIGN DURING 1911
1912	JAN 5 – JAN 29
	OCT 25 – NOV 18
1913	DEC 9 – DEC 31
1914	JAN 1
	OCT 11 – DEC 31
1915	JAN 1 – FEB 6
	NOV 9 – DEC 2
1916	DEC 23 – DEC 31
1917	JAN 1 – JAN 15
	OCT 12 – NOV 7
1918	NOV 24 – DEC 17
1919	NO TRANSIT OF SIGN DURING 1919
1920	JAN 5 – JAN 29
	OCT 25 – NOV 17
1921	DEC 8 – DEC 31
1922	OCT 11 – NOV 28
1923	JAN 3 – FEB 6
	NOV 8 – DEC 1
1924	DEC 22 – DEC 31
1925	JAN 1 – JAN 14
	OCT 12 – NOV 6
1926	NOV 23 – DEC 16
1927	NO TRANSIT OF SIGN DURING 1927
1928	JAN 5 – JAN 29
	OCT 24 – NOV 17

VENUS IN SAGITTARIUS

1929	DEC 8 – DEC 31
1930	OCT 13 – NOV 22
1931	JAN 4 – FEB 6
	NOV 8 – DEC 1
1932	DEC 22 – DEC 31
1933	JAN 1 – JAN 14
	OCT 12 – NOV 6
1934	NOV 23 – DEC 16
1935	NO TRANSIT OF SIGN DURING 1935
1936	JAN 4 – JAN 28
	OCT 24 – NOV 16
1937	DEC 7 – DEC 30
1938	OCT 14 – NOV 15
1939	JAN 5 – FEB 6
	NOV 8 – DEC 1
1940	DEC 21 – DEC 31
1941	JAN 1 – JAN 13
	OCT 11 – NOV 5
1942	NOV 22 – DEC 15
1943	NO TRANSIT OF SIGN DURING 1943
1944	JAN 4 – JAN 28
	OCT 23 – NOV 16
1945	DEC 7 – DEC 30
1946	OCT 17 – NOV 8
1947	JAN 6 – FEB 6
	NOV 7 – NOV 30
1948	DEC 21 – DEC 31
1949	JAN 1 – JAN 13
	OCT 11 – NOV 6
1950	NOV 22 – DEC 14
1951	NO TRANSIT OF SIGN DURING 1951
1952	JAN 3 – JAN 27
	OCT 23 – NOV 15
1953	DEC 6 – DEC 29
1954	OCT 24 – OCT 27
1955	JAN 7 – FEB 6
	NOV 7 – NOV 30
1956	DEC 20 – DEC 31
1957	JAN 1 – JAN 12
	OCT 11 – NOV 5
1958	NOV 21 – DEC 14
1959	NO TRANSIT OF SIGN DURING 1959
1960	JAN 3 – JAN 27
	OCT 22 – NOV 15
1961	DEC 6 – DEC 29
1962	NO TRANSIT OF SIGN DURING 1962
1963	JAN 7 – FEB 5
	NOV 6 – NOV 29
1964	DEC 20 – DEC 31
1965	JAN 1 – JAN 12
	OCT 10 – NOV 5
1966	NOV 21 – DEC 13
1967	NO TRANSIT OF SIGN DURING1967
1968	JAN 2 – JAN 26
	OCT 22 – NOV 14
1969	DEC 5 – DEC 28
1970	NO TRANSIT OF SIGN DURING 1970
1971	JAN 8 – FEB 5
	NOV 6 – NOV 29
1972	DEC 19 – DEC 31
1973	JAN 1 – JAN 11
	OCT 10 – NOV 5
1974	NOV 20 – DEC 13
1975	NO TRANSIT OF SIGN DURING 1975
1976	JAN 2 – JAN 26
	OCT 21 – NOV 14
1977	DEC 5 – DEC 27
1978	NO TRANSIT OF SIGN DURING 1978
1979	JAN 8 – FEB 5
	NOV 5 – NOV 28
1980	DEC 19 – DEC 31
1981	JAN 1 – JAN 11
	OCT 10 – NOV 5

VENUS IN SAGITTARIUS

Year	Dates	Year	Dates
1982	NOV 19 – DEC 12	1992	JAN 1 – JAN 25
1983	NO TRANSIT OF SIGN DURING 1983		OCT 20 – NOV 13
1984	JAN 2 – JAN 25	1993	DEC 3 – DEC 26
	OCT 21 – NOV 13	1994	NO TRANSIT OF SIGN DURING 1994
1985	DEC 4 – DEC 27	1995	JAN 8 – FEB 4
1986	NO TRANSIT OF SIGN DURING 1986		NOV 4 – NOV 27
1987	JAN 8 – FEB 5	1996	DEC 18 – DEC 31
	NOV 4 – NOV 28	1997	JAN 1 – JAN 10
1988	DEC 18 – DEC 31		OCT 9 – NOV 5
1989	JAN 1 – JAN 10	1998	NOV 18 – DEC 11
	OCT 9 – NOV 5	1999	NO TRANSIT OF SIGN DURING 1999
1990	NOV 19 – DEC 12	2000	JAN 1 – JAN 24
1991	NO TRANSIT OF SIGN DURING 1991		OCT 20 – NOV 13

VENUS IN CAPRICORN

Year	Dates	Year	Dates
1850	JAN 5 – JAN 27	1861	JAN 18 – FEB 10
	NOV 16 – DEC 5		NOV 8 – DEC 4
1851	FEB 4 – MAR 7	1862	DEC 20 – DEC 31
	DEC 6 – DEC 29	1863	JAN 1 – JAN 12
1852	NO TRANSIT OF SIGN DURING 1852	1864	FEB 1 – FEB 25
1853	JAN 19 – FEB 11		NOV 20 – DEC 14
	NOV 9 – DEC 4	1865	NO TRANSIT OF SIGN DURING 1865
1854	DEC 20 – DEC 31	1866	JAN 3 – JAN 26
1855	JAN 1 – JAN 12	1867	FEB 5 – MAR 6
1856	FEB 1 – FEB 25		DEC 5 – DEC 28
	NOV 21 – DEC 14	1868	NO TRANSIT OF SIGN DURING 1868
1857	NO TRANSIT OF SIGN DURING 1857	1869	JAN 18 – FEB 10
1858	JAN 4 – JAN 27		NOV 8 – DEC 4
1859	FEB 4 – MAR 6	1870	DEC 19 – DEC 31
	DEC 5 – DEC 28	1871	JAN 1 – JAN 11
1860	NO TRANSIT OF SIGN DURING 1860	1872	JAN 31 – FEB 24
			NOV 20 – DEC 13

VENUS IN CAPRICORN

1873	NO TRANSIT OF SIGN DURING 1873
1874	JAN 3 – JAN 26
1875	FEB 5 – MAR 6
	DEC 4 – DEC 27
1876	NO TRANSIT OF SIGN DURING 1876
1877	JAN 17 – FEB 9
	NOV 8 – DEC 4
1878	DEC 19 – DEC 31
1879	JAN 1 – JAN 11
1880	JAN 31 – FEB 24
	NOV 19 – DEC 13
1881	NO TRANSIT OF SIGN DURING 1881
1882	JAN 2 – JAN 25
1883	FEB 5 – MAR 6
	DEC 4 – DEC 27
1884	NO TRANSIT OF SIGN DURING 1884
1885	JAN 17 – FEB 9
	NOV 7 – DEC 4
1886	DEC 18 – DEC 31
1887	JAN 1 – JAN 10
1888	JAN 30 – FEB 23
	NOV 19 – DEC 12
1889	NO TRANSIT OF SIGN DURING 1889
1890	JAN 2 – JAN 25
1891	FEB 6 – MAR 5
	DEC 3 – DEC 26
1892	NO TRANSIT OF SIGN DURING 1889
1893	JAN 16 – FEB 8
	NOV 7 – DEC 4
1894	DEC 18 – DEC 31
1895	JAN 1 – JAN 10
1896	JAN 30 – FEB 23
	NOV 18 – DEC 12
1897	NO TRANSIT OF SIGN DURING 1897
1898	JAN 1 – JAN 24
1899	FEB 6 – MAR 5
	DEC 3 – DEC 26
1900	NO TRANSIT OF SIGN DURING 1900
1901	JAN 17 – FEB 9
	NOV 8 – DEC 5
1902	DEC 19 – DEC 31
1903	JAN 1 – JAN 11
1904	JAN 31 – FEB 24
	NOV 19 – DEC 13
1905	NO TRANSIT OF SIGN DURING 1905
1906	JAN 2 – JAN 25
1907	FEB 7 – MAR 6
	DEC 4 – DEC 27
1908	NO TRANSIT OF SIGN DURING 1908
1909	JAN 16 – FEB 9
	NOV 8 – DEC 5
1910	DEC 18 – DEC 31
1911	JAN 1 – JAN 10
1912	JAN 30 – FEB 23
	NOV 19 – DEC 12
1913	NO TRANSIT OF SIGN DURING 1913
1914	JAN 2 – JAN 25
1915	FEB 7 – MAR 6
	DEC 3 – DEC 26
1916	NO TRANSIT OF SIGN DURING 1916
1917	JAN 16 – FEB 8
	NOV 8 – DEC 5
1918	DEC 18 – DEC 31
1919	JAN 1 – JAN 10
1920	JAN 30 – FEB 23
	NOV 18 – DEC 12
1921	NO TRANSIT OF SIGN DURING 1921
1922	JAN 1 – JAN 24
1923	FEB 7 – MAR 6

VENUS IN CAPRICORN

1924	NO TRANSIT OF SIGN DURING 1924
1925	JAN 15 – FEB 7
	NOV 7 – DEC 5
1926	DEC 17 – DEC 31
1927	JAN 1 – JAN 9
1928	JAN 30 – FEB 22
	NOV 18 – DEC 12
1929	DEC 31
1930	JAN 1 – JAN 24
1931	FEB 7 – MAR 5
	DEC 2 – DEC 25
1932	JAN 1 – JAN 18
1933	JAN 15 – FEB 7
	NOV 7 – DEC 5
1934	DEC 17 – DEC 31
1935	JAN 1 – JAN 8
1936	JAN 29 – FEB 22
	NOV 17 – DEC 11
1937	DEC 31
1938	JAN 1 – JAN 23
1939	FEB 7 – MAR 5
	DEC 2 – DEC 25
1940	NO TRANSIT OF SIGN DURING 1940
1941	JAN 14 – FEB 6
	NOV 6 – DEC 5
1942	DEC 16 – DEC 31
1943	JAN 1 – JAN 8
1944	JAN 1 – FEB 21
	NOV 17 – DEC 11
1945	DEC 31
1946	JAN 1 – JAN 22
1947	FEB 7 – MAR 5
1948	NO TRANSIT OF SIGN DURING 1948
1949	JAN 14 – FEB 6
	NOV 7 – DEC 6
1950	DEC 15 – DEC 31
1951	JAN 1 – JAN 7
1952	JAN 28 – FEB 21
	NOV 16 – DEC 10
1953	DEC 30 – DEC 31
1954	JAN 1 – JAN 22
1955	FEB 7 – MAR 4
	DEC 1 – DEC 24
1956	NO TRANSIT OF SIGN DURING 1956
1957	JAN 13 – FEB 5
	NOV 6 – DEC 6
1958	DEC 15 – DEC 31
1959	JAN 1 – JAN 7
1960	JAN 28 – FEB 20
	NOV 16 – DEC 10
1961	DEC 30 – DEC 31
1962	JAN 1 – JAN 21
1963	FEB 6 – MAR 4
	NOV 30 – DEC 23
1964	NO TRANSIT OF SIGN DURING 1964
1965	JAN 13 – FEB 5
	NOV 6 – DEC 7
1966	FEB 7 – FEB 25
	DEC 14 – DEC 31
1967	JAN 1 – JAN 6
1968	JAN 27 – FEB 20
	NOV 15 – DEC 9
1969	DEC 29 – DEC 31
1970	JAN 1 – JAN 21
1971	JAN 6 – MAR 4
	NOV 30 – DEC 23
1972	NO TRANSIT OF SIGN DURING 1972
1973	JAN 12 – FEB 4
	NOV 6 – DEC 7
1974	JAN 30 – FEB 28
	DEC 14 – DEC 31
1975	JAN 1 – JAN 6
1976	JAN 27 – FEB 19
	NOV 15 – DEC 9
1977	DEC 28 – DEC 31
1978	JAN 1 – JAN 20
1979	FEB 6 – MAR 3
	NOV 29 – DEC 22

VENUS IN CAPRICORN

1980	JAN 12	–	FEB 4
1981	NOV 6	–	DEC 8
1982	JAN 24	–	MAR 2
	DEC 13	–	DEC 31
1983	JAN 1	–	JAN 5
1984	JAN 26	–	FEB 19
	NOV 14	–	DEC 9
1985	DEC 28	–	DEC 31
1986	JAN 1	–	JAN 20
1987	FEB 6	–	MAR 3
	NOV 29	–	DEC 22
1988	NO TRANSIT OF SIGN DURING 1988		
1989	JAN 11	–	FEB 3
	NOV 6	–	DEC 10
1990	JAN 17	–	MAR 3
	DEC 13	–	DEC 31
1991	JAN 1	–	JAN 5
1992	JAN 26	–	FEB 18
	NOV 14	–	DEC 8
1993	DEC 27	–	DEC 31
1994	JAN 1	–	JAN 19
1995	FEB 5	–	MAR 2
	NOV 28	–	DEC 21
1996	NO TRANSIT OF SIGN DURING 1996		
1997	JAN 11	–	FEB 3
	NOV 6	–	DEC 12
1998	JAN 10	–	MAR 4
	DEC 12	–	DEC 31
1999	JAN 1	–	JAN 4
2000	JAN 25	–	FEB 18
	NOV 14	–	DEC 8

VENUS IN AQUARIUS

1850	JAN 28	–	FEB 20
1851	MAR 8	–	APR 3
	DEC 30	–	DEC 31
1852	JAN 1	–	JAN 22
1853	FEB 12	–	MAR 7
	DEC 5	–	DEC 31
1854	JAN 1	–	JAN 3
1855	JAN 13	–	FEB 5
1856	FEB 26	–	MAR 21
	DEC 15	–	DEC 31
1857	JAN 1	–	JAN 8
1858	JAN 28	–	FEB 20
1859	MAR 7	–	APR 2
	DEC 29	–	DEC 31
1860	JAN 1	–	JAN 22
1861	FEB 11	–	MAR 6
	DEC 5	–	DEC 31
1862	JAN 1	–	JAN 4
	MAR 13	–	MAR 24
1863	JAN 13	–	FEB 5
1864	FEB 26	–	MAR 20
	DEC 15	–	DEC 31
1865	JAN 1	–	JAN 8
1866	JAN 27	–	FEB 19
1867	MAR 7	–	APR 2
	DEC 29	–	DEC 31
1868	JAN 1	–	JAN 21
1869	FEB 11	–	MAR 6
	DEC 5	–	DEC 31
1870	JAN 1	–	JAN 4
	MAR 4	–	MAR 28
1871	JAN 12	–	FEB 4
1872	FEB 25	–	MAR 20
	DEC 14	–	DEC 31
1873	JAN 1	–	JAN 7
1874	JAN 27	–	FEB 19
1875	MAR 7	–	APR 2
	DEC 28	–	DEC 31

VENUS IN AQUARIUS

1876	JAN 1	–	JAN 21
1877	FEB 10	–	MAR 5
	DEC 5	–	DEC 31
1878	JAN 1	–	JAN 5
	FEB 25	–	MAR 30
1879	JAN 12	–	FEB 4
1880	FEB 25	–	MAR 19
	DEC 14	–	DEC 31
1881	JAN 1	–	JAN 7
1882	JAN 26	–	FEB 18
1883	MAR 7	–	APR 1
	DEC 28	–	DEC 31
1884	JAN 1	–	JAN 20
1885	FEB 10	–	MAR 5
	DEC 5	–	DEC 31
1886	JAN 1	–	JAN 6
	FEB 19	–	APR 1
1887	JAN 11	–	FEB 3
1888	FEB 24	–	MAR 19
	DEC 13	–	DEC 31
1889	JAN 1	–	JAN 6
1890	JAN 26	–	FEB 18
1891	MAR 6	–	APR 1
	DEC 27	–	DEC 31
1892	JAN 1	–	JAN 20
1893	FEB 9	–	MAR 4
	DEC 5	–	DEC 31
1894	JAN 1	–	JAN 8
	FEB 13	–	APR 2
1895	JAN 11	–	FEB 3
1896	FEB 24	–	MAR 18
	DEC 13	–	DEC 31
1897	JAN 1	–	JAN 6
1898	JAN 25	–	FEB 17
1899	MAR 6	–	MAR 31
	DEC 27	–	DEC 31
1900	JAN 1	–	JAN 20
1901	FEB 10	–	MAR 5
	DEC 6	–	DEC 31
1902	JAN 1	–	JAN 11
	FEB 7	–	APR 4
1903	JAN 12	–	FEB 4
1904	FEB 25	–	MAR 19
	DEC 14	–	DEC 31
1905	JAN 1	–	JAN 7
1906	JAN 26	–	FEB 18
1907	MAR 7	–	APR 2
	DEC 28	–	DEC 31
1908	JAN 1	–	JAN 20
1909	FEB 10	–	MAR 5
	DEC 6	–	DEC 31
1910	JAN 1	–	JAN 15
	JAN 30	–	APR 5
1911	JAN 11	–	FEB 3
1912	FEB 24	–	MAR 19
	DEC 13	–	DEC 31
1913	JAN 1	–	JAN 7
1914	JAN 26	–	FEB 18
1915	MAR 7	–	APR 1
	DEC 27	–	DEC 31
1916	JAN 1	–	JAN 20
1917	FEB 9	–	MAR 4
	DEC 6	–	DEC 31
1918	JAN 1	–	APR 5
1919	JAN 11	–	FEB 2
1920	FEB 24	–	MAR 18
	DEC 13	–	DEC 31
1921	JAN 1	–	JAN 6
1922	JAN 25	–	FEB 17
1923	MAR 7	–	APR 1
	DEC 26	–	DEC 31
1924	JAN 1	–	JAN 19
1925	FEB 8	–	MAR 4
	DEC 6	–	DEC 13
1926	JAN 1	–	APR 6
1927	JAN 10	–	FEB 2
1928	FEB 23	–	MAR 18
	DEC 13	–	DEC 31
1929	JAN 1	–	JAN 6
1930	JAN 25	–	FEB 16
1931	MAR 6	–	MAR 31
	DEC 26	–	DEC 31

VENUS IN AQUARIUS

1932	JAN 1	– JAN 19
1933	FEB 8	– MAR 3
	DEC 6	– DEC 31
1934	JAN 1	– APR 6
1935	JAN 9	– FEB 1
1936	FEB 23	– MAR 17
	DEC 12	– DEC 31
1937	JAN 1	– JAN 6
1938	JAN 24	– FEB 16
1939	MAR 6	– MAR 31
	DEC 26	– DEC 31
1940	JAN 1	– JAN 18
1941	FEB 7	– MAR 2
	DEC 6	– DEC 31
1942	JAN 1	– APR 6
1943	JAN 9	– FEB 1
1944	FEB 22	– MAR 17
	DEC 12	– DEC 31
1945	JAN 1	– JAN 5
1946	JAN 23	– FEB 15
1947	MAR 6	– MAR 30
	DEC 25	– DEC 31
1948	JAN 1	– JAN 18
1949	FEB 7	– MAR 2
	DEC 7	– DEC 31
1950	JAN 1	– APR 6
1951	JAN 8	– JAN 31
1952	FEB 22	– MAR 16
	DEC 11	– DEC 31
1953	JAN 1	– JAN 5
1954	JAN 23	– FEB 15
1955	MAR 5	– MAR 30
	DEC 25	– DEC 31
1956	JAN 1	– JAN 17
1957	FEB 6	– MAR 1
	DEC 7	– DEC 31
1958	JAN 1	– APR 6
1959	JAN 8	– JAN 31
1960	FEB 21	– MAR 16
	DEC 11	– DEC 31
1961	JAN 1	– JAN 5

1962	JAN 22	– FEB 14
1963	MAR 5	– MAR 30
	DEC 24	– DEC 31
1964	JAN 1	– JAN 17
1965	FEB 6	– MAR 1
	DEC 8	– DEC 31
1966	JAN 1	– FEB 6
	FEB 26	– APR 6
1967	JAN 7	– JAN 30
1968	FEB 21	– MAR 15
	DEC 10	– DEC 31
1969	JAN 1	– JAN 4
1970	JAN 22	– FEB 14
1971	MAR 5	– MAR 29
	DEC 24	– DEC 31
1972	JAN 1	– JAN 16
1973	FEB 5	– FEB 28
	DEC 8	– DEC 31
1974	JAN 1	– JAN 29
	MAR 1	– APR 6
1975	JAN 7	– JAN 30
1976	FEB 20	– MAR 15
	DEC 10	– DEC 31
1977	JAN 1	– JAN 4
1978	JAN 21	– FEB 13
1979	MAR 4	– MAR 29
	DEC 23	– DEC 31
1980	JAN 1	– JAN 16
1981	FEB 5	– FEB 28
	DEC 9	– DEC 31
1982	JAN 1	– JAN 23
	MAR 3	– APR 6
1983	JAN 6	– JAN 29
1984	FEB 20	– MAR 14
	DEC 10	– DEC 31
1985	JAN 1	– JAN 4
1986	JAN 21	– FEB 13
1987	MAR 4	– MAR 28
	DEC 23	– DEC 31
1988	JAN 1	– JAN 15

VENUS IN AQUARIUS

Year	From	To
1989	FEB 4	FEB 27
	DEC 11	DEC 31
1990	JAN 1	JAN 16
	MAR 4	APR 6
1991	JAN 6	JAN 29
1992	FEB 19	MAR 13
	DEC 9	DEC 31
1993	JAN 1	JAN 3
1994	JAN 20	FEB 12
1995	MAR 3	MAR 28
	DEC 22	DEC 31
1996	JAN 1	JAN 15
1997	FEB 4	FEB 27
	DEC 13	DEC 31
1998	JAN 1	JAN 9
	MAR 5	APR 6
1999	JAN 5	JAN 28
2000	FEB 18	MAR 13
	DEC 9	DEC 31

VENUS IN PISCES

Year	From	To
1850	FEB 21	MAR 16
1851	APR 4	APR 29
1852	JAN 23	FEB 16
1853	MAR 8	MAR 31
1854	JAN 4	MAY 6
1855	FEB 6	MAR 1
1856	MAR 22	APR 14
1857	JAN 9	FEB 3
1858	FEB 21	MAR 16
1859	APR 3	APR 28
1860	JAN 23	FEB 15
1861	MAR 7	MAR 30
1862	JAN 5	MAR 12
	MAR 25	MAY 6
1863	FEB 6	MAR 1
1864	MAR 21	APR 14
1865	JAN 9	FEB 3
1866	FEB 20	MAR 15
1867	APR 3	APR 28
1868	JAN 22	FEB 15
1869	MAR 7	MAR 30
1870	JAN 5	MAR 3
	MAR 29	MAY 6
1871	FEB 5	FEB 28
1872	MAR 21	APR 13
1873	JAN 8	FEB 2
1874	FEB 20	MAR 15
1875	APR 3	APR 27
1876	JAN 22	FEB 14
1877	MAR 6	MAR 29
1878	JAN 6	FEB 24
	MAR 31	MAY 6
1879	FEB 5	FEB 28
1880	MAR 20	APR 13
1881	JAN 8	FEB 2
1882	FEB 19	MAR 14
1883	APR 2	APR 27
1884	JAN 21	FEB 14
1885	MAR 6	MAR 29
1886	JAN 7	FEB 18
	APR 2	MAY 6
1887	FEB 4	FEB 27
1888	MAR 20	APR 12
1889	JAN 7	FEB 2
1890	FEB 19	MAR 14
1891	APR 2	APR 26
1892	JAN 21	FEB 13
1893	MAR 5	MAR 28
1894	JAN 9	FEB 12
	APR 3	MAY 5
1895	FEB 4	FEB 27
1896	MAR 19	APR 12
1897	JAN 7	FEB 1
1898	FEB 18	MAR 13

VENUS IN PISCES

Year	From	To
1899	APR 1	APR 26
1900	JAN 21	FEB 13
1901	MAR 6	MAR 29
1902	JAN 12	FEB 6
	APR 5	MAY 7
1903	FEB 5	FEB 28
1904	MAR 20	APR 13
1905	JAN 8	FEB 3
1906	FEB 19	MAR 14
1907	APR 3	APR 27
1908	JAN 21	FEB 14
1909	MAR 6	MAR 29
1910	JAN 16	JAN 29
	APR 6	MAY 7
1911	FEB 4	FEB 27
1912	MAR 20	APR 12
1913	JAN 8	FEB 2
1914	FEB 19	MAR 14
1915	APR 2	APR 22
1916	JAN 21	FEB 13
1917	MAR 5	MAR 28
1918	APR 6	MAY 6
1919	FEB 3	FEB 27
1920	MAR 19	APR 12
1921	JAN 7	FEB 2
1922	FEB 18	MAR 13
1923	APR 2	APR 26
1924	JAN 20	FEB 13
1925	MAR 5	MAR 28
1926	APR 7	MAY 6
1927	FEB 3	FEB 26
1928	MAR 19	APR 11
1929	JAN 7	FEB 2
1930	FEB 17	MAR 12
1931	APR 1	APR 26
1932	JAN 20	FEB 12
1933	MAR 4	MAR 27
1934	APR 7	MAY 6
1935	FEB 2	FEB 26
1936	MAR 18	APR 11
1937	JAN 7	FEB 2

Year	From	To
1938	FEB 17	MAR 12
1939	APR 1	APR 25
1940	JAN 19	FEB 12
1941	MAR 3	MAR 27
1942	APR 7	MAY 6
1943	FEB 2	FEB 25
1944	MAR 18	APR 10
1945	JAN 6	FEB 2
1946	FEB 16	MAR 11
1947	MAR 31	APR 25
1948	JAN 19	FEB 11
1949	MAR 3	MAR 26
1950	APR 7	MAY 5
1951	FEB 1	FEB 24
1952	MAR 17	APR 9
1953	JAN 6	FEB 2
1954	FEB 16	MAR 11
1955	MAR 31	APR 24
1956	JAN 18	FEB 11
1957	MAR 2	MAR 25
1958	APR 7	MAY 5
1959	FEB 1	FEB 24
1960	MAR 17	APR 9
1961	JAN 6	FEB 2
1962	FEB 15	MAR 10
1963	MAR 31	APR 24
1964	JAN 18	FEB 10
1965	MAR 2	MAR 25
1966	APR 7	MAY 5
1967	JAN 31	FEB 23
1968	MAR 16	APR 8
1969	JAN 5	FEB 2
1970	FEB 15	MAR 10
1971	MAR 30	APR 23
1972	JAN 17	FEB 10
1973	MAR 1	MAR 24
1974	APR 7	MAY 4
1975	JAN 31	FEB 23
1976	MAR 16	APR 8
1977	JAN 5	FEB 2
1978	FEB 14	MAR 9

VENUS IN PISCES

1979	MAR 30 – APR 23	1990	APR 7 – MAY 4
1980	JAN 17 – FEB 9	1991	JAN 30 – FEB 22
1981	MAR 1 – MAR 24	1992	MAR 14 – APR 7
1982	APR 7 – MAY 4	1993	JAN 4 – FEB 2
1983	JAN 30 – FEB 22	1994	FEB 13 – MAR 8
1984	MAR 15 – APR 7	1995	MAR 29 – APR 22
1985	JAN 5 – FEB 2	1996	JAN 16 – FEB 9
1986	FEB 14 – MAR 9	1997	FEB 28 – MAR 23
1987	MAR 29 – APR 22	1998	APR 7 – MAY 3
1988	JAN 16 – FEB 9	1999	JAN 29 – FEB 21
1989	FEB 28 – MAR 23	2000	MAR 14 – APR 6

VENUS IN ARIES

Your Venus in Aries makes you demanding of total obeisance from your partner. You need to be told constantly of your mate's devotion to you. You are persuasive in love and really know how to court and be courted. You are always attentive and considerate as a lover, but your incredible ego needs to make conquests of your partners. You're not the type to sit back and wait for the right lover to come along—you *always* take the lead. You need to be the emotional master at all times, and the game must be played *your* way. If your partner doesn't cater to you, you become bored and go out looking for another conquest who will idolize you and bring excitement back into your life. You are idealistic and become depressed when the "love of your life" cools on you. But when love goes *your* way and you're adored on your pedestal, you make a romantic, passionate and intense lover.

VENUS IN TAURUS

Your Venus in Taurus makes you *very* slow and cautious and deliberate in giving your heart, but once you've finally found someone you feel you can really trust, and you've made the decision to become totally involved and demonstrative with your affections, you will never give up until you've won him or her with your incredible determination. A more constant and steady partner doesn't exist in the Zodiac. You are devoted to your mate and never unfaithful, and you expect the same devotion and faithfulness from him or her.

You're not a flirt and won't tolerate flirting. You really love the comfort and predictability of having your mate home every night with you, and don't need the excitement and uncertainty of changing partners. An affair holds no stimulation for you at all. Taurus is a money sign and often Venus in Taurus means a money marriage. Because you're so slow in giving your love, it's difficult for someone attracted to you to have the patience to wait for you to reciprocate. But it's worth the wait.

VENUS IN GEMINI

Your Venus in Gemini is the most fickle and changeable and discontented of all the love signs (remember what I said earlier about JFK). You're mercurial and unpredictable with your feelings—one moment you can desire someone and the next moment you won't—it's as fast and simple as that. You're a game-player and a total tease. You love to keep 'em guessing, which drives most people crazy 'cause no one ever will know with you exactly where he or she stands. You are ruled by your mind, not your body, and for someone to stimulate you, it *must* be a mental turn-on. You love beauty, but you'll take a less attractive person with a sharp brain over an empty-headed god or goddess. Your feelings are quicksilver and keep one on one's toes, but because of the emotional see-saw, after a while the excitement of an affair with you becomes exhausting. Faithfulness is not your thing, and most of the time family life really bores you.

VENUS IN CANCER

Your Venus in Cancer gives you an enormous capacity to love and a deep need for home and family life. You need constant reassurance that you are loved. Because of your great compulsion for emotional security, you will rarely abandon your home and family. You have an inordinate need for emotional intimacy, you are *always* seeking a permanent relationship, and you crave an ideal mate, one with whom you can merge totally—physically, mentally and emotionally. You're extremely sensitive, receptive, tender and affectionate, and until you find your perfect love, you will search the world looking, having many affairs, and because of your sensitive nature, much guilt. But if and when you *do* finally find your ideal, your tenderness and romantic and loving qualities will make for you a perfect union.

VENUS IN LEO

Your Venus in Leo makes you about as dynamic a lover as can exist. You are generous to a fault—you send flowers, cuff-links, diamonds, bow-ties—whatever you can afford. You are flamboyant and demonstrative. You love elegance and romantic displays of your affection. You have a magnetism about you and you know it. You love being around someone who also enjoys the spotlight, but not too much to detract from you. You give great parties and have a flair for drama, particularly in the bedroom. You're a loyal and lavish lover. You never do *anything* halfway—when you fall in love (which you do often), it has to be a *giant* romance. You have to feel the earth shake and see rockets go off. Romance is as important to you as food is to some of the other signs. In fact, you literally couldn't live without romance in your life.

VENUS IN VIRGO

Your Venus in Virgo gives you sincerity, refinement, orderliness and lots of other not-too-romantically exciting qualities. You're *not* a romantic, but you are sexual. Sex is very important to you, but not necessarily in a love relationship. You love and need sex for itself. Many Venus in Virgos never get married, and have lots of affairs. You're not an emotional person, you're very wary in a relationship, and if you *do* get married, it's often later in life. But if you ever do meet a person who convinces you to love and trust him or her, and is patient with you and waits for your love and trust to develop and grow, (how many people do you know with *that* kind of patience?), that love of yours will be exceptionally strong and will last a lifetime. You will also be faithful once you have committed yourself, and your partner will have enormous emotional security, which will make up for the lack of romance, adventure and excitement in your relationship.

VENUS IN LIBRA

Your Venus in Libra makes you a wonderful lover (not necessarily a wonderful wife or husband). You have a problem with indecisiveness in your love life, and because of this, you usually have more than one lover, and can't make a decision about which one you want as a spouse. You treat love as an art and you are the artist. You respond to flattery and need to be praised. You need a lot of attention and constant reassurance, and when you get it there's nothing you won't do to satisfy your mate. You tend to be narcissistic, and you want and need to be turned on physically, mentally and emotionally first, before you turn your partner on. You have a refinement about you and abhor anything vulgar or lewd in sex. Sexual bad taste turns you off. You love beauty in *all* forms—a beautiful body, beautiful lips, beautiful hair, and you need a beautiful setting with soft music for your lovemaking. When these are right, you're a voluptuary, giving your lover anything and everything to satisfy.

VENUS IN SCORPIO

Your Venus in Scorpio is the most selfish of all the love signs. Sexually, you are much more interested in your satisfaction than in your partner's. You have a compulsive need to prove yourself sexually, for you have an incredible insecurity about love and sex. You're also compulsively possessive, which tends to drive love away, and you keep on attracting and repelling through your obsessive domination. In fact, your need to dominate is almost pathological, because it stems from an overwhelming fear that if you don't dominate, you will *be* dominated, which petrifies you. The incredible part of all this is that you are a strong attraction to others, (everyone finds you sexy), and your fear of domination is *only* in your mind. You are never satisfied with one person very long, and you are always looking for new and stimulating conquests. You should really try self-discipline in all these areas, which will help you to finally overcome your love problems, for until you do, you will continue through life being sexually dissatisfied and constantly unhappy.

VENUS IN SAGITTARIUS

Your Venus in Sagittarius makes you extremely open, sincere and frank in all areas of romance. Nothing surreptitious about you. You're always straightforward and are sometimes even tactless in your superhonesty. Fortunately, you have great humor and charm, which helps a lot. You love animals and have a wonderful rapport with them, and they're crazy about you. You're idealistic in love and need a mental and spiritual closeness as much as a feeling one, (it takes a lot of time for you to really trust your feelings). You need your freedom, and you are able to live alone (whereas most people can't), and a lot of you stay single, or if you do marry, it's often later in life. You have emotional needs, but they're often satisfied by work or friends. You prefer pals, companions, to really intense lovers, but once you find your ideal mate, someone who really turns you on and won't fence you in, someone who needs some freedom too, and you two groove together in other areas, you'll give a total commitment and be happy to settle down and will be a faithful mate.

VENUS IN CAPRICORN

Your Venus in Capricorn makes you very ambitious, seeking love affairs which will profit you monetarily, professionally and in the social arena. You are very aware of what is naturally good for you, and instinctively go after it. You are *not* looking for a deep emotional commitment; in fact, feelings frighten you and real romance is not what you're after. You are sharp and astute and can be very calculating as you scan possibilities of lovers. If and when you see someone you want, you pursue him or her slowly and deliberately and relentlessly, until you finally make your catch. You are the most determined of all the signs and just *never* give up if you really set your sights on someone (preferably someone with money and/or power). But while you wait for the big catch, you always make sure your ravenous appetite, which is terribly important to you, is satisfied. You're manipulative and not easy to know, but *you* always know what you're doing. You'll always advance yourself in marriage.

VENUS IN AQUARIUS

Your Venus in Aquarius will make you an honest, dependable lover, with a warm and friendly disposition, who will shy away from a permanent relationship. But once you find the person you feel you can really groove with in every area, you will have a lasting relationship and be totally faithful. You are direct and play straight in everything you do—you're never deceitful or dishonest in your dealings. In romance, you don't play games and you're turned off by people who do. The most important thing to you is to have your lover also your friend, because although you do need love, companionship and friendship are more important to you. You are capable of the tenderest feelings and are very gentle emotionally. You have a vivid imagination, and until you find the right mate, you will lose your self in erotic fantasies, which you prefer, rather than making love to what you consider the wrong person. Your standards are high, and you are perceptive and a great judge of potential lovers. You appear outwardly cool, but underneath it all lies an animal magnetism that would surprise most people.

VENUS IN PISCES

Your Venus in Pisces makes you extremely sensitive in love, and makes you hunger for a mate you can totally assimilate your self with spiritually, mentally and emotionally. You are overly affectionate, terribly sentimental, and need a strong, dominant partner who can give you the stability you need, and make you feel secure. You need constant reassurance that you are loved and needed. You crave a unity that will make you one with your mate. But this happens so seldom in anyone's life that you are constantly frustrated with your relationships, and are hurt much of the time. Because of your enormous need for love, you are willing to give almost anything to satisfy your partner, and when this is not reciprocated, you crawl into your shell to lick your wounds. If you ever *do* find your ideal love, you will dedicate your life to making the union a happy and satisfying one.

7

Your 12 Mars Signs and Chart

Mars symbolizes energy, force, action, fervor, heat, aggression, potency—WOW!!! Whatever sign your Mars is in will show how the forces of energy in your life will be expressed, where your energy will most naturally flow and how you can best use that energy in your life.

Mars rules the strength of your sex drive, your courage, vigor and potency, and is a planet of great power and energy. This can be constructive energy or destructive energy, depending on how you channel it. Used well, Mars can be a tremendous creative force in your romance and in your life.

Your Mars Sign is determined by the year you were born. Your Mars Chart is on the following pages.

Your Mars Chart

HOW TO FIND THE POSITION OF MARS
AT THE TIME OF YOUR BIRTH

1850

Jan 1 – Mar 15	Gemini
Mar 16 – May 14	Cancer
May 15 – Jul 5	Leo
Jul 6 – Aug 22	Virgo
Aug 23 – Oct 7	Libra
Oct 8 – Nov 19	Scorpio
Nov 20 – Dec 30	Sagittarius
Dec 31	Capricorn

1851

Jan 1 – Feb 7	Capricorn
Feb 8 – Mar 17	Aquarius
Mar 18 – Apr 25	Pisces
Apr 26 – Jun 3	Aries
Jun 4 – Jul 15	Taurus
Jul 16 – Aug 29	Gemini
Aug 30 – Oct 24	Cancer
Oct 25 – Dec 31	Leo

1852

Jan 1 – Feb 3	Leo
Feb 4 – Apr 5	Cancer
Apr 6 – Jun 11	Leo
Jun 12 – Aug 1	Virgo
Aug 2 – Sep 17	Libra
Sep 18 – Oct 30	Scorpio
Oct 31 – Dec 9	Sagittarius
Dec 10 – Dec 31	Capricorn

1853

Jan 1 – Jan 17	Capricorn
Jan 18 – Feb 24	Aquarius
Feb 25 – Apr 3	Pisces
Apr 4 – May 13	Aries
May 14 – Jun 23	Taurus
Jun 24 – Aug 5	Gemini
Aug 6 – Sep 22	Cancer
Sep 23 – Nov 16	Leo
Nov 17 – Dec 31	Virgo

1854

Jan 1 – Mar 22	Virgo
Mar 23 – Apr 27	Leo
Apr 28 – Jul 8	Virgo
Jul 9 – Aug 27	Libra
Aug 28 – Oct 10	Scorpio
Oct 11 – Nov 19	Sagittarius
Nov 20 – Dec 28	Capricorn
Dec 29 – Dec 31	Aquarius

1855

Jan 1 – Feb 4	Aquarius
Feb 5 – Mar 14	Pisces
Mar 15 – Apr 23	Aries
Apr 24 – Jun 3	Taurus
Jun 4 – Jul 16	Gemini
Jul 17 – Aug 31	Cancer
Sep 1 – Oct 19	Leo
Oct 20 – Dec 13	Virgo
Dec 14 – Dec 31	Libra

1856

Jan 1 – Jul 30	Libra
Jul 31 – Sep 16	Scorpio
Sep 17 – Oct 28	Sagittarius
Oct 29 – Dec 6	Capricorn
Dec 7 – Dec 31	Aquarius

1857

Jan 1 – Jan 14	Aquarius
Jan 15 – Feb 21	Pisces
Feb 22 – Apr 2	Aries
Apr 3 – May 14	Taurus
May 15 – Jun 26	Gemini
Jun 27 – Aug 11	Cancer
Aug 12 – Sep 27	Leo
Sep 28 – Nov 15	Virgo
Nov 16 – Dec 31	Libra

1858

Jan 1 – Jan 7	Libra
Jan 8 – Mar 21	Scorpio
Mar 22 – Apr 28	Sagittarius
Apr 29 – Aug 12	Scorpio
Aug 13 – Oct 1	Sagittarius
Oct 2 – Nov 12	Capricorn
Nov 13 – Dec 22	Aquarius
Dec 23 – Dec 31	Pisces

1859

Jan 1 – Jan 31	Pisces
Feb 1 – Mar 13	Aries
Mar 14 – Apr 24	Taurus
Apr 25 – Jun 7	Gemini
Jun 8 – Jul 23	Cancer
Jul 24 – Sep 8	Leo
Sep 9 – Oct 26	Virgo
Oct 27 – Dec 13	Libra
Dec 14 – Dec 31	Scorpio

Your Mars Chart

1860

Jan 1 – Jan 30	Scorpio
Jan 31 – Mar 22	Sagittarius
Mar 23 – Jun 9	Capricorn
Jun 10 – Jun 22	Aquarius
Jun 23 – Sep 29	Capricorn
Sep 30 – Nov 20	Aquarius
Nov 21 – Dec 31	Pisces

1861

Jan 1 – Jan 4	Pisces
Jan 5 – Feb 17	Aries
Feb 18 – Apr 2	Taurus
Apr 3 – May 18	Gemini
May 19 – Jul 4	Cancer
Jul 5 – Aug 20	Leo
Aug 21 – Oct 6	Virgo
Oct 7 – Nov 21	Libra
Nov 22 – Dec 31	Scorpio

1862

Jan 1 – Jan 5	Scorpio
Jan 6 – Feb 19	Sagittarius
Feb 20 – Mar 3	Capricorn
Mar 4 – May 17	Aquarius
May 18 – Jul 5	Pisces
Jul 6 – Dec 31	Aries

1863

Jan 1 – Jan 14	Aries
Jan 15 – Mar 8	Taurus
Mar 9 – Apr 27	Gemini
Apr 28 – Jun 15	Cancer
Jun 16 – Aug 2	Leo
Aug 3 – Sep 18	Virgo
Sep 19 – Nov 2	Libra
Nov 3 – Dec 16	Scorpio
Dec 17 – Dec 31	Sagittarius

1864

Jan 1 – Jan 27	Sagittarius
Jan 28 – Mar 8	Capricorn
Mar 9 – Apr 17	Aquarius
Apr 18 – May 27	Pisces
May 28 – Jul 8	Aries
Jul 9 – Aug 25	Taurus
Aug 26 – Dec 31	Gemini

1865

Jan 1 – Mar 30	Gemini
Mar 31 – May 23	Cancer
May 24 – Jul 13	Leo
Jul 14 – Aug 29	Virgo
Aug 30 – Oct 14	Libra
Oct 15 – Nov 26	Scorpio
Nov 27 – Dec 31	Sagittarius

1866

Jan 1 – Jan 6	Sagittarius
Jan 7 – Feb 15	Capricorn
Feb 16 – Mar 25	Aquarius
Mar 26 – May 3	Pisces
May 4 – Jun 12	Aries
Jun 13 – Jul 24	Taurius
Jul 25 – Sep 9	Gemini
Sep 10 – Nov 25	Cancer
Nov 26 – Dec 7	Leo
Dec 8 – Dec 31	Cancer

1867

Jan 1 – Apr 25	Cancer
Apr 26 – Jun 21	Leo
Jun 22 – Aug 10	Virgo
Aug 11 – Sep 25	Libra
Sep 26 – Nov 7	Scorpio
Nov 8 – Dec 18	Sagittarius
Dec 19 – Dec 31	Capricorn

1868

Jan 1 – Jan 26	Capricorn
Jan 27 – Mar 4	Aquarius
Mar 5 – Apr 11	Pisces
Apr 12 – May 20	Aries
May 21 – Jun 30	Taurus
Jul 1 – Aug 13	Gemini
Aug 14 – Oct 1	Cancer
Oct 2 – Dec 5	Leo
Dec 6 – Dec 31	Virgo

1869

Jan 1 – Jan 31	Virgo
Feb 1 – May 22	Leo
May 23 – Jul 18	Virgo
Jul 19 – Sep 4	Libra
Sep 5 – Oct 17	Scorpio
Oct 18 – Nov 27	Sagittarius
Nov 28 – Dec 31	Capricorn

Your Mars Chart

1870

Jan 1	– Jan 5	Capricorn
Jan 6	– Feb 12	Aquarius
Feb 13	– Mar 22	Pisces
Mar 23	– Apr 30	Aries
May 1	– Jun 10	Taurus
Jun 11	– Jul 24	Gemini
Jul 25	– Sep 8	Cancer
Sep 9	– Oct 28	Leo
Oct 29	– Dec 30	Virgo
Dec 31		Libra

1871

Jan 1	– Mar 17	Libra
Mar 18	– Jun 15	Virgo
Jun 16	– Aug 12	Libra
Aug 13	– Sep 26	Scorpio
Sep 27	– Nov 6	Sagittarius
Nov 7	– Dec 15	Capricorn
Dec 16	– Dec 31	Aquarius

1872

Jan 1	– Jan 23	Aquarius
Jan 24	– Mar 1	Pisces
Mar 2	– Apr 10	Aries
Apr 11	– May 21	Taurus
May 22	– Jul 3	Gemini
Jul 4	– Aug 18	Cancer
Aug 19	– Oct 5	Leo
Oct 6	– Nov 24	Virgo
Nov 25	– Dec 31	Libra

1873

Jan 1	– Jan 22	Libra
Jan 23	– May 19	Scorpio
May 20	– Jun 24	Libra
Jun 25	– Aug 29	Scorpio
Aug 30	– Oct 13	Sagittarius
Oct 14	– Nov 22	Capricorn
Nov 23	– Dec 31	Aquarius

1874

Jan 1	– Feb 8	Pisces
Feb 9	– Mar 21	Aries
Mar 22	– May 2	Taurus
May 3	– Jun 15	Gemini
Jun 16	– Jul 30	Cancer
Jul 31	– Sep 15	Leo
Sep 16	– Nov 2	Virgo
Nov 3	– Dec 21	Libra
Dec 22	– Dec 31	Scorpio

1875

Jan 1	– Feb 11	Scorpio
Feb 12	– Apr 19	Sagittarius
Apr 20	– Jun 15	Capricorn
Jun 16	– Aug 31	Sagittarius
Sep 1	– Oct 23	Capricorn
Oct 24	– Dec 5	Aquarius
Dec 6	– Dec 31	Pisces

1876

Jan 1	– Jan 16	Pisces
Jan 17	– Feb 27	Aries
Feb 28	– Apr 10	Taurus
Apr 11	– May 25	Gemini
May 26	– Jul 11	Cancer
Jul 12	– Aug 27	Leo
Aug 28	– Oct 13	Virgo
Oct 14	– Nov 29	Libra
Nov 30	– Dec 31	Scorpio

1877

Jan 1	– Jan 14	Scorpio
Jan 15	– Mar 1	Sagittarius
Mar 2	– Apr 16	Capricorn
Apr 17	– Jun 6	Aquarius
Jun 7	– Dec 9	Pisces
Dec 10	– Dec 31	Aries

1878

Jan 1	– Jan 30	Aries
Jan 31	– Mar 19	Taurus
Mar 20	– May 5	Gemini
May 6	– Jun 22	Cancer
Jun 23	– Aug 9	Leo
Aug 10	– Sep 25	Virgo
Sep 26	– Nov 9	Libra
Nov 10	– Dec 23	Scorpio
Dec 24	– Dec 31	Sagittarius

1879

Jan 1	– Feb 4	Sagittarius
Feb 5	– Mar 18	Capricorn
Mar 19	– Apr 28	Aquarius
Apr 29	– Jun 8	Pisces
Jun 9	– Jul 23	Aries
Jul 24	– Dec 31	Taurus

Your Mars Chart

1880

Jan 1	– Feb 13	Taurus
Feb 14	– Apr 11	Gemini
Apr 12	– Jun 1	Cancer
Jun 2	– Jul 20	Leo
Jul 21	– Sep 5	Virgo
Sep 6	– Oct 21	Libra
Oct 22	– Dec 3	Scorpio
Dec 4	– Dec 31	Sagittarius

1881

Jan 1	– Jan 13	Sagittarius
Jan 14	– Feb 22	Capricorn
Feb 23	– Apr 2	Aquarius
Apr 3	– May 12	Pisces
May 13	– Jun 21	Aries
Jun 22	– Aug 3	Taurus
Aug 4	– Sep 23	Gemini
Sep 24	– Dec 31	Cancer

1882

Jan 1	– Jan 11	Cancer
Jan 12	– Feb 25	Gemini
Feb 26	– May 7	Cancer
May 8	– Jun 30	Leo
Jul 1	– Aug 18	Virgo
Aug 19	– Oct 2	Libra
Oct 3	– Nov 14	Scorpio
Nov 15	– Dec 25	Sagittarius
Dec 26	– Dec 31	Capricorn

1883

Jan 1	– Feb 2	Capricorn
Feb 3	– Mar 12	Aquarius
Mar 13	– Apr 20	Pisces
Apr 21	– May 29	Aries
May 30	– Jul 10	Taurus
Jul 11	– Aug 23	Gemini
Aug 24	– Oct 14	Cancer
Oct 15	– Dec 31	Leo

1884

Jan 1	– Jun 4	Leo
Jun 5	– Jul 27	Virgo
Jul 28	– Sep 12	Libra
Sep 13	– Oct 25	Scorpio
Oct 26	– Dec 5	Sagittarius
Dec 6	– Dec 31	Capricorn

1885

Jan 1	– Jan 12	Capricorn
Jan 13	– Feb 19	Aquarius
Feb 20	– Mar 30	Pisces
Mar 31	– May 8	Aries
May 9	– Jun 18	Taurus
Jun 19	– Jul 31	Gemini
Aug 1	– Sep 16	Cancer
Sep 17	– Nov 8	Leo
Nov 9	– Dec 31	Virgo

1886

Jan 1	– Jul 1	Virgo
Jul 2	– Aug 21	Libra
Aug 22	– Oct 5	Scorpio
Oct 6	– Nov 14	Sagittarius
Nov 15	– Dec 23	Capricorn
Dec 24	– Dec 31	Aquarius

1887

Jan 1	– Jan 30	Aquarius
Jan 31	– Mar 10	Pisces
Mar 11	– Apr 18	Aries
Apr 19	– May 29	Taurus
May 30	– Jul 11	Gemini
Jul 12	– Aug 26	Cancer
Aug 27	– Oct 13	Leo
Oct 14	– Dec 5	Virgo
Dec 6	– Dec 31	Libra

1888

Jan 1	– Feb 26	Libra
Feb 27	– Mar 9	Scorpio
Mar 10	– Jul 21	Libra
Jul 22	– Sep 10	Scorpio
Sep 11	– Oct 22	Sagittarius
Oct 23	– Dec 1	Capricorn
Dec 2	– Dec 31	Aquarius

1889

Jan 1	– Jan 9	Aquarius
Jan 10	– Feb 16	Pisces
Feb 17	– Mar 28	Aries
Mar 29	– May 9	Taurus
May 10	– Jun 22	Gemini
Jun 23	– Aug 6	Cancer
Aug 7	– Sep 22	Leo
Sep 23	– Nov 10	Virgo
Nov 11	– Dec 31	Libra

Your Mars Chart

1890

Jan 1 – Feb 28	Scorpio
Mar 1 – Jun 16	Sagittarius
Jun 17 – Jul 21	Scorpio
Jul 22 – Sep 23	Sagittarius
Sep 24 – Nov 5	Capricorn
Nov 6 – Dec 16	Aquarius
Dec 17 – Dec 31	Pisces

1891

Jan 1 – Jan 25	Pisces
Jan 26 – Mar 7	Aries
Mar 8 – Apr 19	Taurus
Apr 20 – Jun 3	Gemini
Jun 4 – Jul 19	Cancer
Jul 20 – Sep 4	Leo
Sep 5 – Oct 21	Virgo
Oct 22 – Dec 7	Libra
Dec 8 – Dec 31	Scorpio

1892

Jan 1 – Feb 24	Scorpio
Feb 25 – Mar 13	Sagittarius
Mar 14 – May 6	Capricorn
May 7 – Nov 8	Aquarius
Nov 9 – Dec 27	Pisces
Dec 28 – Dec 31	Aries

1893

Jan 1 – Feb 10	Aries
Feb 11 – Mar 28	Taurus
Mar 29 – May 13	Gemini
May 14 – Jun 29	Cancer
Jun 30 – Aug 15	Leo
Aug 16 – Oct 1	Virgo
Oct 2 – Nov 16	Libra
Nov 17 – Dec 31	Scorpio

1894

Jan 1 – Feb 13	Sagittarius
Feb 14 – Mar 27	Capricorn
Mar 28 – May 9	Aquarius
May 10 – Jun 22	Pisces
Jun 23 – Aug 18	Aries
Aug 19 – Oct 12	Taurus
Oct 13 – Dec 30	Aries
Dec 31	Taurus

1895

Jan 1 – Mar 1	Taurus
Mar 2 – Apr 21	Gemini
Apr 22 – Jun 10	Cancer
Jun 11 – Jul 28	Leo
Jul 29 – Sep 13	Virgo
Sep 14 – Oct 30	Libra
Oct 31 – Dec 11	Scorpio
Dec 12 – Dec 31	Sagittarius

1896

Jan 1 – Jan 22	Sagittarius
Jan 23 – Mar 2	Capricorn
Mar 3 – Apr 11	Aquarius
Apr 12 – May 21	Pisces
May 22 – Jul 1	Aries
Jul 2 – Aug 15	Taurus
Aug 16 – Dec 31	Gemini

1897

Jan 1 – Mar 21	Gemini
Mar 22 – May 17	Cancer
May 18 – Jul 8	Leo
Jul 9 – Aug 25	Virgo
Aug 26 – Oct 9	Libra
Oct 10 – Nov 21	Scorpio
Nov 22 – Dec 31	Sagittarius

1898

Jan 1	Sagittarius
Jan 2 – Feb 10	Capricorn
Feb 11 – Mar 20	Aquarius
Mar 21 – Apr 28	Pisces
Apr 29 – Jun 6	Aries
Jun 7 – Jul 18	Taurus
Jul 19 – Sep 2	Gemini
Sep 3 – Oct 30	Cancer
Oct 31 – Dec 31	Leo

1899

Jan 1 – Jan 15	Leo
Jan 16 – Apr 14	Cancer
Apr 15 – Jun 15	Leo
June 16 – Aug 5	Virgo
Aug 6 – Sep 20	Libra
Sep 21 – Nov 2	Scorpio
Nov 3 – Dec 13	Sagittarius
Dec 14 – Dec 31	Capricorn

Your Mars Chart

1900

Jan 1 – Feb 29	Aquarius
Mar 1 – Apr 7	Pisces
Apr 8 – May 16	Aries
May 17 – Jun 26	Taurus
Jun 27 – Aug 9	Gemini
Aug 10 – Sep 26	Cancer
Sep 27 – Nov 22	Leo
Nov 23 – Dec 31	Virgo

1901

Jan 1 – Mar 1	Virgo
Mar 2 – May 10	Leo
May 11 – Jul 13	Virgo
Jul 14 – Aug 31	Libra
Sep 1 – Oct 14	Scorpio
Oct 15 – Nov 23	Sagittarius
Nov 24 – Dec 31	Capricorn

1902

Jan 1	Capricorn
Jan 2 – Feb 8	Aquarius
Feb 9 – Mar 17	Pisces
Mar 18 – Apr 26	Aries
Apr 27 – Jun 6	Taurus
Jun 7 – Jul 20	Gemini
Jul 21 – Sep 4	Cancer
Sep 5 – Oct 23	Leo
Oct 24 – Dec 19	Virgo
Dec 20 – Dec 31	Libra

1903

Jan 1 – Apr 19	Libra
Apr 20 – May 30	Virgo
May 31 – Aug 6	Libra
Aug 7 – Sep 22	Scorpio
Sep 23 – Nov 2	Sagittarius
Nov 3 – Dec 11	Capricorn
Dec 12 – Dec 31	Aquarius

1904

Jan 1 – Jan 19	Aquarius
Jan 20 – Feb 26	Pisces
Feb 27 – Apr 6	Aries
Apr 7 – May 17	Taurus
May 18 – Jun 30	Gemini
Jul 1 – Aug 14	Cancer
Aug 15 – Oct 1	Leo
Oct 2 – Nov 19	Virgo
Nov 20 – Dec 31	Libra

1905

Jan 1 – Jan 13	Libra
Jan 14 – Aug 21	Scorpio
Aug 22 – Oct 7	Sagittarius
Oct 8 – Nov 17	Capricorn
Nov 18 – Dec 27	Aquarius
Dec 28 – Dec 31	Pisces

1906

Jan 1 – Feb 4	Pisces
Feb 5 – Mar 16	Aries
Mar 17 – Apr 28	Taurus
Apr 29 – Jun 11	Gemini
Jun 12 – Jul 27	Cancer
Jul 28 – Sep 12	Leo
Sep 13 – Oct 29	Virgo
Oct 30 – Dec 16	Libra
Dec 17 – Dec 31	Scorpio

1907

Jan 1 – Feb 4	Scorpio
Feb 5 – Apr 1	Sagittarius
Apr 2 – Oct 13	Capricorn
Oct 14 – Nov 28	Aquarius
Nov 29 – Dec 31	Pisces

1908

Jan 1 – Jan 10	Pisces
Jan 11 – Feb 22	Aries
Feb 23 – Apr 6	Taurus
Apr 7 – May 22	Gemini
May 23 – Jul 7	Cancer
Jul 8 – Aug 23	Leo
Aug 24 – Oct 9	Virgo
Oct 10 – Nov 25	Libra
Nov 26 – Dec 31	Scorpio

1909

Jan 1 – Jan 9	Scorpio
Jan 10 – Feb 23	Sagittarius
Feb 24 – Apr 9	Capricorn
Apr 10 – May 25	Aquarius
May 26 – Jul 20	Pisces
Jul 21 – Sep 26	Aries
Sep 27 – Nov 20	Pisces
Nov 21 – Dec 31	Aries

Your Mars Chart

1910

Jan 1 – Feb 22	Aries
Feb 23 – Mar 13	Taurus
Mar 14 – May 1	Gemini
May 2 – Jun 18	Cancer
Jun 19 – Aug 5	Leo
Aug 6 – Sep 21	Virgo
Sep 22 – Nov 6	Libra
Nov 7 – Dec 19	Scorpio
Dec 20 – Dec 31	Sagittarius

1911

Jan 1 – Jan 31	Sagittarius
Feb 1 – Mar 13	Capricorn
Mar 14 – Apr 22	Aquarius
Apr 23 – Jun 2	Pisces
Jun 3 – Jul 15	Aries
Jul 16 – Sep 5	Taurus
Sep 6 – Nov 29	Gemini
Nov 30 – Dec 31	Taurus

1912

Jan 1 – Jan 30	Taurus
Jan 31 – Apr 4	Gemini
Apr 5 – May 27	Cancer
May 28 – Jul 16	Leo
Jul 17 – Sep 2	Virgo
Sep 3 – Oct 17	Libra
Oct 18 – Nov 29	Scorpio
Nov 30 – Dec 31	Sagittarius

1913

Jan 1 – Jan 10	Sagittarius
Jan 11 – Feb 18	Capricorn
Feb 19 – Mar 29	Aquarius
Mar 30 – May 7	Pisces
May 8 – Jun 16	Aries
Jun 17 – Jul 28	Taurus
Jul 29 – Sep 15	Gemini
Sep 16 – Dec 31	Cancer

1914

Jan 1 – May 1	Cancer
May 2 – Jun 25	Leo
Jun 26 – Aug 14	Virgo
Aug 15 – Sep 28	Libra
Sep 29 – Nov 10	Scorpio
Nov 11 – Dec 21	Sagittarius
Dec 22 – Dec 31	Capricorn

1915

Jan 1 – Jan 29	Capricorn
Jan 30 – Mar 9	Aquarius
Mar 10 – Apr 16	Pisces
Apr 17 – May 25	Aries
May 26 – Jul 5	Taurus
Jul 6 – Aug 18	Gemini
Aug 19 – Oct 7	Cancer
Oct 8 – Dec 31	Leo

1916

Jan 1 – May 28	Leo
May 29 – Jul 22	Virgo
Jul 23 – Sep 8	Libra
Sep 9 – Oct 21	Scorpio
Oct 22 – Dec 1	Sagittarius
Dec 2 – Dec 31	Capricorn

1917

Jan 1 – Jan 9	Capricorn
Jan 10 – Feb 16	Aquarius
Feb 17 – Mar 26	Pisces
Mar 27 – May 4	Aries
May 5 – Jun 14	Taurus
Jun 15 – Jul 27	Gemini
Jul 28 – Sep 11	Cancer
Sep 12 – Nov 1	Leo
Nov 2 – Dec 31	Virgo

1918

Jan 1 – Jan 10	Virgo
Jan 11 – Feb 25	Libra
Feb 26 – Jun 23	Virgo
Jun 24 – Aug 16	Libra
Aug 17 – Sep 30	Scorpio
Oct 1 – Nov 10	Sagittarius
Nov 11 – Dec 19	Capricorn
Dec 20 – Dec 31	Aquarius

1919

Jan 1 – Jan 26	Aquarius
Jan 27 – Mar 6	Pisces
Mar 7 – Apr 14	Aries
Apr 15 – May 25	Taurus
May 26 – Jul 8	Gemini
Jul 9 – Aug 22	Cancer
Aug 23 – Oct 9	Leo
Oct 10 – Nov 29	Virgo
Nov 30 – Dec 31	Libra

Your Mars Chart

1920

Jan 1 – Jan 31	Libra
Feb 1 – Apr 23	Scorpio
Apr 24 – Jul 10	Libra
Jul 11 – Sep 4	Scorpio
Sep 5 – Oct 18	Sagittarius
Oct 19 – Nov 27	Capricorn
Nov 28 – Dec 31	Aquarius

1921

Jan 1 – Jan 4	Aquarius
Jan 5 – Feb 12	Pisces
Feb 13 – Mar 24	Aries
Mar 25 – May 5	Taurus
May 6 – Jun 9	Gemini
Jun 10 – Aug 2	Cancer
Aug 3 – Sep 18	Leo
Sep 19 – Nov 6	Virgo
Nov 7 – Dec 25	Libra
Dec 26 – Dec 31	Scorpio

1922

Jan 1 – Feb 18	Scorpio
Feb 19 – Sep 13	Sagittarius
Sep 14 – Oct 30	Capricorn
Oct 31 – Dec 11	Aquarius
Dec 12 – Dec 31	Pisces

1923

Jan 1 – Jan 20	Pisces
Jan 21 – Mar 3	Aries
Mar 4 – Apr 15	Taurus
Apr 16 – May 30	Gemini
May 31 – Jul 15	Cancer
Jul 16 – Aug 31	Leo
Sep 1 – Oct 17	Virgo
Oct 18 – Dec 3	Libra
Dec 4 – Dec 31	Scorpio

1924

Jan 1 – Feb 19	Scorpio
Feb 20 – Mar 6	Sagittarius
Mar 7 – Apr 24	Capricorn
Apr 25 – Jun 24	Aquarius
Jun 25 – Aug 24	Pisces
Aug 25 – Oct 19	Aquarius
Oct 20 – Dec 18	Pisces
Dec 19 – Dec 31	Aries

1925

Jan 1 – Feb 4	Aries
Feb 5 – Mar 23	Taurus
Mar 24 – May 9	Gemini
May 10 – Jun 25	Cancer
Jun 26 – Aug 12	Leo
Aug 13 – Sep 28	Virgo
Sep 29 – Nov 13	Libra
Nov 14 – Dec 27	Scorpio
Dec 28 – Dec 31	Sagittarius

1926

Jan 1 – Feb 8	Sagittarius
Feb 9 – Mar 22	Capricorn
Mar 23 – May 3	Aquarius
May 4 – Jun 14	Pisces
Jun 15 – Jul 31	Aries
Aug 1 – Dec 31	Taurus

1927

Jan 1 – Feb 21	Taurus
Feb 22 – Apr 16	Gemini
Apr 17 – Jun 5	Cancer
Jun 6 – Jul 24	Leo
Jul 25 – Sep 10	Virgo
Sep 11 – Oct 25	Libra
Oct 26 – Dec 7	Scorpio
Dec 8 – Dec 31	Sagittarius

1928

Jan 1 – Jan 18	Sagittarius
Jan 19 – Feb 27	Capricorn
Feb 28 – Apr 7	Aquarius
Apr 8 – May 16	Pisces
May 17 – Jun 25	Aries
Jun 26 – Aug 8	Taurus
Aug 9 – Oct 2	Gemini
Oct 3 – Dec 19	Cancer
Dec 20 – Dec 31	Gemini

1929

Jan 1 – Mar 10	Gemini
Mar 11 – May 12	Cancer
May 13 – Jul 3	Leo
Jul 4 – Aug 21	Virgo
Aug 22 – Oct 5	Libra
Oct 6 – Nov 18	Scorpio
Nov 19 – Dec 28	Sagittarius
Dec 29 – Dec 31	Capricorn

Your Mars Chart

1930

From	To	Sign
Jan 1	Feb 6	Capricorn
Feb 7	Mar 16	Aquarius
Mar 17	Apr 24	Pisces
Apr 25	Jun 2	Aries
Jun 3	Jul 14	Taurus
Jul 15	Aug 27	Gemini
Aug 28	Oct 20	Cancer
Oct 21	Dec 31	Leo

1931

From	To	Sign
Jan 1	Feb 15	Leo
Feb 16	Mar 29	Cancer
Mar 30	Jun 9	Leo
Jun 10	Jul 31	Virgo
Aug 1	Sep 16	Libra
Sep 17	Oct 29	Scorpio
Oct 30	Dec 9	Sagittarius
Dec 10	Dec 31	Capricorn

1932

From	To	Sign
Jan 1	Jan 17	Capricorn
Jan 18	Feb 24	Aquarius
Feb 25	Apr 2	Pisces
Apr 3	May 11	Aries
May 12	Jun 21	Taurus
Jun 22	Aug 3	Gemini
Aug 4	Sep 19	Cancer
Sep 20	Nov 12	Leo
Nov 13	Dec 31	Virgo

1933

From	To	Sign
Jan 1	Jul 5	Virgo
Jul 6	Aug 25	Libra
Aug 26	Oct 8	Scorpio
Oct 9	Nov 18	Sagittarius
Nov 19	Dec 27	Capricorn
Dec 28	Dec 31	Aquarius

1934

From	To	Sign
Jan 1	Feb 3	Aquarius
Feb 4	Mar 13	Pisces
Mar 14	Apr 21	Aries
Apr 22	Jun 1	Taurus
Jun 2	Jul 14	Gemini
Jul 15	Aug 29	Cancer
Aug 30	Oct 17	Leo
Oct 18	Dec 10	Virgo
Dec 11	Dec 31	Libra

1935

From	To	Sign
Jan 1	Jul 28	Libra
Jul 29	Sep 15	Scorpio
Sep 16	Oct 27	Sagittarius
Oct 28	Dec 6	Capricorn
Dec 7	Dec 31	Aquarius

1936

From	To	Sign
Jan 1	Jan 13	Aquarius
Jan 14	Feb 21	Pisces
Feb 22	Mar 31	Aries
Apr 1	May 12	Taurus
May 13	Jun 24	Gemini
Jun 25	Aug 9	Cancer
Aug 10	Sep 25	Leo
Sep 26	Nov 13	Virgo
Nov 14	Dec 31	Libra

1937

From	To	Sign
Jan 1	Mar 12	Scorpio
Mar 13	May 13	Sagittarius
May 14	Aug 7	Scorpio
Aug 8	Sep 29	Sagittarius
Sep 30	Nov 10	Capricorn
Nov 11	Dec 20	Aquarius
Dec 21	Dec 31	Pisces

1938

From	To	Sign
Jan 1	Jan 29	Pisces
Jan 30	Mar 11	Aries
Mar 12	Apr 22	Taurus
Apr 23	Jun 6	Gemini
Jun 7	Jul 21	Cancer
Jul 22	Sep 6	Leo
Sep 7	Oct 24	Virgo
Oct 25	Dec 10	Libra
Dec 11	Dec 31	Scorpio

1939

From	To	Sign
Jan 1	Jan 28	Scorpio
Jan 29	Mar 20	Sagittarius
Mar 21	May 23	Capricorn
May 24	Jul 20	Aquarius
Jul 21	Sep 23	Capricorn
Sep 24	Nov 18	Aquarius
Nov 19	Dec 31	Pisces

Your Mars Chart

1940

Jan 1 – Jan 2	Pisces
Jan 3 – Feb 16	Aries
Feb 17 – Mar 31	Taurus
Apr 1 – May 16	Gemini
May 17 – Jul 2	Cancer
Jul 3 – Aug 18	Leo
Aug 19 – Oct 4	Virgo
Oct 5 – Nov 19	Libra
Nov 20 – Dec 31	Scorpio

1941

Jan 1 – Jan 3	Scorpio
Jan 4 – Feb 16	Sagittarius
Feb 17 – Apr 1	Capricorn
Apr 2 – May 15	Aquarius
May 16 – Jul 1	Pisces
Jul 2 – Dec 31	Aries

1942

Jan 1 – Jan 10	Aries
Jan 11 – Mar 6	Taurus
Mar 7 – Apr 25	Gemini
Apr 26 – Jun 13	Cancer
Jun 14 – Jul 31	Leo
Aug 1 – Sep 16	Virgo
Sep 17 – Oct 31	Libra
Nov 1 – Dec 15	Scorpio
Dec 16 – Dec 31	Sagittarius

1943

Jan 1 – Jan 25	Sagittarius
Jan 26 – Mar 7	Capricorn
Mar 8 – Apr 16	Aquarius
Apr 17 – May 26	Pisces
May 27 – Jun 6	Aries
Jun 7 – Aug 22	Taurus
Aug 23 – Dec 31	Gemini

1944

Jan 1 – Mar 27	Gemini
Mar 28 – May 21	Cancer
May 22 – Jul 11	Leo
Jul 12 – Aug 28	Virgo
Aug 29 – Oct 12	Libra
Oct 13 – Nov 24	Scorpio
Nov 25 – Dec 31	Sagittarius

1945

Jan 1 – Jan 4	Sagittarius
Jan 5 – Feb 13	Capricorn
Feb 14 – Mar 24	Aquarius
Mar 25 – May 1	Pisces
May 2 – Jun 10	Aries
Jun 11 – Jul 22	Taurus
July 23 – Sep 6	Gemini
Sep 7 – Nov 10	Cancer
Nov 11 – Dec 25	Leo
Dec 26 – Dec 31	Cancer

1946

Jan 1 – Apr 21	Cancer
Apr 22 – Jun 19	Leo
Jun 20 – Aug 8	Virgo
Aug 9 – Sep 23	Libra
Sep 24 – Nov 5	Scorpio
Nov 6 – Dec 16	Sagittarius
Dec 17 – Dec 31	Capricorn

1947

Jan 1 – Jan 24	Capricorn
Jan 25 – Mar 3	Aquarius
Mar 4 – Apr 10	Pisces
Apr 11 – May 20	Aries
May 21 – Jun 30	Taurus
Jul 1 – Aug 12	Gemini
Aug 13 – Sep 30	Cancer
Oct 1 – Nov 30	Leo
Dec 1 – Dec 31	Virgo

1948

Jan 1 – Feb 11	Virgo
Feb 12 – May 17	Leo
May 18 – Jul 16	Virgo
Jul 17 – Sep 2	Libra
Sep 3 – Oct 16	Scorpio
Oct 17 – Nov 25	Sagittarius
Nov 26 – Dec 31	Capricorn

1949

Jan 1 – Jan 3	Capricorn
Jan 4 – Feb 10	Aquarius
Feb 11 – Mar 20	Pisces
Mar 21 – Apr 29	Aries
Apr 30 – Jun 9	Taurus
Jun 10 – Jul 22	Gemini
Jul 23 – Sep 6	Cancer
Sep 7 – Oct 26	Leo
Oct 27 – Dec 25	Virgo
Dec 26 – Dec 31	Libra

Your Mars Chart

1950

Jan 1 – Mar 27	Libra
Mar 28 – Jun 10	Virgo
Jun 11 – Aug 9	Libra
Aug 10 – Sep 24	Scorpio
Sep 25 – Nov 5	Sagittarius
Nov 6 – Dec 14	Capricorn
Dec 15 – Dec 31	Aquarius

1951

Jan 1 – Jan 21	Aquarius
Jan 22 – Feb 28	Pisces
Mar 1 – Apr 9	Aries
Apr 10 – May 20	Taurus
May 21 – Jul 2	Gemini
Jul 3 – Aug 17	Cancer
Aug 18 – Oct 3	Leo
Oct 4 – Nov 23	Virgo
Nov 24 – Dec 31	Libra

1952

Jan 1 – Jan 19	Libra
Jan 20 – Aug 26	Scorpio
Aug 27 – Oct 11	Sagittarius
Oct 12 – Nov 20	Capricorn
Nov 21 – Dec 29	Aquarius
Dec 30 – Dec 31	Pisces

1953

Jan 1 – Feb 7	Pisces
Feb 8 – Mar 19	Aries
Mar 20 – Apr 30	Taurus
May 1 – Jun 13	Gemini
Jun 14 – Jul 29	Cancer
Jul 30 – Sep 14	Leo
Sep 15 – Nov 1	Virgo
Nov 2 – Dec 19	Libra
Dec 20 – Dec 31	Scorpio

1954

Jan 1 – Feb 8	Scorpio
Feb 9 – Apr 11	Sagittarius
Apr 12 – Jul 2	Capricorn
Jul 3 – Aug 23	Sagittarius
Aug 24 – Oct 20	Capricorn
Oct 21 – Dec 3	Aquarius
Dec 4 – Dec 31	Pisces

1955

Jan 1 – Jan 14	Pisces
Jan 15 – Feb 25	Aries
Feb 26 – Apr 9	Taurus
Apr 10 – May 25	Gemini
May 26 – Jul 10	Cancer
Jul 11 – Aug 26	Leo
Aug 27 – Oct 12	Virgo
Oct 13 – Nov 28	Libra
Nov 29 – Dec 31	Scorpio

1956

Jan 1 – Jan 13	Scorpio
Jan 14 – Feb 27	Sagittarius
Feb 28 – Apr 13	Capricorn
Apr 14 – Jun 2	Aquarius
Jun 3 – Dec 5	Pisces
Dec 6 – Dec 31	Aries

1957

Jan 1 – Feb 27	Aries
Feb 28 – Mar 16	Taurus
Mar 17 – May 3	Gemini
May 4 – Jun 20	Cancer
Jun 21 – Aug 7	Leo
Aug 8 – Sep 23	Virgo
Sep 24 – Nov 7	Libra
Nov 8 – Dec 22	Scorpio
Dec 23 – Dec 31	Sagittarius

1958

Jan 1 – Feb 2	Sagittarius
Feb 3 – Mar 16	Capricorn
Mar 17 – Apr 26	Aquarius
Apr 27 – Jun 6	Pisces
Jun 7 – Jul 20	Aries
Jul 21 – Sep 20	Taurus
Sep 21 – Oct 28	Gemini
Oct 29 – Dec 31	Taurus

1959

Jan 1 – Feb 9	Taurus
Feb 10 – Apr 9	Gemini
Apr 10 – May 31	Cancer
Jun 1 – Jul 19	Leo
Jul 20 – Sep 4	Virgo
Sep 5 – Oct 20	Libra
Oct 21 – Dec 2	Scorpio
Dec 3 – Dec 31	Sagittarius

Your Mars Chart

1960

Jan 1 – Jan 13 .... Sagittarius
Jan 14 – Feb 22 .... Capricorn
Feb 23 – Apr 1 .... Aquarius
Apr 2 – May 10 .... Pisces
May 11 – Jun 19 .... Aries
Jun 20 – Aug 1 .... Taurus
Aug 2 – Sep 20 .... Gemini
Sep 21 – Dec 31 .... Cancer

1961

Jan 1 – May 5 .... Cancer
May 6 – Jun 27 .... Leo
Jun 28 – Aug 16 .... Virgo
Aug 17 – Sep 30 .... Libra
Oct 1 – Nov 12 .... Scorpio
Nov 13 – Dec 23 .... Sagittarius
Dec 24 – Dec 31 .... Capricorn

1962

Jan 1 – Jan 31 .... Capricorn
Feb 1 – Mar 11 .... Aquarius
Mar 12 – Apr 18 .... Pisces
Apr 19 – May 27 .... Aries
Mar 28 – Jul 8 .... Taurus
Jul 9 – Aug 21 .... Gemini
Aug 22 – Oct 10 .... Cancer
Oct 11 – Dec 31 .... Leo

1963

Jan 1 – Jun 2 .... Leo
Jun 3 – Jul 26 .... Virgo
Jul 27 – Sep 11 .... Libra
Sep 12 – Oct 24 .... Scorpio
Oct 25 – Dec 4 .... Sagittarius
Dec 5 – Dec 31 .... Capricorn

1964

Jan 1 – Jan 12 .... Capricorn
Jan 13 – Feb 19 .... Aquarius
Feb 20 – Mar 28 .... Pisces
Mar 29 – May 6 .... Aries
May 7 – Jun 16 .... Taurus
Jun 17 – Jul 29 .... Gemini
Jul 30 – Sep 14 .... Cancer
Sep 15 – Nov 5 .... Leo
Nov 6 – Dec 31 .... Virgo

1965

Jan 1 – Jun 28 .... Virgo
Jun 29 – Aug 19 .... Libra
Aug 20 – Oct 3 .... Scorpio
Oct 4 – Nov 13 .... Sagittarius
Nov 14 – Dec 22 .... Capricorn
Dec 23 – Dec 31 .... Aquarius

1966

Jan 1 – Jan 29 .... Aquarius
Jan 30 – Mar 8 .... Pisces
Mar 9 – Apr 16 .... Aries
Apr 17 – May 27 .... Taurus
May 28 – Jul 10 .... Gemini
Jul 11 – Aug 24 .... Cancer
Aug 25 – Oct 11 .... Leo
Oct 12 – Dec 3 .... Virgo
Dec 4 – Dec 31 .... Libra

1967

Jan 1 – Feb 11 .... Libra
Feb 12 – Mar 31 .... Scorpio
Apr 1 – Jul 18 .... Libra
Jul 19 – Sep 9 .... Scorpio
Sep 10 – Oct 22 .... Sagittarius
Oct 23 – Nov 30 .... Capricorn
Dec 1 – Dec 31 .... Aquarius

1968

Jan 1 – Jan 8 .... Aquarius
Jan 9 – Feb 16 .... Pisces
Feb 17 – Mar 26 .... Aries
Mar 27 – May 7 .... Taurus
May 8 – Jun 20 .... Gemini
Jun 21 – Aug 4 .... Cancer
Aug 5 – Sep 20 .... Leo
Sep 21 – Oct 8 .... Virgo
Oct 9 – Dec 28 .... Libra
Dec 29 – Dec 31 .... Scorpio

1969

Jan 1 – Feb 24 .... Scorpio
Feb 25 – Sep 20 .... Sagittarius
Sep 21 – Nov 3 .... Capricorn
Nov 4 – Dec 13 .... Aquarius
Dec 14 – Dec 31 .... Pisces

Your Mars Chart

1970

Jan 1 – Jan 23	Pisces
Jan 24 – Mar 6	Aries
Mar 7 – Apr 17	Taurus
Apr 18 – Jun 1	Gemini
Jun 2 – Jul 17	Cancer
Jul 18 – Sep 2	Leo
Sep 3 – Oct 19	Virgo
Oct 20 – Dec 5	Libra
Dec 6 – Dec 31	Scorpio

1971

Jan 1 – Jan 23	Scorpio
Jan 24 – Mar 12	Sagittarius
Mar 13 – May 3	Capricorn
May 4 – Nov 6	Aquarius
Nov 7 – Dec 26	Pisces
Dec 27 – Dec 31	Aries

1972

Jan 1 – Feb 10	Aries
Feb 11 – Mar 27	Taurus
Mar 28 – May 12	Gemini
May 13 – Jun 28	Cancer
Jun 29 – Aug 15	Leo
Aug 16 – Sep 30	Virgo
Oct 1 – Nov 15	Libra
Nov 16 – Dec 30	Scorpio
Dec 31	Sagittarius

1973

Jan 1 – Feb 12	Sagittarius
Feb 13 – Mar 26	Capricorn
Mar 27 – May 8	Aquarius
May 9 – Jun 20	Pisces
Jun 21 – Aug 12	Aries
Aug 13 – Oct 29	Taurus
Oct 30 – Dec 24	Aries
Dec 25 – Dec 31	Taurus

1974

Jan 1 – Feb 27	Taurus
Feb 28 – Apr 20	Gemini
Apr 21 – Jun 9	Cancer
Jun 10 – Jul 27	Leo
Jul 28 – Sep 12	Virgo
Sep 13 – Oct 28	Libra
Oct 29 – Dec 10	Scorpio
Dec 11 – Dec 31	Sagittarius

1975

Jan 1 – Jan 21	Sagittarius
Jan 22 – Mar 3	Capricorn
Mar 4 – Apr 11	Aquarius
Apr 12 – May 21	Pisces
May 22 – Jul 1	Aries
Jul 2 – Aug 14	Taurus
Aug 15 – Oct 17	Gemini
Oct 18 – Nov 25	Cancer
Nov 26 – Dec 31	Gemini

1976

Jan 1 – Mar 18	Gemini
Mar 19 – May 16	Cancer
May 17 – Jul 6	Leo
Jul 7 – Aug 24	Virgo
Aug 25 – Oct 8	Libra
Oct 9 – Nov 20	Scorpio
Nov 21 – Dec 31	Sagittarius

1977

Jan 1	Sagittarius
Jan 2 – Feb 9	Capricorn
Feb 10 – Mar 20	Aquarius
Mar 21 – Apr 27	Pisces
Apr 28 – Jun 6	Aries
Jun 7 – Jul 17	Taurus
Jul 18 – Sep 1	Gemini
Sep 2 – Oct 26	Cancer
Oct 27 – Dec 31	Leo

1978

Jan 1 – Jan 26	Leo
Jan 27 – Apr 10	Cancer
Apr 11 – Jun 14	Leo
Jun 15 – Aug 30	Virgo
Aug 31 – Sep 7	Libra
Sep 8 – Nov 2	Scorpio
Nov 3 – Dec 12	Sagittarius
Nov 13 – Dec 31	Capricorn

1979

Jan 1 – Jan 20	Capricorn
Jan 21 – Feb 27	Aquarius
Feb 28 – Apr 7	Pisces
Apr 8 – May 16	Aries
May 17 – Jun 26	Taurus
Jun 27 – Aug 8	Gemini
Aug 9 – Sep 24	Cancer
Sep 25 – Nov 19	Leo
Nov 20 – Dec 31	Virgo

Your Mars Chart

1980

Jan 1 – Mar 11	Virgo
Mar 12 – May 4	Leo
May 5 – Jul 10	Virgo
Jul 11 – Aug 29	Libra
Aug 30 – Oct 12	Scorpio
Oct 13 – Nov 22	Sagittarius
Nov 23 – Dec 30	Capricorn
Dec 31	Aquarius

1981

Jan 1 – Feb 6	Aquarius
Feb 7 – Mar 17	Pisces
Mar 18 – Apr 25	Aries
Apr 26 – Jun 5	Taurus
Jun 6 – Jul 18	Gemini
Jul 19 – Sep 29	Cancer
Sep 30 – Oct 21	Leo
Oct 22 – Dec 16	Virgo
Dec 17 – Dec 31	Libra

1982

Jan 1 – Aug 3	Libra
Aug 4 – Sep 20	Scorpio
Sep 21 – Oct 31	Sagittarius
Nov 1 – Dec 10	Capricorn
Dec 11 – Dec 31	Aquarius

1983

Jan 1 – Jan 17	Aquarius
Jan 18 – Feb 25	Pisces
Feb 26 – Apr 5	Aries
Apr 6 – May 16	Taurus
May 17 – Jun 29	Gemini
Jun 30 – Aug 13	Cancer
Aug 14 – Sep 30	Leo
Oct 1 – Nov 18	Virgo
Nov 19 – Dec 31	Libra

1984

Jan 1 – Jan 11	Libra
Jan 12 – Aug 17	Scorpio
Aug 18 – Oct 30	Sagittarius
Oct 31 – Nov 15	Capricorn
Nov 16 – Dec 25	Aquarius
Dec 26 – Dec 31	Pisces

1985

Jan 1 – Feb 27	Pisces
Feb 28 – Mar 15	Aries
Mar 16 – Apr 26	Taurus
Apr 27 – Jun 9	Gemini
Jun 10 – Jul 25	Cancer
Jul 26 – Sep 10	Leo
Sep 11 – Oct 27	Virgo
Oct 28 – Dec 14	Libra
Dec 15 – Dec 31	Scorpio

1986

Jan 1 – Feb 2	Scorpio
Feb 3 – Mar 28	Sagittarius
Mar 29 – Oct 9	Capricorn
Oct 10 – Nov 26	Aquarius
Nov 27 – Dec 31	Pisces

1987

Jan 1 – Jan 8	Pisces
Jan 9 – Feb 20	Aries
Feb 21 – Apr 5	Taurus
Apr 6 – May 21	Gemini
May 22 – Jul 6	Cancer
Jul 7 – Aug 22	Leo
Aug 23 – Oct 8	Virgo
Oct 9 – Nov 24	Libra
Nov 25 – Dec 31	Scorpio

1988

Jan 1 – Jan 8	Scorpio
Jan 9 – Feb 22	Sagittarius
Feb 23 – Apr 6	Capricorn
Apr 7 – May 22	Aquarius
May 23 – Jul 13	Pisces
Jul 14 – Oct 23	Aries
Oct 24 – Nov 1	Pisces
Nov 2 – Dec 31	Aries

1989

Jan 1 – Jan 19	Aries
Jan 20 – Mar 11	Taurus
Mar 12 – Apr 29	Gemini
Apr 30 – Jun 16	Cancer
Jun 17 – Aug 3	Leo
Aug 4 – Sep 19	Virgo
Sep 20 – Nov 4	Libra
Nov 5 – Dec 18	Scorpio
Dec 19 – Dec 31	Sagittarius

Your Mars Chart

1990

Jan 1 – Jan 29	Sagittarius
Jan 30 – Mar 11	Capricorn
Mar 12 – Apr 20	Aquarius
Apr 21 – May 31	Pisces
Jun 1 – Jul 12	Aries
Jul 13 – Aug 31	Taurus
Sep 1 – Dec 14	Gemini
Dec 15 – Dec 31	Taurus

1991

Jan 1 – Jan 21	Taurus
Jan 22 – Apr 3	Gemini
Apr 4 – May 26	Cancer
May 27 – Jul 15	Leo
Jul 16 – Sep 1	Virgo
Sep 2 – Oct 16	Libra
Oct 17 – Nov 29	Scorpio
Nov 30 – Dec 31	Sagittarius

1992

Jan 1 – Jan 9	Sagittarius
Jan 10 – Feb 18	Capricorn
Feb 19 – Mar 28	Aquarius
Mar 29 – May 5	Pisces
May 6 – Jun 14	Aries
Jun 15 – Jul 26	Taurus
Jul 27 – Sep 12	Gemini
Sep 13 – Dec 31	Cancer

1993

Jan 1 – Apr 27	Cancer
Apr 28 – Jun 23	Leo
Jun 24 – Aug 12	Virgo
Aug 13 – Sep 27	Libra
Sep 28 – Nov 9	Scorpio
Nov 10 – Dec 20	Sagittarius
Dec 21 – Dec 31	Capricorn

1994

Jan 1 – Jan 28	Capricorn
Jan 29 – Mar 7	Aquarius
Mar 8 – Apr 14	Pisces
Apr 15 – May 23	Aries
May 24 – Jul 3	Taurus
Jul 4 – Aug 16	Gemini
Aug 17 – Oct 4	Cancer
Oct 5 – Dec 12	Leo
Dec 13 – Dec 31	Virgo

1995

Jan 1 – Jan 22	Virgo
Jan 23 – May 25	Leo
May 26 – Jul 21	Virgo
Jul 22 – Sep 7	Libra
Sep 8 – Oct 20	Scorpio
Oct 21 – Nov 30	Sagittarius
Dec 1 – Dec 31	Capricorn

1996

Jan 1 – Jan 8	Capricorn
Jan 9 – Feb 15	Aquarius
Feb 16 – Mar 24	Pisces
Mar 25 – May 2	Aries
May 3 – Jun 12	Taurus
Jun 13 – Jul 25	Gemini
Jul 26 – Sep 9	Cancer
Sep 10 – Oct 30	Leo
Oct 31 – Dec 31	Virgo

1997

Jan 1 – Jan 3	Virgo
Jan 4 – Mar 8	Libra
Mar 9 – Jun 19	Virgo
Jun 20 – Aug 14	Libra
Aug 15 – Sep 28	Scorpio
Sep 29 – Nov 9	Sagittarius
Nov 10 – Dec 18	Capricorn
Dec 19 – Dec 31	Aquarius

1998

Jan 1 – Jan 25	Aquarius
Jan 26 – Mar 4	Pisces
Mar 5 – Apr 13	Aries
Apr 14 – May 24	Taurus
May 25 – Jul 6	Gemini
Jul 7 – Aug 20	Cancer
Aug 21 – Oct 7	Leo
Oct 8 – Nov 27	Virgo
Nov 28 – Dec 31	Libra

Your Mars Chart

1999		
Jan 1 – Jan 26	....	Libra
Jan 27 – May 5	....	Scorpio
May 6 – Jul 5	....	Libra
Jul 6 – Sep 2	....	Scorpio
Sep 3 – Oct 17	....	Sagittarius
Oct 18 – Nov 26	....	Capricorn
Nov 27 – Dec 31	....	Aquarius

2000		
Jan 1 – Jan 4	....	Aquarius
Jan 5 – Feb 12	....	Pisces
Feb 13 – Mar 23	....	Aries
Mar 24 – May 3	....	Taurus
May 4 – Jun 16	....	Gemini
Jun 17 – Aug 1	....	Cancer
Aug 2 – Sep 17	....	Leo
Sep 18 – Nov 4	....	Virgo
Nov 5 – Dec 23	....	Libra
Dec 24 – Dec 31	....	Scorpio

MARS IN ARIES

Your Mars in Aries gives you your boldness and your impulsiveness mixed with your need for excitement, with little regard for the effects of your sometimes rash behavior. You are not a tease and don't want to be teased. You want what you want when you want it. There are no games here. You have a passion for adventure and are *very* adventurous in your passion. Your romances are fierce, fast and furious, but *always* positive.

MARS IN TAURUS

Your Mars in Taurus gives you your steadfastness in your sexual drive and your unflagging desire for sexual experiences. You Taureans *love* to make love, not to prove anything, not to get rid of tension,—you just really *enjoy* sex for its own sake. You are lusty, earthy and sensual, and have incredible staying-power. You are attracted to those with money and power (they sexually go together), and if you *do* marry, it will further you monetarily or in your professional career.

MARS IN GEMINI

Your Mars in Gemini gives you your quicksilver restlessness in all your love relationships, and lovers are drawn to you like flies to honey. You are very exciting in the boudoir in a teasing sort of way. In fact, you invented the word "tease" when it comes to sex, and this makes the opposite sex desire you even more. It's *very* difficult for you to be faithful to one partner; in fact, I'm not really sure it's possible. You tend to be critical. You like to keep your lovers on a string, so when you're tired of one, you always have another to run to, and when *that* bores you (as it will) you've got the other dangling.

MARS IN CANCER

Your Mars in Cancer gives you a great depth of feeling and a strong sex drive, but rarely gives you sexual satisfaction. You need constant encouragement in love, you are highly imaginative and tend to dramatize your love affairs, and often create an attachment of great emotional intensity with someone who hardly knows you're alive. You have the ability to become emotionally intimate very quickly, and are able to move on to new loves whenever your old loves fade.

MARS IN LEO

Your Mars in Leo gives you great sexual energy and the strength to enjoy it. You love being dominant in a sex relationship, and as king or queen, you are able to rule your lover regally. You must *never* be teased—when someone promises with a wink and a flirt, he or she had better deliver. You also have a fiery temper, and you believe that you, Leo the Lion, are *always* right, which isn't exactly easy for your mate to put up with. But you're usually forgiven because you're such a robust and dynamic lover.

MARS IN VIRGO

Your Mars in Virgo gives you considerable sexual desires, but you're not a romantic at all. To you, sex is a need, and a great one, but it's not necessarily tied in with love. And plain old healthy and wholesome sex bores you—you go for the unusual and different, and depravity turns you on. You are sometimes a voyeur and get your kicks in this kinky way, but you keep this a secret. You aren't especially imaginative, but you *are* open to suggestion, so make sure your partner is uninhibited.

MARS IN LIBRA

Your Mars in Libra gives you ardor, fervor, eagerness, optimism and assurance in le boudoir—you love everything about sex and work hard to maintain your terrific sex life. Libra is a thoughtful lover, and you *always* treat your lover the way *you* want to be treated. You have the talent to sense exactly what to do to turn someone on at precisely the right time, and you always seem to find the exact right spot. Your enthusiasm is contagious and you will always have a happy partner (partners?).

MARS IN SCORPIO

Your Mars in Scorpio gives you a magnetic quality which seems to strongly attract sexual partners to you. You are compulsive about sex and will do almost anything to satisfy your ravenous sexual appetite. Your lovemaking can either rise like the Eagle to great heights of passion, or sink like the Scorpion to the depths of depravity. It's difficult for you to fall deeply in love, you have a cruel streak (which is a turn-on to some), and you are rarely gentle and affectionate. Your passion is all-consuming, you are stimulated by your intense feelings and you are prone to sudden attachments and equally sudden splits, which will probably bewilder your lovers.

MARS IN SAGITTARIUS

Your Mars in Sagittarius gives you a need for freedom in your relationships. You love to travel and love the freedom to fool around a lot on all your trips. Sex itself isn't *nearly* as important as the chase; in fact, the intimacy that comes with a permanent sexual alliance makes you very nervous, so you prefer less involvement with more than one lover. You are a sexual adventurer and you may go from one romance to another before you feel you're ready for marriage, (you *do* love your freedom). You often make a mistake when you finally settle down.

MARS IN CAPRICORN

Your Mars in Capricorn gives you enormous ambition that you fulfill in your love alliances. You always seek to improve your self in every way by attaching yourself to someone either socially or professionally who will advance you up the ladder of success. You are passionate, strongly sensual, and like weaker partners that you can dominate in bed. If your sexual advances are not reciprocated, you are not above using force. With just a little push, you could become cruel, so look for a partner with a masochistic streak whom you can really turn on. You have a gluttonous sexual appetite and are a virtuoso lover.

MARS IN AQUARIUS

Your Mars in Aquarius makes you more of a great friend than a great lover. You genuinely like people and have a lot of warmth and geniality about you. You are also a person of discernment and taste, so your sex life is not wild and crazy, but on the quieter side. However, you are a true artist in lovemaking and love long and varied foreplay, so much so that you tend to get hung up in that area and not go on to the main event. That can drive your partner almost crazy with desire, and he or she may have to actively let you know it's time for the main event, or you might never end the preliminaries.

MARS IN PISCES

Your Mars in Pisces gives you a constant need for reassurance and a steady flow of affection from your lover. You have a tendency to be turned on by master-slave relationships, (where you are the slave). You are incredibly romantic, and need the emotional support of a stronger partner. Sex is important to you, but not *nearly* as important as the courtship—the hugs and kisses and "I love you's" that you thrive on.

8

Your 12 Jupiter Signs and Chart

Jupiter is your opportunity sign. It rules your superconscious, and has a great effect on your reasoning powers and on your understanding of your mind and spirit and how your feelings are shaped. Jupiter is your antenna, your feeler for opportunity and chance, and depending on where it's found in your chart, fame, fortune and ambitions (including love ambitions) will turn out the way you want them.

Your Jupiter Sign is determined by the year your were born. Your Jupiter Chart is on the following pages.

Your Jupiter Chart

JAN 1, 1850—SEP 10,1850 . . . . . . VIR
SEP 11, 1850—OCT 11, 1851 . . . . LIB
OCT 12, 1851—NOV 7, 1852 . . SCO
NOV 8, 1852—DEC 1, 1853 . . . . SAG
DEC 2, 1853—DEC 18, 1854 . . . . CAP
DEC 19, 1854—MAY 11, 1855 . . AQU
MAY 12, 1855—AUG 2, 1855 . . . . PIS
AUG 3, 1855—DEC 27, 1855 . . . AQU
DEC 28, 1855—MAY 8, 1856 . . . . PIS
MAY 9, 1856—NOV 3, 1856 . . . . ARI
NOV 4, 1856—DEC 14, 1856 . . . . PIS
DEC 15, 1856—MAY 14, 1857 . . . ARI
MAY 15, 1857—MAY 25, 1858 . . TAU
MAY 26, 1858—JUN 9, 1859 . . . GEM
JUN 10, 1859—JUN 29, 1860 . . . CAN
JUN 30, 1860—JUL 25, 1861 . . . . LEO
JUL 26, 1861—AUG 24, 1862 . . . . VIR
AUG 25, 1862—SEP 24, 1863 . . . . LIB
SEP 25, 1863—OCT 22, 1864 . . . SCO
OCT 23, 1864—NOV 14, 1865 . . SAG
NOV 15, 1865—NOV 29, 1866 . . CAP
NOV 30, 1866—APR 14, 1867 . . AQU
APR 15, 1867—SEP 15, 1867 . . . . . PIS
SEP 16, 1867—NOV 30, 1867 . . AQU
DEC 1, 1867—APR 19, 1868 . . . . . PIS
APR 20, 1868—APR 28, 1869 . . . . ARI
APR 29, 1869—MAY 9, 1870 . . . . TAU
MAY 10, 1870—MAY 23, 1871 . GEM
MAY 24, 1871—JUN 11, 1872 . . CAN
JUN 12, 1872—NOV 15, 1872 . . . LEO
NOV 16, 1872—JAN 16, 1873 . . . VIR
JAN 17, 1873—JUL 7, 1873 . . . . . LEO
JUL 8, 1873—DEC 12, 1873 . . . . . VIR
DEC 13, 1873—FEB 18, 1874 . . . . . LIB
FEB 19, 1874—AUG 6, 1874 . . . . . VIR
AUG 7, 1874—JAN 12, 1875 . . . . . LIB
JAN 13, 1875—MAR 20, 1875 . . SCO
MAR 21, 1875—SEP 6, 1875 . . . . . LIB
SEP 7, 1875—FEB 9, 1876 . . . . . . SCO
FEB 10, 1876—APR 23, 1876 . . . . SAG
APR 24, 1876—OCT 3, 1876 . . . SCO
OCT 4, 1876—FEB 28, 1877 . . . . SAG
MAR 1, 1877—JUN 9, 1877 . . . . . CAP
JUN 10, 1877—OCT 25, 1877 . . . SAG
OCT 26, 1877—MAR 14, 1878 . . CAP
MAR 15, 1878—AUG 11, 1878 . AQU
AUG 12, 1878—NOV 3, 1878 . . . CAP
NOV 4, 1878—MAR 25, 1879 . . AQU
MAR 26, 1879—APR 2, 1880 . . . . . PIS
APR 3, 1880—APR 11, 1881 . . . . . ARI
APR 12, 1881—APR 21, 1882 . . . TAU
APR 22, 1882—SEP 19, 1882 . . . GEM
SEP 20, 1882—NOV 17, 1882 . . . CAN
NOV 18, 1882—MAY 4, 1883 . . GEM
MAY 5, 1883—SEP 26, 1883 . . . . CAN
SEP 27, 1883—JAN 16, 1884 . . . . LEO
JAN 17, 1884—MAY 21, 1884 . . CAN
MAY 22, 1884—OCT 17, 1884 . . LEO
OCT 18, 1884—FEB 25, 1885 . . . . VIR
FEB 26, 1885—JUN 14, 1885 . . . . LEO
JUN 15, 1885—NOV 15, 1885 . . . VIR
NOV 16, 1885—MAR 29, 1886 . . . LIB
MAR 30, 1886—JUL 15, 1886 . . . . VIR
JUL 16, 1886—DEC 16, 1886 . . . . . LIB
DEC 17, 1886—APR 28, 1887 . . . SCO
APR 29, 1887—AUG 15, 1887 . . . . LIB
AUG 16, 1887—JAN 14, 1888 . . SCO
JAN 15, 1888—JUN 3, 1888 . . . . SAG
JUN 4, 1888—SEP 10, 1888 . . . . SCO
SEP 11, 1888—FEB 5, 1889 . . . . . SAG
FEB 6, 1889—JUL 23, 1889 . . . . . CAP
JUL 24, 1889—SEP 25, 1889 . . . . SAG
SEP 26, 1889—FEB 22, 1890 . . . . CAP
FEB 23, 1890—MAR 7, 1891 . . . AQU
MAR 8, 1891—MAR 16, 1892 . . . . PIS
MAR 17, 1892—MAR 24, 1893 . . . ARI
MAR 25, 1893—AUG 20, 1893 . . TAU
AUG 21, 1893—OCT 19, 1893 . . GEM
OCT 20, 1893—APR 1, 1894 . . . . TAU
APR 2, 1894—AUG 18, 1894 . . . GEM

Your Jupiter Chart

AUG 19, 1894—JAN 1, 1895 ... CAN
JAN 2, 1895—APR 10, 1895 ... GEM
APR 11, 1895—SEP 4, 1895 ... CAN
SEP 5, 1895—FEB 29, 1896 ... LEO
MAR 1, 1896—APR 17, 1896 ... CAN
APR 18, 1896—SEP 27, 1896 ... LEO
SEP 28, 1896—OCT 27, 1897 ... VIR
OCT 28, 1897—NOV 26, 1898 ... LIB
NOV 27, 1898—DEC 25, 1899 .. SCO
DEC 26, 1899—JAN 19, 1901 ... SAG
JUN 20, 1901—FEB 6, 1902 ... CAP
FEB 7, 1902—FEB 20, 1903 ... AQU
FEB 21, 1903—FEB 28, 1904 ... PIS
FEB 29, 1904—AUG 8, 1904 ... ARI
AUG 9, 1904—AUG 31, 1904 ... TAU
SEP 1, 1904—MAR 7, 1905 ... ARI
MAR 8, 1905—JUL 21, 1905 ... TAU
JUL 22, 1905—DEC 4, 1905 ... GEM
DEC 5, 1905—MAR 9, 1906 ... TAU
MAR 10, 1906—JUL 30, 1906 ... GEM
JUL 31, 1906—AUG 18, 1907 ... CAN
AUG 19, 1907—SEP 12, 1908 ... LEO
SEP 13, 1908—OCT 11, 1909 ... VIR
OCT 12, 1909—NOV 11, 1910 ... LIB
NOV 12, 1910—DEC 10, 1911 .. SCO
DEC 11, 1911—JAN 2, 1913 ... SAG
JAN 3, 1913—JAN 21, 1914 ... CAP
JAN 22, 1914—FEB 4, 1915 ... AQU
FEB 5, 1915—FEB 12, 1916 ... PIS
FEB 13, 1916—JUN 26, 1916 ... ARI
JUN 27, 1916—OCT 26, 1916 ... TAU
OCT 27, 1916—FEB 12, 1917 ... ARI
FEB 13, 1917—JUN 29, 1917 ... TAU
JUN 30, 1917—JUL 13, 1918 ... GEM
JUL 14, 1918—AUG 2, 1919 ... CAN
AUG 3, 1919—AUG 27, 1920 ... LEO
AUG 28, 1920—SEP 25, 1921 ... VIR
SEP 26, 1921—OCT 26, 1922 ... LIB
OCT 27, 1922—NOV 24, 1923 . SCO
NOV 25, 1923—DEC 18, 1924 .. SAG
DEC 19, 1924—JAN 6, 1926 ... CAP
JAN 7, 1926—JAN 18, 1927 ... AQU
JAN 19, 1927—JUN 6, 1927 ... PIS
JUN 7, 1927—SEP 11, 1927 ... ARI
SEP 12, 1927—JAN 23, 1928 ... PIS
JAN 24, 1928—JUN 4, 1928 ... ARI
JUN 5, 1928—JUN 12, 1929 ... TAU
JUN 13, 1929—JUN 26, 1930 ... GEM
JUN 27, 1930—JUL 17, 1931 ... CAN
JUL 18, 1931—AUG 11, 1932 ... LEO
AUG 12, 1932—SEP 10, 1933 ... VIR
SEP 11, 1933—OCT 11, 1934 ... LIB
OCT 12, 1934—NOV 9, 1935 .. SCO
NOV 10, 1935—DEC 2, 1936 ... SAG
DEC 3, 1936—DEC 20, 1937 ... CAP
DEC 21, 1937—MAY 14, 1938 .. AQU
MAY 15, 1938—JUL 30, 1938 ... PIS
JUL 31, 1938—DEC 29, 1938 ... AQU
DEC 30, 1938—MAY 11, 1939 ... PIS
MAY 12, 1939—OCT 30, 1939 ... ARI
OCT 31, 1939—DEC 20, 1939 ... PIS
DEC 21, 1939—MAY 16, 1940 ... ARI
MAY 17, 1940—MAY 26, 1941 .. TAU
MAY 27, 1941—JUN 10, 1942 .. GEM
JUN 11, 1942—JUN 29, 1943 ... CAN
JUN 30, 1943—JUL 26, 1944 ... LEO
JUL 27, 1944—AUG 25, 1945 ... VIR
AUG 26, 1945—SEP 25, 1946 ... LIB
SEP 26, 1946—OCT 24, 1947 ... SCO
OCT 25, 1947—NOV 15, 1948 .. SAG
NOV 16, 1948—APR 12, 1949 ... CAP
APR 13, 1949—JUN 27, 1949 ... AQU
JUN 28, 1949—NOV 29, 1949 .. CAP
NOV 30, 1949—APR 15, 1950 .. AQU
APR 16, 1950—SEP 15, 1950 ... PIS
SEP 16, 1950—DEC 1, 1950 ... AQU
DEC 2, 1950—APR 21, 1951 ... PIS
APR 22, 1951—APR 28, 1952 ... ARI
APR 29, 1952—MAY 9, 1953 ... TAU
MAY 10, 1953—MAY 24, 1954 . GEM

Your Jupiter Chart

MAY 25, 1954—JUN 13, 1955 . . CAN
JUN 14, 1955—NOV 17, 1955. . . LEO
NOV 18, 1955—JAN 18, 1956 . . . VIR
JAN 19, 1956—JUL 7, 1956 . . . . . LEO
JUL 8, 1956—DEC 13, 1956 . . . . . VIR
DEC 14, 1956—FEB 18, 1957. . . . . LIB
FEB 20, 1957—AUG 7, 1957 . . . . . VIR
AUG 8, 1957—JAN 13, 1958 . . . . . LIB
JAN 14, 1958—MAR 20, 1958 . . SCO
MAR 21, 1958—SEP 7, 1958 . . . . . LIB
SEP 8, 1958—FEB 10, 1959 . . . . . SCO
FEB 11, 1959—APR 24, 1959 . . . . SAG
APR 25, 1959—OCT 5, 1959 . . . SCO
OCT 6, 1959—MAR 1, 1960 . . . . SAG
MAR 2, 1960—JUN 10, 1960. . . . CAP
JUN 11, 1960—OCT 25, 1960. . . SAG
OCT 26, 1960—MAR 15, 1961 . . CAP
MAR 16, 1961—AUG 12, 1961 . AQU
AUG 13, 1961—NOV 4, 1961 . . . CAP
NOV 5, 1961—MAR 25, 1962 . . AQU
MAR 26, 1962—APR 4, 1963 . . . . . PIS
APR 5, 1963—APR 12, 1964 . . . . . ARI
APR 13, 1964—APR 22, 1965 . . . TAU
APR 23, 1965—SEP 21, 1965 . . . GEM
SEP 22, 1965—NOV 17, 1965. . . CAN
NOV 18, 1965—MAY 5, 1966 . . GEM
MAY 6, 1966—SEP 27, 1966. . . . CAN
SEP 28, 1966—JAN 16, 1967 . . . . LEO
JAN 17, 1967—MAY 23, 1967 . . CAN
MAY 24, 1967—OCT 19, 1967 . . LEO
OCT 20, 1967—FEB 27, 1968 . . . . VIR
FEB 28, 1968—JUN 15, 1968 . . . . LEO
JUN 16, 1968—NOV 15, 1968 . . . VIR
Nov 16, 1968—MAR 30, 1969. . . . LIB
MAR 31, 1969—JUL 15, 1969 . . . . VIR
JUL 16, 1969—DEC 16, 1969. . . . . LIB
DEC 17, 1969—APR 30, 1970 . . . SCO
MAY 1, 1970—AUG 15, 1970 . . . . LIB
AUG 16, 1970—JAN 23, 1971 . . SCO
JAN 24, 1971—JUN 5, 1971 . . . . SAG
JUN 6, 1971—SEP 11, 1971 . . . . SCO
SEP 12, 1971—FEB 6, 1972 . . . . . SAG
FEB 7, 1972—FEB 23, 1973 . . . . . CAP
FEB 24, 1973—MAR 8, 1974 . . . AQU
MAR 9, 1974—MAR 18, 1975 . . . . PIS
MAR 19, 1975—MAR 26, 1976. . . ARI
MAR 27, 1976—AUG 23, 1976 . . TAU
AUG 24, 1976—OCT 16, 1976. . GEM
OCT 17, 1976—APR 3, 1977. . . . TAU
APR 4, 1977—AUG 20, 1977 . . . GEM
AUG 21, 1977—DEC 30, 1977 . . CAN
DEC 31, 1977—APR 12, 1978. . . GEM
APR 13, 1978—SEP 5, 1978. . . . . CAN
SEP 6, 1978—SEP 29, 1979. . . . . . LEO
SEP 30, 1979—OCT 27, 1980 . . . . VIR
OCT 28, 1980—NOV 27, 1981 . . . LIB
NOV 28, 1981—DEC 26, 1982 . . SCO
DEC 27, 1982—JAN 19, 1984 . . . SAG
JAN 20, 1984—FEB 6, 1985 . . . . . CAP
FEB 7, 1985—FEB 20, 1986. . . . . AQU
FEB 21, 1986—MAR 2, 1987 . . . . . PIS
MAR 3, 1987—MAR 8, 1988. . . . . ARI
MAR 9, 1988—MAR 11, 1989 . . . TAU
MAR 12, 1989—JUL 30, 1989. . . GEM
JUL 31, 1989—AUG 18, 1990 . . . CAN
AUG 19, 1990—SEP 12, 1991 . . . LEO
SEP 13, 1991—OCT 10, 1992 . . . . VIR
OCT 11, 1992—NOV 10, 1993 . . . LIB
NOV 11, 1993—DEC 9, 1994. . . SCO
DEC 10, 1994—JAN 3, 1996 . . . . SAG
JAN 4, 1996—JAN 21, 1997. . . . . CAP
JAN 22, 1997—FEB 4, 1998 . . . . AQU
FEB 5, 1998—FEB 13, 1999 . . . . . . PIS
FEB 14, 1999—JUN 28, 1999. . . . . ARI
JUN 29, 1999—OCT 23, 1999. . . TAU
OCT 24, 1999—FEB 14, 2000 . . . . ARI
FEB 15, 2000—JUN 30, 2000. . . . TAU
JUL 1, 2000—DEC 31, 2000 . . . . GEM

JUPITER IN ARIES

Your Jupiter in Aries gives you a fiery imagination and lots of creativity to help you achieve a position of authority—you are a leader, *not* a follower. You're a dynamo—just don't lose your enthusiasm.

JUPITER IN TAURUS

Your Jupiter in Taurus gives you your ability to make money—and gives you a desire to work hard for it. You're slow and steady, but you get there. You love to amass material possessions, from houses and property, to lots of money.

JUPITER IN GEMINI

Your Jupiter in Gemini gives you your sharp-as-a-tack mind and your versatility. You're always doing more than one thing—it's usually two totally different things, but sometimes as many as three or four. You're a whiz with words.

JUPITER IN CANCER

Your Jupiter in Cancer gives you your need for emotional security and your desire for a home and family. Your deepest fulfillment comes from a loving and romantic mate who tells you what a wonderful lover you are.

JUPITER IN LEO

Your Jupiter in Leo gives you your colossal self-confidence and belief that you can conquer the world. Your enthusiasm is contagious and people are drawn to you. You have power and people know it. You make a good boss.

JUPITER IN VIRGO

Your Jupiter in Virgo makes you a tireless worker, full of efficiency and orderliness, who will quietly out-perform the razzle-dazzle crowd. You're very good in the health area and generally take good care of your self.

JUPITER IN LIBRA

Your Jupiter in Libra gives you an innate sense of good taste and great style. You're easy to get along with, have a marvelous temperament, and are talented in anything artistic.

JUPITER IN SCORPIO

Your Jupiter in Scorpio gives you your resourcefulness and ability to carry out business matters. You have a penetrating way about you—you're able to get right to the core of things, and you're extremely adroit. With your keen discernment and intuition, you'll go far.

JUPITER IN SAGITTARIUS

Your Jupiter in Sagittarius makes you an adventurer who loves all kinds of excitement. Travel turns you on, but you don't want to go alone. You like to be around lots of people to share your humor and fun. You can use your sharp instincts in business.

JUPITER IN CAPRICORN

Your Jupiter in Capricorn gives you your endless patience and enormous determination which, when blended with your tremendous capacity for work, almost always ensures success at anything you really want. It will take a while, but you'll eventually get it.

JUPITER IN AQUARIUS

Your Jupiter in Aquarius makes you a humanitarian interested in all kinds of welfare, particularly in government. You're eccentric, but charmingly so, and have an originality about you that just won't quit. You're very inventive and can always come up with a new way of doing something.

JUPITER IN PISCES

Your Jupiter in Pisces gives you the temperament to be a sympathetic listener. You have a great deal of empathy, and people respond to this by unloading their troubles on you. You make a wonderful psychologist, psychiatrist or psychoanalyst, or just a friendly ear.

9

Your 12 Saturn Signs and Chart

Saturn is the planet of self-preservation and defense, of form and organization and justice, and gives the ability and talent to analyze a situation and then to use great determination in reaching a goal. Whatever sign your Saturn is in will decide how you will use your powers of self-preservation, and whether you will be defensive in your strivings or whether you will turn your defenses into ambitions and goals(your best defense is a good offense). Another good motto for Saturn is, "Desire without determination and hard work will bring you nothing."

Your Venus may be more influential in attracting love, but Saturn's influence will help you to keep that love.

Your Saturn Sign is determined by the year you were born. Your Saturn Chart is on the following pages.

Your Saturn Chart

JAN 1, 1850—JUN 3, 1851 ...... ARI
JUN 4, 1851—NOV 4, 1851 .... TAU
NOV 5, 1851—FEB 22, 1852..... ARI
FEB 23, 1852—JUL 29, 1853 .... TAU
JUL 30, 1853—OCT 29, 1853 ... GEM
OCT 30, 1853—APR 14, 1854 ... TAU
APR 15, 1854—MAY 27, 1856 .. GEM
MAY 28, 1856—JUL 9, 1858 .... CAN
JUL 10, 1858—AUG 25, 1860 ... LEO
AUG 26, 1860—OCT 22, 1862 ... VIR
OCT 23, 1862—APR 22, 1863 .... LIB
APR 23, 1863—JUL 9, 1863...... VIR
JUL 10, 1863—JAN 20, 1865 ..... LIB
JAN 21, 1865—FEB 27, 1865.... SCO
FEB 28, 1865—SEP 29, 1865 ..... LIB
SEP 30, 1865—DEC 16, 1867 ... SCO
DEC 17, 1867—JUN 28, 1868 ... SAG
JUN 29, 1868—SEP 5, 1868 .... SCO
SEP 6, 1868—DEC 14, 1870..... SAG
DEC 15, 1870—MAR 13, 1873 .. CAP
MAR 14, 1873—JUL 13, 1873 .. AQU
JUL 14, 1873—DEC 10, 1873.... CAP
DEC 11, 1873—FEB 29, 1876 ... AQU
MAR 1, 1876—MAY 14, 1878 .... PIS
MAY 15, 1878—SEP 15, 1878 .... ARI
SEP 16, 1878—FEB 5, 1879 ...... PIS
FEB 6, 1879—APR 5, 1881....... ARI
APR 6, 1881—MAY 23, 1883.... TAU
MAY 24, 1883—JUL 5, 1885.... GEM
JUL 6, 1885—AUG 18, 1887 .... CAN
AUG 19, 1887—OCT 6, 1889 ... LEO
OCT 7, 1889—FEB 24, 1890 ..... VIR
FEB 25, 1890—JUN 27, 1890 .... LEO
JUN 28, 1890—DEC 26, 1891 .... VIR
DEC 27, 1891—JAN 22, 1892 .... LIB
JAN 23, 1892—AUG 29, 1892.... VIR
AUG 30, 1892—NOV 6, 1894 .... LIB
NOV 7, 1894—FEB 6, 1897..... SCO
FEB 7, 1897—APR 9, 1897 ...... SAG
APR 10, 1897—OCT 26, 1897
OCT 27, 1897—JAN 20, 1900 ... SAG
JAN 21, 1900—JUL 18, 1900 .... CAP
JUL 19, 1900—OCT 16, 1900 ... SAG
OCT 17, 1900—JAN 19, 1903 ... CAP
JAN 20, 1903—APR 12, 1905 ... AQU
APR 13, 1905—AUG 16, 1905 .... PIS
AUG 17, 1905—JAN 7, 1906 ... AQU
JAN 8, 1906—MAR 18, 1908 ..... PIS
MAR 19, 1908—MAY 16, 1910... ARI
MAY 17, 1910—DEC 14, 1910 .. TAU
DEC 15, 1910—JAN 19, 1911 .... ARI
JAN 20, 1911—JUL 6, 1912 ..... TAU
JUL 7, 1912—NOV 30, 1912 ... GEM
DEC 1, 1912—MAR 25, 1913 ... TAU
MAR 26, 1913—AUG 24, 1914 . GEM
AUG 25, 1914—DEC 6, 1914 ... CAN
DEC 7, 1914—MAY 11, 1915 ... GEM
MAY 12, 1915—OCT 16, 1916.. CAN
OCT 17, 1916—DEC 7, 1916.... LEO
DEC 8, 1916—JUN 23, 1917.... CAN
JUN 24, 1917—AUG 11, 1919... LEO
AUG 12, 1919—OCT 7, 1921 .... VIR
OCT 8, 1921—DEC 19, 1923..... LIB
DEC 20, 1923—APR 5, 1924.... SCO
APR 6, 1924—SEP 13, 1924 ...... LIB
SEP 14, 1924—DEC 2, 1926 .... SCO
DEC 3, 1926—MAR 29, 1929 ... SAG
MAR 30, 1929—MAY 4, 1929 ... CAP
MAY 5, 1929—NOV 29, 1929... SAG
NOV 30, 1929—FEB 22, 1932 ... CAP
FEB 23, 1932—AUG 12, 1932 .. AQU
AUG 13, 1932—NOV 18, 1932.. CAP
NOV 19, 1932—FEB 13, 1935 .. AQU
FEB 14, 1935—APR 24, 1937 ..... PIS
APR 25, 1937—OCT 17, 1937.... ARI
OCT 18, 1937—JAN 13, 1938 .... PIS
JAN 14, 1938—JUL 5, 1939...... ARI
JUL 6, 1939—SEP 21, 1939 ..... TAU
SEP 22, 1939—MAR 19, 1940 .... ARI
MAR 20, 1940—MAY 7, 1942 ... TAU

Your Saturn Chart

MAY 8, 1942—JUN 19, 1944 . . . GEM
JUN 20, 1944—AUG 1, 1946 . . . CAN
AUG 2, 1946—SEP 18, 1948 . . . . LEO
SEP 19, 1948—APR 2, 1949. . . . . . VIR
APR 3, 1949—MAY 28, 1949 . . . . LEO
MAY 29, 1949—NOV 19, 1950 . . VIR
NOV 20, 1950—MAR 6, 1951 . . . . LIB
MAR 7, 1951—AUG 12, 1951. . . . VIR
AUG 13, 1951—OCT 21, 1953 . . . LIB
OCT 22, 1953—JAN 11, 1956. . . SCO
JAN 12, 1956—MAY 13, 1956 . . . SAG
MAY 14, 1956—OCT 9, 1956. . . SCO
OCT 10, 1956—JAN 4, 1959 . . . . SAG
JAN 5, 1959—JAN 9, 1962. . . . . . CAP
JAN 10, 1962—DEC 16, 1964. . . AQU
DEC 17, 1964—MAR 3, 1967 . . . . PIS
MAR 4, 1967—APR 29, 1969 . . . . ARI
APR 30, 1969—JUN 18, 1971 . . . TAU
JUN 19, 1971—JAN 10, 1972 . . . GEM
JAN 11, 1972—FEB 21, 1972 . . . . TAU
FEB 22, 1972—AUG 1, 1973. . . . GEM
AUG 2, 1973—JAN 7, 1974 . . . . CAN
JAN 8, 1974—APR 18, 1974 . . . . GEM
APR 19, 1974—SEP 17, 1975. . . . CAN
SEP 18, 1975—JAN 14, 1976 . . . . LEO
JAN 15, 1976—JUN 5, 1976 . . . . CAN
JUN 6, 1976—NOV 17, 1977. . . . LEO
NOV 18, 1977—JAN 5, 1978 . . . . VIR
JAN 6, 1978—JUL 26, 1978 . . . . . LEO
JUL 27, 1978—SEP 21, 1980 . . . . . VIR
SEP 22, 1980—NOV 29, 1982 . . . . LIB
NOV 30, 1982—MAY 6, 1983 . . SCO
MAY 7, 1983—AUG 24, 1983 . . . . LIB
AUG 25, 1983—NOV 17, 1985 . SCO
NOV 18, 1985—FEB 13, 1988 . . . SAG
FEB 14, 1988—JUN 10, 1988 . . . . CAP
JUN 11, 1988—NOV 12, 1988 . . SAG
NOV 13, 1988—FEB 6, 1991 . . . . CAP
FEB 7, 1991—MAY 21, 1993 . . . AQU
MAY 22, 1993—JUN 30, 1993. . . . PIS
JUL 1, 1993—JAN 28, 1994 . . . . AQU
JAN 29, 1994—APR 7, 1996. . . . . . PIS
APR 8, 1996—JUN 9, 1998 . . . . . . ARI
JUN 10, 1998—OCT 25, 1998. . . TAU
OCT 26, 1998—MAR 1, 1999. . . . ARI
MAR 2, 1999—AUG 10, 2000 . . . TAU
AUG 11, 2000—OCT 16, 2000. . GEM
OCT 17, 2000—DEC 31, 2000 . . TAU

SATURN IN ARIES

Your Saturn in Aries helps to mollify your enormous ego and turn some of your egocentricity outward. Try to remember you're not the center of the universe. And work on your stick-to-it-ive-ness. And your temper.

SATURN IN TAURUS

Your Saturn in Taurus will let you see how insensitive you really can be. It's up to you to change and bring some empathy and feeling for those around you. You also have a lot of insecurity about money, and with just a little self-discipline, you can whip your self in shape financially.

SATURN IN GEMINI

Your Saturn in Gemini will help you realize how scattered your forces are, and how frustrated and discontented you are in your dual personality. Can you try to pull yourself together? In unity is strength.

SATURN IN CANCER

Your Saturn in Cancer influences the sometimes too-close relationships you have with your home and family. You're too dependent on others—try developing a little self-reliance.

SATURN IN LEO

Your Saturn in Leo will heighten your awareness of your colossal superiority complex, which tends to make you a pain to be around. A little humility will go a long way.

SATURN IN VIRGO

Your Saturn in Virgo makes you aware that your constant criticism and pickiness are terrible off-putters to everyone around you—and besides that, it's awful for *you*, because you're also constantly criticizing your self. "Judge not that ye be not judged."

SATURN IN LIBRA

Your Saturn in Libra helps you unbalance the balance. You're so hung up in weighing everything in your innate scales, that you have a terrible time making decisions. When you recognize this and make an effort to make a decision, any decision, right or wrong, you'll be on the way to a new-found strength.

SATURN IN SCORPIO

Your Saturn in Scorpio shows you how to lessen your relentless drive for control and your obsession with power—if only you'll pay attention. Your cunning ways will reap you nothing but anguish and pain. Use your psychic abilities and intuitive mind and try to change.

SATURN IN SAGITTARIUS

Your Saturn in Sagittarius bestows a strength of practicality on you which allows you to see yourself as a mental wanderer. You won't really accomplish anything till you get it all together and become more trustworthy and reliable, particularly to your self.

SATURN IN CAPRICORN

Your Saturn in Capricorn gives you that brass ring you've tried so hard for all your life. You set your sights, determined to get what you want, worked day and night, and now you've got it. Your persistence paid off. Whoopee!

SATURN IN AQUARIUS

Your Saturn in Aquarius brings you a little down-to-earth from your humanitarian perch. Of course you want to save the whole world, but don't forget that the world is made up of people. Try helping just *one* person.

SATURN IN PISCES

Your Saturn in Pisces will light a fire under your behind to get you off your lazy, clinging, nobody-loves-or-understands-me kick. Use some of that creative and spiritual talent, make some decisions and get moving.

10

Your 12 Uranus Signs and Chart

Uranus is the revolutionary planet which rules the unusual and the innovative, the unexpected and everything futuristic and visionary. It never lets any one condition last too long, and rules your ability to be creatively original, and to respond to change. Mighty changes can happen overnight under Uranus' influence.

Your Uranus Sign is determined by the year you were born. Your Uranus Chart is on the following pages.

Your Uranus Chart

JAN 1,1850—APR 14, 1851 . . . . . . ARI
APR 15, 1851—MAY 31, 1858 . . . TAU
JUN 1, 1858—JAN 3, 1859 . . . . . GEM
JAN 4, 1859—MAR 11, 1859 . . . . TAU
MAR 12, 1859—JUN 25, 1865 . . GEM
JUN 26, 1865—SEP 12, 1871 . . . CAN
SEP 13, 1871—JAN 1, 1872 . . . . . LEO
JAN 2, 1872—JUN 27, 1872 . . . . CAN
JUN 28, 1872—AUG 24, 1878 . . . LEO
AUG 25, 1878—OCT 13, 1884 . . . VIR
OCT 14, 1884—APR 11, 1885 . . . . LIB
APR 12, 1885—JUL 28, 1885 . . . . . VIR
JUL 29, 1885—DEC 9, 1890 . . . . . . LIB
DEC 10, 1890—APR 4, 1891 . . . . SCO
APR 5, 1891—SEP 25, 1891 . . . . . . LIB
SEP 26, 1891—DEC 1, 1897 . . . . SCO
DEC 2, 1897—JUL 3, 1898 . . . . . . SAG
JUL 4, 1898—SEP 10, 1898 . . . . . SCO
SEP 11, 1898—DEC 19, 1904 . . . . SAG
DEC 20, 1904—JAN 30, 1912 . . . CAP
JAN 31, 1912—SEP 4, 1912 . . . . AQU
SEP 5, 1912—NOV 11, 1912 . . . . CAP
NOV 12, 1912—MAR 31, 1919 . AQU
APR 1, 1919—AUG 16, 1919 . . . . . PIS
AUG 17, 1919—JAN 21, 1920 . . AQU
JAN 22, 1920—MAR 30, 1927 . . . . PIS
MAR 31, 1927—NOV 4, 1927 . . . ARI
NOV 5, 1927—JAN 12, 1928 . . . . . PIS
JAN 13, 1928—JUN 6, 1934 . . . . . ARI
JUN 7, 1934—OCT 9, 1934 . . . . . TAU
OCT 10, 1934—MAR 28, 1935 . . . ARI
MAR 29, 1935—AUG 6, 1941 . . . TAU
AUG 7, 1941—OCT 4, 1941 . . . . GEM
OCT 5, 1941—MAY 13, 1942 . . . TAU
MAY 14, 1942—AUG 29, 1948 . GEM
AUG 30, 1948—NOV 11, 1948 . CAN
NOV 12, 1948—JUN 9, 1949 . . . GEM
JUN 10, 1949—AUG 23, 1955 . . CAN
AUG 24, 1955—JAN 27, 1956 . . . LEO
JAN 28, 1956—JUN 8, 1956 . . . . CAN
JUN 9, 1956—OCT 31, 1961 . . . . LEO
NOV 1, 1961—JAN 11, 1962 . . . . VIR
JAN 12, 1962—AUG 8, 1962 . . . . LEO
AUG 9, 1962—SEP 27, 1968 . . . . . VIR
SEP 28, 1968—MAY 20, 1969 . . . . LIB
MAY 21, 1969—JUN 24, 1969 . . . VIR
JUN 25, 1969—NOV 21, 1974 . . . LIB
NOV 22, 1974—MAY 1, 1975 . . SCO
MAY 2, 1975—SEP 6, 1975 . . . . . . LIB
SEP 7, 1975—NOV 16, 1981 . . . . SCO
NOV 17, 1981—FEB 15, 1988 . . . SAG
FEB 16, 1988—JUN 10, 1988 . . . . CAP
JUN 11, 1988—DEC 2, 1988 . . . . SAG
DEC 3, 1988—APR 1, 1995 . . . . . CAP
APR 2, 1995—JUN 9, 1995 . . . . . AQU
JUN 10, 1995—JAN 12, 1996 . . . . CAP
JAN 13, 1996—DEC 31, 2000 . . . AQU

URANUS IN ARIES

Your Uranus in Aries makes you tend to lose interest in any project you're working on, from business to social to romantic, and go off in another, totally different direction and begin all over again. You also tend to be so sure of your own ideas that you don't want to listen to any others. Curb your impulses.

URANUS IN TAURUS

Your Uranus in Taurus upsets your life-course and makes for turbulence on every front, particularly in areas of business and money. Be more practical in your day-to-day dealings, and less headstrong. Watch your moodiness.

URANUS IN GEMINI

Your Uranus in Gemini gives you roving feet and a roving mind which leads to intellectual stimulation and excitement, but your roving eye can only lead to trouble. People love to be around you and you love having them around, but only if they stimulate you with new ideas. You can't stand even a *smidgen* of boredom.

URANUS IN CANCER

Your Uranus in Cancer induces eruption in your family life, eruption that can be terribly unpleasant, but fortunately you've an abundance of understanding to work your way through these problems. You're very changeable and impatient, and need to work on strengthening your inner self so that all the things that annoy you and tend to make you so irritable will roll off you and not bother you, because you won't *let* them.

URANUS IN LEO

Your Uranus in Leo makes you fiery and extroverted—a born business leader—and even though you will encounter some upsets, your creativity and dynamism won't ever let you stay down. But you really should curb your arrogance if want to *stay* successful.

URANUS IN VIRGO

Your Uranus in Virgo leads to business upheavals, but your diagnostic nature and conscientiousness with details will pull you through. You have an independent streak and are rather set in your ways, but you're very clever. Stay prudent.

URANUS IN LIBRA

Your Uranus in Libra will threaten your partnerships with sudden and unforeseen conditions, but your cooperativeness and ability to see both sides will tip the scales in your favor. You should curb your tendency to want things only your way and you'll have a lot fewer problems with associates.

URANUS IN SCORPIO

Your Uranus in Scorpio thrives on the unanticipated and your life will be full of surprises, but your magnetism and resourcefulness will enable you to perceive the laws of nature and keep an inner calm. You have incredible willpower, and your powers of concentration are acute. Don't be so secretive and mysterious.

URANUS IN SAGITTARIUS

Your Uranus in Sagittarius makes you impulsive, particularly in the travel area, and you're able to hop on a plane to anywhere in a minute's notice. You love the unexpected. But you *don't* love being restricted in any way, and you must have your freedon in all areas.

URANUS IN CAPRICORN

Your Uranus in Capricorn will throw up many sudden and unexpected obstacles to upset your ambitions and curb your aspirations, but you are *so* determined and persistent that you will never give up till you get everything you want. You love authority and the power it gives you.

URANUS IN AQUARIUS

Your Uranus in Aquarius tends to restrain your revolutionary ideas. But you're such an innovator that as one unique idea is shot down, you'll come up with two more. You like and need to be around people who are eccentric.

URANUS IN PISCES

Your Uranus in Pisces gives you quick insight and sudden hunches about most things in your life. You're very aware of people and ideas, and extremely receptive to them. You dream a lot and your dreams often show you the future. Use your psychic abilities and play those hunches.

11

Your 12 Neptune Signs and Chart

Neptune rules your intuition, spiritually and extrasensory perception, and this is of great help to anyone in business, where snap decisions are often called for.

Neptune governs anyone who is sensitive, imaginative and a dreamer, and this includes poets, artists, musicians and mystics.

Your Neptune Sign is determined by the year you were born. Your Neptune chart is below.

Your Neptune Chart

HOW TO FIND YOUR NEPTUNE

JAN 1, 1850—APR 13, 1861...... PIS
APR 14, 1861—APR 6, 1875 ..... ARI
APR 7, 1875—MAR 20, 1889.... TAU
MAR 21, 1889—JUL 19, 1901... GEM
JUL 20, 1901—DEC 25, 1901 ... CAN
DEC 26, 1901—MAY 19, 1902 .. GEM
MAY 20, 1902—SEP 22, 1914... CAN
SEP 23, 1914—DEC 14, 1914.... LEO
DEC 15, 1914—JUL 18, 1915 ... CAN
JUL 19, 1915—MAR 19, 1916 ... LEO
MAR 20, 1916—MAY 1, 1916... CAN
MAY 2, 1916—SEP 20, 1928 .... LEO
SEP 21, 1928—FEB 19, 1929...... VIR
FEB 20, 1929—JUL 23, 1929..... LEO
JUL 24, 1929—OCT 3, 1942 ..... VIR
OCT 4, 1942—APR 18, 1943..... LIB
APR 19, 1943—AUG 2, 1943 .... VIR
AUG 3, 1943—DEC 22, 1955 .... LIB
DEC 23, 1955—MAR 12, 1956 .. SCO
MAR 13, 1956—OCT 19, 1956 ... LIB
OCT 20, 1956—JUN 15, 1957 .. SCO
JUN 16, 1957—AUG 6, 1957..... LIB
AUG 7, 1957—JAN 4, 1970 .... SCO
JAN 5, 1970—MAY 3, 1970..... SAG
MAY 4, 1970—NOV 6, 1970 ... SCO
NOV 7, 1970—JAN 19, 1984.... SAG
JAN 20, 1984—JUN 23, 1984.... CAP
JUN 24, 1984—NOV 21, 1984 .. SAG
NOV 22, 1984—JAN 29, 1998... CAP
JAN 30, 1998—AUG 23, 1998 .. AQU
AUG 24, 1998—NOV 27, 1998.. CAP
NOV 28, 1998—DEC 31, 2000 . AQU

NEPTUNE IN ARIES

Neptune in Aries is a time of some problems. Reason and logic don't prevail, and much thought and coolness of head is needed to rise above the turmoil.

NEPTUNE IN TAURUS

Neptune in Taurus is a period of strong feelings of intuition in business leading to success in making money. If there's a deal cooking, instincts will sniff out the right moves to make and keep the wrong ones from being made. In romance, those strong instincts that are listened to in business work also for love.

NEPTUNE IN GEMINI

Neptune in Gemini is a time of superficiality, where depth of feeling is suspect. Change is needed in all dealings, but particularly in business. Restlessness is rampant and this is ruinous to many business deals, where patience and waiting usually pay off.

NEPTUNE IN CANCER

Neptune in Cancer is a depressed period which needs strength to be overcome. Mysticism and sensitivity are expressed, plus discernment in others sharing sensitivity. Others' moods must not be allowed to influence anything.

NEPTUNE IN LEO

Neptune in Leo is a time of rashness and impetuosity. No one wants to be told what to do in any area now—personal, business, or pleasure. It's a period when everyone wants to be in charge at all times, and most would not be too considerate of others. Strong egos prevail, plus a tendency to be selfish and restless in dealings.

NEPTUNE IN VIRGO

Neptune in Virgo is a time for all kinds of new ideas, and quick minds to pick up on them. Basics and details are most important now, and details are what all big things are made of. Without the basement and ground floor, there couldn't *be* a skyscraper. These basics are now very positive.

NEPTUNE IN LIBRA

All partnerships are in Libra, and marriage is the ultimate partnership, so Neptune in this placement brings about new and revolutionary ideas pertaining to marriage and relationships. This is a time of a romance and partnership revolution.

NEPTUNE IN SCORPIO

Neptune in Scorpio is a time of great progress in areas of technology, from biology to chemistry to every field of science. And Scorpio ruling the sexual organs leads Neptune into a sexual rebellion, a breaking out of restricted areas and expansion of great changes.

NEPTUNE IN SAGITTARIUS

Neptune in Sagittarius brings a searching and seeking, and an opening up of new and advanced ideas of polity, regulations, government, religion, psychology and philosophy. It's a time of consciousness-expanding and inner probing. An experiencing of a new kind of freedom.

NEPTUNE IN CAPRICORN

Neptune in Capricorn is a period of progress and attainment of goals, a determination of ambitions and an unrelenting drive toward success in realizing aspirations, the things everyone is working so hard for. And hard work is the solution.

NEPTUNE IN AQUARIUS

Neptune in Aquarius is a time of realization of a feeling of oneness with the universe, a breaking of boundaries and advancing into uncharted territory. There is a striving for utopia, and this is the closest we've come so far.

NEPTUNE IN PISCES

Neptune in Pisces is causing some problems, but they're solvable, because we're learning to sublimate baser urges and express the higher ones. And as time goes on, the realization is that this isn't just an answer—this is the *only* answer.

12

Your 12 Pluto Signs and Chart

Your Pluto is found by the year you were born, and it remains in one sign for from two months to almost thirty years. Pluto is the planet that makes new conditions possible to replace old ones. And as we become more aware of our selves and of astrology, we'll find that in looking back on world changes (which of course affect each one of us), Pluto was the force causing these changes.

Being a planet of mystery and extremes, Pluto's changes often take us by surprise, and by the time we realize we're changing, the transformation is complete.

When you look at the Pluto chart and notice the transition dates, you'll see they coincide with many social changes and world changes, and you'll notice that people born within certain dates have inclinations different from groups of people born within other dates. Within certain dates of Cancer's influence were born people who grew up very conservative, home-loving and marriage-conscious. During a period of Leo's influence were born people who caused the sexual revolution of the sixties. Cancer is conservative and home-loving, and Leo is revolutionary and forceful. Then Pluto moves into Virgo, which is back to conservatism. Virgo is also practical and orderly, a bit inhibited and into perfectionism, so these people born under Pluto in Virgo are part of a conservative-leaning group. And so the pendulum swings back and forth. After Virgo comes Libra, with a leaning toward justice and the arts, then Scorpio, inclining toward all things psychic, and so the planetary circles goes round and round.

By looking at the dates on the Pluto chart and recalling past history, we have an idea of what to expect in the future as Pluto moves into different planetary influences.

Your Pluto chart is on the following page.

Your Pluto Chart

JAN 1, 1870—JUL 29, 1882 ..... TAU
JUL 30, 1882—SEP 27, 1882 .... GEM
SEP 28, 1882—JUN 24, 1883 .... TAU
JUN 25, 1883—NOV 27, 1883 .. GEM
NOV 28, 1883—APR 23, 1884 .. TAU
APR 24, 1884—SEP 11, 1912 ... GEM
SEP 12, 1912—OCT 20, 1912 ... CAN
OCT 21, 1912—JUL 9, 1913 .... GEM
JUL 10, 1913—DEC 28, 1913 ... CAN
DEC 29, 1913—MAY 26, 1914 .. GEM
MAY 27, 1914—OCT 7, 1937 ... CAN
OCT 8, 1937—NOV 25, 1937 ... LEO
NOV 26, 1937—AUG 3, 1938 .. CAN
AUG 4, 1938—FEB 7, 1939 ..... LEO
FEB 8, 1939—JUN 14, 1939 .... CAN
JUN 15, 1939—OCT 20, 1956 ... LEO
OCT 21, 1956—JAN 15, 1957 .... VIR
JAN 16, 1957—AUG 19, 1957 ... LEO
AUG 20, 1957—APR 11, 1958 ... VIR
APR 12, 1958—JUN 10, 1958 .... LEO
JUN 11, 1958—OCT 5, 1971 .... VIR
OCT 6, 1971—APR 17, 1972 ..... LIB
APR 18, 1972—JUL 30, 1972 ..... VIR
JUL 31, 1972—NOV 5, 1983 ..... LIB
NOV 6, 1983—MAY 18, 1984 ... VIR
MAY 19, 1984—AUG 28, 1984 ... LIB
AUG 29, 1984—JAN 16, 1995 .. SCO
JAN 17, 1995—APR 21, 1995 .... SAG
APR 22, 1995—NOV 10, 1995 .. SCO
NOV 11, 1995—DEC 31, 2000 .. SAG

PLUTO IN ARIES

The positive aspect is a radical changing of political leadership and a beginning of new social and political ideas.

The negative aspect is a pioneering in warlike tactics and an egocentric and jingoistic "we are best" attitude.

PLUTO IN TAURUS

The positive aspect is an inclination toward economic growth, and a gradual sexual awakening.

The negative aspect is a tendency toward avarice and greed and "Thou shalt covet *everything*."

PLUTO IN GEMINI

The positive aspect is a loosening of mental, emotional and spiritual bonds, with a leaning toward transcendentalism.

The negative aspect is an intellectual arrogance, and a propensity to multiple dealings with no real concentration on any.

PLUTO IN CANCER

The positive aspect is a centering on familial ties, with a strengthening of marriage and home life.

The negative aspect is an ostrich view that family unity becomes the answer to *all* problems.

PLUTO IN LEO

The positive aspect is a flourishing of inner strength that brings a sense of confidence leading to positive action.

The negative aspect is a vanity in the extreme, and a feeling of being part of royalty, therefore above the law.

PLUTO IN VIRGO

The positive aspect is a desire to improve everything through changing the basics—*preventive* medicine, *self-help* politics, *do-it-yourself* businesses.

The negative aspect is a super-critical attitude which kills spontaneity and makes for self-consciousness and rigid thinking.

PLUTO IN LIBRA

The positive aspect is an artistic burgeoning that helps to strengthen all creative forces.

The negative aspect is an extreme involvement in self with a tendency to forget others while in a narcissistic haze.

PLUTO IN SCORPIO

The positive aspect is a psychic awareness that initiates the expansion of inner spiritual resources.

The negative aspect is a need for secrecy, and a selfishness that closes off most avenues of communication.

PLUTO IN SAGITTARIUS

The positive aspect is an increase of exploration and travel which unlocks more of the secrets of the universe than ever before.

The negative aspect is a lack of emotionalism and feeling, leading to cold and calculating dealings in all areas.

PLUTO IN CAPRICORN

The positive aspect is the perseverance of the rationale that honor is the quality to strive for above all other qualities.

The negative aspect is a conventional thinking in the extreme leading to rigid conformity.

PLUTO IN AQUARIUS

The positive aspect is the use of perception and innovative thinking to transform scientific study and speculation to brand new and totally original ideas.

The negative aspect is the tendency to build a skyscraper of thoughts without a basement and foundation.

PLUTO IN PISCES

The positive is the expansion of spiritual growth and the evolution of new origins of energy leading to mind over matter.

The negative aspect is in getting submerged in supernatural phenomena and drugs, and losing the essence of reality.

13

Celebrity Birth Days

By Dates, 366 Days

Aries

MARCH

21	Johann Sebastian Bach Modest Moussorgorsky John D. Rockefeller III	Phyllis McGinley James Coco Ed Begley	Patrick Lucey Manny Sanguillen
22	Sir Anthony Van Dyck Karl Malden Stephen Sondheim	Werner Klemperer William Shatner Sen. Orin Hatch	Marcel Marceau Chico Marx Andrew Lloyd Webber
23	Joan Crawford	Wernher von Braun Marty Allen	Lee May
24	Byron Janis Thomas Dewey	Steve McQueen William Goetz	Harry Houdini
25	Gloria Steinem Howard Cosell Simone Signoret Bela Bartok	Frankie Carle Monique Van Vooren Elton John Aretha Franklin	David Lean Arturo Toscanini Leonard Nimoy Anita Bryant
26	Robert Frost Tennessee Williams Alan Arkin Al Jolson	Diana Ross James Caan Sterling Hayden Pierre Boulez	Vicki Lawrence Erica Jong Bob Woodward
27	Budd Schulberg Nathaniel Currier Gloria Swanson David Janssen	Ferde Grofé Sarah Vaughan Edward Steichen	Michael York Cyrus Vance Wilhelm Roentgen
28	Rudolph Serkin Edmund Muskie Paul Whiteman August Busch	Nelson Algren Irving Lazar Spyros Skouras	Rick Barry Pandro Berman Carolyn Jones
29	Eugene McCarthy Pres. John Tyler Walt Frazier Dirk Bogarde	Eileen Heckart Pearl Bailey Howard Lindsay Denny McClain	Arthur O'Connell Warner Baxter Cy Young
30	McGeorge Bundy Francisco Goya Vincent Van Gogh John Astin	Turhan Bey Warren Beatty Frankie Laine	Paul Verlaine Eric Clapton Richard Helm
31	Franz Joseph Haydn Cesar Chavez René Descartes Arthur Godfrey	Red Norvo Jack Johnson Shirley Jones	Herb Alpert Richard Chamberlain Richard Kiley

Aries

APRIL

1	Otto Von Bismarck Ali MacGraw Debbie Reynolds	Jane Powell Emil Mosbacher Wallace Beery	Lon Chaney William Manchester
2	Alec Guinness Max Ernst Buddy Ebsen	Charlemagne Jack Webb Gary Stevens	Emile Zola Casanova
3	George Jessel Marlon Brando Doris Day Arthur Murray	Henry Luce Wayne Newton George Stevens, Jr. Washington Irving	Tony Orlando Herb Caen Sally Rand
4	Howard Koch Anthony Perkins Gil Hodges	John Cameron Swayze Elmer Bernstein Maya Angelou	Frances Langford Arthur Murray
5	Herbert Von Karajan Melvyn Douglas Gregory Peck Joseph Lister Frank Gorshin	Jean Fragonard Bette Davis Spencer Tracy Chester Bowles Gale Storm	Roger Corman Goddard Lieberson Maxine Cheshire Michael Moriarity
6	André Previn Lowell Thomas	Raphael Merle Haggard	Billy Dee Williams Walter Huston
7	David Frost Walter Winchell Percy Faith	Irene Castle Ravi Shankar	Jerry Brown Francis Ford Coppola
8	Ilka Chase Mary Pickford Yip Harburg Warren Avis Sonja Henie	Franco Corelli Jacques Brel Michael Bennett Catfish Hunter	John Gavin Connie Stevens Betty Ford Julian Lennon Clementine Churchill
9	Sen. William J. Fullbright Sen. Abraham Ribicoff Paul Robeson Mary Pickford	Jean-Paul Belmondo Hugh Hefner Sol Hurok	Tommy Manville Charles Baudelaire Ward Bond
10	Clare Boothe Luce Arthur Ashe, Jr. David Halberstam	Omar Sharif Chuck Connors Commodore Perry	George Arliss William Booth

Aries

APRIL

11	Joel Grey Oleg Cassini	Ethel Kennedy Quentin Reynolds	Dean Acheson Gov. Hugh Carey
12	Henry Clay Ann Miller	Lily Pons Tiny Tim	David Letterman David Cassidy
13	Pres. Thomas Jefferson Howard Keel	Don Adams Butch Cassidy	F. W. Woolworth Harold Stassen
14	Julie Christie Rod Steiger Brad Dillman	John Gielgud Loretta Lynn	Pete Rose Sir James Clark
15	Leonardo Da Vinci Alfred Bloomingdale Claudia Cardinale	Elizabeth Montgomery Bessie Smith	Roy Clark Algernon Swinburne
16	Nikita Khrushchev Charlie Chaplin Peter Ustinov Wilbur Wright	Henry Mancini Edie Adams Kareem Abdul-Jabbar	Jimmy Osmond Dusty Springfield Bobby Vinton
17	Gregor Piatigorsky William Holden Harry Reasoner	Thornton Wilder James Garner Billie Holiday	J. P. Morgan Anne Shirley
18	Leopold Stokowski Hayley Mills	Huntington Hartford	Philippe Junot
19	Kenneth Battelle Jayne Mansfield	Dudley Moore Hugh O'Brian	Don Adams
20	Adolf Hitler Ryan O'Neal Joan Miró	Harvey Firestone, Jr. Lionel Hampton Harold Lloyd	Nina Foch Bob Braun

Taurus

April

21	Queen Elizabeth II Elaine May Anthony Quinn	Charlotte Brontë Charles Grodin Rollo May	Catherine the Great Hans Christian Andersen
22	Eddie Albert Immanuel Kant Glenn Campbell	Yehudi Menuhin Vera Maxwell	Jack Nicholson Peter Frampton
23	Bernadette Devlin Sergei Prokofiev Sergei Rachmaninoff Janet Blair Lee Majors Shirley Temple (Black)	Warren Spahn Pres. James Buchanan Vladimir Nabokov Stephen A. Douglas Halston	Sandra Dee Pres. Franklin Pierce William Shakespeare Valerie Bertinelli Frank Borzage
24	Shirley MacLaine Barbra Streisand	William De Kooning Jill Ireland	Leslie Howard
25	Al Pacino Guglielmo Marconi Ella Fitzgerald	Edward R. Murrow Melissa Hayden Oliver Cromwell	King Edward II William Brennan
26	Carol Burnett I. M. Pei Bernard Malamud Jules Stein	Anita Loos Sal Maglie J. P. Donleavy John James Audubon	Emperor Marcus Aurelius Rudolph Hess Bobby Rydell Charles Richter
27	Coretta King Sandy Dennis Samuel F. B. Morse	Pres. Ulysses S. Grant Rogers Hornsby Jack Klugman	Mary Wollstonecraft Judy Carne Anouk Aimée
28	Ann-Margret Eugène Delacroix	Pres. James Monroe Lionel Barrymore	Carolyn Jones
29	Zubin Mehta Rod McKuen Duke Ellington Tom Ewell	Fred Zinnemann George Allen William Randolph Hearst, Sr.	Celeste Holm Emperor Hirohito Zizi Jeanmaire
30	Eve Arden Sheldon Harnick Marlon Brando	Jill Clayburgh Cloris Leachman	Willie Nelson Conductor Robert Shaw

Taurus

May

1	Scott Carpenter Glenn Ford Jack Paar Calamity Jane	Danielle Darrieux Kate Smith Gen. Mark Clark	Judy Collins Rita Coolidge Duke of Wellington
2	Dr. Benjamin Spock Bing Crosby Lorenz Hart	Theodore Bikel Brian Aherne Engelbert Humperdinck	Sidney Skolsky Larry Gatlin Lesley Gore
3	Niccolò Machiavelli Mary Astor Sugar Ray Robinson Betty Comden Earl Blackwell	Earl Wilson Walter Slezak James Brown Pete Seeger William Inge	Tom O'Horgan Frankie Valli Doug Henning Golda Meir
4	Roberta Peters Vladimir Lenin Audrey Hepburn	Francis Cardinal Spellman Luther Adler	Moshe Dayan El Cordobes
5	Karl Marx Giorgio Di Sant' Angelo Søren Kierkegaard	James Beard Alice Faye Tammy Wynette	Tyrone Power Nelly Bly Freeman Gosden
6	Orson Welles Weeb Ewbank Willie Mays Carmen Cavallero	Robespierre Sigmund Freud Robert Perry Theodore White	Ross Hunter Rudolph Valentino Stewart Granger Ayatollah Khomeini
7	Johannes Brahms Peter Ilyitch Tchaikovsky Anne Baxter Teresa Brewer Archibald MacLeish	Johnny Unitas Darren McGavin Gabby Hayes Robert Browning	Edwin Land Eva Perón Janis Ian Gary Cooper
8	Fulton J. Sheen Don Rickles Pres. Harry S. Truman Roberto Rossellini	Ricky Nelson Melissa Gilbert Sonny Liston Peter Benchley	Toni Tennille Angel Cordero Fernandel
9	Daniel Berrigan Albert Finney Glenda Jackson Mike Wallace	Pancho Gonzalez Candice Bergen J. M. Barrie	Hank Snow Billy Joel Henry J. Kaiser
10	Dmitri Tiomkin Fred Astaire Max Steiner	Nancy Walker David O. Selznick Carl Albert	John Wilkes Booth Ella Grasso

Taurus

May

11	Phil Silvers Valentino Doug McClure	Martha Graham Irving Berlin	Mort Sahl Denver Pyle
12	Yogi Berra Burt Bacharach Howard K. Smith Philip Wylie	George Carlin Florence Nightingale	Tom Snyder Ron Ziegler Judith Crist
13	Georges Braque Joe Louis Walt Whitman	Joseph Pulitzer, Jr. Clive Barnes Bea Arthur	Stevie Wonder Empress Maria Theresa
14	Patrice Munsel Bobby Darin	Dante Thomas Gainesborough	Tony Perez
15	Mayor Richard J. Daley Pierre Curie Clifton Fadiman Jasper Johns James Mason	Richard Avedon Katherine Anne Porter Joseph Cotten Anna Maria Alberghetti Metternich	L. Frank Baum Joseph Califano Eddy Arnold Paul Zindel Trini Lopez
16	Henry Fonda Liberace	Billy Martin Woody Herman	James Arness Margaret Sullavan
17	Stewart Alsop Birgit Nilsson	Edward Jenner Maureen O'Sullivan	Dennis Hopper
18	Jacob Javits Robert Morse Pierre Balmain Reggie Jackson Brooks Robinson	Margot Fonteyn Pope John Paul II Meredith Willson Frank Capra	Perry Como Ezio Pinza Bertrand Russell Czar Nicholas II
19	Ho Chi Minh Malcolm X	Sarah Peale David Hartman	Steven Ford
20	James Stewart Adela Rogers St. Johns George Gobel	Honoré De Balzac Cher Dolly Madison	Henri Rousseau Joe Cocker
21	Harold Robbins Raymond Burr Peggy Cass	Dennis Day Robert Montgomery	Fats Waller Albrecht Durer

Gemini

MAY

22	Richard Wagner Richard Benjamin Laurence Olivier Judith Crist	Charles Aznavour Mary Cassatt Susan Strasberg Vance Packard	Peter Nero Marisol Arthur Conan Doyle
23	Scat Man Crothers Rosemary Clooney	Joan Collins Douglas Fairbanks, Sr.	Barbara Ward
24	Wilbur Mills Queen Victoria Siobhan McKenna	Bob Dylan Jane Byrne Fatty Arbuckle	George Washington Carver Lilli Palmer
25	Beverly Sills Leslie Uggams John Weitz Hal David Lindsey Nelson	Gene Tunney Mary Wells Lawrence Ralph Waldo Emerson Claude Akins	Miles Davis Marshal Tito Kitty Kallen Jeanne Crain
26	James Arness John Wayne Aldo Gucci	Peggy Lee Laurance Rockefeller Alec McGowen	Artie Shaw Norma Talmadge
27	Hubert Humphrey Henry Kissinger Vincent Price Wild Bill Hickok	Rachel Carson Georges Rouault Sam Snead John Cheever	Christopher Lee Herman Wouk Isadora Duncan Louis Gossett, Jr.
28	Dietrich Fisher-Dieskau Carroll Baker Stephen Birmingham	Barry Commoner Gladys Knight	Jim Thorpe Dionne Quintuplets
29	Bob Hope Patrick Henry Pres. John F. Kennedy	Herb Shriner Helmut Berger	Beatrice Lillie King Charles II
30	Cornelia Otis Skinner Billy Baldwin Benny Goodman Irving Thalberg Christine Jorgenson	Frank Blair Keir Dullea James Farley Stepin Fetchit	Mel Blanc Clint Walker Gale Sayers Michael J. Pollard
31	Henry Jackson Clint Eastwood Joe Namath Norman Vincent Peale	Edward Bennett Williams Don Ameche Brooke Shields Rainer Werner Fassbinder	Johnny Paycheck Fred Allen Shirley Verrett

Gemini

JUNE

1	Andy Griffith Pat Boone Brigham Young	René Auberjonois Marilyn Monroe	David Rockefeller Joan Caulfield
2	Marvin Hamlisch Hedda Hopper Stacy Keach	Marquis de Sade Chuck Barris Martha Washington	Johnny Weissmuller Sally Kellerman
3	Jan Peerce Marcus Tullius Cicero Jefferson Davis Colleen Dewhurst Josephine Baker	Tony Curtis Paulette Goddard Allen Ginsberg Maurice Evans	Abel Green Bert Lance King George V Marion Davies
4	Rosalind Russell Robert Merrill Charles Collingwood	Dennis Weaver Gene Barry	Bruce Dern King George III
5	Bill Boyd (Hopalong Cassidy)	Pancho Villa Bill Hayes	Bill Moyers
6	Achmed Sukarno Roy Innes Nathan Hale Ted Lewis	Bjorn Borg Thomas Mann Jimmie Lunceford Walter Abel	Diego Velasquez Empress Alexandra of Russia Pushkin
7	Tom Jones Jessica Tandy Rocky Graziano	Paul Gauguin Thurman Munson	Beau Brummel Fred Waring
8	Frank Lloyd Wright Robert Schumann	Robert Preston Alexis Smith	Nancy Sinatra, Jr. James Darren
9	Fred Waring Robert McNamara Peter the Great	Cole Porter Jackie Mason George Axelrod	Jackie Wilson Les Paul Happy Rockefeller
10	Frederick Loewe Donald Brooks Prince Philip	Robert Alan Aurthur F. Lee Bailey Hattie McDaniel	Saul Bellow Judy Garland Robert Cummings

Gemini

JUNE

11	Jacques Cousteau Richard Strauss Chad Everett Gene Wilder	Paul Mellon William Styron Risë Stevens	Vince Lombardi Michael Cacoyannis Joey Dee
12	George Bush David Rockefeller	Vic Damone Jim Nabors	Ivan Tors Irwin Allen
13	Luis Alvarez Don Budge Prince Aly Kahn	Richard Thomas Basil Rathbone	Paul Lynde Red Grange
14	Harriet Beecher Stowe Cy Coleman Burl Ives	Gene Barry Margaret Bourke-White	Dorothy McGuire Pierre Salinger
15	Saul Steinberg David Rose Erroll Garner	Robert Russell Bennett June Lockhart Edvard Grieg	Malcolm MacDowell Morris Udall
16	Joyce Carol Oates Erich Segal Helen Traubel	Katharine Graham Stan Laurel	Derrick Sanderson Jack Albertson
17	Ralph Bellamy John Hersey Sammy Fain Igor Stravinsky	Dean Martin Charles Gounod Elroy "Crazylegs" Hirsch Dave Concepcion	Barry Manilow John Wesley Red Foley
18	John D. Rockefeller IV E. G. Marshall Sylvia Porter Bud Collyer Tom Wicker	Sammy Cahn Jeanette MacDonald Richard Boone Kay Kyser	Paul McCartney Anastasia Lou Brock James Brolin
19	Louis Jourdan Guy Lombardo Gena Rowlands	Dame May Whitty Charles Coburn	King James I Lou Gehrig
20	Jacques Offenbach André Watts Lillian Hellman	Mack Gordon Audie Murphy Chet Atkins	Errol Flynn Anne Murray
21	Judy Holliday Maureen Stapleton Jean-Paul Sartre Jane Russell	Mary McCarthy Lalo Schifrin Ernest Hemingway Al Hirschfeld	Willie Mosconi Françoise Sagan Meredith Baxter-Birney Mariette Hartley

Cancer

JUNE

22	Bill Blass Gower Champion Erich Maria Remarque Lindsay Wagner Buddy Adler	Billy Wilder Katherine Dunham Pete Maravich Joseph Papp Kris Kristofferson	Anne Morrow Lindberg John Dillinger Freddie Prinze Meryl Streep Mike Todd
23	Bob Fosse Dr. Alfred Kinsey June Carter Cash	Kind Edward VIII (Duke of Windsor) William Rogers Empress Josephine	Jean Anouilh George Abbott
24	Phil Harris Norman Cousins Billy Casper	Henry Ward Beecher Jack Dempsey	Claude Chabrol Margot Stewart
25	Sidney Lumet George Abbott	Marusia Carly Simon	June Lockhart Willis Reed
26	John Tunney Anna Moffo Pearl Buck	Peter Lorre Stuart Symington	Richard Maltby Jeanne Eagles
27	Emma Goldman William G. Armstrong	Helen Keller	Bob "Captain Kangaroo" Keeshan
28	King Henry VIII Richard Rodgers Ashley Montagu	Max Gordon Jean-Jacques Rousseau Mel Brooks	Lester Flatt Rachel Perry
29	Peter Paul Rubens Frank Loesser Nelson Eddy Harmon Killebrew	Egon Von Furstenberg Robert Evans Leroy Anderson Slim Pickens	Stokely Carmichael William Mayo Ruth Warrick
30	William Zeckendorf Susan Hayward	Buddy Rich Lena Horne	June Valli

Cancer

JULY

1	Princess Diana William Wyler Leslie Caron Olivia De Havilland	Tab Hunter Karen Black Jamie Farr	Charles Laughton George Sand Geneviève Bujold
2	Thurgood Marshall Robert Sarnoff	Arthur Treacher David Webb	Dan Rowan Cheryl Ladd
3	George M. Cohan Paul Anka George Sanders	Stravros Niarchos Earl Butz Michael Cole	Geraldo Rivera Pete Fountain
4	Neil Simon Tokyo Rose Garibaldi Louis B. Mayer Stephen Foster Virginia Graham George Murphy	Nathaniel Hawthorne George Steinbrenner Eva Marie Saint Pres. Calvin Coolidge Louis Armstrong Alec Templeton Mitch Miller	Rube Goldberg Gina Lollobrigida Ann Landers (Esther Pauline "Eppie" Friedman) Abigail "Dear Abby" Van Buren (Pauline Esther "Popo" Friedman)
5	Henry Cabot Lodge Mack David Katherine Helmond	Julie Nixon Eisenhower P. T. Barnum	Cecil Rhodes Jean Cocteau
6	Andrei Gromyko Merv Griffin Dorothy Kirsten Janet Leigh Sebastian Cabot	Emperor Maximilian John Paul Jones Nancy Reagan Ned Beatty Louis Bellson	Susan Ford Vance Sylvester Stallone Della Reese Bill Haley
7	Gustav Mahler Gian-Carlo Menotti William Kunstler Doc Severinson	Pierre Cardin Marc Chagall George Cukor Vittorio De Sica	Ringo Starr Leroy "Satchel" Paige Ezzard Charles
8	Nelson Rockefeller George Romney Walter Kerr Faye Emerson	Roone Arledge Steve Lawrence Billy Eckstine	Kim Darby John D. Rockefeller Count Ferdinand von Zeppelin
9	O. J. Simpson Ed Ames	Elias Howe Barbara Cartland	Lee Hazelwood
10	Jean Kerr John Calvin Saul Bellow Marcel Proust	Jimmy McHugh James Whistler David Brinkley Max Von Sydow	Fred Gwynne Eunice Kennedy Shriver Arlo Guthrie Sue Lyons
11	E. B. White Pres. John Quincy Adams	Yul Brynner	Tab Hunter

Cancer

JULY

12	Mark Hatfield Milton Berle Bill Cosby Van Cliburn	Julius Caesar Modigliani Andrew Wyeth Oscar Hammerstein	Henry David Thoreau Josiah Wedgewood George Eastman
13	Dave Garroway Cheech Marin	Sudie Bond Jack Kemp	Harrison Ford
14	Ingmar Bergman Irving Stone Pres. Gerald R. Ford Polly Bergen	John Chancellor Woody Guthrie Dale Robertson	Rosey Grier Pete Rose Terry-Thomas
15	Rembrandt Dorothy Fields Harding Lawrence	Alex Karras Clement Moore Linda Ronstadt	Barry Goldwater, Jr. Jim Dale Mother Cabrini
16	Jean Corot Sir Joshua Reynolds Ginger Rogers	Barbara Stanwyck Margaret Smith Court Mary Baker Eddy	Ronald Amundson Sonny Tufts
17	Phyllis Diller Isaac Bashevis Singer James Cagney Geo."Machine Gun" Kelly	Art Linkletter Eleanor Steber Diahann Carroll Lou Boudreau	Donald Sutherland Hardy Amies Erle Stanley Gardner Lucie Arnaz
18	Red Skelton John Glenn Hume Cronyn	Dick Button Chill Wills Harriet Hilliard Nelson	Joe Torre Dione Dimucci
19	George McGovern Duchess of Windsor Ilie Nastase	Edgar Degas A. J. Cronin Charles Horace Mayo	Vikki Carr Samuel Colt
20	Natalie Wood Diana Rigg	Tony Oliva Elliott Richardson	Sir Edmund Hillary
21	Isaac Stern Ernest Hemingway Francis Parkinson Keyes Marshall McLuhan	Robin Williams Don Knotts Kaye Stevens	Kay Starr Cat Stevens C. Aubrey Smith
22	Robert Dole Karl Menninger Amy Vanderbilt Rose Kennedy	Oscar De La Renta Alexander Calder Jason Robards, Jr. Orson Bean	Sparky Lyle Licia Albanese Raymond Chandler
23	Haile Selassie Vincent Sardi, Jr. Don Drysdale	Pee Wee Reese Gloria De Haven Bert Convy	Michael Wilding Harry Cohn

Leo

JULY

24	Bella Abzug Amelia Earhart	Alexandre Dumas Ruth Buzzi	Alex Cohen Simon Bolívar
25	Frank Church Thomas Eakins Walter Brennan	Erick Hoffer Stanley Dancer	Joseph Kennedy, Jr. Louise Brown (1st test tube baby)
26	George Bernard Shaw Gracie Allen Stanley Kubrick	Mick Jagger Carl Jung Dorothy Hamill	Blake Edwards Aldous Huxley Vitas Gerulaitis
27	Leo Durocher Keenan Wynn	Peggy Fleming Bobbie Gentry	Norman Lear
28	Jacques D'Amboise Sally Struthers Rudy Vallee Joe E. Brown	Harry Bridges Jacqueline Kennedy Onassis Peter Duchin	Vida Blue Bill Bradley David Brown
29	Sigmund Romberg Dag Hammarskjold Benito Mussolini	Melvin Belli Rasputin William Powell	Robert Horton Booth Tarkington
30	Emily Brontë Casey Stengel Henri Moore	Paul Anka Henry Ford	Edd "Kookie" Byrnes Peter Bogdanovich
31	Milton Friedman Evonne Goolagong Irv Kupcinet	Jean Dubuffet Ahmet Ertegun Curt Gowdy	Geraldine Chaplin Don Murray Hank Bauer

Leo

AUGUST

1	Yves St. Laurent Jack Kramer	Herman Melville Giancarlo Giannini	Francis Scott Key Robert Todd Lincoln
2	Jack Warner James Baldwin Myrna Loy	Peter O'Toole Westbrook Pegler	Linda Fratianne Carroll O'Connor
3	Leon Uris Dolores Del Rio Tony Bennett	Martin Sheen Rupert Brooke Ted Ashley	John Eisenhower Jay North Marilyn Maxwell
4	Percy Bysshe Shelley	Isaac Babbitt Cleon Jones	Queen Mother Elizabeth
5	John Huston Neil Armstrong Geraldine Stutz	Roman Gabriel Robert Taylor	Loni Anderson Guy de Maupassant
6	Lucille Ball Robert Mitchum Clara Bow	Franz Allers William B. Williams Louella Parsons	Alfred, Lord Tennyson Rosemary "the B. W." Wilson
7	Billie Burke Lana Cantrell Mata Hari	Ralph Bunche Dr. Louis Leakey Stan Freberg	B. J. Thomas Don Larson
8	Arthur Goldberg Rudi Gernreich Victor Young Andy Warhol	Dino De Laurentis Dustin Hoffman Sylvia Sidney Esther Williams	Connie Stevens Joan Mondale Larry Wilcox Mel Tillis
9	Rod Laver Bob Cousy Robert Shaw	Tom Agee Isaac Walton	Robert Aldrich David Steinberg
10	Jimmy Dean Herbert Hoover	Harry Richman Norma Shearer	Rhonda Fleming Eddie Fisher
11	Arlene Dahl Buddy Hackett Mike Douglas	Alex Haley Lyle Stuart Liz Holtzman	Lloyd Nolan Chuck Connors
12	Wilt Chamberlain George Hamilton Jane Wyatt Michael Kidd	Buck Owens Parnelli Jones Cecil B. DeMille	John Derek Diamond Jim Brady Christy Mathewson

Leo

AUGUST

13	Menachem Begin Alfred Hitchcock George Shearing	Ben Hogan Bert Lahr Alfred Krupp	Annie Oakley Fidel Castro Neville Brand
14	Russell Baker John Ringling North Wellington Mara Susan St. James	Earl Weaver Bricktop Buddy Greco	John Galsworthy Lina Wertmuller Robyn Smith
15	Napoleon Bonaparte Sir Walter Scott Bil Baird Signe Hasso Phyllis Schlafly Princess Anne Lillian Carter	Thomas Hart Benton Ethel Barrymore Jill Haworth Edna Ferber Lawrence of Arabia Mike Connors	Julia Child Robert Bolt Jim Webb Oscar Peterson Vernon Jordan, Jr. Wendy Hiller
16	George Meany Eydie Gormé	Frank Gifford Robert Culp	Fess Parker Ann Blyth
17	Orville Wright Mae West Maureen O'Hara	Larry Rivers Robert De Niro Boog Powell	Merriwether Lewis (Lewis and Clark) Davy Crockett Franklin D. Roosevelt, Jr.
18	Roman Polanski Rafer Johnson Robert Redford Ogden Nash	Shelley Winters Gus Edwards Otto Harbach Antonio Salieri	Roslyn Carter Roberto Clemente Caspar Weinberger Emperor Franz Joseph
19	Alfred Lunt Jill St. John Ogden Nash Willie Shoemaker	Bernard Baruch Coco Chanel Malcolm Forbes Debra Paget	Randi Oakes Madame Du Barry Orville Wright
20	Jackie Susann Pres. Benjamin Harrison	Isaac Hayes Paul Tillich	Graig Nettles
21	William "Count" Basie Princess Margaret	Kenny Rogers Carrie Fisher	Melvin Van Peebles
22	Claude Debussy Carl Yastrzemski Theonis V. Aldredge	Jacques Lipchitz William Bradbury Valerie Harper	Ray Bradbury Cindy Williams Honor Blackman
23	Louis XVI Gene Kelly Richard Adler	Vera Miles Tex Williams Barbara Eden	Bob Crosby Dorothy Parker

Virgo

AUGUST

24	Jorge Luis Borges Richard Cardinal Cushing	Monty Hall Preston Foster	Mason Williams
25	Carter Burden George C. Wallace Leonard Bernstein Mel Ferrer Willis Reed	Van Johnson Ruby Keeler Regis Philbin Sean Connery	Monty Hall Walt Kelly Ivan The Terrible
26	Dr. Albert Sabin Jay Pritzker Christopher Isherwood	Lee De Forest Prince Albert	Vic Dana Jan Clayton
27	Martha Raye Samuel Goldwyn Frank Leahy	Darryl Dragon Georg Hegel Pres. Lyndon B. Johnson	Tommy Sands Tuesday Weld
28	Richard Tucker Charles Boyer Ben Gazzara Bruno Bettelheim	Donald O'Connor Sam Levene Lou Piniella Mother Elizabeth Seton	Ron Guidry Wayne Osmond Goethe
29	Jean Ingres Ingrid Bergman Elliott Gould Mr. Blackwell	George Montgomery Barry Sullivan Dinah Washington Michael Jackson	Sir Richard Attenborough Oliver Wendell Holmes William Friedkin
30	Roy Wilkins Geoffrey Beene Joan Blondell Shirley Booth Fred MacMurray	Raymond Massey Tug McGraw Timothy Bottoms Regina Resnick	Jean Claude Killy Elizabeth Ashley Huey Long Donald O'Connor
31	Eldridge Cleaver William Saroyan Frank Robinson Ted Williams Caligula	Fredric March Alan Jay Lerner Arthur Godfrey Buddy Hackett	Maria Montessori Richard Basehart Dore Schary James Coburn

Virgo

SEPTEMBER

1	Lily Tomlin Rocky Marciano Yvonne De Carlo	Don Wilson Walter Reuther Edgar Rice Burroughs	Conway Twitty Barry Gibb
2	Jean Dalrymple Cleveland Amory	Joan Kennedy Jimmy Connors	Marge Champion Martha Mitchell
3	Kitty Carlisle Hart Alan Ladd, Sr. Valerie Perrine	Eddie Stanky Al Jardine	Chuck Glaser Tompall Glaser
4	Henry Ford II Mitzi Gaynor	Ken Harrelson	Senator Thomas Eagleton
5	Bob Newhart Darryl F. Zanuck Frank Yerby King Louis XIV	Arthur Nielsen Carol Lawrence John Mitchell	Raquel Welch Jesse James Jack Valenti
6	Billy Rose Joanne Worley Mike McCoy	Richard Barr Jane Addams	Joseph P. Kennedy Marquis De Lafayette
7	Dr. Michael DeBakey Queen Elizabeth I Elia Kazan	Taylor Caldwell Peter Lawford Anthony Quale	Buddy Holly Grandma Moses Richard Roundtree
8	Sid Caesar Anton Dvorak Peter Sellers	Howard Dietz Frankie Avalon Patsy Cline	King Richard I Penny Singleton
9	Cliff Robertson Frankie Frisch Sylvia Miles	Colonel Sanders Joseph E. Levine Leo Tolstoy	Rod Laver Alf Landon
10	Leonard Lyons Arnold Palmer Roger Maris	Fay Wray José Feliciano Charles Kuralt	Tommy Overstreet Jerome Bradshaw
11	D. H. Lawrence	Tom Landry Pres. Ferdinand Marcos	O. Henry Paul "Bear" Bryant
12	Alfred A. Knopf Terry Bradshaw Eddy Howard Maurice Chevalier	Tina Leser Cannonball Adderly Ben Blue	Henry Hudson Jesse Owens H. L. Mencken

Virgo

SEPTEMBER

13	Arnold Schoenberg Jacqueline Bisset Claudette Colbert Leonard Feather	Mel Tormé Eileen Fulton Leland Hayward Herbert Berghof	Dr. Walter Reed Gen. John J. Pershing Dick Haymes Barbara Bain
14	Kate Millett Margaret Sanger	Zoe Caldwell Ivan Pavlov	Joey Heatherton
15	Agatha Christie William Howard Taft Jackie Cooper	Bobby Short Robert Benchley	Gaylord Perry Roy Acuff
16	Lauren Bacall Peter Falk	J. C. Penney Allen Funt	Sir Alexander Korda Janis Paige
17	Warren Burger Anne Bancroft	Roddy McDowall John Ritter	Hank Williams, Sr. Ben Turpin
18	Greta Garbo Rossano Brazzi	Frankie Avalon Eddie "Rochester" Anderson	Robert Blake
19	Lewis Powell, Jr. Twiggy Joseph Pasternak Duke Snider	Blanche Thebom Clifton Daniel David McCallum	Adam West Leon Jaworski Brook Benton
20	James Galanos Sophia Loren	Rachel Roberts Upton Sinclair	Pia Lindstrom Alexander The Great
21	Larry Hagman H. G. Wells	Hamilton Jordan Artis Gilmore	Dickie Lee Leonard Cohen
22	John Houseman Erich Von Stroheim Martha Scott	Joe Valachi Tom Lasorda Debby Boone	Scott Baio Ingemar Johansson
23	Walter Lippman Louise Nevelson Mickey Rooney	Walter Pidgeon Ray Charles Romy Schneider	Bruce Springsteen Augustus Caesar

Libra

SEPTEMBER

24	F. Scott Fitzgerald Anthony Newley Cheryl Crawford	"Mean" Joe Green Linda McCartney Jim Henson	Eric Soderholm Jim McKay
25	Dmitri Shostakovich Barbara Walters Sheila MacRae Red Smith	Phil Rizzuto William Faulkner Cesare Borgia Mark Hamill	Christopher Reeve Michael Douglas Juliet Prowse Anson Williams
26	Pope Paul VI George Gershwin T. S. Eliot	George Raft Julie London	Olivia Newton-John Marty Robbins
27	Sam Ervin Sen. Charles Percy Louis Auchincloss	Vincent Youmans Arthur Penn Greg Morris	Jayne Meadows Shaun Cassidy William Conrad
28	Al Capp William S. Paley Brigitte Bardot Marcello Mastroianni	Elmer Rice Ed Sullivan Bonnie Cashin Peter Finch	Ben E. King Tom Harmon Confucius
29	Stanley Kramer Gene Autry Naura Hayden Anita Ekberg Cervantes Brenda Marshall	Greer Garson Trevor Howard Michelangelo Antonioni Lord Nelson Enrico Fermi	Madeline Kahn Lizabeth Scott Jerry Lee Lewis Mike Frankovich Beth Forcelledo
30	Lester Maddox Angie Dickinson Deborah Kerr	Truman Capote Johnny Mathis	Jody Powell Barry Williams

Libra

OCTOBER

1	William Rehnquist Vladimir Horowitz Pres. Jimmy Carter Faith Baldwin Julie Andrews	Walter Matthau George Peppard James Whitmore Rod Carew Bonnie Parker	Tom Bosley Laurence Harvey Edward Villella Stella Stevens
2	Mahatma Gandhi Graham Greene Rex Reed	Groucho Marx Clay Felker Hindenberg	Maury Wills Bud Abbott
3	Gore Vidal Pierre Bonnard Chubby Checker Gertrude Berg	Eleonora Duse Thomas Wolfe Leo McCarey James Darren	Emily Post Warner Oland Damon Runyon
4	Pres. Rutherford B. Hayes Charlton Heston Sam Huff	Jan Murray Susan Sarandon Buster Keaton	Pancho Villa LeRoy Van Dyke Felicia Farr
5	Phillip Berrigan Joshua Logan Pres. Chester A. Arthur	Bill Dana Glynis Johns	Jean Louis Steve Miller
6	Britt Ekland Shana Alexander Thor Heyerdahl	Jenny Lind Jack Sharkey	Carole Lombard George Westinghouse
7	Henry Wallace Leroi Jones Meyer Levin Janet Gaynor	Andy Devine Vaughn Monroe Alfred Drake June Allyson	Heinrich Himmler José Cardenal Al Martino Ralph Rainger
8	Rev. Jesse Jackson Dr. Christiaan Barnard	Eddie Rickenbacker Danny Murtaugh	Rona Barrett Chevy Chase
9	Aimee Semple McPherson John Lennon Sean Ono Lennon	Walter O'Malley John Entwistle	Freddie Patek Jackson Browne
10	Giuseppi Verdi Harold Pinter Tanya Tucker	Helen Hayes Vernon Duke	Johnny Green Thelonious Monk Adlai Stevenson, Jr.

Libra

OCTOBER

11	Joseph Alsop	Eleanor Roosevelt	Daryl Hall
	Jerome Robbins	Ron Leibman	Dottie West
	Charles Revson	King Richard III	
12	Dick Gregory	Joe Cronin	Brian Hyland
	Perle Mesta	Luciano Pavarotti	
	Tony Kubek		
13	Yves Montand	Paul Simon	Pamela Tiffin
	Herblock	Margaret Thatcher	Lenny Bruce
	Lillie Langtry	Demond Wilson	Burr Tillstrom
	Laraine Day	Marie Osmond	Anita Kerr
	Cornel Wilde	Eddie Mathews	
14	William Penn	Roger Moore	Allan Jones
	Dwight D. Eisenhower	Paul Muni	Hannah Arendt
	Lillian Gish	John Dean	
15	Arthur Schlesinger, Jr.	Lee Iacocca	Penny Marshall
	Mario Puzo	Mervyn Leroy	José Quintero
	P. G. Wodehouse	Linda Lavin	Richard Carpenter
	King Carol II	John Kenneth Galbraith	Jean Peters
	Friedrich Nietzsche	King James II	
16	David Ben Gurion	Eugene O'Neill	Dave De Busschere
	William O. Douglas	Linda Darnell	Suzanne Somers
	Oscar Wilde	Günter Grass	Noah Webster
	Angela Lansbury	Robert Ardrey	Bert Kaempfert
17	Arthur Miller	Jean Arthur	Irene Ryan
	Evel Knievel	Spring Byington	Margot Kidder
	Montgomery Clift	Pope Paul I	Jim Seals
	Vince Van Patten	Jimmy Breslin	Rita Hayworth
	Tom Poston		
18	Pierre Trudeau	George C. Scott	Martina Navratilova
	Lotte Lenya	Hilly Elkins	James Gaffney
	Melina Mercouri	Laura Nyro	
19	Jack Anderson	Jeannie C. Riley	George McCrae
	Amy Carter	Lyn Dickey	
20	Dr. Joyce Brothers	Herschel Bernardi	Jerry Orbach
	Art Buchwald	Arlene Francis	Bela Lugosi
	Stuart Hamblen	Mickey Mantle	Christopher Wren

Libra

OCTOBER

21	Georg Solti Dizzy Gillespie Whitey Ford Christopher Columbus	Carrie Fisher Samuel Taylor Coleridge Bill Russell	Michael Landon Jade Jagger Manfred Mann
22	Timothy Leary Franz Liszt Constance Bennett	Catherine Deneuve Joan Fontaine Sarah Bernhardt	Teresa Wright Annette Funicello Dore Previn
23	Johnny Carson Pelé	Jim Bunning Diana Dors	Adlai Euwing Stevenson

Scorpio

OCTOBER

24	Y. A. Tittle	David Nelson Bill Wyman	Jackie Coogan Chester Marcol
25	Georges Bizet Admiral Richard Byrd Pablo Picasso Barbara Cook	Johann Strauss Helen Reddy Tony Franciosa	Minnie Pearl Bobby Thompson Dave Cowens
26	Leon Trotsky Mahalia Jackson Shah of Iran (Mohammed Reza Pahlavi)	Sen. Edward Brooke P. M. Francois Mitterand	Jaclyn Smith Mike Hargrove
27	Niccolò Paganini C. L. Sulzberger Pres. Theodore Roosevelt Sylvia Plath	Ruby Dee Carrie Snodgress Kyle Rote	Ralph Kiner Nanette Fabray Roy Lichtenstein
28	Jonas Salk Bowie Kuhn Edith Head	James Cook Elsa Lanchester Jane Alexander	Erasmus Evelyn Waugh Suzy Parker
29	James Boswell Melba Moore Bill Mauldin	Fanny Brice Joseph Goebbels	Richard Dreyfuss Kate Jackson
30	Ruth Gordon Ezra Pound Henry Winkler	Gordon Parks Grace Slick Pres. John Adams	Mickey Rivers Christopher Columbus
31	Chiang Kai-Shek John Keats Barbara Bel Geddes Ethel Waters	Vermeer Dan Rather Michael Landon Lee Grant	Brian Piccolo Jane Pauley Dale Evans

Scorpio

NOVEMBER

1	Gary Player Stephen Crane	Betsy Palmer Grantland Rice	Larry Flynt Bill Anderson
2	Burt Lancaster Pres. James Polk	Pres. Warren G. Harding Marie Antoinette Luchino Visconti	Daniel Boone Benvenuto Cellini
3	James Reston Bob Feller Charles Bronson	Terrence McNally Lulu	Sen. Russell Long William Cullen Bryant
4	Martin Balsam Art Carney Walter Cronkite	Gig Young Pauline Trigère Loretta Swit	Bob Considine Will Rogers
5	Elke Sommer Eugene V. Debs Vivian Leigh	Tatum O'Neal Andrea McArdle Ike Turner	Roy Rogers Art Garfunkel
6	James Jones John Philip Sousa	Mike Nichols Sally Field	Ray Coniff John Candelaria
7	Joan Sutherland Marie Curie Billy Graham	Al Hirt Joni Mitchell Dean Jagger	Johnny Rivers Archie Campbell
8	Katherine Hepburn Alain Delon	June Havoc Patti Page	Bonnie Raitt
9	Spiro Agnew Sargent Shriver Ed Wynn Hedy Lamarr	Dorothy Dandridge King Edward VII Tom Weiskopf	Mary Travers Marie Dressler Bob Gibson
10	Mackenzie Phillips Richard Burton William Hogarth	Dave Loggins Martin Luther Friedrich Schiller	Roy Scheider Donna Fargo
11	Bibi Andersson Jonathan Winters Fyodor Dostoevsky Pat O'Brien	William Proxmire Kurt Vonnegut, Jr. René Clair Sam Spiegel	Robert Ryan Gen. George Patton Abigail Adams
12	Elizabeth Cady Stanton Harry Blackmun Nadia Comaneci	Richard Whiting Charles Manson Rodin Baha "U" Llah	Kim Hunter Princess Grace of Monaco Stephanie Powers

Scorpio

NOVEMBER

13	Louis Brandeis Linda Christian Nathaniel Benchley	Jean Seberg Robert Louis Stevenson	Hermione Baddeley Oskar Werner
14	Howard Baker Claude Monet Barbara Hutton Harrison E. Salisbury William of Orange Aaron Copland	St. Augustine Jawaharlal Nehru Dick Powell Mamie Eisenhower Morton Downey William Steig	Brian Keith Prince Charles Robert Fulton Jimmy Piersall McLean Stevenson King Hussein
15	Georgia O'Keefe Daniel Barenboim Averell Harriman	Gen. Rommel Ed Asner Petula Clark	Sam Waterston C. W. McCall Dave Clark
16	Eddie Condon Burgess Meredith George S. Kaufman	Emperor Tiberius Chi Coltrane	Jim "Fibber McGee" Jordan W. C. Handy
17	Rock Hudson Tom Seaver Billy Graham	Lee Strasberg Lauren Hutton Gene Clark	Dino Martin Gordon Lightfoot
18	Brenda Vaccaro George Gallup Eugene Ormandy	Dorothy Collins Alan Shepard	Johnny Mercer Paderewski
19	Jody Foster Roy Campanella Pres. James A. Garfield Dick Cavett	George Rogers Clark Tommy Dorsey Indira Gandhi Clifton Webb	King Charles I Calvin Klein Martin Luther
20	Emilio Pucci Robert F. Kennedy Estelle Parsons Alistair Cooke	Dick Smothers Kaye Ballard Judy Canova Bo Derek	Art Buchwald Sen. Robert Byrd Gene Tierney
21	Goldie Hawn Marlo Thomas Voltaire Stan Musial	Harpo Marx Jim Bishop Eleanor Powell Vivian Blaine	Martha Deane David Hemmings Hetty Green Georgia Frontieri
22	Geraldine Page Billie Jean King Doris Duke Charles De Gaulle	Benjamin Britten Hoagy Carmichael Rodney Dangerfield	George Eliot André Gide Robert Vaughn

Sagittarius

NOVEMBER

23	Charles Berlitz Pres. Franklin Pierce	Boris Karloff Jerry Bock	Billy The Kid Louis Tiant
24	Toulouse-Lautrec Pres. Zachary Taylor Martin Charnin	Howard Duff William F. Buckley, Jr. Garson Kanin	John V. Lindsay Father Junipero Serra Scott Joplin
25	Joe DiMaggio Pope John XXIII Arthur Schwartz Ricardo Montalban	Carry Nation Murray Schisgal Andrew Carnegie	John F. Kennedy, Jr. Kathryn Grant Crosby Spinoza
26	Eric Sevareid Charles Schulz Robert Goulet	Emlyn Williams Michael Butler Eugene Ionesco	Rich Little Tina Turner Jan Stenerud
27	Jimi Hendrix Alfred Gwynne Vanderbilt	David Merrick Caroline Kennedy	Bruce Lee Eddie Rabbit
28	Hope Lange William Blake Brooks Atkinson José Iturbi	Randy Newman Natalia Makarova Berry Gordy, Jr. Sen. James Eastland	Gloria Graham Anton Rubinstein Sen. Gary Hart
29	John Gary Adam Clayton Powell, Jr. Willie Morris David Reuben	Busby Berkeley Suzy Chaffee Tom Hayden	Chuck Mangione Louisa May Alcott Merle Travis
30	Efrem Zimbalist, Jr. Angier Biddle Duke Abbie Hoffman Shirley Chisholm Samuel "Mark Twain" Clements	Sir Winston Churchill Dick Clark Jonathan Swift Robert Guillaume Virginia Mayo	Joan Ganz Cooney Jacques Barzun June Pointer Richard Crenna

Sagittarius

DECEMBER

1	Bette Midler Woody Allen Lee Trevino Mary Martin	Charlene Tilton Cyril Ritchard Richard Pryor George Foster	Diane Lennon Walter Alston
2	Alexander Haig Walter Hoving Georges Seurat	Tracy Austin Julie Harris Adolph Green	Maggie Smith
3	Andy Williams Maria Callas	Jean-Luc Godard Joseph Conrad	Ferlin Husky
4	Robert Vesco Stewart Mott Pappy Boyington Lillian Russell	Rainer Maria Rilke Francisco Franco Jeff Bridges	Deanna Durbin Dennis Wilson Freddy Cannon
5	Otto Preminger Pres. Martin Van Buren Strom Thurmond	Walt Disney Nunnally Johnson Jim Plunkett	Little Richard Gen. George Custer
6	Lynn Fontanne Agnes Moorehead Ira Gershwin	Joyce Kilmer Dave Brubeck	Wally Cox "Baby Face" Nelson
7	Noam Chomsky Giovanni Lorenzo Bernini Eli Wallach Rudolf Friml Rod Cameron	Louis Prima Ted Knight Leonard Goldenson Harry Chapin Mary, Queen of Scots	Willa Cather Johnny Bench Ellen Burstyn Madame Tussaud
8	Flip Wilson Eli Whitney Adele Simpson Diego Rivera	John Rubinstein Maximillian Schell Jean Sibelius Greg Allman	Sammy Davis, Jr. David Carradine Jules Dassin
9	Thomas O'Neill John Milton Lee J. Cobb Hermione Gingold Joel Chandler Harris Dick Butkus	Broderick Crawford Kirk Douglas Douglas Fairbanks, Jr. Dina Merrill Beau Bridges Redd Foxx	Emmett Kelly Willie Hartack Dick Van Patten John Cassavetes Margaret Hamilton
10	Emily Dickinson Chet Huntley	Morton Gould Dorothy Lamour	Victor McLaglen Johnny Rodriguez

Sagittarius

DECEMBER

11	Carlo Ponti Hector Berlioz Rita Moreno	Jean-Louis Trintignant Brenda Lee	Jermaine Jackson Christina Onassis
12	Frank Sinatra Edward G. Robinson Paul Hornung	Bob Barker Dionne Warwick	Connie Francis John Osborne
13	Dick Van Dyke Carlos Montoya Christopher Plummer	Richard Zanuck Mary Todd Lincoln	Dick Haymes John Davidson
14	Margaret Chase Smith Patty Duke Astin Morey Amsterdam James Aubrey	Spike Jones Lee Remick Nostradamus Dan Dailey	King George VI Charlie Rich Jimmy Doolittle
15	Maxwell Anderson Gladys Shelley Kermit Bloomgarden	Emperor Nero Jerry Wallace Tim Conway	Alan Freed J. Paul Getty
16	Jane Austin Margaret Mead Liv Ullmann	Noel Coward Ludwig Van Beethoven	George Santayana George Schaefer
17	Samuel Crompton Arthur Fiedler	Erskine Caldwell	John Greenleaf Whittier
18	Keith Richards Ramsey Clark Paul Klee Abe Burroughs	John O. Hayden George Stevens Ty Cobb Ossie Davis	Willy Brandt Betty Grable Roger Smith
19	David Susskind Al Kaline Robert Urich Piaf	Ford Frick Charlotte Curtis Galt McDermot	Sir Ralph Richardson Cicely Tyson Leonid Brezhnev
20	Uri Geller Irene Dunne Ted Fiorito Paul Francis Webster	Sen. Harry Byrd Branch Rickey Hortense Calisher Max Lerner	Jenny Agutter Harvey Firestone Dr. Samuel Mudd
21	Benjamin Disraeli Joseph Stalin Kurt Waldheim Heinrich Böll	Michael Tilson Thomas Chris Evert Lloyd Jane Fonda	John Avildsen Thomas à Becket Joe Paterno

Capricorn

DECEMBER

22	Giacomo Puccini Jose Greco Lady Bird Johnson	André Kostelanetz Maurice Gibb Robin Gibb	Steve Garvey Steve Carleton
23	Eric Blore	Harry Guardino	Paul Hornung Dave May Connie Mack
24	Howard Hughes Ava Gardner	Harry Warren Kit Carson	Michael Curtiz Mike Curb
25	Anwar Sadat Sir Isaac Newton Conrad Hilton Rod Serling	Raphael Soyer Cab Calloway Tony Martin Gladys Swarthout	Larry Csonka Clara Barton Sissy Spacek Barbara Mandrell
26	Alan King Mao Tse-tung Henry Miller	Steve Allen Richard Widmark Doris Lilly	Carleton Fisk Phil Spector
27	Dr. William Masters Louis Pasteur Cyrus Eaton	Sidney Greenstreet Marlene Dietrich Oscar Levant	Dave Tebet Roy White
28	Sam Levenson Pres. Woodrow Wilson Maggie Smith	Earl "Fatha" Hines Lew Ayres Herb Gardner	Cliff "Charlie Weaver" Arquette Johnny Otis
29	Pablo Casals Madame de Pompadour Pres. Andrew Johnson	Gen. Billy Mitchell Mary Tyler Moore	Jon Voight William Gladstone
30	Sandy Koufax Jack Lord Marie Wilson	Rudyard Kipling Al Smith Bert Parks	Davey Jones Mike Nesmith
31	Nathan Milstein Diane Von Furstenberg Henri Matisse Jule Styne	Joe Dallesandro Sarah Miles Gen. George Marshall	Rex Allen Pola Negri John Denver

Capricorn

JANUARY

1	E. M. Forster J. D. Salinger Betsy Ross J. Edgar Hoover	Peter Beard Barry Goldwater Xavier Cugat Dana Andrews	Hank Greenberg Pope Alexander VI Clay Cole Paul Revere
2	Jack Nicklaus Rudolf Bing Isaac Asimov	Vera Zorina Julius La Rosa	Helen Taft Roger Miller
3	Betty Furness Ray Milland Anna Pavlova	Bobby Hull J. R. R. Tolkien Victor Borge	Victoria Principal Zasu Pitts
4	Everett Dirksen Jane Wyman Floyd Patterson Grace Bumbry	Don Shula Phyllis Battelle William Bendix Maureen Reagan	Dyan Cannon Louis Braille Barbara Rush
5	Alvin Ailey Konrad Adenauer Jean-Pierre Aumont	Robert Duvall Diane Keaton Jeanne Dixon	Zebulon Pike V. P. Walter Mondale
6	Danny Thomas Loretta Young Carl Sandburg Kahlil Gibran Joan Of Arc	Louis Harris Sam Rayburn Joey Adams Vic Tayback Capucine	John Lilly Earl Scruggs Tom Mix Nancy Lopez
7	Pres. Millard Fillmore Adolph Zukor	Vincent Gardenia Charles Addams	Terry Moore William Peter Blatty
8	José Ferrer Elvis Presley Sherman Adams Giorgio Tozzi	Peter Arno Little Anthony David Bowie Shirley Bassey	Soupy Sales Sander Vanocur Yvette Mimieux
9	Simone de Beauvoir Fernando Lamas Joan Baez	Crystal Gayle George Balanchine Susannah York	Pres. Richard M. Nixon John Ellsworth Hayden Bart Starr
10	Ray Bolger Willie McCovey Jim Croce Johnnie Ray	Paul Henreid Meyer Davis Rod Stewart Ethan Allen	Sal Mineo George Foreman Frank Sinatra, Jr. Francis X. Bushman

Capricorn

JANUARY

11	Rod Taylor Eva Le Gallienne	John Ericsson Alexander Hamilton	Tex Ritter
12	Patsy Kelly John Singer Sargent Jack London	José Limon Hermann Goering Luise Rainer	Drew Pearson Nijinsky Paul Revere
13	Gwen Verdon Robert Stack	Ralph Edwards Sophie Tucker	Garry Moore A. C. Fuller (brush)
14	Faye Dunaway Thomas Tryon Cecil Beaton Jack Jones	Yukio Mishima Julian Bond William Bendix	Joseph Losey Albert Schweitzer Russ Columbo
15	Lloyd Bridges Thomas P. Hoving Martin Luther King, Jr. Margaret O'Brien	Cy Feurer Gene Krupa Goodman Ace Molière	President Nasser Chuck Berry Aristotle Onassis
16	Marilyn Horne Dizzy Dean	Ethel Merman Eartha Kitt	Katy Jurado A. J. Foyt
17	James Earl Jones Joe Frazier	Benjamin Franklin Al Capone	Shari Lewis
18	Cary Grant Danny Kaye Oliver Hardy	Peter Mark Roget Daniel Webster Bobby Goldsboro	Sol Yurick Muhammad Ali
19	Paul Cézanne Edgar Allan Poe Jean Stapleton Janis Joplin	Robert E. Lee Richard Lester Dolly Parton	Desi Arnaz, Jr. Shelley Fabares Phil Everly
20	Patricia Neal Edwin "Buzz" Aldrin George Burns	Federico Fellini Leon Ames Joy Adamson	Ruth St. Denis Joan Rivers

Aquarius

JANUARY

21	Placido Domingo Mac Davis	Telly Savalas "Stonewall" Jackson	Gardner Cowles
22	George Balanchine Lord Byron Sen. Birch Bayh Piper Laurie Carl Hubbell	Bill Bixby Linda Blair Ray Anthony Sam Cooke D. W. Griffith	Harold Geneen Rosa Ponselle August Strindberg Ann Sothern Francis Bacon
23	Edouard Manet John Hancock Ernie Kovacs	Stendhal Jeanne Moreau Danny Arnold	Randolph Scott Humphrey Bogart Eisenstein
24	Ernest Borgnine Robert Motherwell Oral Roberts	Maria Tallchief Neil Diamond Desmond Morris	Frederick The Great John Belushi
25	Mildred Dunnock Edwin Newman Somerset Maugham	Virginia Woolf Robert Burns	Dean Jones Benedict Arnold
26	Paul Newman Angela Davis Gen. Douglas MacArthur	Jimmy Van Heusen Jules Feiffer	Roger Vadim Gabe Katzka
27	William Randolph Hearst, Jr. Wolfgang Amadeus Mozart Skitch Henderson Jerome Kern	Donna Reed Troy Donohue Samuel Gompers Kaiser Wilhelm II	Lewis Carroll Ross Bagdasarian Princess Caroline of Monaco Karon Cullen
28	Joseph Green Claes Oldenburg Mikhail Baryshnikov	Artur Rubinstein Alan Alda Colette	Ernst Lubitsch Barbi Benton
29	John Forsythe Pres. William McKinley Anton Chekov Claudine Longet	Paddy Chayevsky Frederick Delius Germaine Greer Victor Mature	W. C. Fields Thomas Paine Katherine Ross
30	Gene Hackman Vanessa Redgrave Pres. Franklin Delano Roosevelt	Barbara Tuchman Harold Prince John Ireland	David Wayne Tammy Grimes Dick Martin
31	Jean Simmons Norman Mailer Franz Schubert Eddie Cantor John O'Hara	Ernie Banks Jackie Robinson Carol Channing Suzanne Pleshette Jessica Walter	Mario Lanza Tallulah Bankhead Nolan Ryan Zane Grey

Aquarius

FEBRUARY

1	Victor Herbert S. J. Perelman Hildegarde	Clark Gable Langston Hughes Carroll Righter	John Ford Don Everly Stuart Whitman
2	Jascha Heifitz Charles Talleyrand James Joyce Tommy Smothers Gale Gordon	Burton Lane Anne Fogarty Elaine Stritch Farrah Fawcett	Havelock Ellis Christopher Marlowe Stan Getz Fritz Kreisler
3	Felix Mendelssohn James Michener Gertrude Stein Shelley Berman	Melanie Bob Griese Fran Tarkenton Norman Rockwell	Nick Kenny Charles Correll Joey Bishop Horace Greeley
4	Betty Friedan Erich Leinsdorf	Charles Lindbergh Ida Lupino	Alice Cooper
5	Adlai Stevenson Arthur Ochs Sulzberger Hank Aaron	Roger Staubach Craig Morton Red Buttons	Norton Simon John Carradine
6	Pres. Ronald Reagan François Truffaut Louis Nizer Mamie Van Doren	Rip Torn Zsa Zsa Gabor Fabian Claudio Arrau	Babe Ruth Natalie Cole Aaron Burr
7	Eubie Blake Buster Crabbe Jim Brown	Thomas More Eddie Bracken Keefe Brasselle	Sinclair Lewis Charles Dickens
8	Jack Lemmon Lana Turner James Dean	John Ruskin Dame Edith Evans Gary Coleman	Jules Verne Gen. William Tecumseh Sherman
9	Dean Rusk Pres. William Henry Harrison Mia Farrow Kathryn Grayson	Bill Veeck Gypsy Rose Lee Brian Donlevy Carole King	Roger Mudd Ernest Tubb Ronald Colman
10	Leontyne Price Mark Spitz Judith Anderson Jimmy Durante	Robert Wagner Allie Reynolds Lon Chaney, Jr.	Bill Tilden Roberta Flack Bertold Brecht

Aquarius

FEBRUARY

11	Joseph Mankiewicz Virginia Johnson Thomas Edison	Sergio Mendes Eva Gabor Burt Reynolds	Matt Dennis King Farouk Kim Stanley
12	Charles Darwin John L. Lewis Pres. Abraham Lincoln Lorne Greene	Bill Russell Joe Garagiola Ted Mack Gen. Omar Bradley	Forrest Tucker Joe Don Baker Franco Zeffirelli Alice Roosevelt Longworth
13	Joey Bishop Grant Wood Kim Novak Eileen Farrell	Bess Truman Patty Berg Georges Simenon Oliver Reed	Tennessee Ernie Ford George Segal Carol Lynley
14	Jack Benny James Hoffa Hugh Downs	Woody Hayes Carl Bernstein Mel Allen	Thelma Ritter Gregory Hines Florence Henderson
15	Galileo Galilei King Louis XV Harold Arlen Cesar Romero	Cyrus McCormick Adolfo Claire Bloom Walter Donaldson	John Barrymore Susan B. Anthony James R. Schlesinger
16	Katherine Cornell Edgar Bergen	Sonny Bono Patty Andrews	John McEnroe
17	Marian Anderson H. L. Hunt Hal Holbrook	Margaret Truman Daniels Red Barber	Alan Bates Arthur Kennedy
18	Andres Segovia Helen Gurley Brown Jack Palance Milos Forman Saint-Subber	Zero Mostel Queen Mary I John Travolta George Kennedy Cybill Shepherd	Yoko Ono Bill Cullen Adolphe Menjou Sen. John Warner
19	Eddie Arcaro Lee Marvin Merle Oberon Stan Kenton	Adelina Patti Carson McCullers Sir Cedric Hardwicke Mama Cass Elliot	Prince Andrew of England David Garrick Copernicus John Frankenheimer

Pisces

FEBRUARY

20	Gloria Vanderbilt Nancy Wilson Robert Altman C. V. "Sonny" Whitney Buffy Sainte-Marie	Alexei Kosygin Sandy Duncan Jennifer O'Neill Ansel Adams Edward Albert	Russell Crouse Mary Garden John Daly Amanda Blake Patty Hearst
21	Erma Bombeck Larry Hagman Zachary Scott Ann Sheridan	W. H. Auden Nina Simone Sam Peckinpah	Tricia Nixon Cox Prince Michael Romanoff Barbara Jordan
22	Sen. Edward M. Kennedy Arthur Schopenhauer John Mills David Dubinsky Luis Buñuel	Robert Young Frederic Chopin Pres. George Washington Roy Cohn William Seabrook	Edna St. Vincent Millay Charlie Finley Julius "Dr. J" Erving Albert "Cubby" Broccoli
23	George Frederick Handel Peter Fonda	Elston Howard, Sr. Samuel Pepys	Sally Victor
24	Sidney Poitier Honus Wagner	Marjorie Main Winslow Homer	James Farentino Michel Legrand
25	John Foster Dulles Enrico Caruso Renoir	Jim Backus Adelle Davis George Harrison	Zeppo Marx Jed Harris
26	Jackie Gleason Godfrey Cambridge Honoré Daumier Johnny Cash	Victor Hugo Tony Randall Betty Hutton Robert Alda	"Buffalo Bill" Cody Madeleine Carroll Fats Domino Tom Courtenay
27	John Connally Ralph Nader Irwin Shaw Franchot Tone John Steinbeck	Joan Bennett Elizabeth Taylor Joanne Woodward Marian Anderson	David "General" Sarnoff Peter De Vries Henry W. Longfellow Guy Mitchell
28	Vincente Minnelli Linus Pauling Zero Mostel Ben Hecht	Jo Copeland Molly Picon Gavin MacLeod	Bernadette Peters Mario Andretti Brian Jones
29	Jimmy Dorsey	Gioacchino Rossini	John Boyd Dunlop

Pisces

MARCH

1	David Niven Robert Lowell Harry Belafonte	Harry Winston Terence Cardinal Cooke Dinah Shore	Pete Rozelle Ron Howard Robert Conrad
2	Pope Pius XII Kurt Weill Jennifer Jones Desi Arnaz	Mel Ott Tom Wolfe Sam Houston	Karen Carpenter Jay Osmond Theodore "Dr. Seuss" Geisel
3	Alexander Graham Bell Jean Harlow	Lee Radziwill Julius Boros	Gen. Matthew Ridgeway
4	Charles Goren John Garfield	Paula Prentiss Chastity Bono	Barbara McNair Count Casimir Pulaski
5	Rex Harrison James Ives Samantha Eggar	King Henry II Dean Stockwell	Rocky Bleier Jack Cassidy
6	Ed McMahon John Fairchild Lefty Grove	Lou Costello Stephen Schwartz Merle Haggard	Rob Reiner Michelangelo Elizabeth Barrett Browning
7	Piet Mondrian Anna Magnani Franco Harris	Morton Da Costa Luther Burbank	Anthony Armstrong-Jones Maurice Ravel
8	Lynn Redgrave Sam Jaffee Cyd Charisse	Jim Bouton Claire Trevor Oliver Wendell Holmes	Mickey Dolenz Richie Allen Frances Whyatt
9	Mickey Spillane Thomas Schippers Edward Durell Stone Joyce Van Patten Irene Pappas	James Buckley Samuel Barber Keely Smith Arthur Goldberg	Leland Stanford Amerigo Vespucci Trish Van Devere Marty Ingals
10	Barry Fitzgerald Prince Edward	James Earl Ray Sherman Billingsley	Pamela Mason Bayard Rustin
11	Dorothy Schiff Ralph Abernathy Harold Wilson	Robert Paine "Johnny Appleseed" Chapman	Lawrence Welk Salvador Dali

Pisces

MARCH

12	Liza Minnelli Valery Panov Edward Albee Roger Stevens	Gordon MacRae Nijinsky James Taylor John Bainbridge	Gabrielle D'Annunzio Barbara Feldon Walter Schirra
13	Walter Annenberg Sammy Kaye	John A. Roosevelt Neil Sedaka	Joseph Priestly
14	Michael Caine Albert Einstein	Les Brown Prince Albert (Albert Grimaldi)	Frank Borman Casey Jones
15	Marjorie Merriweather Post Harry James George Brent	Judd Hirsch Lew Wasserman Michael Ford	Sly Stone Pres. Andrew Jackson
16	Pres. James Madison Mike Mansfield Daniel Patrick Moynihan	Pat Nixon Erik Estrada Rosa Bonheur	Bernardo Bertolucci Jerry Lewis Henny Youngman
17	Rudolf Nureyev Alfred Newman Sonny Werblin	Patrick Duffy Frederick Brisson Nat King Cole	Marquis Childs Mercedes McCambridge
18	Mollie Parnis Grover Cleveland George Plimpton Peter Graves Edgar Cayce	John Updike Nikolay Rimsky-Korsakov Neville Chamberlin Edward Everett Horton John C. Calhoun	Robert Donat Dane Clark Charley Pride Smiley Burnette Rudolf Diesel
19	Ursula Andress Philip Roth Irving Wallace Earl Warren	Sir Richard Burton Jo Mielziner William Jennings Bryan Adolf Eichmann	Wyatt Earp Lynda Bird Johnson David Livingstone
20	Hal Linden Bobby Orr Henrik Ibsen	Carl Reiner Lauritz Melchior Ozzie Nelson	Frank Stanton John Erlichman Michael Redgrave

Celebrity Birth Days

By Occupations and Professions

ACTORS AND PERSONALITIES
(Movies, TV and Theater)

Edie Adams—Apr. 16, 1929
Walter Abel—Jun. 6, 1898
Luther Adler—May 4, 1903
Jenny Agutter—Dec. 20, 1952
Brian Aherne—May 2, 1902
Anouk Aimée—Apr. 27, 1932
Claude Akins—May 25, 1918
Anna Maria Alberghetti—May 15, 1936
Eddie Albert—Apr. 22, 1908
Edward Albert—Feb. 20, 1951
Alan Alda—Jan. 28, 1936
Robert Alda—Feb. 26, 1914
Jane Alexander—Oct. 28, 1939
Fred Allen—May 31, 1894
Rex Allen—Dec. 31, 1922
Steve Allen—Dec. 26, 1921
June Allyson—Oct. 7, 1923
Don Ameche—May 31, 1908
Leon Ames—Jan. 20, 1903
Eddie "Rochester" Anderson—Sep. 18, 1905
Dame Judith Anderson—Feb. 10, 1898
Bibi Andersson—Nov. 11, 1933
Ursula Andress—Mar. 19, 1936
Dana Andrews—Jan. 1, 1909
Julie Andrews—Oct. 1, 1935
Fatty Arbuckle—May 24, 1887
Ann-Margret—Apr. 28, 1941
Eve Arden—Apr. 30, 1912
Alan Arkin—Mar. 26, 1934
George Arliss—Apr. 10, 1868
Desi Arnaz—Mar. 2, 1917
Desi Arnaz Jr.—Jan. 19, 1953
Lucie Arnaz—Jul. 17, 1951
James Arness—May 26, 1923
Cliff Arquette—Dec. 28, 1905
Beatrice Arthur—May 13, 1926
Jean Arthur—Oct. 17, 1905
Elizabeth Ashley—Aug. 30, 1939
Ed Asner—Nov. 15, 1929
John Astin—Mar. 30, 1930
Patty Duke Astin—Dec. 14, 1946
Mary Astor—May 3, 1906
Richard Attenborough—Aug. 29, 1923
René Auberjonois—Jun. 1, 1940
Jean-Pierre Aumont—Jan. 5, 1909
Gene Autry—Sep. 29, 1907
Lew Ayres—Dec. 28, 1908
Lauren Bacall—Sep. 16, 1924
Jim Backus—Feb. 25, 1913
Hermione Baddeley—Nov. 13, 1906
Carroll Baker—May 28, 1931
Joe Don Baker—Feb. 12, 1936
Josephine Baker—Jun. 3, 1906
Lucille Ball—Aug. 6, 1911
Martin Balsam—Nov. 4, 1919
Anne Bancroft—Sep. 17, 1931
Tallulah Bankhead—Jan. 31, 1903
Brigitte Bardot—Sep. 28, 1934
Rona Barrett—Oct. 8, 1936
Gene Barry—Jun. 14, 1921
Ethel Barrymore—Aug. 15, 1879
John Barrymore—Feb. 15, 1882
Lionel Barrymore—Apr. 28, 1878
Richard Basehart—Aug. 31, 1914
Alan Bates—Feb. 17, 1934
Anne Baxter—May 7, 1923
Warner Baxter—Mar. 29, 1891

ACTORS AND PERSONALITIES (Movies, TV and Theater) *(cont.)*

Ned Beatty—Jul. 6, 1937
Warren Beatty—Mar. 30, 1937
Wallace Beery—Apr. 1, 1885
Ed Begley—Mar. 21, 1901
Barbara Bel Geddes—Oct. 31, 1922
Ralph Bellamy—Jun. 17, 1904
Jean-Paul Belmondo—Apr. 9, 1933
John Belushi—Jan. 24, 1951
Turhan Bey—Mar. 30, 1920
William Bendix—Jan. 14, 1906
Richard Benjamin—May 22, 1938
Constance Bennett—Oct. 22, 1904
Joan Bennett—Feb. 27, 1910
Barbi Benton—Jan. 28, 1950
Candice Bergen—May 9, 1946
Edgar Bergen—Feb. 16, 1903
Polly Bergen—Jul. 14 1930
Helmut Berger—May 29, 1944
Ingrid Bergman—Aug. 29, 1915
Herschel Bernardi—Oct. 20, 1923
Sarah Bernhardt—Oct. 22, 1844
Theodore Bikel—May 2, 1924
Jacqueline Bisset—Sep. 13, 1944
Bill Bixby—Jan. 22, 1934
Karen Black—Jul. 1, 1942
Vivian Blaine—Nov. 21, 1921
Frank Blair—May 30, 1915
Janet Blair—Apr. 23, 1921
Linda Blair—Jan. 22, 1959
Amanda Blake—Feb. 20, 1931
Robert Blake—Sep. 18, 1933
Mel Blanc—May 30, 1908
Joan Blondell—Aug. 30, 1909
Claire Bloom—Feb. 15, 1931
Eric Blore—Dec. 23, 1887
Ann Blyth—Aug. 16, 1928
Dirk Bogarde—Mar. 29, 1921
Humphrey Bogart—Jan. 23, 1899
Ray Bolger—Jan. 10, 1904
Ward Bond—Apr. 9, 1903
Richard Boone—June 18, 1917
Shirley Booth—Aug. 30, 1907
Clara Bow—Aug. 6, 1905
Ernest Borgnine—Jan. 24, 1915
Timothy Bottoms—Aug. 30, 1950
Charles Boyer—Aug. 28, 1899
Eddie Bracken—Feb. 7, 1920
Marlon Brando—Apr. 3, 1924
Keefe Brasselle—Feb. 7, 1923
Rossanno Brazzi—Sep. 18, 1918
Walter Brennan—Jul. 25, 1894
George Brent—Mar. 15, 1904
Beau Bridges—Dec. 9, 1941
Jeff Bridges—Dec. 4, 1949
Lloyd Bridges—Jan. 13, 1913
David Brinkley—Jul. 10, 1920
Charles Bronson—Nov. 3, 1922
Joe E. Brown—Jul. 28, 1892
Yul Brynner—Jul. 11, 1915
Geneviève Bujold—Jul. 1, 1942
Billie Burke—Aug. 7, 1885
Raymond Burr—May 21, 1917
Ellen Burstyn—Dec. 7, 1932
Richard Burton—Nov. 10, 1925
Francis X. Bushman—Jan. 10, 1883
Ruth Buzzi—Jul. 24, 1936
Spring Byington—Oct. 17, 1892
Edd Byrnes—Jul. 30, 1933
James Caan—Mar. 26, 1940 (39)
Sebastian Cabot—Jul. 6, 1918
James Cagney—Jul. 1, 1899
Michael Caine—Mar. 14, 1933
Zoe Caldwell—Sep 14, 1933
Claudia Cardinale—Apr. 15, 1939
Kitty Carlisle (Hart)—Sep. 3, 1915
Judy Carne—Apr. 27, 1939
Art Carney—Nov. 4, 1918
Leslie Caron—Jul. 1, 1931
David Carradine—Dec. 8, 1936
John Carradine—Feb. 5, 1906
Diahann Carroll—Jul. 17, 1935
Madeleine Carroll—Feb. 26, 1906
Peggy Cass—May 21, 1925
John Cassavetes—Dec. 9, 1929
David Cassidy—Apr. 12, 1950
Jack Cassidy—Mar. 5, 1927
Shaun Cassidy—Sep. 27, 1958
Dick Cavett—Nov. 19, 1936
Richard Chamberlain—Mar. 31, 1935
John Chancellor—Jul. 14, 1927
Lon Chaney—Apr. 1, 1883
Lon Chaney, Jr.—Feb. 10, 1906
Carol Channing—Jan. 31, 1921
Charlie Chaplin—Apr. 16, 1889
Geraldine Chaplin—Jul. 31, 1944
Ilka Chase—Apr. 8, 1905
Cher—May 20, 1946
Maurice Chevalier—Sep. 12, 1888
Julie Christie—Apr. 14, 1941
Petula Clark—Nov. 15, 1932

ACTORS AND PERSONALITIES (Movies, TV and Theater) *(cont.)*

Jill Clayburgh—Apr. 30, 1944
Montgomery Clift—Oct. 17, 1920
Lee J. Cobb—Dec. 9, 1911 (8)
James Coburn—Aug. 31, 1928
James Coco—Mar. 21, 1929
Claudette Colbert—Sep. 13, 1907
Gary Coleman—Feb. 8, 1968
Charles Collingwood—Jun. 4, 1917
Joan Collins—May 23, 1933
Bud Collyer—Jun. 18, 1908
Ronald Colman—Feb. 9, 1891
Sean Connery—Aug. 25, 1930
Chuck Connors—Apr. 10, 1921
Mike Connors—Aug. 15, 1925
Robert Conrad—Mar. 1, 1935
Jackie Coogan—Oct. 24, 1914
Alistair Cook—Nov. 20, 1908
Barbara Cook—Oct. 25, 1927
Gary Cooper—May 7, 1901
Jackie Cooper—Sep. 15, 1922
Katherine Cornell—Feb. 16, 1898
Howard Cosell—Mar. 25, 1920
Joseph Cotten—May 15, 1905
Tom Courtenay—Feb. 26, 1937
Noel Coward—Dec. 16, 1889
Wally Cox—Dec. 6, 1924
Buster Crabbe—Feb. 7, 1908
Jeanne Crain—May 25, 1925
Broderick Crawford—Dec. 9, 1911
Joan Crawford—Mar. 23, 1904
Richard Crenna—Nov. 30, 1926
Walter Cronkite—Nov. 4, 1916
Hume Cronyn—Jul. 18, 1911
Bing Crosby—May 2, 1904
Robert Culp—Aug. 16, 1930
Bill Cullen—Feb. 18, 1920
Bob Cummings—Jun. 10, 1910
Tony Curtis—Jun. 3, 1925
Arlene Dahl—Aug. 11, 1928
Dan Dailey—Dec. 14, 1914
Jim Dale—Jul. 15, 1935
Joe D'Allesandro—Dec. 31, 1948
John Daly—Feb. 20, 1915
Linda Darnell—Oct. 16, 1923
Danielle Darrieux—May 1, 1917
Marion Davies—Jun. 3, 1897
Bette Davis—Apr. 5, 1908
Ossie Davis—Dec. 18, 1917
Dennis Day—May 21, 1917
Doris Day—Apr. 3, 1924
Laraine Day—Oct. 13, 1920
James Dean—Feb. 8, 1931
Yvonne DeCarlo—Sep. 1, 1922
Ruby Dee—Oct. 27, 1924
Sandra Dee—Apr. 23, 1942
Gloria deHaven—Jul. 23, 1924
Olivia De Havilland—Jul. 1, 1916
Alain Delon—Nov. 8, 1935
Dolores Del Rio—Aug. 3, 1905
Catherine Deneuve—Oct. 22, 1943
Robert DeNiro—Aug. 17, 1943
Sandy Dennis—Apr. 27, 1939
Bo Derek—Nov. 20, 1956
John Derek—Aug. 12, 1926
Bruce Dern—Jun. 4, 1936
Andy Devine—Oct. 7, 1905
Colleen Dewhurst—Jun. 3, 1926
Angie Dickinson—Sep. 30, 1931
Marlene Dietrich—Dec. 27, 1904
Brad Dillman—Apr. 14, 1930
Robert Donat—Mar. 18, 1905
Brian Donlevy—Feb. 9, 1899
Troy Donahue—Jan. 27, 1936
Diana Dors—Oct. 23, 1931
Kirk Douglas—Dec. 9, 1916
Melvyn Douglas—Apr. 5, 1901
Michael Douglas—Sep. 25, 1944
Mike Douglas—Aug. 11, 1925
Hugh Downs—Feb. 14, 1921
Alfred Drake—Oct. 7, 1914
Marie Dressler—Nov. 9, 1869
Richard Dreyfuss—Oct. 29, 1947
Howard Duff—Nov. 14, 1917
Keir Dullea—May 30, 1936
Faye Dunaway—Jan. 14, 1941
Sandy Duncan—Feb. 20, 1946
Irene Dunne—Dec. 20, 1904
Mildred Dunnock—Jan. 25, 1906
Jimmy Durante—Feb. 10, 1893
Deanna Durbin—Dec. 4, 1922
Eleanora Duse—Oct. 3, 1859
Robert Duvall—Jan. 5, 1931
Jeanne Eagles—Jun. 26, 1894
Clint Eastwood—May 31, 1930
Buddy Ebsen—Apr. 2, 1908
Nelson Eddy—Jun. 29, 1901
Barbara Eden—Aug. 23, 1934
Ralph Edwards—June 13, 1913
Samantha Eggar—Mar. 5, 1939
Anita Ekberg—Sep. 29, 1931

ACTORS AND PERSONALITIES (Movies, TV and Theater) *(cont.)*

Britt Ekland—Oct. 6, 1942
Faye Emerson—Jul. 8, 1917
Dale Evans—Oct. 31, 1912
Dame Edith Evans—Feb. 8, 1888
Maurice Evans—Jun. 3, 1901
Chad Everett—Jun. 11, 1936
Tom Ewell—Apr. 29, 1909
Shelley Fabares—Jan. 19, 1944
Nanette Fabray—Oct. 27, 1920
Clifton Fadiman—May 15, 1904
Douglas Fairbanks, Jr.—Dec. 9, 1909
Douglas Fairbanks, Sr.—May 23, 1883
Peter Falk—Sep. 16, 1927
James Farentino—Feb. 24, 1938
Felicia Farr—Oct. 4, 1932
Mia Farrow—Feb. 9, 1945
Farrah Fawcett—Feb. 2, 1946
Alice Faye—May 5, 1915
Barbara Feldon—Mar. 12, 1941
José Ferrer—Jan. 8, 1912
Mel Ferrer—Aug. 25, 1917
Sally Field—Nov. 6, 1946
W. C. Fields—Jan. 29, 1880
Peter Finch—Sep. 28, 1916
Albert Finney—May 9, 1936
Carrie Fisher—Oct. 21, 1956
Barry Fitzgerald—Mar. 10, 1888
Rhonda Fleming—Aug. 10, 1923
Errol Flynn—Jun. 20, 1909
Nina Foch—Apr. 20, 1924
Henry Fonda—May 16, 1905
Jane Fonda—Dec. 21, 1937
Peter Fonda—Feb. 23, 1939
Joan Fontaine—Oct. 22, 1917
Lynn Fontanne—Dec. 6, 1887
Glenn Ford—May 1, 1916
Harrison Ford—Jul. 13, 1942
Steve Ford—May 19, 1956
John Forsythe—Jan. 29, 1918
Jody Foster—Nov. 19, 1962
Arlene Francis—Oct. 20, 1912
David Frost—Apr. 7, 1939
Annette Funicello—Oct. 22, 1942
Betty Furness—Jan. 3, 1916
Clark Gable—Feb. 1, 1901
Eva Gabor—Feb. 11, 1924
Zsa Zsa Gabor—Feb. 6, 1920
Greta Garbo—Sep. 18, 1905
Ava Gardner—Dec. 24, 1922
Judy Garland—Jun. 10, 1922
James Garner—Apr. 17, 1928
David Garrick—Feb. 19, 1717
Dave Garroway—Jul. 13, 1913
Greer Garson—Sep. 29, 1908
John Gavin—Apr. 8, 1928
Janet Gaynor—Oct. 6, 1906
Mitzi Gaynor—Sep. 4, 1931
Ben Gazzara—Aug. 28, 1930
Giancarlo Giannini—Aug. 1, 1942
John Gielgud—Apr. 14, 1904
Melissa Gilbert—May 8, 1964
Hermione Gingold—Dec. 9, 1897
Lillian Gish—Oct. 14, 1896
Paulette Goddard—Jun. 3, 1911
Arthur Godfrey—Mar. 31, 1903
Ruth Gordon—Oct. 30, 1896
Louis Gossett, Jr.—May 27, 1937
Elliott Gould—Aug. 29, 1938
Betty Grable—Dec. 18, 1916
Princess Grace of Monaco—Nov. 12, 1929
Gloria Graham—Nov. 28, 1925
Virginia Graham—Jul. 4, 1912
Steward Granger—May 6, 1913
Cary Grant—Jan. 18, 1904
Kathryn Grant Crosby—Nov. 25, 1933
Lee Grant—Oct. 31, 1927
Peter Graves—Mar. 18, 1925
Kathryn Grayson—Feb. 9, 1921
Lorne Greene—Feb. 12, 1915
Joel Gray—Apr. 11, 1932
Merv Griffin—Jul. 6, 1925
Andy Griffith—Jun. 1, 1926
Tammy Grimes—Jan. 30, 1934
Charles Grodin—Apr. 21, 1935
Harry Guardino—Dec. 23, 1925
Alec Guinness—Apr. 2, 1914
Gene Hackman—Jan. 30, 1931
Monty Hall—Aug. 25, 1923
Mark Hamill—Sep. 25, 1952
George Hamilton—Aug. 12, 1939
Margaret Hamilton—Dec. 9, 1902
Oliver Hardy—Jan. 18, 1892
Sir Cedric Hardwicke—Feb. 19, 1883
Jean Harlow—March 3, 1911
Valerie Harper—Aug. 22, 1940
Julie Harris—Dec. 2, 1925
Phil Harris—Jun. 24, 1906
Mariette Hartley—Jun. 21, 1941
Rex Harrison—Mar. 5, 1908
David Hartman—May 19, 1937

ACTORS AND PERSONALITIES (Movies, TV and Theater) *(cont.)*

Laurence Harvey—Oct. 1, 1928
June Havoc—Nov. 8, 1916
Goldie Hawn—Nov. 21, 1945
Sterling Hayden—Mar. 26, 1916
Helen Hayes—Oct. 10, 1900
Susan Hayward—Jun. 30, 1917
Rita Hayworth—Oct. 17, 1919
Eileen Heckart--Mar. 29, 1919
David Hemmings—Nov. 18, 1941
Florence Henderson—Feb. 14, 1934
Sonja Henie—Apr. 8, 1913
Doug Henning—May 3, 1947
Paul Henreid—Jan. 10, 1908
Audrey Hepburn—May 4, 1929
Katharine Hepburn—Nov. 8, 1909
Charlton Heston—Oct. 4, 1923
Hildegarde—Feb. 1, 1906
Wendy Hiller—Aug. 15, 1912
Gregory Hines—Feb. 14, 1946
Dustin Hoffman—Aug. 8, 1937
Hal Holbrook—Feb. 17, 1925
William Holden—Apr. 17, 1918
Judy Holliday—Jun. 21, 1921
Celeste Holm—Apr. 29, 1919
Dennis Hopper—May 17, 1936
Edward Everett Horton—Mar. 18, 1887
Harry Houdini—Mar. 24, 1874
John Houseman—Sep. 22, 1902
Leslie Howard—Apr. 24, 1893
Ron Howard—Mar. 1, 1954
Trevor Howard—Sep. 29, 1916
Rock Hudson—Nov. 17, 1925
Kim Hunter—Nov. 12, 1922
Tab Hunter—Jul. 1, 1931
Chet Huntley—Dec. 10, 1911
Walter Huston—Apr. 6, 1884
Betty Hutton—Feb. 26, 1921
Lauren Hutton—Nov. 17, 1943
Jill Ireland—Apr. 24, 1936
Glenda Jackson—May 9, 1936
Kate Jackson—Oct. 29, 1948
Sam Jaffe—Mar. 8, 1897
David Janssen—Mar. 27, 1930
Van Johnson—Aug. 25, 1916
Al Jolson—Mar. 26, 1886
Carolyn Jones—Mar. 28, 1933
Dean Jones—Jan. 25, 1933
James Earl Jones—Jan. 17, 1931
Jennifer Jones—Mar. 2, 1919
Shirley Jones—Mar. 31, 1934
Tom Jones—Jun. 7, 1940
Madeline Kahn—Sep. 29, 1942
Boris Karloff—Nov. 23, 1887
Danny Kaye—Jan. 18, 1913
Stacy Keach—Jun. 2, 1941
Diane Keaton—Jan. 5, 1946
Howard Keel—Apr. 13, 1917
Ruby Keeler—Aug. 25, 1909
Brian Keith—Nov. 14, 1921
Sally Kellerman—Jun. 2, 1938
Emmett Kelly—Dec. 9, 1898
Patsy Kelly—Jan. 12, 1910
Arthur Kennedy—Feb. 17, 1914
George Kennedy—Feb. 18, 1925
Deborah Kerr—Sep. 30, 1921
Margot Kidder—Oct. 17, 1948
Richard Kiley—Mar. 31, 1922
Jack Klugman—Apr. 27, 1922
Evel Knievel—Oct. 17, 1938
Alan Ladd—Sep. 3, 1913
Cheryl Ladd—Jul. 2, 1951
Bert Lahr—Aug. 13, 1895
Hedy Lamarr—Nov. 9, 1913
Fernando Lamas—Jan. 9, 1920
Dorothy Lamour—Dec. 10, 1914
Burt Lancaster—Nov. 2, 1913
Elsa Lanchester—Oct. 28, 1902
Michael Landon—Oct. 21, 1937
Hope Lange—Nov. 28, 1933
Lillie Langtry—Oct. 13, 1853
Angela Lansbury—Oct. 16, 1925
Charles Laughton—Jul. l, 1899
Piper Laurie—Jan. 22, 1932
Peter Lawford—Sep. 7, 1921
Cloris Leachman—Apr. 30, 1926
Christopher Lee—May 27, 1922
Gypsy Rose Lee—Feb. 9, 1914
Vivian Leigh—Nov. 5, 1913
Jack Lemmon—Feb. 8, 1925
Lotte Lenya—Oct. 18, 1898
Sam Levene—Aug 28, 1905
Shari Lewis—Jan. 17, 1934
Ted Lewis—Jun. 6, 1891
Beatrice Lillie—May 29, 1898
Doris Lilly—Dec. 26, 1926
Hal Linden—Mar. 20, 1931
Art Linkletter—Jul. 17, 1912
Harold Lloyd—Apr. 20, 1894
Gina Lollobrigida—Jul. 4, 1927
Carole Lombard—Oct. 6, 1908

ACTORS AND PERSONALITIES (Movies, TV and Theater) *(cont.)*

Julie London—Sep. 26, 1926
Jack Lord—Dec. 30, 1928
Sophia Loren—Sep. 20, 1934
Peter Lorre—Jun. 26, 1904
Myrna Loy—Aug. 2, 1905
Bela Lugosi—Oct. 20, 1882
Alfred Lunt—Aug. 19, 1892
Ida Lupino—Feb. 4, 1918
Carol Lynley—Feb. 13, 1942
Jeanette MacDonald—Jun. 18, 1901
Malcolm MacDowell—Jun. 15, 1943
Ali MacGraw—Apr. l, 1939
Shirley MacLaine—Apr. 24, 1934
Fred MacMurray—Aug. 30, 1908
Gordon MacRae—Mar. 12, 1921
Bill Macy—May 18, 1922
Anna Magnani—Mar. 7, 1908
Lee Majors—Apr. 23, 1942
Karl Malden—Mar. 22, 1913
Jayne Mansfield—Apr. 19, 1933
Marcel Marceau—Mar. 22, 1923
Fredric March—Aug. 31, 1897
E. G. Marshall—Jun. 18, 1919
Penny Marshall—Oct. 15, 1942
Dean Martin—Jun. 17, 1917
Mary Martin—Dec. 1, 1913
Lee Marvin—Feb. 19, 1924
James Mason—May 15, 1909
Pamela Mason—Mar. 10, 1918
Raymond Massey—Aug. 30, 1896
Marcello Mastroianni—Sep. 28, 1924
Walter Matthau—Oct. 1, 1920
Victor Mature—Jan. 29, 1916
Elaine May—Apr. 21, 1932
Virginia Mayo—Nov. 30, 1920
Andrea McArdle—Nov. 5, 1963
Mercedes McCambridge—Mar. 17, 1918
Hattie McDaniel—Jun. 10, 1893
Roddy McDowell—Sep. 17, 1928
Darren McGavin—May 7, 1922
Alec McGowen—May 26, 1925
Dorothy McGuire—Jun. 14, 1919
Siobhan McKenna—May 24, 1923
Victor McLaglen—Dec. 10, 1886
Ed McMahon—Mar. 6, 1923
Steve McQueen—Mar. 24, 1930
Jayne Meadows—Sep. 27, 1923
Adolphe Menjou—Feb. 18, 1890
Melina Mercouri—Oct. 18, 1925
Ethel Merman—Jan. 16, 1909
Dina Merrill—Dec. 9, 1925
Bette Midler—Dec. 1, 1945
Sarah Miles—Dec. 31, 1943
Sylvia Miles—Sep. 9, 1932
Vera Miles—Aug. 23, 1929
Ray Milland—Jan. 3, 1907
Ann Miller—Apr. 12, 1919
Hayley Mills—Apr. 18, 1946
John Mills—Feb. 22, 1908
Yvette Mimieux—Jan. 8, 1941
Sal Mineo—Jan. 10, 1939
Liza Minnelli—Mar. 12, 1946
Robert Mitchum—Aug. 6, 1917
Marilyn Monroe—Jun. 1, 1926
Ricardo Montalban—Nov. 25, 1920
Yves Montand—Oct. 13, 1921
Elizabeth Montgomery—Apr. 15, 1933
Dudley Moore—Apr. 19, 1935
Garry Moore—Jan. 13, 1915
Mary Tyler Moore—Dec. 29, 1937
Melba Moore—Oct. 29, 1945
Roger Moore—Oct. 14, 1927
Terry Moore—Jan. 7, 1929
Agnes Moorehead—Dec. 6, 1906
Jeanne Moreau—Jan. 23, 1928
Rita Moreno—Dec. 11, 1931
Michael Moriarity—Apr. 5, 1941
Greg Morris—Sep. 27, 1934
Robert Morse—May 18, 1931
Zero Mostel—Feb. 28, 1915
George Murphy—Jul. 4, 1902
Roger Mudd—Feb. 9, 1929
Edward R. Murrow—Apr. 25, 1908
Jim Nabors—Jun. 12, 1932
Patricia Neal—Jan. 20, 1926
Pola Negri—Dec. 31, 1894
Anthony Newley—Sep. 24, 1931
Edwin Newman—Jan. 25, 1919
Paul Newman—Jan. 26, 1925
Wayne Newton—Apr. 3, 1944
Jack Nicholson—Apr. 22, 1937
Leonard Nimoy—Mar. 25, 1931
David Niven—Mar. 1, 1910
Kim Novak—Feb. 13, 1933
Merle Oberon—Feb. 19, 1911
Hugh O'Brian—Apr. 19, 1925
Margaret O'Brien—Jan. 15, 1937
Pat O'Brien—Nov. 11, 1899
Arthur O'Connell—Mar. 29, 1908
Carroll O'Connor—Aug. 2, 1925

ACTORS AND PERSONALITIES (Movies, TV and Theater) *(cont.)*

Donald O'Connor—Aug. 30, 1925
Maureen O'Hara—Aug. 17, 1921
Laurence Olivier—May 22, 1907
Ryan O'Neal—Apr. 20, 1941
Tatum O'Neal—Nov. 5, 1963
Jennifer O'Neill—Feb. 20, 1948
Jerry Orbach—Oct. 20, 1935
Peter O'Toole—Aug. 2, 1933
Jack Paar—May 1, 1918
Al Pacino—Apr. 25, 1940
Geraldine Page—Nov. 22, 1924
Jack Palance—Feb. 18, 1919
Lilli Palmer—May 24, 1914
Fess Parker—Aug. 16, 1927
George Peppard—Oct. 1, 1928
Anthony Perkins—Apr. 4, 1932
Mackenzie Phillips—Nov. 10, 1959
Mary Pickford—Apr. 8, 1893
Molly Picon—Feb. 28, 1898
Walter Pidgeon—Sep. 23, 1897
Zasu Pitts—Jan. 3, 1898
Suzanne Pleshette—Jan. 31, 1937
Christopher Plummer—Dec. 13, 1927
Sidney Poitier—Feb. 24, 1920
Paula Prentiss—Mar. 4, 1939
Robert Preston—Jun. 8, 1919
Dick Powell—Nov. 14, 1904
Eleanor Powell—Nov. 21, 1912
Jane Powell—Apr. 1, 1929
William Powell—Jul. 29, 1892
Tyrone Power—May 5, 1913
Stephanie Powers—Nov. 12, 1942
Vincent Price—May 27, 1911
Freddie Prinz—Jun 22, 1954
Richard Pryor—Dec. 1, 1940
Anthony Quayle—Sep. 7, 1913
Anthony Quinn—Apr. 21, 1915
George Raft—Sep. 26, 1895
Luise Rainer—Jan. 12, 1910
Tony Randall—Feb. 26, 1920
Basil Rathbone—June 13, 1892
Harry Reasoner—Apr. 17, 1923
Robert Redford—Aug. 18, 1937
Lynn Redgrave—Mar. 8, 1943
Michael Redgrave—Mar. 20, 1908
Vanessa Redgrave—Jan. 30, 1937
Donna Reed—Jan. 27, 1921
Oliver Reed—Feb. 13, 1938
Rex Reed—Oct. 2, 1939
Lee Remick—Dec. 14, 1935
Burt Reynolds—Feb. 11, 1936
Debbie Reynolds—Apr. 1, 1932
Sir Ralph Richardson—Dec. 19, 1902
Diana Rigg—Jul. 20, 1938
Cyril Ritchard—Dec. 1, 1898
John Ritter—Sep. 17, 1948
Tex Ritter—Jan 11, 1907
Thelma Ritter—Feb. 14, 1905
Geraldo Rivera—Jul. 3, 1943
Jason Robards, Jr.—Jul. 22, 1922
Rachel Roberts—Sep. 20, 1927
Cliff Robertson—Sep. 9, 1925
Edward G. Robinson—Dec. 12, 1893
Ginger Rogers—Jul. 16, 1911
Will Rogers—Nov. 4, 1879
Cesar Romero—Feb. 15, 1907
Mickey Rooney—Sep. 23, 1920
Katherine Ross—Jan. 29, 1942
Gena Rowlands—Jun. 19, 1934
John Rubinstein—Dec. 8, 1946
Jane Russell—Jun. 4, 1911
Lillian Russell—Dec. 4, 1861
Rosalind Russell—Jun. 4, 1911
Irene Ryan—Oct. 17, 1903
Robert Ryan—Nov. 11, 1913
Eva Marie Saint—Jul. 4, 1924
Susan St. James—Aug. 14, 1946
Jill St. John—Aug. 19, 1940
George Sanders—Jul. 3, 1906
Susan Sarandon—Oct. 4, 1946
Telly Savalas—Jan. 21, 1925
Maximillian Schell—Dec. 8, 1930
Romy Schneider—Sep. 23, 1938
George C. Scott—Oct. 18, 1927
Lizabeth Scott—Sep. 29, 1922
Randolph Scott—Jan. 23, 1903
Zachary Scott—Feb. 21, 1914
Jean Seberg—Nov. 13, 1938
George Segal—Feb. 13, 1934
Peter Sellers—Sep. 8, 1925
Eric Sevareid—Nov. 26, 1912
Omar Sharif—Apr. 10, 1932
William Shatner—Mar. 22, 1931
Robert Shaw—Aug. 9, 1927
Norma Shearer—Aug. 10, 1905
Martin Sheen—Aug. 3, 1940
Cybill Shepherd—Feb. 18, 1950
Ann Sheridan—Feb. 21, 1915
Dinah Shore—Mar. 1, 1917
Sylvia Sidney—Aug. 8, 1910

ACTORS AND PERSONALITIES (Movies, TV and Theater) *(cont.)*

Simone Signoret—Mar. 25, 1921
Jean Simmons—Jan. 31, 1929
Frank Sinatra—Dec. 12, 1917
Penny Singleton—Sep. 8, 1908
Cornelia Otis Skinner—May 30, 1901
Walter Slezak—May 3, 1902
Alexis Smith—Jun. 8, 1921
Howard K. Smith—May 12, 1914
Jaclyn Smith—Oct. 26, 1945
Kate Smith—May 1, 1909
Maggie Smith—Dec. 28, 1934
Dick Smothers—Nov. 20, 1938
Tommy Smothers—Feb. 2, 1937
Tom Snyder—May 12, 1936
Elke Sommer—Nov. 5, 1940
Suzanne Somers—Oct. 16, 1946
Ann Sothern—Jan. 22, 1909
Sissy Spacek—Dec. 25, 1949
Robert Stack—Jan. 13, 1919
Sylvester Stallone—Jul. 6, 1946
Kim Stanley—Feb. 11, 1925
Barbara Stanwyck—Jul. 16, 1907
Jean Stapleton—Jan. 19, 1923
Maureen Stapleton—Jun. 21, 1925
Rod Steiger—Apr. 14, 1925
James Stewart—May 20, 1908
Stella Stevens—Oct. 1, 1936
Gale Storm—Apr. 5, 1922
Lee Strasberg—Nov. 17, 1901
Susan Strasberg—May 22, 1928
Meryl Streep—Jun. 22, 1949
Barbra Streisand—Apr. 24, 1942
Sally Struthers—Jul. 28, 1948
Margaret Sullavan—May 16, 1911
Barry Sullivan—Aug. 29, 1912
Ed Sullivan—Sep. 28, 1902
Donald Sutherland—Jul. 17, 1934
Gloria Swanson—Mar. 27, 1899
John Cameron Swayze—Apr. 4, 1906
Norma Talmadge—May 26, 1897
Jessica Tandy—Jun. 7, 1909
Elizabeth Taylor—Feb. 27, 1932
Robert Taylor—Aug. 5, 1911
Rod Taylor—Jan. 11, 1930
Shirley Temple (Black)—Apr. 23, 1928
Danny Thomas—Jan. 6, 1914
Lowell Thomas—Apr. 6, 1892
Marlo Thomas—Nov. 21, 1938
Richard Thomas—Jun. 15, 1951
Gene Tierney—Nov. 20, 1920
Charlene Tilton—Dec. 1, 1958
Lily Tomlin—Sep. 1, 1936
Franchot Tone—Feb. 27, 1903
Rip Torn—Feb. 6, 1931
Spencer Tracy—Apr. 5, 1900
John Travolta—Feb. 18, 1954
Arthur Treacher—Jul. 2, 1894
Claire Trevor—Mar. 8, 1909
Jean-Louis Trintignant—Dec. 11, 1930
Forrest Tucker—Feb. 12, 1919
Sonny Tufts—Jul. 16, 1911
Lana Turner—Feb. 8, 1920
Twiggy (Leslie Hornby)—Sep. 19, 1949
Cicely Tyson—Dec. 19, 1932
Leslie Uggams—May 25, 1943
Liv Ullmann—Dec. 16, 1939
Peter Ustinov—Apr. 16, 1921
Brenda Vaccaro—Nov. 18, 1939
Rudolph Valentino—May 6, 1895
Rudy Vallee—Jul. 28, 1901
Trish Van DeVere—Mar. 9, 1945
Mamie Van Doren—Feb. 6, 1933
Dick Van Dyke—Dec. 13, 1925
Dick Van Patten—Dec. 9, 1928
Joyce Van Patten—Mar. 9, 1934
Vince Van Patten—Oct. 17, 1957
Melvin Van Peebles—Aug. 21, 1932
Sander Vanocur—Jan. 8, 1928
Robert Vaughn—Nov. 22, 1932
Gwen Verdon—Jan. 13, 1925
Jon Voight—Dec. 29, 1938
Erich Von Stroheim—Sep. 22, 1885
Max Von Sydow—Jul. 10, 1929
Lindsay Wagner—Jun. 22, 1949
Robert Wagner—Feb. 10, 1930
Nancy Walker—May 10, 1922
Mike Wallace—May 9, 1918
Eli Wallach—Dec. 7, 1915
Barbara Walters—Sep. 25, 1931
Ruth Warrick—Jun. 29, 1915
Ethel Waters—Oct. 31, 1900
Sam Waterston—Nov. 15, 1940
David Wayne—Jan. 30, 1914
John Wayne—May 26, 1907
Dennis Weaver—Jun. 4, 1924
Clifton Webb—Nov. 19, 1891
Jack Webb—Apr. 2, 1920
Johnny Weissmuller—Jan. 2, 1904
Raquel Welch—Sep. 5, 1940
Tuesday Weld—Aug. 27, 1943

ACTORS AND PERSONALITIES (Movies, TV and Theater) *(cont.)*

Orson Welles—May 6, 1915
Oskar Werner—Nov. 13, 1922
Mae West—Aug. 17, 1892
Stuart Whitman—Feb. 1, 1929
Richard Widmark—Dec. 26, 1914
Cornel Wilde—Oct. 13, 1915
Gene Wilder—Jun. 11, 1935
Andy Williams—Dec. 3, 1928
Anson Williams—Sep. 25, 1948
Billy Dee Williams—Apr. 6, 1937
Cindy Williams—Aug. 22, 1947
Emlyn Williams—Nov. 26, 1905
Esther Williams—Aug. 8, 1923
Don Wilson—Sep. 1, 1900
Marie Wilson—Dec. 30, 1917
Walter Winchell—Apr. 7, 1897
Shelley Winters—Aug. 18, 1922
Natalie Wood—Jul. 20, 1938
Joanne Woodward—Feb. 27, 1930
Fay Wray—Sep. 10, 1907
Jane Wyatt—Aug. 12, 1912
Jane Wyman—Jan. 4, 1914
Keenan Wynn—Jul. 27, 1916
Michael York—Mar. 27, 1942
Susannah York—Jan. 9, 1942
Gig Young—Nov. 4, 1913
Loretta Young—Jan. 6, 1913
Robert Young—Feb. 22, 1907
Efram Zimbalist, Jr.—Nov. 30, 1918

ARTISTS

Thomas Hart Benton—Aug. 15, 1889
Giovanni Lorenzo Bernini—Dec. 7, 1598
William Blake—Nov. 28, 1757
Rosa Bonheur—Mar. 16, 1822
Pierre Bonnard—Oct. 3, 1867
Georges Braque—May 13, 1882
Alexander Calder—Jul. 22, 1898
Mary Cassatt—May 22, 1845
Paul Cézanne—Jan. 19, 1839
Marc Chagall—Jul. 7, 1887
Jean Corot—Jul. 16, 1796
Nathaniel Currier—Mar. 27, 1813
Salvador Dali—Mar. 11, 1904
Honoré Daumier—Feb. 26, 1808
Leonardo Da Vinci—Apr. 1452
Edgar Degas—Jul. 19, 1834
William de Kooning—Apr. 24, 1904
Eugène Delacroix—Apr. 28, 1798
Jean Dubuffet—Jul. 31, 1901
Thomas Eakins—Jul. 25, 1844
Max Ernst—Apr. 2, 1891
Jean Fragonard—Apr. 5, 1732
Thomas Gainsborough—May 14, 1727
Paul Gauguin—Jun. 7, 1848
Francisco Goya—Mar. 30, 1746
William Hogarth—Nov. 10, 1697
Winslow Homer—Feb. 24, 1836
Jean Ingres—Aug. 29, 1780
James Ives—Mar. 5, 1824
Jasper Johns—May 15, 1930
Paul Klee—Dec. 18, 1879
Roy Lichtenstein—Oct. 27, 1923
Jacques Lipchitz—Aug. 22, 1891
Edouard Manet—Jan. 23, 1832
Marisol—May 22, 1930
Henri Matisse—Dec. 31, 1869
Michelangelo (Buonarroti)—Mar. 6, 1475
Joan Miró—Apr. 20, 1893
Amedeo Modigliani—Jul. 12, 1884
Piet Mondrian—Mar. 7, 1872
Claude Monet—Nov. 14, 1840
Henri Moore—Jul. 30, 1898
Grandma Moses—Sep. 7, 1860
Robert Motherwell—Jan. 24, 1915
Louise Nevelson—Sep. 23, 1900
Georgia O'Keefe—Nov. 15, 1887
Claes Oldenburg—Jan. 28, 1929
Pablo Picasso—Oct. 25, 1881
Raphael (Sanzio)—Apr. 6, 1483
Rembrandt (Van Rijn)—Jul. 15, 1606
Auguste Renoir—Feb. 25, 1841
Sir Joshua Reynolds—Jul. 16, 1723
Diego Rivera—Dec. 8, 1886
Larry Rivers—Aug. 17, 1923
Norman Rockwell—Feb. 3, 1894
Georges Rouault—May 27, 1871
Henri Rousseau—May 20, 1844
Peter Paul Rubens—Jun. 29, 1577
John Singer Sargent—Jan. 12, 1856
Georges Seurat—Dec. 2, 1859

ARTISTS *(cont.)*

Raphael Soyer—Dec. 25, 1899
Saul Steinberg—Jun. 15, 1914
Toulouse-Lautrec—Nov. 24, 1864
Sir Anthony Van Dyck—Mar. 22, 1599
Vincent Van Gogh—Mar. 30, 1853
Diego Velasquez—Jun. 6, 1599
Vermeer—Oct. 31, 1632
Andy Warhol—Aug. 8, 1927
James Whistler—Jul. 10, 1834
Grant Wood—Feb. 13, 1891
Andrew Wyeth—Jul. 12, 1917

COMEDIANS

Bud Abbot—Oct. 2, 1898
Don Adams—Apr. 19, 1927
Joey Adams—Jan. 6, 1912
Gracie Allen—Jul. 26, 1902
Marty Allen—Mar. 23, 1930
Steve Allen—Dec. 26, 1921
Woody Allen—Dec. 1, 1935
Morey Amsterdam—Dec. 14, 1912
Fatty Arbuckle—May 24, 1887
Lucille Ball—Aug. 6, 1911
Kaye Ballard—Nov. 20, 1926
Orson Bean—Jul. 22, 1928
Jack Benny—Feb. 14, 1894
Milton Berle—Jul. 12, 1908
Shelley Berman—Feb. 3, 1924
Joey Bishop—Feb. 13, 1918
Ben Blue—Sep. 12, 1901
Victor Borge—Jan. 3, 1908
Fanny Brice—Oct. 29, 1891
Mel Brooks—Jun. 28, 1926
Lenny Bruce—Oct. 13, 1925
Carol Burnett—Apr. 26, 1933
George Burns—Jan. 20, 1896
Red Buttons—Feb. 5, 1919
Ruth Buzzi—Jul. 24, 1936
Sid Caesar—Sep. 8, 1922
Godfrey Cambridge—Feb. 26, 1933
Judy Canova—Nov. 20, 1916
Eddie Cantor—Jan. 31, 1892
George Carlin—May 12, 1938
Johnny Carson—Oct. 23, 1925
Dick Cavett—Nov. 19, 1936
Bill Cosby—Jul. 12, 1937
Wally Cox—Dec. 6, 1924
Bill Dana—Oct. 5, 1924
Rodney Dangerfield—Nov. 22, 1921
Phyllis Diller—Jul. 17, 1917
Jimmy Durante—Feb. 10, 1893
Fernandel—May 8, 1903
Stepin Fetchit—May 30, 1902
W. C. Fields—Jan. 29, 1880
Redd Foxx—Dec. 9, 1922
Stan Freberg—Aug. 7, 1926
Jackie Gleason—Feb. 26, 1916
George Gobel—May 20, 1920
Frank Gorshin—Apr. 5, 1935
Dick Gregory—Oct. 12, 1932
Buddy Hackett—Aug. 31, 1924
Bob Hope—May 29, 1903
Marty Ingals—Mar. 9, 1936
George Jessel—Apr. 3, 1898
Danny Kaye—Jan. 18, 1913
Buster Keaton—Oct. 4, 1895
Patsy Kelly—Jan. 12, 1910
Alan King—Dec. 26, 1927
Don Knotts—Jul. 21, 1924
Ernie Kovacs—Jan. 23, 1919
Bert Lahr—Aug. 13, 1895
Stan Laurel—Jun. 16, 1890
Sam Levenson—Dec. 28, 1911
Jerry Lewis—Mar. 16, 1926
Rich Little—Nov. 26, 1938
Cheech Marin—Jul. 13, 1946
Dick Martin—Jan. 30, 1922
Chico Marx—Mar. 22, 1887
Groucho Marx—Oct. 2, 1895
Harpo Marx—Nov. 21, 1893
Zeppo Marx—Feb. 25, 1901
Elaine May—Apr. 21, 1932
Jan Murray—Oct. 4, 1917
Bob Newhart—Sep. 5, 1929
Mike Nichols—Nov. 6, 1931
Richard Pryor—Dec. 1, 1940
Tony Randall—Feb. 26, 1920
Martha Raye—Aug. 27, 1916
Carl Reiner—Mar. 20, 1922
Don Rickles—May 8, 1926
Joan Rivers—Jan. 20, 1937

COMEDIANS *(cont.)*

Mort Sahl—May ll, 1927
Soupy Sales—Jan. 8, 1926
Phil Silvers—May ll, 1912
Red Skelton—Jul. 18, 1913
Dick Smothers—Nov. 20, 1939
Tommy Smothers—Feb. 2, 1937
Danny Thomas—Jan. 6, 1914
Terry-Thomas—Jul. 14, 1911
Lily Tomlin—Sep. 1, 1939
Ben Turpin—Sep. 17, 1874
Dick Van Dyke—Dec. 13, 1925
Nancy Walker—May 10, 1922
Robin Williams—Jul. 21, 1952
Flip Wilson—Dec. 8, 1933
Jonathan Winters—Nov. 11, 1925
Joanne Worley—Sep. 6, 1927
Ed Wynn—Nov. 9, 1889

DANCERS

Alvin Ailey—Jan. 5, 1931
Fred Astaire—May 10, 1899
George Balanchine—Jan. 22, 1904
Mikhail Baryshnikov—Jan. 28, 1948
Ray Bolger—Jan. 10, 1904
Irene Castle—Apr. 7, 1893
Gower Champion—Jun. 22, 1921
Cyd Charisse—Mar. 8, 1923
Jacques D'Amboise—Jul. 28, 1934
Isadora Duncan—May 27, 1878
Katherine Dunham—Jun. 22, 1910
Margot Fonteyn—May 18, 1919
Bob Fosse—Jun. 23, 1927
Martha Graham—May 11, 1894
José Greco—Dec. 22, 1918
Zizi Jeanmaire—Apr. 29, 1924
Gene Kelly—Aug. 23, 1912
Michael Kidd—Aug. 12, 1919
José Limon—Jan. 12, 1908
Natalia Makarova—Nov. 28, 1940
Arthur Murray—Apr. 4, 1895
George Murphy—Jul. 4, 1903
Nijinsky—Jan. 12, 1890
Rudolf Nureyev—Mar. 17, 1938
Donald O'Connor—Aug. 28, 1925
Valery Panov—Mar. 12, 1939
Anna Pavlova—Jan. 3, 1885
Eleanor Powell—Nov. 21, 1913
Juliet Prowse—Sep. 25, 1936
Sally Rand—Apr. 3, 1904
Jerome Robbins—Oct. 11, 1918
Ruth St. Denis—Jan. 20, 1878
Maria Tallchief—Jan. 24, 1925
Gwen Verdon—Jan. 13, 1926
Edward Villella—Oct. 1, 1937
Vera Zorina—Jan. 2, 1917

FASHION FIGURES

Adolfo—Feb. 15, 1933
Hardy Amies—Jul. 17, 1909
Richard Avedon—May 15, 1923
Pierre Balmain—May 18, 1914
Geoffrey Beene—Aug. 30, 1927
Bill Blass—Jun. 22, 1922
Donald Brooks—Jun. 10, 1928
Bonnie Cashin—Sep. 28, 1915
Oleg Cassini—Apr. 11, 1913
Jo Copeland—Feb. 28, 1903
Oscar de la Renta—Jul. 22, 1932
Giorgio Di Sant'Angelo—May 5, 1939
Anne Fogarty—Feb. 2, 1919
James Galanos—Sep. 20, 1924
Rudi Gernreich—Aug. 8, 1922
Aldo Gucci—May 26, 1909
Halston—Apr. 23, 1932
Edith Head—Oct. 28, 1907
Kenneth (Battelle)—Apr. 19, 1927
Calvin Klein—Nov. 19, 1942
Tina Leser—Sep. 12, 1910
Jean Louis—Oct. 5, 1907
Marusia—Jun. 25, 1918
Vera Maxwell—Apr. 22, 1901
Mollie Parnis—Mar. 18, 1905
Emilio Pucci—Nov. 20, 1914

FASHION FIGURES *(cont.)*

Yves St. Laurent—Aug. 1, 1936
Adele Simpson—Dec. 8, 1903
Pauline Trigère—Nov. 4, 1912
Valentino—May 11, 1932
Gloria Vanderbilt—Feb. 20, 1924
Sally Victor—Feb. 23, 1905
Diane Von Furstenberg—Dec. 31, 1946
Egon Von Furstenberg—Jun. 29, 1946
David Webb—Jul. 2, 1925
John Weitz—May 25, 1923

GOVERNMENT & POLITICAL FIGURES

Bella Abzug—Jul. 24, 1920
Dean Acheson—Apr. 11, 1893
Sherman Adams—Jan. 8, 1899
Spiro Agnew—Nov. 9, 1918
Carl Albert—May 10, 1908
Walter Annenberg—Mar. 13, 1909
Howard Baker—Nov. 14, 1925
Bernard Baruch—Aug. 19, 1870
Birch Bayh—Jan. 22, 1928
Menachem Begin—Aug. 13, 1913
David Ben Gurion—Oct. 16, 1886
Harry Blackmun—Nov. 12, 1908
Julian Bond—Jan. 14, 1940
Chester Bowles—Apr. 5, 1901
Willy Brandt—Dec. 18, 1913
Leonid Brezhnev—Dec. 19, 1906
Edward Brooke—Oct. 26, 1919
Jerry Brown—Apr. 7, 1938
James Buckley—Mar. 9, 1923
McGeorge Bundy—Mar. 30, 1919
Carter Burden—Aug. 25, 1941
Warren Burger—Sep. 17, 1907
George Bush—Jun. 12, 1924
Jane Byrne—May 24, 1934
Gov. Hugh Carey—Apr. 11, 1919
Fidel Castro—Aug. 13, 1926
Neville Chamberlain—Mar. 18, 1869
Chiang Kai-Shek—Oct. 31, 1887
Shirley Chisholm—Nov. 30, 1924
Frank Church—Jul. 25, 1925
Winston Churchill—Nov. 30, 1874
Ramsey Clark—Dec. 18, 1927
John Connally—Feb. 27, 1917
Richard J. Daley—May 15, 1902
Jefferson Davis—Jun. 3, 1808
Moshe Dayan—May 4, 1915
Eugene V. Debs—Nov. 5, 1855
Charles De Gaulle—Nov. 22, 1890
Thomas Dewey—Mar. 24, 1902
Everett Dirksen—Jan. 4, 1896
Benjamin Disraeli—Dec. 21, 1804
Robert Dole—Jul. 22, 1923
William O. Douglas—Oct. 16, 1898
John Foster Dulles—Feb. 25, 1888
Thomas Eagleton—Sep. 4, 1920
John Ehrlichman—Mar. 20, 1925
Sam Ervin—Sep. 27, 1896
James Farley—May 30, 1888
King Farouk—Feb. 11, 1920
William Fulbright—Apr. 9, 1905
John Kenneth Galbraith—Oct. 15, 1908
Indira Gandhi—Nov. 19, 1917
Mahatma Gandhi—Oct. 2, 1869
Arthur Goldberg—Aug. 8, 1908
Barry Goldwater—Jan. 1, 1909
Ella Grasso—May 10, 1919
Andrei Gromyko—Jul. 6, 1909
Alexander Haig—Dec. 2, 1924
Dag Hammarskjold—Jul. 29, 1905
Averell Harriman—Nov. 15, 1891
Mark Hatfield—Jul. 12, 1922
Tom Hayden—Nov. 29, 1940
Adolf Hitler—Apr. 20, 1889
Ho Chi Minh—May 19, 1890
Elizabeth Holtzman—Aug. 11, 1941
Hubert Humphrey—May 27, 1911
King Hussein—Nov. 14, 1935
Henry Jackson—May 31, 1912
Jacob Javits—May 18, 1904
Barbara Jordan—Feb. 21, 1936
Vernon Jordan, Jr.—Aug. 15, 1935
Edward M. Kennedy—Feb. 22, 1932
Robert F. Kennedy—Nov. 20, 1925
Henry Kissinger—May 27, 1923
Nikita Khrushchev—Apr. 16, 1894
Melvin Laird—Sep. 1, 1922
John V. Lindsay—Nov. 24, 1921
Henry Cabot Lodge—Jul. 5, 1902
Huey P. Long—Aug. 30, 1893
Clare Boothe Luce—Apr. 10, 1903

GOVERNMENT & POLITICAL FIGURES *(cont.)*

Patrick Lucey—Mar. 21, 1918
Lester Maddox—Sep. 30, 1915
Mike Mansfield—Mar. 16, 1903
Mao Tse-tung—Dec. 26, 1893
Ferdinand Marcos—Sep. 11, 1917
Thurgood Marshall—Jul. 2, 1908
Karl Marx—May 5, 1818
Eugene McCarthy—Mar. 29, 1916
George McGovern—Jul. 19, 1922
Robert McNamara—Jun. 9, 1916
Golda Meir—May 3, 1898
Wilbur Mills—May 24, 1909
John Mitchell—Sep. 5, 1913
Walter Mondale—Jan. 5, 1928
Daniel Patrick Moynihan—Mar. 16, 1927
Edmund Muskie—Mar. 28, 1914
Benito Mussolini—Jul. 29, 1883
Jawaharlal Nehru—Nov. 14, 1889
Thomas O'Neill—Dec. 9, 1912
Charles Percy—Sep. 27, 1919
Lewis Powell, Jr.—Sep. 19, 1907
William Proxmire—Nov. 11, 1915
Sam Rayburn—Jan. 6, 1882
William Rehnquist—Oct. 1, 1924
Abraham Ribicoff—Apr. 9, 1910
John D. Rockefeller IV—Jun. 18, 1937
Nelson Rockefeller—Jul. 8, 1908
George Romney—Jul. 8, 1907
Dean Rusk—Feb. 9, 1909
Bayard Rustin—Mar. 10, 1910
Anwar Sadat—Dec. 25, 1918
Pierre Salinger—Jun. 14, 1925
Arthur Schlesinger, Jr.—Oct. 15, 1917
James R. Schlesinger—Feb. 15, 1929
Haile Selassie—Jul. 23, 1892
Sargent Shriver—Nov. 9, 1915
Al Smith—Dec. 30, 1873
Margaret Chase Smith—Dec. 14, 1897
Joseph Stalin—Dec. 21, 1897
Harold Stassen—Apr. 13, 1907
Adlai Stevenson—Feb. 5, 1900
Achmed Sukarno—Jun. 6, 1901
Stuart Symington—Jun. 26, 1901
Strom Thurmond—Dec. 5, 1902
Josip Broz Tito—May 25, 1892
Pierre Trudeau—Oct. 18, 1919
John Tunney—Jun. 26, 1934
Cyrus Vance—Mar. 27, 1917
Kurt Waldheim—Dec. 21, 1918
George C. Wallace—Aug. 25, 1919
Henry Wallace—Oct. 7, 1888
John Warner—Feb. 18, 1927
Earl Warren—Mar. 19, 1891
Harold Wilson—Mar. 11, 1916

HISTORICAL FIGURES

Alexander The Great—Sep. 20, 356 b.c.
Ethan Allen—Jan. 10, 1738
Marie Antoinette—Nov. 2, 1775
Benedict Arnold—Jan. 25, 1741
Francis Bacon—Jan. 22, 1561
Amelia Bloomer—May 27, 1818
Napoleon Bonaparte—Aug. 15, 1769
Simon Bolivar—Jul. 24, 1783
Beau Brummel—Jun. 7, 1778
Sir Richard Burton—Mar. 19, 1821
Admiral Richard Byrd—Oct. 25, 1888
Lord Byron—Jan. 22, 1788
Augustus Caesar—Sep. 23, 63 b.c.
Julius Caesar—Jul. 12, 100 b.c.
King Carol II—Oct. 15, 1893
Butch Cassidy—Apr. 13, 1866
Catherine the Great—Apr. 21, 1729
King Charles II—May 29, 1630
Marcus Tullius Cicero—Jun. 3, 106 b.c.
Henry Clay—Apr. 12, 1777
"Buffalo Bill" Cody—Feb. 26, 1846
Christopher Columbus—Oct. 30, 1451
Davy Crockett—Aug. 17, 1786
Confucius—Sep. 28, 551 b.c.
Jefferson Davis—Jun. 3, 1808
Marquis de Lafayette—Sep. 6, 1757
Madame de Pompadour—Dec. 29, 1721
Marquis de Sade—Jun. 2, 1740
Benjamin Disraeli—Dec. 21, 1804
Wyatt Earp—Mar. 19, 1848
King Edward VII—Nov. 9, 1841
King Edward VIII (Duke of Windsor)—Jun. 23, 1894
Queen Elizabeth I—Sep. 1, 1533
Queen Elizabeth II—Apr. 21, 1926
Benjamin Franklin—Jan. 17, 1706

HISTORICAL FIGURES *(cont.)*

Mahatma Gandhi—Oct. 2, 1869
William Gladstone—Dec. 29, 1809
Samuel Gompers—Jan. 27, 1850
Horace Greeley—Feb. 3, 1811
Nathan Hale—Jun. 6, 1775
Alexander Hamilton—Jan. 11, 1757
John Hancock—Jan. 23, 1737
King Henry VIII—Jun. 28, 1491
Patrick Henry—May 29, 1736
Thor Heyerdahl—Oct. 6, 1914
Emperor Hirohito—Apr. 29, 1901
Adolf Hitler—Apr. 20, 1889
Henry Hudson—Sep. 12, 1575
Stonewall Jackson—Jan. 21, 1824
John Paul Jones—Jul. 6, 1747
Francis Scott Key—Aug. 1, 1779
Robert E. Lee—Jan. 19, 1807
Nikolai Lenin—May 4, 1870
David Livingstone—Mar. 19, 1812
King Louis XIV—Sep. 5, 1638
King Louis XV—Feb. 15, 1710
King Louis XVI—Aug. 23, 1754
Gen. Douglas MacArthur—Jan. 26, 1880
Niccolo Machiavelli—May 3, 1469
Mao Tse-tung—Dec. 26, 1893
Karl Marx—May 5, 1818
Sir Thomas More—Feb. 7, 1478
Benito Mussolini—Jul. 29, 1883
Lord Nelson—Sep. 29, 1758
Thomas Paine—Jan. 29, 1737
William Penn—Oct. 14, 1644
Samuel Pepys—Feb. 23, 1633
Eva Peron—May 7, 1919
Commodore Matthew Perry—Apr. 10, 1794
Robert Perry—May 6, 1856
Gen. John J. Pershing—Sep. 13, 1860
Peter the Great—Jun. 9, 1762
Count Casimir Pulaski—Mar. 4, 1748
King Richard III—Oct. 11, 1452
Betsy Ross—Jan. 1, 1752
Sir Walter Scott—Aug. 15, 1771
Gen. William Tecumseh Sherman—Feb. 8, 1820
Charles Talleyrand—Feb. 2, 1754
Leo Tolstoy—Sep. 9, 1828
Leon Trotsky—Oct. 26, 1879
Amerigo Vespucci—Mar. 9, 1451
Queen Victoria—May 24, 1819
Otto Von Bismarck—Apr. 1, 1815
Daniel Webster—Jan. 18, 1782
Noah Webster—Oct. 16, 1758
Duke of Wellington—May 1, 1769

INDUSTRY AND BUSINESS FIGURES

Sherman Billingsley—Mar. 10, 1900
Alfred Bloomingdale—Apr. 15, 1916
Harry Bridges—Jul. 28, 1901
August Busch—Mar. 28, 1899
Cesar Chavez—Mar. 31, 1927
Eugene V. Debs—Nov. 5, 1855
David Dubinsky—Feb. 22, 1892
Cyrus Eaton—Dec. 27, 1883
Harvey Firestone, Jr.—Apr. 20, 1898
Henry Ford—Jul. 30, 1863
Henry Ford II—Sep. 4, 1917
Harold Geneen—Jan. 22, 1910
J. Paul Getty—Dec. 15, 1892
Huntington Hartford—Apr. 18, 1911
Hugh Hefner—Apr. 9, 1926
Conrad Hilton—Dec. 25, 1887
James Hoffa—Feb. 14, 1913
Howard Hughes—Dec. 24, 1905
H. L. Hunt—Feb. 17, 1889
Lee Iacocca—Oct. 15, 1924
Edwin Land—May 7, 1909
Harding Lawrence—Jul. 15, 1920
Mary Wells Lawrence—May 25, 1928
John L. Lewis—Feb. 12, 1880
George Meany—Aug. 16, 1894
Paul Mellon—Jun. 11, 1907
Stavros Niarchos—Jul. 3, 1909
Aristotle Onassis—Jan. 15, 1906
William Paley—Sep. 28, 1901
J. C. Penney—Sep. 16, 1875
Charles Revson—Oct. 11, 1906
David Rockefeller—Jun. 12, 1915
John D. Rockefeller III—Mar. 21, 1906
Laurance Rockefeller—May 26, 1910
Colonel Harlan Sanders—Sep. 9, 1890
Vincent Sardi, Jr.—Jul. 23, 1915
Robert Sarnoff—Jul. 2, 1918
Norton Simon—Feb. 5, 1907

INDUSTRY AND BUSINESS FIGURES *(cont.)*

Leland Stanford—Mar. 9, 1824
Jules Stein—Apr. 26, 1896
Geraldine Stutz—Aug. 5, 1924
Alfred Gwynne Vanderbilt—Nov. 27, 1843
Lew Wasserman—Mar. 15, 1913
Cornelius Vanderbilt "C. V." Whitney —Feb. 20, 1899
F. W. Woolworth—Apr. 13, 1852
Robert Vesco—Dec. 4, 1935
William Zeckendorf—Jun. 30, 1905

LITERARY FIGURES

Louisa May Alcott—Nov 29, 1832
Nelson Algren—Mar. 28, 1909
Hans Christian Andersen—Apr. 21, 1805
Maya Angelou—Apr. 4, 1928
Isaac Asimov—Jan. 2, 1920
Robert Ardrey—Oct. 16, 1908
Louis Auchincloss—Sep. 27, 1917
John Bainbridge—Mar. 12, 1913
Faith Baldwin—Oct. 1, 1893
James Baldwin—Aug. 2, 1924
(Honoré De) Balzac—May 20, 1799
J. M. Barrie—May 9, 1860
Jacques Barzun—Nov. 30, 1907
Saul Bellow—Jul. 10, 1915
Nathaniel Benchley—Nov. 13, 1915
Peter Benchley—May 8, 1940
Stephen Birmingham—May 28, 1931
Heinrich Böll—Dec. 21, 1917
Jorge Luis Borges—Aug. 24, 1899
James Boswell—Oct. 29, 1740
Ray Bradbury—Aug. 22, 1920
Charlotte Brontë—Apr. 21, 1816
Emily Brontë—Jul. 30, 1818
Rupert Brooke—Aug. 3, 1887
Elizabeth Barrett Browning—Mar. 6, 1806
Robert Burns—Jan. 25, 1759
Lord Byron—Jan. 22, 1788
Erskine Caldwell—Dec. 17, 1903
Taylor Caldwell—Sep. 7, 1900
Hortense Calisher—Dec. 20, 1911
Truman Capote—Sep. 30, 1924
Lewis Carroll—Jan. 27, 1832
Rachel Carson—May 27, 1907
Barbara Cartland—Jul. 9, 1901
Willa Cather—Dec. 7, 1876
Raymond Chandler—Jul. 22, 1888
John Cheever—May 27, 1912
Anton Chekov—Jan. 29, 1860
Agatha Christie—Sep. 15, 1890
Jean Cocteau—Jul. 5, 1889
Samuel Taylor Coleridge—Oct. 21, 1772
Colette—Jan. 28, 1873
A. J. Cronin—Jul. 19, 1896
Gabriele D'Annunzio—Mar. 12, 1863
Simone de Beauvoir—Jan. 9, 1908
Guy de Maupassant—Aug. 5, 1850
Marquis De Sade—Jun. 2, 1740
Peter De Vries—Feb. 27, 1918
Charles Dickens—Feb. 7, 1812
Emily Dickinson—Dec. 10, 1830
Fyodor Dostoevsky—Nov. 11, 1821
Alexandre Dumas—Jul. 24, 1802
T. S. Eliot—Sep. 26, 1888
Ralph Waldo Emerson—May 25, 1803
William Faulkner—Sep. 25, 1897
F. Scott Fitzgerald—Sep. 24, 1896
E. M. Forster—Jan. 1, 1879
Robert Frost—Mar. 26, 1874
Erle Stanley Gardner—Jul. 17, 1889
André Gide—Nov. 22, 1869
Allen Ginsburg—Jun. 3, 1926
Goethe—Aug. 28, 1749
Günter Grass—Oct. 16, 1927
Zane Grey—Jan. 31, 1875
Graham Greene—Oct. 2, 1904
Alex Haley—Aug. 11, 1921
Nathaniel Hawthorne—Jul. 4, 1804
Joel Chandler Harris—Dec. 9, 1848
Lillian Hellman—Jun. 20, 1905
Ernest Hemingway—Jun. 21, 1899
John Hersey—Jun. 17, 1914
Langston Hughes—Feb. 1, 1902
Victor Hugo—Feb. 26, 1802
Aldous Huxley—Jul. 26, 1894
Henrik Ibsen—Mar. 20, 1828
Washington Irving—Apr. 3, 1753
Christopher Isherwood—Aug. 26, 1904
James Jones—Nov. 6, 1921
Erica Jong—Mar. 26, 1942
James Joyce—Feb. 2, 1882

LITERARY FIGURES *(cont.)*

John Keats—Oct. 31, 1795
Jean Kerr—Jul. 10, 1923
Frances Parkinson Keyes—Jul. 21, 1885
D. H. Lawrence—Sep. 11, 1885
Max Lerner—Dec. 20, 1902
Meyer Levin—Oct. 7, 1905
Sinclair Lewis— Feb. 7, 1885
Jack London—Jan. 12, 1876
Henry Longfellow—Feb. 27, 1807
Anita Loos—Apr. 26, 1893
Robert Lowell—Mar. 1, 1917
Archibald MacLeish—May 7, 1892
Norman Mailer—Jan. 31, 1923
Bernard Malamud—Apr. 26, 1914
William Manchester—Apr. 1, 1922
Thomas Mann—Jun. 6, 1875
Somerset Maugham—Jan. 25, 1874
Mary McCarthy—Jun. 21, 1912
Carson McCullers—Feb. 19, 1917
Rod McKuen—Apr. 29, 1933
Herman Melville—Aug. 1, 1819
James Michener—Feb. 3, 1907
Edna St. Vincent Millay—Feb. 22, 1892
Henry Miller—Dec. 26, 1891
John Milton—Dec. 9, 1608
Yukio Mishima—Jan. 14, 1925
Clement Moore—Jul. 15, 1779
Willie Morris—Nov. 29, 1934
Vladimir Nabokov—Apr. 23, 1899
Ogden Nash—Aug. 19, 1902
Louis Nizer—Feb. 6, 1902
Joyce Carol Oates—Jun. 16, 1938
Eugene O'Neill—Oct. 16, 1888
Vance Packard—May 22, 1914
Dorothy Parker—Aug. 23, 1893
S. J. Perelman—Feb. 1, 1904
Edgar Alan Poe—Jan. 19, 1809
Katherine Anne Porter—May 15, 1890
Ezra Pound—Oct. 30, 1885
Mario Puzo—Oct. 15, 1921
Erich Maria Remarque—Jun. 22, 1898
Rainer Maria Rilke—Dec. 4, 1875
Peter Mark Roget—Jan. 18, 1779
Harold Robbins—May 21, 1916
Philip Roth—Mar. 19, 1933
John Ruskin—Feb. 8, 1819
J. D. Salinger—Jan. 1, 1919
Françoise Sagan—Jun. 21, 1935
Carl Sandburg—Jan. 6, 1878
George Sand—Jul. 1, 1804
William Saroyan—Aug. 31, 1908
Jean-Paul Sartre—Jun. 21, 1905
Budd Schulberg—Mar. 27, 1917
Sir Walter Scott—Aug. 15, 1771
William Seabrook—Feb. 22, 1896
Erich Segal—Jun. 16, 1937
Theodore "Dr. Seuss" Geisel—Mar. 2, 1904
George Bernard Shaw—Jul. 26, 1856
Irwin Shaw—Feb. 27, 1913
Percy Bysshe Shelley—Aug. 4, 1792
Georges Simenon—Feb. 13, 1903
Upton Sinclair—Sep. 20, 1878
Isaac Bashevis Singer—Jul. 17, 1904
Mickey Spillane—Mar. 9, 1918
Gertrude Stein—Feb. 3, 1874
John Steinbeck—Feb. 27, 1902
Stendhal—Jan. 23, 1783
Robert Louis Stevenson—Nov. 13, 1850
Irving Stone—Jul. 14, 1903
Harriet Beecher Stowe—Jun. 14, 1811
August Strindberg—Jan. 22, 1849
William Styron—Jun. 11, 1925
Jacqueline Susann—Aug. 20, 1926
Algernon Charles Swinburne—Apr. 15, 1837
Booth Tarkington—Jul. 29, 1861
Alfred, Lord Tennyson—Aug. 6, 1809
Henry David Thoreau—Jul. 12, 1817
J. R. R. Tolkien—Jan. 3, 1892
Leo Tolstoy—Sep. 9, 1828
Thomas Tryon—Jan. 14, 1926
Barbara Tuchman—Jan. 30, 1912
Mark Twain—Nov. 30, 1835
John Updike—Mar. 18, 1932
Leon Uris—Aug. 3, 1924
Paul Verlaine—Mar. 30, 1844
Jules Verne—Feb. 8, 1828
Gore Vidal—Oct. 3, 1925
Voltaire—Nov. 21, 1694
Kurt Vonnegut, Jr.—Nov. 11, 1922
Irving Wallace—Mar. 19, 1916
H. G. Wells—Sep. 21, 1866
E. B. White—Jul. 11, 1899
Theodore White—May 6, 1915
Walt Whitman—May 13, 1819
Oscar Wilde—Oct. 16, 1854
Thornton Wilder—Apr. 17, 1897
Tennessee Williams—Mar. 26, 1911
P. G. Wodehouse—Oct. 15, 1881

LITERARY FIGURES *(cont.)*

Thomas Wolfe—Oct. 3, 1900
Tom Wolfe—Mar. 2, 1931
Mary Wollstonecraft—Apr. 27, 1759
Virginia Woolf—Jan. 25, 1882
Herman Wouk—May 27, 1915
Philip Wylie—May 12, 1902
Frank Yerby—Sep. 5, 1916
Emile Zola—Apr. 2, 1840

MEDICAL, PHILOSOPHY AND PSYCHIATRY FIGURES

Hannah Arendt—Oct. 14, 1906
Dr. Christiaan Barnard—Oct. 8, 1922
Bruno Bettelheim—Aug. 28, 1903
Dr. Joyce Brothers—Oct. 20, 1928
Dr. Michael DeBakey—Sep. 7, 1908
René Descartes—Mar. 31, 1596
Havelock Ellis—Feb. 2, 1859
Sigmund Freud—May 6, 1856
Goethe—Aug. 18, 1749
Georg Hegel—Aug. 27, 1770
Eric Hoffer—Jul. 25, 1902
Edward Jenner—May 17, 1749
Virginia Johnson—Feb. 11, 1925
Carl Gustav Jung—Jul. 26, 1875
Immanuel Kant—Apr. 22, 1724
Søren Kierkegaard—May 5, 1813
Karl Marx—May 5, 1818
Dr. William Masters—Dec. 27, 1915
Rollo May—Apr. 21, 1909
Karl Menninger—Jul. 22, 1893
Friedrich Nietzsche—Oct. 15, 1844
David Reuben—Nov. 29, 1933
Jean-Jacques Rousseau—Jun. 28, 1712
Bertrand Russell—May 18, 1872
Albert Sabin—Aug. 26, 1906
Jonas Salk—Oct. 28, 1914
George Santayana—Dec. 16, 1863
Jean-Paul Sartre—Jun. 21, 1905
Arthur Schopenhauer—Feb. 22, 1788
Spinoza—Nov. 25, 1632
Dr. Benjamin Spock—May 2, 1903

MISCELLANEOUS FIGURES

Abigail Adams—Nov. 11, 1744
Ansel Adams—Feb. 20, 1902
Joy Adamson—Jan. 20, 1910
Charles Addams—Jan. 7, 1912
Prince Albert of Monaco—Mar. 14, 1958
Edwin "Buzz" Aldrin—Jan. 20, 1930
Shana Alexander—Oct. 6, 1925
Cleveland Amory—Sep. 2, 1917
Prince Andrew (England)—Feb. 19, 1960
Susan B. Anthony—Feb. 15, 1820
Richard Avedon—May 15, 1923
F. Lee Bailey—Jun. 10, 1933
Bil Baird—Aug. 15, 1904
Billy Baldwin—May 30, 1903
James Beard—May 5, 1903
Peter Beard—Jan. 1, 1938
Cecil Beaton—Jan. 14, 1904
Alexander Graham Bell—Mar. 3, 1847
Melvin Belli—Jul. 29, 1907
Bill Blass—Jun. 22, 1922
"Diamond Jim" Brady—Aug. 12, 1856
Gen. Omar Bradley—Feb. 12, 1893
William Jennings Bryan—Mar. 19, 1860
Aaron Burr—Feb. 6, 1756
Dick Button—Jul. 18, 1929
Al Capone—Jan. 17, 1899
Al Capp—Sep. 28, 1909
Princess Caroline (Monaco)—Jan. 27, 1957
Casanova—Apr. 2, 1725
Lillian Carter—Aug. 15, 1898
Rosalyn Carter—Aug. 18, 1927
Julia Child—Aug. 15, 1912
Noam Chomsky—Dec. 7, 1928
Clementine Churchill—Apr. 8, 1885
Gen. Mark Clark—May 1, 1896
Roy Cohn—Feb. 22, 1927
Barry Commoner—May 28, 1917
Tricia Nixon Cox—Feb. 21, 1946
Adelle Davis—Feb. 25, 1904
Martha Deane—Nov. 21, 1909

MISCELLANEOUS FIGURES *(cont.)*

John Dillinger—Jun. 22, 1902
Dionne Quintuplets—May 28, 1934
Walt Disney—Dec. 5, 1901
Angier Biddle Duke—Nov. 30, 1915
Doris Duke—Nov. 22, 1912
Amelia Earhart—Jul. 24, 1898
Prince Edward—Mar. 10, 1964
Mamie Eisenhower—Nov. 14, 1896
Julie Nixon Eisenhower—Jul. 5, 1948
Thomas Edison—Feb. 11, 1847
Queen Mother Elizabeth—Aug. 4, 1900
Betty Ford—Apr. 8, 1918
A. J. Foyt—Jan. 16, 1935
Betty Friedan—Feb. 4, 1921
Milton Friedman—Jul. 31, 1912
George Gallup—Nov. 18, 1901
Charles Goren—Mar. 4, 1901
Alexander Hamilton—Jan. 11, 1757
Mata Hari—Aug. 7, 1876
Louis Harris—Jan. 6, 1921
Huntington Hartford—Apr. 18, 1911
Sir Edmund Hillary—Jul. 20, 1919
J. Edgar Hoover—Jan. 1, 1895
Harry Houdini—Mar. 24, 1874
Thomas P. Hoving—Jan. 15, 1931
Barbara Hutton—Nov. 14, 1912
Lady Bird Johnson—Dec. 22, 1912
Lynda Bird Johnson Robb—Mar. 19, 1944
Phillipe Junot—Apr. 18, 1940
Helen Keller—Jun. 27, 1880
George "Machine Gun" Kelly—Jul. 17, 1900
Ethel Kennedy—Apr. 11, 1928
Joan Kennedy—Sep. 2, 1937
Joseph P. Kennedy—Sep. 6, 1888
Joseph Kennedy Jr.—Jul. 25, 1915
Rose Kennedy—Jul. 22, 1890
Kenneth (Battelle)—Apr. 19, 1927
Prince Aly Khan—Jun. 13, 1911
Alexsei Kosygin—Feb. 20, 1904
William Kunstler—Jul. 7, 1919
T. E. Lawrence (of Arabia)—Aug. 15, 1888
Irving Lazar—Mar. 28, 1907
Gypsy Rose Lee—Feb. 9, 1914
Charles Lindberg—Feb. 4, 1902
Claudine Longet—Jan. 29, 1942
Alice Roosevelt Longworth—Feb. 12, 1884
Gen. Douglas MacArthur—Jan. 26, 1880
Dolly Madison—May 20, 1768
Tommy Manville—Apr. 9, 1894
Guglielmo Marconi—Apr. 25, 1874
Marshall McLuhan—Jul. 21, 1911
Paul Mellon—Jun. 11, 1907
Perle Mesta—Oct. 12, 1891
Martha Mitchell—Sep. 2, 1918
Maria Montessori—Aug. 31, 1870
Ralph Nader—Feb. 27, 1934
Carry Nation—Nov. 25, 1846
Arthur Nielsen—Sep. 5, 1897
Florence Nightingale—May 12, 1820
Pat Nixon—Mar. 16, 1912
Louis Nizer—Feb. 6, 1902
Annie Oakley—Aug. 13, 1860
Jacqueline Kennedy Onassis—Jul. 28, 1929
Yoko Ono—Feb. 18, 1933
I. M. Pei—Apr. 26, 1917
Prince Philip—Jun. 10, 1921
George Plimpton—Mar. 18, 1927
Sylvia Porter—Jun. 18, 1913
Marjorie Merriweather Post—Mar. 15, 1887
Joseph Pulitzer, Jr.—May 13, 1913
Lee Radziwill—Mar. 3, 1933
James Earl Ray—Mar. 10, 1928
Nancy Reagan—Jul. 6, 1923
Eddie Rickenbacker—Oct. 8, 1890
Carroll Righter—Feb. 1, 1908
Adela Rogers St. Johns—May 20, 1894
Gen. Rommel—Nov. 15, 1891
John A. Roosevelt—Mar. 13, 1916
Margaret Sanger—Sep. 14, 1883
Charles Schulz—Nov. 26, 1922
Albert Schweitzer—Jan. 14, 1875
Theodore "Dr. Seuss" Geisel—Mar. 2, 1904
Shah of Iran (Mohammed Reza Pahlevi)—Oct. 26, 1919
Al Smith—Dec. 30, 1873
Gloria Steinem—Mar. 25, 1936
Edward Steichen—Mar. 27, 1879
Adlai Stevenson—Feb. 5, 1900
Edward Durrell Stone—Mar. 9, 1902
Bess Truman—Feb. 13, 1885
Margaret Truman (Daniels)—Feb. 17, 1924
Alfred Gwynne Vanderbilt—Sep. 22, 1912
Amy Vanderbilt—Jul. 22, 1908
Pancho Villa—Jun. 5, 1878
Booker T. Washington—Apr. 5, 1856
Martha Washington—Jun. 2, 1731
C. V. "Sonny" Whitney—Feb. 20, 1899

MISCELLANEOUS FIGURES *(cont.)*

Eli Whitney—Dec. 8, 1765
Edward Bennett Williams—May 31, 1920
Duchess of Windsor—Jul. 19, 1896
Duke of Windsor—Jun. 23, 1894
Harry Winston—Mar. 1, 1896
Frank Lloyd Wright—Jun. 8, 1869
Orville Wright—Aug. 17, 1871
Wilbur Wright—Apr. 16, 1867

MOVIES AND TV—PRODUCERS, DIRECTORS AND WRITERS

Goodman Ace—Jan. 15, 1899
Buddy Adler—Jun. 22, 1909
Robert Aldrich—Aug. 9, 1918
Irwin Allen—Jun. 12, 1916
Robert Altman—Feb. 20, 1925
Michelangelo Antonioni—Sep. 29, 1912
Roone Arledge—Jul. 8, 1931
Danny Arnold—Jan. 23, 1925
Ted Ashley—Aug. 3, 1922
Robert Alan Aurthur—Jun. 10, 1922
John Avildsen—Dec. 21, 1935
Chuck Barris—Jun. 2, 1929
Ingmar Bergman—Jul. 14, 1918
Busby Berkeley—Nov. 29, 1895
Pandro Berman—Mar. 28, 1905
Elmer Bernstein—Apr. 4, 1922
Bernardo Bertolucci—Mar. 16, 1941
Peter Bogdanovich—Jul. 30, 1939
Robert Bolt—Aug. 15, 1924
Frank Borzage—Apr. 23, 1893
Frederick Brisson—Mar. 17, 1917
Albert "Cubby" Broccoli—Feb. 22, 1900
David Brown—Jul. 28, 1916
Luis Buñuel—Feb. 22, 1900
Abe Burrows—Dec. 18, 1910
Michael Cacoyannis—Jun. 11, 1922
Frank Capra—May 18, 1897
John Cassavetes—Dec. 9, 1923
Claude Chabrol—Jun. 24, 1930
Paddy Chayevsky—Jan. 29, 1923
René Clair—Nov. 11, 1898
Harry Cohn—Jul. 23, 1891
Joan Ganz Cooney—Nov. 30, 1929
Francis Ford Coppola—Apr. 7, 1939
Roger Corman—Apr. 5, 1926
Judith Crist—May 12, 1922
George Cukor—Jul. 7, 1899
Michael Curtiz—Dec. 24, 1888
Jules Dassin—Dec. 8, 1911
Dino De Laurentiis—Aug. 8, 1918
Cecil B. De Mille—Aug. 12, 1881
Vittorio De Sica—Jul. 7, 1902
Walt Disney—Dec. 5, 1901
Blake Edwards—Jul. 26, 1922
Eisenstein—Jan. 23, 1898
Robert Evans—Jun. 29, 1930
Rainer Werner Fassbinder—May 31, 1946
Federico Fellini—Jan. 20, 1920
John Ford—Feb. 1, 1895
Milos Forman—Feb. 18, 1932
John Frankenheimer—Feb. 19, 1930
Mike Frankovich—Sep. 29, 1910
William Friedkin—Aug. 29, 1939
Allen Funt—Sep. 16, 1914
Jean-Luc Godard—Dec. 3, 1930
William Goetz—Mar. 24, 1903
Leonard Goldenson—Dec. 7, 1905
Samuel Goldwyn—Aug. 27, 1882
Joseph Green—Jan. 28, 1935
D. W. Griffith—Jan. 22, 1875
Alfred Hitchcock—Aug. 13, 1899
Ross Hunter—May 6, 1924
John Huston—Aug. 5, 1906
Nunnally Johnson—Dec. 5, 1897
Sir Alexander Korda—Sep. 16, 1893
Stanley Kramer—Sep. 29, 1913
Stanley Kubrick—Jul. 26, 1928
David Lean—Mar. 25, 1908
Norman Lear—Jul. 27, 1922
Mervyn LeRoy—Oct. 15, 1900
Richard Lester—Jan. 19, 1932
Joseph E. Levine—Sep. 9, 1905
Joseph Losey—Jan. 14, 1909
Ernst Lubitsch—Jan. 28, 1892
Sidney Lumet—Jun. 25, 1924
Joseph Mankiewicz—Feb. 11, 1909
Louis B. Mayer—Jul. 4, 1885
Leo McCarey—Oct. 3, 1898
Vincente Minnelli—Feb. 28, 1913
William S. Paley—Sep. 28, 1901
Gordon Parks—Oct. 30, 1912
Joseph Pasternak—Sep. 19, 1901

MOVIES AND TV—PRODUCERS, DIRECTORS AND WRITERS *(cont.)*

Sam Peckinpah—Feb. 21, 1925
Roman Polanski—Aug. 18, 1933
Carlo Ponti—Dec. 11, 1913
Otto Preminger—Dec. 5, 1906
Roberto Rossellini—May 8, 1906
David "General" Sarnoff—Feb. 27, 1891
Robert Sarnoff—Jul. 2, 1918
Dore Schary—Aug. 31, 1905
Budd Schulberg—Mar. 27, 1917
David O. Selznick—May 10, 1902
Rod Serling—Dec. 25, 1924
Spyros Skouras—Mar. 28, 1893
Sam Spiegel—Nov. 11, 1901
Frank Stanton—Mar. 20, 1908
George Stevens—Dec. 18, 1904
George Stevens, Jr.—Apr. 3, 1932
David Susskind—Dec. 19, 1920
Irving Thalberg—May 30, 1899
Mike Todd—Jun. 22, 1907
Ivan Tors—Jun. 12, 1916
François Truffaut—Feb. 6, 1932
Roger Vadim—Jan. 26, 1928
Jack Valenti—Sep. 5, 1921
Luchino Visconti—Nov. 2, 1906
Jack Warner—Aug. 2, 1892
Lina Wertmuller—Aug. 14, 1928
Billy Wilder—Jun. 22, 1906
William Wyler—Jul. 1, 1902
Darryl F. Zanuck—Sep. 5, 1902
Richard Zanuck—Dec. 13, 1934
Franco Zeffirelli—Feb. 12, 1923
Fred Zinnemann—Apr. 29, 1907
Adolph Zukor—Jan. 7, 1873

MUSIC—CLASSICAL ARTISTS

Licia Albanese—Jul. 22, 1913
Franz Allers—Aug. 6, 1905
Marian Anderson—Feb. 17, 1902
Claudio Arrau—Feb. 6, 1903
Johann Sebastian Bach—Mar. 21, 1685
Samuel Barber—Mar. 9, 1910
Daniel Barenboim—Nov. 15, 1942
Hector Berlioz—Dec. 11, 1803
Elmer Bernstein—Apr. 4, 1922
Leonard Bernstein—Aug. 25, 1918
Rudolph Bing—Jan. 2, 1902
Georges Bizet—Oct. 25, 1838
Pierre Boulez—Mar. 26, 1925
Johannes Brahms—May 7, 1833
Benjamin Britten—Nov. 22, 1913
Grace Bumbry—Jan. 4, 1937
Maria Callas—Dec. 3, 1923
Enrico Caruso—Feb. 25, 1873
Pablo Casals—Dec. 29, 1876
Frederic Chopin—Feb. 22, 1810
Van Cliburn—Jul. 12, 1934
Aaron Copland—Nov. 14, 1900
Franco Corelli—Apr. 8, 1923
Claude Debussy—Aug. 22, 1862
Frederick Delius—Jan. 29, 1862
Placido Domingo—Jan. 21, 1941
Anton Dvorak—Sep. 8, 1841
Eileen Farrell—Feb. 13, 1920
Arthur Fiedler—Dec. 17, 1894
Dietrich Fischer-Dieskau—May 28, 1925
George Frederick Handel—Feb. 23, 1685
Franz Joseph Haydn—Mar. 31, 1732
Jascha Heifetz—Feb. 2, 1901
Marilyn Horne—Jan. 16, 1934
Vladimir Horowitz—Oct. 1, 1904
José Iturbi—Nov. 28, 1895
Byron Janis—Mar. 24, 1928
Dorothy Kirsten—Jul. 6, 1919
Werner Klemperer—Mar. 22, 1920
André Kostelanetz—Dec. 22, 1901
Mario Lanza—Jan. 31, 1921
Erich Leinsdorf—Feb. 4, 1912
Franz Liszt—Oct. 22, 1811
Gustav Mahler—Jul. 7, 1860
Zubin Mehta—Apr. 29, 1936
Lauritz Melchior—Mar. 20, 1890
Felix Mendelssohn—Feb. 3, 1809
Gian-Carlo Menotti—Jul. 7, 1911
Yehudi Menuhin—Apr. 22, 1916
Robert Merrill—Jun. 4, 1919
Nathan Milstein—Dec. 31, 1904
Anna Moffo—Jun. 26, 1935
Carlos Montoya—Dec. 13, 1903
Wolfgang Amadeus Mozart—Jan. 27, 1756
Patrice Munsel—May 14, 1925
Modest Mussorgsky—Mar. 21, 1839

MUSIC—CLASSICAL ARTISTS *(cont.)*

Birgit Nilsson—May 17, 1918
Jacques Offenbach—Jun. 20, 1819
Eugene Ormandy—Nov. 18, 1889
Niccolò Paganini—Oct. 27, 1782
Adelina Patti—Feb. 19, 1843
Jan Peerce—Jun. 3, 1904
Roberta Peters—May 4, 1930
Gregor Piatigorsky—Apr. 17, 1903
Lily Pons—Apr. 12, 1904
Rosa Ponselle—Jan. 22, 1897
André Previn—Apr. 6, 1929
Leontyne Price—Feb. 10, 1927
Sergei Prokofiev—Apr. 23, 1891
Giacomo Puccini—Dec. 22, 1858
Sergei Rachmaninoff—Apr. 23, 1873
Maurice Ravel—Mar. 27, 1875
Regina Resnick—Aug. 30, 1924
Nikolay Rimsky-Korsakov—Mar. 18, 1844
Paul Robeson—Apr. 9, 1898
Artur Rubinstein—Jan. 28, 1887
Antonio Salieri—Aug. 18, 1750
Thomas Schippers—Mar. 9, 1930
Arnold Schoenberg—Sep. 13, 1874
Franz Schubert—Jan. 31, 1797
Robert Schumann—Jun. 8, 1810
Andres Segovia—Feb. 18, 1894
Rudolf Serkin—Mar. 28, 1903
Dmitri Shostakovich—Sep. 25, 1906
Jean Sibelius—Dec. 8, 1865
Beverly Sills—May 25, 1929
Georg Solti—Oct. 21, 1912
John Philip Sousa—Nov. 6, 1854
Isaac Stern—Jul. 21, 1920
Risë Stevens—Jun. 11, 1913
Leopold Stokowski—Apr. 18, 1882
Richard Strauss—Jun. 11, 1864
Joan Sutherland—Nov. 7, 1926
Gladys Swarthout—Dec. 25, 1904
Peter Ilyitch Tchaikovsky—May 7, 1840
Blanche Thebom—Sep. 19, 1919
Michael Tilson Thomas—Dec. 21, 1944
Dmitri Tiomkin—May 10, 1899
Giorgio Tozzi—Jan. 8, 1923
Helen Traubel—Jun. 16, 1903
Richard Tucker—Aug. 28, 1913
Giuseppe Verdi—Oct. 10, 1813
Shirley Verrett—May 31, 1933
Herbert Von Karajan—Apr. 5, 1908
Richard Wagner—May 22, 1813
André Watts—Jun. 10, 1946

MUSIC—POPULAR ARTISTS

Roy Acuff—Sep. 15, 1903
Greg Allman—Dec. 8, 1947
Herb Alpert—Mar. 31, 1937
Ed Ames—Jul. 9, 1929
Leroy Anderson—Jun. 29, 1908
Paul Anka—Jul. 30, 1941
Little Anthony (Gourdine)—Jan. 8, 1941
Patty Andrews—Feb. 16, 1920
Ray Anthony—Jan. 22, 1922
Harold Arlen—Feb. 15, 1905
Louis Armstrong—Jul. 4, 1900
Eddie Arnold—May 15, 1918
Chet Atkins—Jun. 20, 1924
Frankie Avalon—Sep. 18, 1939
Charles Aznavour—May 22, 1924
Burt Bacharach—May 12, 1929
Joan Baez—Jan. 9, 1941
Pearl Bailey—Mar. 29, 1918
Josephine Baker—Jun. 3, 1906
Count Basie—Aug. 21, 1904
Shirley Bassey—Jan. 18, 1937
Harry Belafonte—Mar. 1, 1927
Louis Bellson—Jul. 6, 1924
Tony Bennett—Aug. 3, 1926
Brook Benton—Sep. 19, 1933
Irving Berlin—May 11, 1888
Chuck Berry—Jan. 15, 1926
Sonny Bono—Feb. 16, 1935
Pat Boone—Jun. 1, 1934
David Bowie—Jan. 8, 1948
James Brown—May 3, 1934
Dave Brubeck—Dec. 6, 1920
Anita Bryant—Mar. 25, 1940
Sammy Cahn—Jun. 18, 1913
Cab Calloway—Dec. 25, 1907
Glen Campbell—Apr. 22, 1938
Lana Cantrell—Aug. 7, 1944
Hoagy Carmichael—Nov. 22, 1899
Diahann Carroll—Jul. 17, 1935
Johnny Cash—Feb. 26, 1932

MUSIC—POPULAR ARTISTS *(cont.)*

June Carter Cash—Jun. 23, 1931
Harry Chapin—Dec. 7, 1942
Ray Charles—Sep. 23, 1930
Chubby Checker—Oct. 3, 1941
Cher—May 20, 1946
Eric Clapton—Mar. 30, 1945
Dick Clark—Nov. 30, 1929
Roy Clark—Apr. 15, 1933
Patsy Cline—Sep. 8, 1932
Rosemary Clooney—May 23, 1928
Joe Cocker—May 20, 1944
Nat King Cole—Mar. 17, 1919
Natalie Cole—Feb. 6, 1950
Judy Collins—May 1, 1939
Russ Columbo—Jan. 14, 1908
Perry Como—May 18, 1912
Sam Cooke—Jan. 22, 1935
Rita Coolidge—May 1, 1945
Alice Cooper—Feb. 4, 1948
Noel Coward—Dec. 16, 1899
Jim Croce—Jan. 10, 1943
Bing Crosby—May 2, 1904
Xavier Cugat—Jan. 1, 1900
Vic Damone—Jun. 12, 1928
Dorothy Dandridge—Nov. 9, 1923
Bobby Darin—May 14, 1936
James Darren—Oct. 3, 1936
Hal David—May 25, 1921
Mac Davis—Jan. 21, 1942
Meyer Davis—Jan. 10, 1893
Miles Davis—May 25, 1926
Sammy Davis, Jr.—Dec. 8, 1925
Doris Day—Apr. 3, 1924
Joey Dee—Jun. 11, 1940
Neil Diamond—Jan. 24, 1941
Howard Dietz—Sep. 8, 1896
Dion Dimucci—Jul. 18, 1940
Walter Donaldson—Feb. 15, 1893
Tommy Dorsey—Nov. 19, 1905
Morton Downey—Nov. 14, 1902
Darryl Dragon—Aug. 27, 1943
Alfred Drake—Oct. 7, 1914
Peter Duchin—Jul. 28, 1937
Vernon Duke—Oct. 10, 1903
Bob Dylan—May 24, 1941
Billy Eckstine—Jul. 8, 1914
Duke Ellington—Apr. 29, 1899
Cass Elliot—Feb. 19, 1943
Ahmet Ertegun—Jul. 31, 1923
Don Everly—Feb. 1, 1937
Fabian—Feb. 6, 1943
Sammy Fain—Jun. 17, 1902
Percy Faith—Apr. 7, 1908
Donna Fargo—Nov. 10, 1945
José Feliciano—Sep. 10, 1945
Dorothy Fields—Jul. 15, 1905
Eddie Fisher—Aug. 10, 1928
Ella Fitzgerald—Apr. 25, 1918
Roberta Flack—Feb. 10, 1940
Tennessee Ernie Ford—Feb. 13, 1919
Peter Frampton—Apr. 22, 1950
Connie Francis—Dec. 12, 1938
Aretha Franklin—Mar. 25, 1942
Alan Freed—Dec. 15, 1922
Rudolf Friml—Dec. 7, 1879
Art Garfunkel—Nov. 5, 1941
Erroll Garner—Jun. 15, 1921
Crystal Gayle—Jan. 9, 1956
George Gershwin—Sep. 26, 1898
Ira Gershwin—Dec. 6, 1896
Stan Getz—Feb. 2, 1927
Barry Gibb—Sep. 1, 1946
Maurice & Robin Gibb—Dec. 22, 1949
Dizzy Gillespie—Oct. 21, 1917
Bobby Goldsboro—Jan. 18, 1940
Benny Goodman—May 30, 1909
Berry Gordy, Jr.—Nov. 28, 1930
Eydie Gormé—Aug. 16, 1932
Morton Gould—Dec. 10, 1913
Robert Goulet—Nov. 26, 1933
Johnny Green—Oct. 10, 1908
Arlo Guthrie—Jul. 10, 1947
Woody Guthrie—Jul. 14, 1912
Merle Haggard—Mar. 6, 1937
Marvin Hamlisch—Jun. 2, 1944
Lionel Hampton—Apr. 20, 1913
E. Y. "Yip" Harburg—Apr. 8, 1898
Phil Harris—Jun. 24, 1906
George Harrison—Feb. 25, 1943
Isaac Hayes—Aug. 20, 1942
Dick Haymes—Dec. 13, 1916
Skitch Henderson—Jan. 27, 1918
Jimi Hendrix—Nov. 27, 1942
Victor Herbert—Feb. 1, 1859
Woody Herman—May 16, 1913
Gregory Hines—Feb. 14, 1946
Billie Holiday—Apr. 17, 1915
Buddy Holly—Sep. 7, 1936
Lena Horne—Jun. 30, 1917
Engelbert Humperdinck—May 2, 1936

MUSIC—POPULAR ARTISTS *(cont.)*

Janice Ian—May 7, 1950
Burl Ives—Jun. 14, 1909
Mahalia Jackson—Oct. 26, 1911
Michael Jackson—Aug. 29, 1956
Mick Jagger—Jul. 26, 1943
Harry James—Mar. 15, 1916
Billy Joel—May 9, 1949
Elton John—Mar. 25, 1947
Allan Jones—Oct. 14, 1908
Jack Jones—Jan. 14, 1938
Tom Jones—Jun. 7, 1940
Janis Joplin—Jan. 19, 1943
Sammy Kaye—Mar. 13, 1913
Jerome Kern—Jan. 27, 1885
Carole King—Feb. 9, 1942
Eartha Kitt—Jan. 16, 1928
Gladys Knight—May 28, 1944
Fritz Kreisler—Feb. 2, 1875
Kris Kristofferson—Jun. 22, 1936
Gene Krupa—Jan. 15, 1909
Kay Kyser—Jun. 18, 1897
Frankie Laine—Mar. 30, 1913
Burton Lane—Feb. 2, 1912
Frances Langford—Apr. 4, 1913
Steve Lawrence—Jul 8, 1935
Vicki Lawrence—Mar. 26, 1949
Brenda Lee—Dec. 11, 1944
Peggy Lee—May 26, 1920
Michel Legrand—Feb. 24, 1932
John Lennon—Oct. 9, 1940
Julian Lennon—Apr. 8, 1963
Jerry Lee Lewis—Sep. 29, 1935
Liberace—May 16, 1919
Goddard Lieberson—Apr. 5, 1911
Frank Loesser—Jun. 29, 1910
Frederick Loewe—Jun. 10, 1901
Kenny Loggins—Jan. 7, 1948
Guy Lombardo—Jun. 19, 1902
Julie London—Sep. 26, 1926
Trini Lopez—May 15, 1937
Loretta Lynn—Apr. 14, 1932
Galt MacDermot—Dec. 19, 1928
Barry Manilow—Jun. 17, 1946
Henry Mancini—Apr. 16, 1924
Barbara Mandrell—Dec. 25, 1948
Toriy Martin—Dec. 25, 1912
Al Martino—Oct. 7, 1926
Johnny Mathis—Sep. 30, 1935
Paul McCartney—Jun. 18, 1942
Jimmy McHugh—Jul. 10, 1894
Melanie—Feb. 3, 1939
Sergio Mendez—Feb. 11, 1941
Johnny Mercer—Nov. 18, 1909
Mitch Miller—Jul. 4, 1911
Steve Miller—Oct. 5, 1943
Thelonius Monk—Oct. 10, 1918
Vaughn Monroe—Oct. 7, 1912
Anne Murray—Jun. 20, 1946
Rick Nelson—May 8, 1940
Willy Nelson—Apr. 30, 1933
Peter Nero—May 22, 1934
Wayne Newton—Apr. 3, 1941
Olivia Newton-John—Sep. 26, 1947
Laura Nyro—Oct. 18, 1947
Tony Orlando—Apr. 3, 1944
Buck Owens—Aug. 12, 1929
Patti Page—Nov. 8, 1927
Dolly Parton—Jun. 19, 1946
Les Paul—Jun. 9, 1907
Johnny Paycheck—May 31, 1941
Minnie Pearl—Dec. 19, 1915
Oscar Peterson—Aug. 15, 1925
Edith Piaf—Dec. 19, 1915
Cole Porter—Jun. 9, 1891
Elvis Presley—Jan. 8, 1935
Dore Previn—Oct. 22, 1929
Louis Prima—Dec. 7, 1911
Ralph Rainger—Oct. 7, 1900
Johnny Ray—Jan. 10, 1927
Buddy Rich—Jun. 30, 1917
Jeannie C. Riley—Oct. 19, 1945
Richard Rodgers—Jun. 28, 1902
Kenny Rogers—Aug. 21, 1938
Linda Ronstadt—Jul. 15, 1946
David Rose—Jun. 15, 1910
Diana Ross—Mar. 26, 1944
Buffy Saint Marie—Feb. 20, 1941
Tommy Sands—Aug. 27, 1937
Arthur Schwartz—Nov. 25, 1900
Neil Sedaka—Mar. 13, 1939
Pete Seeger—May 3, 1919
Doc Sevrinson—Jul. 7, 1927
Ravi Shankar—Apr. 7, 1920
Artie Shaw—May 26, 1910
Robert Shaw—Apr. 30, 1916
George Shearing—Aug. 13, 1919
Bobby Short—Sep. 15, 1926
Carly Simon—Jun. 25. 1944
Paul Simon—Oct. 13, 1941
Nina Simone—Feb. 21, 1935

MUSIC—POPULAR ARTISTS *(cont.)*

Frank Sinatra—Dec. 12, 1915
Frank Sinatra, Jr.—Jan 10, 1944
Nancy Sinatra—Jun. 8, 1940
Grace Slick—Oct. 30, 1941
Bessie Smith—Apr. 15, 1894
Kate Smith—May 1, 1909
Keely Smith—Mar. 9, 1932
Dusty Springfield—Apr. 16, 1941
Bruce Springsteen—Sep. 23, 1949
Ringo Starr—Jul. 7, 1940
Connie Stevens—Aug. 8, 1938
Rod Stewart—Jan. 10, 1945
Sly Stone—Mar. 15, 1944
Jule Styne—Dec. 31, 1905
James Taylor—Mar. 12, 1948
Toni Tenille—May 8, 1943
B. J. Thomas—Aug. 7, 1945
Tiny Tim—Apr. 12, 1930
Mel Tormé—Sep. 13, 1925
Ernest Tubb—Feb. 9, 1914
Sophie Tucker—Jan. 13, 1884
Rudy Vallee—Jul. 28, 1901
Frankie Valli—May 3, 1937
Jimmy Van Heusen—Jan. 26, 1913
Sarah Vaughan—Mar. 27, 1924
Bobby Vinton—Apr. 16, 1935
Fats Waller—May 21, 1904
Fred Waring—Jun. 7, 1900
Jim Webb—Aug. 15, 1946
Lawrence Welk—Mar. 11, 1903
Meredith Willson—May 18, 1902
Nancy Wilson—Feb. 20, 1937
Stevie Wonder—May 13, 1950
Tammy Wynette—May 5, 1942

NEWSPAPER AND PUBLISHING FIGURES

Joseph Alsop—Oct. 11, 1910
Stewart Alsop—May 17, 1914
Jack Anderson—Oct. 19, 1922
Peter Arno—Jan. 8, 1904
Brooks Atkinson—Nov. 28, 1894
Russell Baker—Aug. 14, 1925
Phyllis Battelle—Jan. 4, 1922
Robert Benchley—Sep. 15, 1889
Carl Bernstein—Feb. 14, 1944
Jim Bishop—Nov. 21, 1907
Earl Blackwell—May 3, 1917
Erma Bombeck—Feb. 21, 1927
Jimmy Breslin—Oct. 17, 1930
Helen Gurley Brown—Feb. 18, 1922
Art Buchwald—Oct. 20, 1925
William F. Buckley, Jr.—Nov. 24, 1925
Edgar Rice Burroughs—Sep. 1, 1875
Herb Caen—Apr. 3, 1916
Al Capp—Sep. 28, 1909
Maxine Cheshire—Apr. 5, 1930
Marquis Childs—Mar. 17, 1903
Bob Considine—Nov. 4, 1906
Norman Cousins—Jun. 24, 1915
Gardner Cowles—Jan. 21, 1921
Charlotte Curtis—Dec. 19, 1928
Clifton Daniel—Sep. 19, 1912
John Fairchild—Mar. 6, 1927
Jules Feiffer—Jan. 26, 1929
Clay Felker—Oct. 2, 1928
Larry Flynt—Nov. 1, 1942
Rube Goldberg—Jul. 4, 1883
Katherine Graham—Jun. 16, 1917
Abel Green—Jun. 3, 1900
David Halberstam—Apr. 10, 1934
William Randolph Hearst, Jr.—Jan. 27, 1908
William Randolph Hearst, Sr.—Apr. 29, 1863
Hugh Hefner—Apr. 9, 1926
Herblock—Oct. 13, 1909
Al Hirschfeld—Jun. 21, 1903
Hedda Hopper—Jun. 2, 1890
Walt Kelly—Aug. 25, 1913
Alfred A. Knopf—Sep. 12, 1892
Irv Kupcinet—Jul. 31, 1912
Ann Landers—Jul. 4, 1918
Walter Lippman—Sep. 23, 1889
Leonard Lyons—Sep. 10, 1906
Bill Mauldin—Oct. 29, 1921
Louella Parsons—Aug. 6, 1893
Rex Reed—Oct. 2, 1940
James Reston—Nov. 3, 1909
Adela Rogers St. Johns—May 20, 1894
James Reston—Nov. 3, 1909

NEWSPAPER AND PUBLISHING FIGURES *(cont.)*

Harrison E. Salisbury—Nov. 14, 1908
Dorothy Schiff—Mar. 11, 1903
Charles Schultz—Nov. 26, 1922
Sidney Skolsky—May 2, 1905
William Steig—Nov. 14, 1917
Lyle Stuart—Aug. 11, 1922
Arthur Ochs Sulzberger—Feb. 5, 1926
C. L. Sulzberger—Oct. 27, 1912
Abigail Van Buren—Jul. 4, 1918
Amy Vanderbilt—Jul. 22, 1908
Tom Wicker—Jun. 18, 1926
Earl Wilson—May 3, 1907
Walter Winchell—Apr. 7, 1897
Bob Woodward—Mar. 26, 1943

POLITICAL ACTIVISTS

Ralph Abernathy—Mar, 11, 1926
Daniel Berrigan—May 9, 1921
Phillip Berrigan—Oct. 5, 1923
Godfrey Cambridge—Feb. 26, 1933
Eldridge Cleaver—Aug. 31, 1935
Angela Davis—Jan. 26, 1944
Bernadette Devlin—Apr. 23, 1947
Betty Friedan—Feb. 4, 1921
Emma Goldman—Jun. 27, 1869
Germaine Greer—Jan. 29, 1939
Abbie Hoffman—Nov. 30, 1936
Roy Innis—Jun. 6, 1934
Jesse Jackson—Oct. 8, 1941
Coretta Scott King—Apr. 27, 1927
Martin Luther King, Jr.—Jan. 15, 1929
Malcolm X (Little)—May 19, 1925
Kate Millett—Sep. 14, 1934
Margaret Sanger—Sep. 14, 1883
Elizabeth Cady Stanton—Nov. 12, 1815
Gloria Steinem—Mar. 25, 1935
Roy Wilkins—Aug. 30, 1901

PRESIDENTS

George Washington—Feb. 22, 1732
John Adams—Oct. 30, 1735
Thomas Jefferson—Apr. 13, 1743
James Madison—Mar. 16, 1751
James Monroe—Apr. 28, 1758
John Quincy Adams—Jul. 11, 1767
Andrew Jackson—Mar. 15, 1767
Martin Van Buren—Dec. 5, 1782
William Henry Harrison—Feb. 9, 1773
John Tyler—Mar. 29, 1790
James Polk—Nov. 2, 1795
Zachary Taylor—Nov. 24, 1784
Millard Fillmore—Jan. 7, 1800
Franklin Pierce—Apr. 23, 1804
James Buchanan—Apr. 23, 1791
Abraham Lincoln—Feb. 12, 1809
Andrew Johnson—Dec. 29, 1808
Ulysses S. Grant—Apr. 27, 1822
Rutherford B. Hayes—Oct. 4, 1822
James A. Garfield—Nov. 19, 1831
Chester A. Arthur—Oct. 5, 1829
Grover Cleveland—Mar. 18, 1837
Benjamin Harrison—Aug. 20, 1833
William McKinley—Jan. 29, 1843
Theodore Roosevelt—Oct. 27, 1858
William Howard Taft—Sep. 15, 1857
Woodrow Wilson—Dec. 28, 1856
Warren G. Harding—Nov. 2, 1865
Calvin Coolidge—Jul. 4, 1872
Herbert C. Hoover—Aug. 10, 1874
Franklin Delano Roosevelt—Jan. 30, 1882
Harry S. Truman—May 8, 1884
Dwight D. Eisenhower—Oct. 14, 1890
John Fitzgerald Kennedy—May 29, 1917
Lyndon Baines Johnson—Aug. 27, 1908
Richard M. Nixon—Jan. 9, 1913
Gerald R. Ford—Jul. 14, 1913
Jimmy (James Earl) Carter—Oct. 1, 1924
Ronald Reagan—Feb. 6, 1911

RELIGIOUS FIGURES

Henry Ward Beecher—Jun. 24, 1813
St. Francis Xavier Cabrini—Jul. 15, 1850
John Calvin—Jul. 10, 1509
Terence Cardinal Cooke—Mar. 1, 1921
Richard Cardinal Cushing—Aug. 24, 1895
Mary Baker Eddy—Jul. 16, 1821
Billy Graham—Nov. 17, 1918
Joan of Arc—Jan. 6, 1412
Ayatollah Khomeini—May 6, 1900
Martin Luther—Nov. 10, 1483
Aimee Semple McPherson—Oct. 9, 1890
Norman Vincent Peale—May 31, 1898
Pope Alexander VI—Jan. 1, 1431
Pope John XXIII—Nov. 25, 1881
Pope Paul I—Oct. 17, 1912
Pope John Paul II—May 18, 1920
Pope Paul VI—Sep. 26, 1897
Pope Pius XIII—Mar. 2, 1876
Oral Roberts—Jan. 24, 1918
Elizabeth Seton—Aug. 28, 1774
Fulton J. Sheen—May 8, 1895
Francis Cardinal Spellman—May 4, 1889
Paul Tillich—Aug. 20, 1886
Baha 'U' Llah—Nov. 12, 1817
John Wesley—Jun. 17, 1703
Brigham Young—Jun. 1, 1801

SCIENCE FIGURES

Edwin "Buzz" Aldrin—Jan. 20, 1930
Luis Alvarez—Jun. 13, 1911
Robert Ardrey—Oct. 16, 1908
Neil Armstrong—Aug. 5, 1930
Luther Burbank—Mar. 7, 1849
Scott Carpenter—May 1, 1925
Noam Chomsky—Dec. 7, 1928
Nicolaus Copernicus—Feb. 19, 1473
Jacques Cousteau—Jun. 11, 1910
Marie Curie—Nov. 7, 1867
Pierre Curie—May 15, 1859
Charles Darwin—Feb. 12, 1809
Lee DeForest—Aug. 26, 1873
George Eastman—Jul. 12, 1854
Albert Einstein—Mar. 14, 1878
Enrico Fermi—Sep. 29, 1901
Galileo Galilei—Feb. 15, 1564
John Glenn—Jul. 18, 1921
Virginia Johnson—Feb. 11, 1925
Dr. Alfred Kinsey—Jun. 23, 1894
John Lilly—Jan. 6, 1915
Sir Joseph Lister—Apr. 5, 1827
Guglielmo Marconi—Apr. 25, 1874
Dr. William Masters—Dec. 27, 1915
Marshall McLuhan—Jul. 21, 1911
Margaret Mead—Dec. 16, 1901
Ashley Montagu—Jun. 28, 1905
Desmond Morris—Jan. 24, 1918
Samuel F. B. Morse—Apr. 27, 1791
Sir Isaac Newton—Dec. 25, 1642
Louis Pasteur—Dec. 27, 1822
Linus Pauling—Feb. 28, 1901
Ivan Pavlov—Sep. 14, 1849
Charles Richter—Apr. 26, 1900
Dr. Albert Sabin—Aug. 26, 1906
Jonas Salk—Oct. 28, 1914
Alan Shepard—Nov. 18, 1923
Wernher von Braun—Mar. 23, 1912

SPORTS FIGURES

Hank Aaron—Feb. 5, 1934
Kareem Abdul-Jabbar—Apr. 16, 1947
Muhammad Ali—Jan. 18, 1942
Mel Allen—Feb. 14, 1913
Mario Andretti—Feb. 28, 1940
Eddie Arcaro—Feb. 19, 1916
Arthur Ashe, Jr.—Apr. 10, 1943
Ernie Banks—Jan. 31, 1931
Red Barber—Feb. 17, 1908
Rick Barry—Mar. 28, 1944
Hank Bauer—Jul. 31, 1922
Johnny Bench—Dec. 7, 1947
Patty Berg—Feb. 13, 1918
Yogi Berra—May 12, 1925

SPORTS FIGURES *(cont.)*

Vida Blue—Jul. 28, 1949
Bjorn Borg—Jun. 6, 1956
Julius Boros—Mar. 3, 1920
Lou Boudreau—Jul. 17, 1917
Jim Bouton—Mar. 8, 1939
Bill Bradley—Jul. 28, 1943
Terry Bradshaw—Sep. 12, 1948
Jim Brown—Feb. 7, 1935
Dick Butkus—Dec. 9, 1942
Roy Campanella—Nov. 19, 1921
Rod Carew—Oct. 1, 1945
Billy Casper—Jun. 24, 1931
Wilt Chamberlain—Aug. 12, 1936
Ezzard Charles—Jul. 7, 1921
Roberto Clemente—Aug. 18, 1934
Jimmy Connors—Sep. 2, 1952
Howard Cosell—Mar. 25, 1920
Margaret Court—Jul. 16, 1942
Bob Cousy—Aug. 9, 1928
Larry Csonka—Dec. 25, 1946
Alvin Dark—Jan. 7, 1922
Dizzy Dean—Jan. 16, 1911
Jack Dempsey—Jun. 24, 1895
Joe DiMaggio—Nov. 25, 1914
Don Drysdale—Jul. 23, 1936
Leo Durocher—Jul. 27, 1906
Julius Erving—Feb. 22, 1950
Chris Evert Lloyd—Dec. 21, 1964
Weeb Ewbank—May 6, 1907
Bob Feller—Nov. 3, 1918
Charlie Finley—Feb. 22, 1918
Bobby Fischer—Mar. 9, 1943
Peggy Fleming—Jul. 27, 1948
Whitey Ford—Oct. 21, 1928
George Foreman—Jan. 10, 1949
Joe Frazier—Jan. 17, 1944
Walt Frazier—Mar. 29, 1945
Ford Frick—Dec. 19, 1894
Roman Gabriel—Aug. 5, 1940
Joe Garagiola—Feb. 12, 1926
Steve Garvey—Dec. 22, 1948
Vitas Gerulaitis—Jul. 26, 1954
Lou Gehrig—Jun. 19, 1903
Frank Gifford—Aug. 16, 1930
Pancho Gonzalez—May 9, 1928
Evonne Goolagong—Jul. 31, 1951
Curt Gowdy—Jul. 31, 1919
Red Grange—Jun. 13, 1903
Rocky Graziano—Jun. 7, 1922
Hank Greenberg—Jan. 1, 1911
Bob Griese—Feb. 3, 1945
Ron Guidry—Aug. 28, 1950
Tom Harmon—Sep. 28, 1919
Franco Harris—Mar. 7, 1950
John Havlicek—Apr. 8, 1940
Woody Hayes—Feb. 14, 1913
Elroy "Crazylegs" Hirsch—Jun. 17, 1923
Gil Hodges—Apr. 4, 1924
Ben Hogan—Aug. 13, 1912
Paul Hornung—Dec. 12, 1935
Elston Howard, Sr.—Feb. 23, 1929
Sam Huff—Oct. 4, 1934
Bobby Hull—Jan. 3, 1939
Catfish Hunter—Apr. 8, 1946
Kareem Abdul-Jabbar—Apr. 16, 1947
Reggie Jackson—May 18, 1946
Tommy John—May 22, 1943
Jack Johnson—Mar. 31, 1878
Rafer Johnson—Aug. 18, 1935
Cleon Jones—Aug. 4, 1942
Parnelli Jones—Aug. 12, 1933
Al Kaline—Dec. 19, 1934
Jean-Claude Killy—Aug. 30, 1943
Billie Jean King—Nov. 22, 1943
Evel Knievel—Oct. 17, 1938
Sandy Koufax—Dec. 30, 1935
Jack Kramer—Aug. 1, 1921
Bowie Kuhn—Oct. 28, 1926
Tom Landry—Sep. 11, 1924
Rod Laver—Aug. 9, 1938
Frank Leahy—Aug. 27, 1908
Sonny Liston—May 8, 1932
Vince Lombardi—Jun. 11, 1913
Davey Lopes—May 3, 1946
Nancy Lopez—Jan. 6, 1957
Joe Louis—May 13, 1914
Connie Mack—Dec. 23, 1862
Mickey Mantle—Oct. 20, 1931
Wellington Mara—Aug. 14, 1916
Pete Maravich—Jun. 22, 1948
Rocky Marciano—Sep. 1, 1924
Roger Maris—Sep. 10, 1934
Billy Martin—May 16, 1931
Christy Mathewson—Aug. 12, 1866
Willie Mays—May 6, 1931
Willie McCovey—Jan. 10, 1939
John McEnroe—Feb. 16, 1959
Craig Morton—Feb. 5, 1943
Emil Mosbacher—Apr. 1, 1922
Willie Mosconi—Jun. 21, 1913

SPORTS FIGURES *(cont.)*

Danny Murtaugh—Oct. 8, 1917
Stan Musial—Nov. 21, 1920
Thurman Munson—Jun. 7, 1947
Joe Namath—May 31, 1943
Ilie Nastase—Jul. 19, 1949
Lindsey Nelson—May 25, 1919
Graig Nettles—Aug. 20, 1944
Jack Nicklaus—Jan 2, 1940
Annie Oakley—Aug. 13, 1860
Tony Oliva—Jul. 20, 1941
Bobby Orr—Mar. 20, 1948
Jesse Owens—Sep. 12, 1913
Leroy "Satchel" Paige—Jul. 7, 1906
Arnold Palmer—Sep. 10, 1929
Floyd Patterson—Jan. 4, 1935
Pelé—Oct. 23, 1940
Lou Piniella—Aug. 28, 1943
Gary Player—Nov. 1, 1935
Jim Plunkett—Dec. 5, 1947
Boog Powell—Aug. 17, 1941
Willis Reed—Aug. 25, 1942
Allie Reynolds—Feb. 10, 1919
Branch Rickey—Dec. 20, 1881
Phil Rizzuto—Sep. 25, 1981
Brooks Robinson—May 18, 1937
Frank Robinson—Aug. 31, 1935
Jackie Robinson—Jan. 31, 1919
Sugar Ray Robinson—May 3, 1921
Knute Rockne—Mar. 4, 1888
Pete Rose—Apr. 14, 1942
Pete Rozelle—Mar. 1, 1926
Bill Russell—Feb. 12, 1934
Babe Ruth—Feb. 6, 1895
Manny Sanguillen—Mar. 21, 1944
Gale Sayers—May 30, 1943
Tom Seaver—Nov. 17, 1944
Jack Sharkey—Oct. 6, 1902
Willie Shoemaker—Aug. 19, 1931
Don Shula—Jan. 4, 1930
O. J. Simpson—Jul. 9, 1947
Red Smith—Sep. 25, 1904
Robyn Smith—Aug. 14, 1944
Sam Snead—May 27, 1912
Duke Snider—Sep. 19, 1926
Warren Spahn—Apr. 23, 1921
Mark Spitz—Feb. 10, 1950
Eddie Stanky—Sep. 3, 1916
Bart Starr—Jan. 9, 1934
Roger Staubach—Feb. 5, 1942
George Steinbrenner—Jul. 4, 1930
Casey Stengel—Jul. 30, 1891
Fran Tarkenton—Feb. 3, 1940
Jim Thorpe—May 28, 1888
Bill Tilden—Feb. 10, 1893
Mike Torrez—Aug. 28, 1946
Lee Trevino—Dec. 1, 1939
Gene Tunney—May 25, 1898
Johnny Unitas—May 7, 1933
Bill Veeck—Feb. 9, 1914
Earl Weaver—Aug. 14, 1930
Ted Williams—Aug. 31, 1918
Maury Wills—Oct. 2, 1932
Carl Yastrzemski—Aug. 22, 1939
Cy Young—Mar. 29, 1867

THEATER FIGURES

George Abbott—Jun. 23, 1887
Luther Adler—May 4, 1903
Richard Adler—Aug. 23, 1923
Edward Albee—Mar. 12, 1928
Theoni V. Aldredge—Aug. 22, 1932
Maxwell Anderson—Dec. 15, 1888
Maya Angelou—Apr. 4, 1928
Jean Anouilh—Jun. 23, 1910
Harold Arlen—Feb. 15, 1905
Robert Alan Aurthur—Jun. 10, 1922
George Axelrod—Jun. 9, 1922
Clive Barnes—May 13, 1927
Richard Barr—Sep. 6, 1917
P. T. Barnum—Jul. 5, 1810
Michael Bennett—Apr. 8, 1943
Robert Russell Bennett—Jun. 15, 1894
Herbert Berghof—Sep. 13, 1909
Kermit Bloomgarden—Dec. 15, 1904
Jerry Bock—Nov. 23, 1928
Bertold Brecht—Feb. 10, 1898
Jacques Brel—Apr. 8, 1929
Abe Burroughs—Dec. 18, 1910
Michael Butler—Nov. 26, 1936
Paddy Chayevsky—Jan. 29, 1923
George M. Cohan—Jul. 3, 1878
Alexander Cohen—Jul 24, 1920

THEATER FIGURES *(cont.)*

Betty Comden—May 3, 1919
Cheryl Crawford—Sep. 24, 1902
Russell Crouse—Feb. 20, 1893
Morton Da Costa—Mar. 7, 1918
Jean Dalrymple—Sep. 2, 1910
Hilly Elkins—Oct. 18, 1929
Cy Feuer—Jan. 15, 1911
Herb Gardner—Dec. 28, 1934
Max Gordon—Jun. 28, 1892
Adolph Green—Dec. 2, 1918
Sheldon Harnick—Apr. 30, 1924
Jed Harris—Feb. 25, 1900
Leland Hayward—Sep. 13, 1902
Ben Hecht—Feb. 28, 1893
Lillian Hellman—Jun. 20, 1905
Sol Hurok—Apr. 9, 1888
William Inge—May 3, 1913
Eugene Ionesco—Nov. 26, 1912
Christopher Isherwood—Aug. 26, 1904
Leroi Jones—Oct. 7, 1934
Garson Kanin—Nov. 24, 1912
George S. Kaufman—Nov. 16, 1889
Elia Kazan—Sep. 7, 1909
Jean Kerr—Jul. 10, 1923
Walter Kerr—Jul. 8, 1913
Alan Jay Lerner—Aug. 31, 1918
Howard Lindsay—Mar. 29, 1889
Joshua Logan—Oct. 5, 1908
David Merrick—Nov. 27, 1912
Jo Mielziner—Mar. 19, 1901
Arthur Miller—Oct. 17, 1915
Mike Nichols—Nov. 6, 1931
Tom O'Horgan—May 3, 1926
John Osborne—Dec. 12, 1929
Joseph Papp—Jun. 22, 1921
Arthur Penn—Sep. 27, 1922
Harold Pinter—Oct. 10, 1930
Harold Prince—Jan. 30, 1928
José Quintero—Oct. 15, 1924
Billy Rose—Sep. 6, 1899
Saint-Subber—Feb. 18, 1918
William Saroyan—Aug. 31, 1908
Murray Schisgal—Nov. 25, 1926
Stephen Schwartz—Jul. 4, 1927
Stephen Sondheim—Mar. 22, 1930
Roger Stevens—Mar. 12, 1910
Lee Strasberg—Nov. 17, 1901
Jule Styne—Dec. 31, 1905
Tennessee Williams—Mar. 26, 1911
Meredith Willson—May 18, 1902
Paul Zindel—May 15, 1936

Afterword

Now you've hopefully done a chart on your self and you've found lots of good qualities that have been lying dormant all your life. You've also found a few negs that explain why you've had so many problems in so many areas of your life. But just finding these things out and not doing anything about them is not enough. It's up to you to change your life for the better, to strengthen your positive qualities that will ensure the success you've dreamed about and hoped for all your life, and eliminate as much as you can the negative qualities that are holding you back from having all those wonderful things that you deserve. You may not feel right *now* that you deserve great things, but as you eliminate, or at least begin to elminate, those negs, you'll actually start to like your self better than you *ever* have (and some of you maybe for the very first time).

And as you like your self better, you'll un-loose some of those wonderful dreams that you've kept hidden and chained for years because you gave up hope on them, and begin to see that maybe it *is* possible to aspire to great and wonderful things. Maybe you'll even begin to realize that God created you and *deliberately* gave you your specific strengths *and* weaknesses for the precise reason that as you *do* work to eliminate your weaknesses, that will strengthen you enough for you to reach all the goals that your positive qualities will lead you to.

God's plan is for us to have all the things that we want and need, and it's up to us to realize this and to *work* at getting them!

I may have forgotten or inadvertently left out some celebrity's birthday. If you know a world-famous figure's birthday (from the dawn of history up to the present), please send it to me with your source of information and it will be printed in our next edition.

Please send to:

Naura Hayden
c/o Bibli O'Phile
P. O. Box #5189
New York, New York 10022

Frank Mastro

About the Author

Naura Hayden has so much energy she's able to accomplish what many less energetic women or men can't. She's an actress, singer, songwriter, and a best-selling author with three books to her credit.* Her successful and widely acclaimed line of health foods, which she formulated and developed, is sold all over the United States.** She has her own radio show on New York's WMCA, "Naura's Good News," which will soon be syndicated nationally on radio and television.

Naura lives in and has a *passion* for New York City, even though she was raised in California. She's probably Manhattan's number one fan. Her household includes a turtle named Oswald (a Capricorn) a cat named Nathan (a Taurus), and a dog named Seymour (an Aquarius).

*Listed on page 2.

**Dynamite Milk Shake, Dynamite Energy Bar (a candy bar), and Dynamite Pak (vitamins).